Lecture Notes in Computer Science 9895

Commenced Publication in 1973
Founding and Former Series Editors:
Gerhard Goos, Juris Hartmanis, and Jan van Leeuwen

More information about this series at http://www.springer.com/series/7410

Sara Foresti · Javier Lopez (Eds.)

Information Security Theory and Practice

10th IFIP WG 11.2 International Conference, WISTP 2016
Heraklion, Crete, Greece, September 26–27, 2016
Proceedings

 Springer

Editors
Sara Foresti
Università degli Studi di Milano
Crema
Italy

Javier Lopez
University of Malaga
Malaga
Spain

ISSN 0302-9743   ISSN 1611-3349   (electronic)
Lecture Notes in Computer Science
ISBN 978-3-319-45930-1   ISBN 978-3-319-45931-8   (eBook)
DOI 10.1007/978-3-319-45931-8

Library of Congress Control Number: 2016950232

LNCS Sublibrary: SL4 – Security and Cryptology

Printed on acid-free paper

This Springer imprint is published by Springer Nature
The registered company is Springer International Publishing AG Switzerland

Preface

The widespread and fast development of ICT is changing the information society in which we live as well as our interactions with the surrounding environment and among each other. This evolution of ICT is bringing unprecedented advantages, but its success will depend on how secure ICT systems are and on the security and privacy guarantees that these systems offer.

These proceedings contain the papers selected for presentation at the 10th WISTP International Conference on Information Security Theory and Practice (WISTP 2016), held in Heraklion, Crete, Greece, on September 26–27, 2016, in conjunction with the 21st European Symposium On Research In Computer Security (ESORICS 2016).

In response to the call for papers, 29 papers were submitted to the conference from 14 different countries. Each paper was reviewed by at least three members of the Program Committee, and evaluated on the basis of its significance, novelty, and technical quality. As in previous years, reviewing was "double-blind", that is, the identities of the authors were not revealed to the reviewers of the papers and the identities of the reviewers were not revealed to the authors. The Program Committee's work was carried out electronically, yielding intensive discussions. Of the submitted papers, the Program Committee accepted 13 full papers (resulting in an acceptance rate of 44.8 %) and 5 short papers for presentation at the conference.

WISTP 2016 was organized in cooperation with the IFIP WG 11.2: Pervasive Systems Security and was sponsored by FORTH Institute of Computer Science.

The success of an event like this depends on the voluntary effort of many individuals. There is a long list of people who volunteered their time and energy to organize the conference, and who deserve special thanks. We would like to thank all the members of the Program Committee and all the external reviewers, for all their hard work in evaluating all the papers in a short time window, and for their active participation in the discussion and selection process. We would like to express our sincere gratitude to the WISTP Steering Committee, and its Chair Damien Sauveron in particular, for their support in the organization of the conference. Thanks to Ruggero Donida Labati for taking care of publicity. We are also very grateful to Ioannis Askoxylakis (WISTP General Chair) and to the local organizers for their support in the conference organization and logistics. We would also like to thank the keynote speakers for accepting our invitation and for their enlightening and interesting talks.

Last but certainly not least, our thanks goes to all the authors who submitted papers and to all the conference's attendees. We hope you find the program of WISTP 2016 interesting, stimulating, and inspiring for your future research.

September 2016

Sara Foresti
Javier Lopez

Organization

General Chair

Ioannis Askoxylakis   FORTH-ICS, Greece

Program Chairs

Sara Foresti   Università degli Studi di Milano, Italy
Javier Lopez   University of Malaga, Spain

Publicity Chair

Ruggero Donida Labati   Università degli Studi di Milano, Italy

Steering Committee

Raja Naeem Akram   Royal Holloway University of London, UK
Angelos Bilas   FORTH-ICS, Greece
Sushil Jajodia   George Mason University, USA
Konstantinos   Royal Holloway University of London, UK
  Markantonakis
Joachim Posegga   University of Passau, Germany
Jean-Jacques Quisquater   UCL, Belgium
Damien Sauveron (chair)   University of Limoges, France

Program Committee

Ioannis Askoxylakis   FORTH-ICS, Greece
Lejla Batina   Radboud University Nijmegen, The Netherlands
Kim-Kwang Raymond   University of Texas at San Antonio, USA
  Choo
Jorge Cuellar   Siemens AG, Germany
Sabrina De Capitani di   Università degli Studi di Milano, Italy
  Vimercati
Jose Fernandez   École Polytechnique de Montréal, Canada
Flavio Garcia   University of Birmingham, UK
Dieter Gollmann   Hamburg University of Technology, Germany
Stefanos Gritzalis   University of the Aegean, Greece
Dimitris Gritzalis   AUEB, Greece
Brahim Hamid   IRIT Research Laboratory, France
Xinyi Huang   Fujian Normal University, China

Michael Hutter	Cryptography Research, USA
Sushil Jajodia	George Mason University, USA
Vasilis Katos	Bournemouth University, UK
Sokratis Katsikas	NTNU, Norway
Florian Kerschbaum	SAP, Germany
Maryline Laurent	Institut Mines-Télécom, France
Giovanni Livraga	Università degli Studi di Milano, Italy
Evangelos Markatos	FORTH-ICS and University of Crete, Greece
Fabio Martinelli	CNR, Italy
Vashek Matyas	Masaryk University, Czech Republic
Sjouke Mauw	University of Luxembourg, Luxembourg
Alessio Merlo	University of Genoa, Italy
Haris Mouratidis	University of Brighton, UK
David Naccache	École Normale Suprieure, France
Rolf Oppliger	eSECURITY Technologies, Switzerland
Stefano Paraboschi	Università degli Studi di Bergamo, Italy
Gerardo Pelosi	Politecnico di Milano, Italy
Pedro Peris-Lopez	Carlos III University, Spain
Günther Pernul	Universität Regensburg, Germany
Milan Petkovic	TU Eindhoven, The Netherlands
Frank Piessens	Katholieke Universiteit Leuven, Belgium
Joachim Posegga	University of Passau, Germany
Jean-Jacques Quisquater	UCL, Belgium
Silvio Ranise	FBK, Italy
Kui Ren	State University of New York at Buffalo, USA
Rodrigo Roman	University of Malaga, Spain
Kouichi Sakurai	Kyushu University, Japan
Pierangela Samarati	Università degli Studi di Milano, Italy
Dave Singelée	Katholieke Universiteit Leuven, Belgium
Miguel Soriano	Universitat Politècnica de Catalunya, Spain
Willy Susilo	University of Wollongong, Australia
Guilin Wang	Huawei International Pte Ltd, Singapore
Meng Yu	University of Texas at San Antonio, USA

External Reviewers

Joonsang Baek	Jan Tobias Muehlberg	Zisis Tsiatsikas
Boutheyna Belgacem	Theodore Ntouskas	Theodoros Tzouramanis
Antonio de La Piedra	Juan D. Parra Rodriguez	Yoshifumi Ueshige
Stelios Dritsas	Alexander Puchta	Ding Wang
Sigrid Guergens	Henrich C. Pöhls	Artsiom Yautsiukhin
Ravi Jhawar	Andreea-Ina Radu	Jiangshan Yu
Christos Kalloniatis	Giada Sciarretta	Yuexin Zhang
Eduard Marin	Raoul Strackx	
Pedro Maat Massolino	Johannes Sänger	

Contents

Authentication and Key Management

Securing Transactions with the eIDAS Protocols

Frank Morgner[1], Paul Bastian[1], and Marc Fischlin[2(✉)]

[1] Bundesdruckerei GmbH, Berlin, Germany
[2] Technische Universität Darmstadt, Darmstadt, Germany
marc.fischlin@cryptoplexity.de

Abstract. The proposed European system for electronic identities, authentication, and trust services (eIDAS) enables remote authentication of an identity card (and selected data of the card) to an eID service. The core system has already been running on the German identity card since 2010. We analyze an extension proposed by Bundesdruckerei that enables the protocol to authenticate further transaction data such as phone numbers or PGP keys. In particular we prove cryptographically that the extension provides strong authenticity guarantees. We also discuss privacy aspects of the solution, preventing the card and the service provider of the eIDAS system to learn the actual transaction data.

1 Introduction

With Regulation EU No 910/2014 about electronic identification, authentication, and trust services for electronic transactions (eIDAS) in 2014, the European parliament has paved the way for a common electronic identity system for Europe. Driven by German and French IT security offices, namely BSI and ANSSI, the first technical proposal for such eIDAS tokens has been put forward in [2] in February 2015. The proposal extends a previous specification for the new German identity cards [1], and as the cards have been issued since November 2010, this means that the basic eIDAS system proposal is already effectively running at this point.

1.1 The Basic eIDAS System

The system of the German identity card adopted early the idea to use the identity card securely for internet services. The basic steps of the protocol are outlined in Fig. 1. The identity card is securely connected to a local card reader at the user's computer via the password-authenticated connection establishment (PACE) protocol. The reader itself is equipped with a small tamper-proof display and is connected (through an application interface on the user's computer) with a service running the eID server. The connection from the computer to the server may be secured through TLS.

The ID card and the eID server then execute the extended access control (EAC) protocol which consists of a terminal authentication (TA) and a chip

© IFIP International Federation for Information Processing 2016
Published by Springer International Publishing Switzerland 2016. All Rights Reserved
S. Foresti and J. Lopez (Eds.): WISTP 2016, LNCS 9895, pp. 3–18, 2016.
DOI: 10.1007/978-3-319-45931-8_1

authentication (CA). In the TA step the eID server authenticates and transmits the credentials for accessing some fields on the ID card, such as for age verification or the address. The human user confirms access to the fields via the reader, by verifying the request on the reader's display. Then the card authenticates itself and the requested data through the CA step.

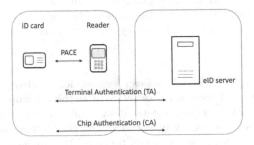

Fig. 1. Extended Access Control (EAC) for online services, consisting of the terminal authentication (TA) step and the chip authentication (CA) step.

1.2 Securing Transactions Through the eID System

Based on a proposal by Bundesdruckerei [3], we discuss how to use the German identity card system (and consequently, the anticipated European eIDAS system) to secure further transaction data. As an example assume that the eID system is used in an online banking service, and that the bank would also like to authenticate the mobile phone number of the user (e.g., for establishing a reliable communication channel for authentication of bank transactions). This phone number is not present on the identity card and thus cannot, per se, be authenticated through the eID system.

The idea of building a transaction system on top of the eID system is to use the auxiliary-data field, originally provisioned for refinements in the data authentication (e.g., the eID server has to commit to the current date for age verification). In order to show that one can securely use this entry for authenticating data like the phone number one needs to show that (a) the solution really validates the transaction, and that (b) it is indeed possible to smoothly extend the existing system to incorporate such checks. The feasibility has already been reported in [3], and we briefly revisit the details at the end of the work, such that it remains to show that the scheme is indeed secure.

We therefore first present a cryptographic description of the transaction system of Bundesdruckerei, called eIDAS transaction system here. The idea is depicted in Fig. 2 and consists of the following steps. (1) The card holder and the service provider first agree upon the transaction T. (2) Then the service provider initiates the eID server for a hash value H(T) of the transaction. (3) The card holder also forwards the transaction in clear to the reader. (4) The original eID components run the TA step, including H(T) as auxiliary data. (5) The reader verifies T against H(T), and the user verifies the transaction via the reader's display. (6) To approve the transaction the user initiates chip authentication.

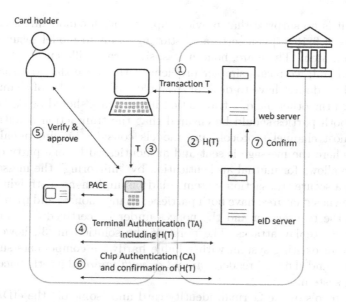

Fig. 2. The eIDAS transaction system

(7) The eID server reports back approval of the transaction if chip authentication terminates successfully.

Our contribution is to put the security of the eIDAS transaction system on formal grounds. To this end we first discuss a security model which ensures that a transaction system satisfying the requirements in the model provides strong authenticity properties of transactions. The model basically guarantees that both parties, card holder and service provider, can have confidence that they agree on the same transaction with the intended partner in a certain session. By this the security model captures for example replay attacks or cloning of transactions across executions, such that the secure transaction system remains immune against such attacks.

An extra feature of the eIDAS transaction system is that the transaction data can be hidden from the underlying eID service. That is, instead of passing the transaction in clear to the service, one can forward a hashed (or committed) version to the service. Our other contribution is to analyze, too, the privacy guarantees given through such a step formally.

We note again that [3] presents an implementation of the above protocol which requires only minor modifications on the reader's side, but is otherwise based on the existing software and hardware for the German identity card. We report on this briefly in Sect. 5.

1.3 Related Work

Since we model transactions as digital data, the authenticity problem of transaction systems at the core resembles the authenticity problem in secure channels.

Therefore, it is no surprise that previous approaches for modeling secure channels such as [4,9,16,17] can serve as a starting point to model security for the transaction system. There are, nonetheless, significant differences.

On one hand, we face a simpler problem in the sense that transactions are atomic and we do not have to deal for example with the order of channel transmissions. On the other hand, a transaction in our sense should be authenticated *mutually*: both parties should be ensured that the transaction is authentic. In contrast, most channel protocols and models consider unidirectional message transfers, where the message is sent and authenticated by one party only. This in principle allows for mutual authentication by "mirroring" the message back.

In fact, a secure transaction system could be implemented straightforwardly in principle via signatures: have both parties exchange nonces and then have each party sign the transaction and the nonces under its certified key. The nonces would prevent replay attacks. The point of the solution in [3], however, is to build upon an existing system with reliable hardware components such as the identity card and the card reader, *without or with minimal* interference with the underlying system.

The protocols of the German identity card and (some of) the eIDAS extensions have been analyzed in a series of works [5–8,10–13,15]. In fact, supporting the protocols by security arguments in form of cryptographic proofs has been a key point in the marketing strategy. We do not directly rely on these results, but we draw on the EAC analysis in [11] for showing that the CA ensures transaction authenticity for the service provider.

2   The eIDAS Transaction System

We first define transaction systems abstractly, and then present the eIDAS transaction system of Bundesdruckerei in our notation.

2.1   Transaction Systems

A *transaction system* TS is given by an interactive protocol between one type of parties, called card holders (or clients) and another type of parties, denoted as service providers (or servers). This is formally specified through a pair of (stateful) algorithms Π_C, Π_S which describe the next message the corresponding party sends upon receiving a message from the other partner. In addition to the interactive protocol the system also comprises key generation algorithms KGC_C and KG_S for both types of parties. The key generation algorithms generate key pairs (sk, pk) for the corresponding party, together with a certificate *cert*.

We assume uniqueness of the certificates and it is convenient to view some unique identifier in a certificate, such as the serial number, as the party's (administrative) identity id. We often use *cert* interchangeably as the identifier id. The certification process is prepared by a general Setup algorithm which creates public parameters such as the root key pk_{CVCA} for verification of certificate chains, as well as secret parameters for certificate generation, typically signing keys.

The interactive protocol execution between a card holder and service provider starts with both parties receiving their keys and certificate as input. Both parties also get the public data of the Setup algorithm as additional input. Each party usually also receives a transaction T as input which it tries to authenticate. A party may abort the execution at any time; it may also accept and terminate. We assume the usual completeness requirement that, if running on genuine parameters and the same transaction, both parties accept.

A *preportioned* transaction system does not hand over the transaction T to the parties in clear. Instead, it uses another algorithm H (as a mnemonic for a hash function) to first compute H(T) before handing the value to the party. The parameters of this algorithm can be specified through the Setup algorithm, and it may be even be a probabilistic algorithm: $H(T; r)$ for random string r.[1] We nonetheless often simply refer to H(T) instead of $H(T; r)$, as the difference becomes relevant only for the privacy setting. Note that the actual transaction system can then only ensure validity of H(T) and that this extends to T must be checked by some other mean, e.g., as in the eIDAS transaction system providing the card reader also with T, r and having it check these values against the hash value used in the underlying transaction system.

2.2 The eIDAS Transaction System

The eIDAS transaction system basically consists of the EAC system where we use the auxiliary data field A_T to transport the (hidden) transaction H(T). Since our goal is to build upon the existing scheme, we do not argue about the specific choices of the EAC system here but instead refer to [1,2] for information about the design ratio. In more detail, both parties first execute the so-called Terminal Authentication (TA) steps of the extended access control.[2] In this step, the terminal picks a fresh ephemeral key pair (esk_T, epk_T) for the domain parameters D_C describing the elliptic curve, sends over its certificate for the long-term key pk_T (which is also included in $cert_T$) and a compressed version Compr(epk_T) of the ephemeral public key. The compression function can be for example the projection onto the x-coordinate of the elliptic curve point. For our analysis we merely assume that Compr is R-regular, meaning that each image has exactly R pre-images.

The chip replies with a random nonce r_C and the terminal then signs this nonce, together with Compr(epk_T). In this step, the eID server of the service provider augments the signature step by the hash value H(T) it has received from the web server. This assumes that the forwarding of H(T) to the eID server

---

[1] In combination with the yet-to-be-specified security properties this makes the algorithm rather a commitment algorithm but which, in turn, can be implemented via a hash function.

[2] We skip the card holder's internal execution of the PACE protocol and assume a trustworthy reader and a secure connection between ID card and reader. This is justified by the fact that PACE has been shown to be a secure password-authenticated key exchange protocol [7] and that we anyhow require a trustworthy display for the user to check the transaction in clear.

is carried out securely; else it is easy to replace the otherwise unprotected transaction T in the communication with the card holder. Note that in the TA protocol both parties also use some chip identifier id_C, not to be confused with our administrative identifier id, for signature generation and verification. Since this value is irrelevant for our security analysis we do not comment further on this value. The chip finally verifies the signature.

Upon successful completion of the TA step, the reader verifies that the given transaction T matches the augmented data H(T) from the TA step and then displays the transaction to the user. Upon confirmation of the user, the reader initiates the Chip Authentication (CA) step between the card and the eID server. In this step the chip sends its certificate $cert_C$ and public key pk_C, and the terminal replies with its ephemeral public key epk_T (in clear).

Finally, both parties compute the Diffie-Hellman key of pk_C and epk_T with the corresponding secret key they hold, and derive an encryption key K_{enc} (which is irrelevant here) and the MAC key K_{mac} with the help of the corresponding key derivation functions KDF_{Enc} and KDF_M. This step again involves a random nonce r'_C of the chip. The chip computes the MAC over epk_T and sends it to the terminal. If this phase is completed successfully then the eID server reports to the web server that the transaction has been confirmed. This, again, must be done in a secure way.

The protocol details of the TA and CA phase are depicted in Fig. 3. For administrative purposes in light of the security model it is convenient to also specify a point in time in the execution in which a session identifier sid is set. This session identifier can be thought of as a quasi unique, purely administrative value, although the parties can determine the identifier easily themselves. Note that both parties output the identifier sid at different points of the execution, due to the sequential order of the authentication steps.

Analogously, we let the protocol specify a partner identifier, pid, which should represent the identity of the intended partner. Since we assume a one-to-one correspondence between certificates and administrative identities, we extract the correct identity out of the certificate. Completeness requires that both session identifier and partner identifier are set upon acceptance, that session identifiers are identical for both parties in genuine executions, and that the partner identifiers correctly point to the corresponding parties.

3   Unforgeability of Transactions

In this section we provide our security analysis of the eIDAS transaction system. For this we first introduce a demanding security model for unforgeability, then we discuss that the eIDAS transaction system achieves this property.

3.1   Defining Unforgeability

Attack Model. We assume that all parties, divided exclusively into card holders from set C and service providers from a set S, receive their (certified) key pairs

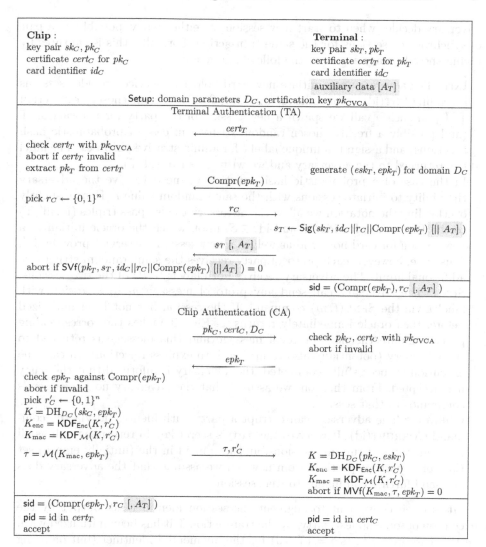

Fig. 3. EAC protocol, consisting of Terminal Authentication (TA) and Chip Authentication (CA). All operations are modulo q resp. over the elliptic curve. The gray part shows the (in EAC optional) auxiliary data field, which we deploy here for securing the transaction.

as initial input at the outset of the attack. We furthermore presume security of the certification in the sense that parties will only accept certified keys. This follows from the unforgeability of the underlying signature scheme used to create certificate, or even certificate chains, but we omit this here for sake of simplicity.

In the attack model the network is fully controlled by the adversary, implying that the adversary decides when to deliver messages to sessions and if to modify transmissions or even to inject new messages. We even assume that the adversary decides when to start new sessions at either party, possibly as a pair of synchronized sessions for the same transaction. Formally, this is captures by giving the adversary access to the following oracles:

- INIT: The adversary can initiate new card holder or service provider sessions by calling INIT(id, T) for some identity id $\in \mathcal{C} \cup \mathcal{S}$ and some chosen transaction T. Upon such a call we spawn a new session of the party for transaction T (and possibly a freshly chosen random string r in case of probabilistic hash functions) and assign it a unique label ℓ for administrative purposes. The label ℓ is returned to the adversary and we write $\ell \leftarrow$ INIT(id, T).

  In the case of a probabilistic hash function we need to give the adversary the ability to initiate sessions with the same random value r. Hence, slightly overloading the notation we allow the adversary to also pass triples (id, id', T) to the INIT oracle for id $\in \mathcal{C}$ and id' $\in \mathcal{S}$, upon which the oracle initializes a new session for card holder id as well as a new session for service provider id'. This time, however, each protocol party receives the same random string r as additional input. The adversary receives both labels (ℓ, ℓ') of the two sessions.

- SEND: The adversary can send any protocol message m to a session with label ℓ via the SEND(ℓ, m) command. If the session has not been initialized before, then oracle immediately returns $\perp$. Else, it makes the corresponding party compute the next protocol message and this message is returned to the adversary (potentially also returning $\perp$ to express rejection). In case the execution is successfully completed, the adversary is informed that the party has accepted. From then on, we assume that the adversary no longer sends commands to that session.

- CORRUPT: The adversary can corrupt a party with identity id via the command CORRUPT(id). It receives the party's secret key in return, as well as all internal states of running sessions, and we put id in the (initially empty) set Corrupt of corrupt parties. From now on, we assume that the adversary does not send further commands to that session.

It is often convenient to augment the session identifier sid, output by the execution of some honest party, by the transaction T it has been initialized with. In this case we write tsid $= (T, sid)$ for the augmented identifier (but omitting the random string r potentially used for computing the probabilistic hash value).

We also use the following self-explanatory notation. We write TSID(ℓ) for the value tsid of the session with label ℓ, where potentially TSID(ℓ) $= \perp$ if the session identifier has not been set by the session yet. Analogously, we write ACC(ℓ) for the acceptance status of the session (true or false), ID(ℓ) for the identity id of the session owner, and PID(ℓ) for the intended partner pid, possibly pid $= \perp$ at this point.

Session-definite unforgeability. We define a very strong notion of unforgeability: if some (honest) card holder accepts a transaction in some execution, then there must be an execution in which a service provider has issued that transaction. Furthermore, this execution of the service provider points to a single card-holder session only. Note that this straightforwardly implies other desirable notions of unforgeability, such as plain unforgeability—if a card holder accepts some transaction then it must have been issued by some service provider—or replay resistance—that no card holder accepts a transaction twice. The latter follows from the fact that there is a one-to-one correspondence between service-provider sessions and card-holder sessions. We call our notion *session-definite unforgeability*.

More formally, we say that the adversary $\mathcal{A}$ wins the session-definite unforgeability game in Fig. 4 if during the execution an honest card-holder party id $\in \mathcal{C} \setminus$ Corrupt *accepts* a transaction T under some session identifier tsid but such that there the partner id pid is not pointing to a corrupt provider and that provider has not set their local identifier to sid at that point. The latter corresponds to the fact that the service provider has issued the transaction. By symmetry, we demand the same for accepting sessions of honest service providers, i.e., that there must be a corresponding card-holder session.

Experiment $\mathsf{SessUnf}_{\mathcal{A}}^{\mathcal{TS}}(n)$

---

1 : **foreach** $i \in \mathcal{C} \cup \mathcal{S}$ **do**

2 :   **if** $i \in \mathcal{C}$ **then** $(sk_i, pk_i, cert_i) \leftarrow \mathsf{KG}_{\mathcal{C}}(1^n)$ **fi**

3 :   **if** $i \in \mathcal{S}$ **then** $(sk_i, pk_i, cert_i) \leftarrow \mathsf{KG}_{\mathcal{S}}(1^n)$ **fi**

4 : **endforeach**

5 : $pks \leftarrow \{(pk_i, cert_i) \mid i \in \mathcal{C} \cup \mathcal{S}\}$

6 : $\mathcal{A}^{\mathrm{INIT}(\cdot,\cdot),\mathrm{SEND}(\cdot,\cdot),\mathrm{CORRUPT}(\cdot)}(1^n, pks)$

7 : $b \leftarrow \mathsf{SessUnfPred}$ // evaluate predicate SessUnfPred on execution state

8 : **return** $\bar{b}$ // where $\bar{b} = \mathrm{NOT}(b)$

Fig. 4. Session-definite unforgeability of transaction system.

In addition, we assume that session identifiers only appear in matching pairs on the sides. This implies that there cannot be session-identifier collisions on the card-holder side, nor on the service-provider side. This also means that it suffices to demand for the first property above that every accepting session has a matching partner; together with collision-freeness of session identifiers on one side the matching session must be on the other party's side. The formal predicate capturing these requirements is depicted in Fig. 5 and called as a subroutine in the attack game.

Definition 1 (Session-definite unforgeability). *A transaction system* $\mathcal{TS}$ *is session-definite unforgeable if for any efficient adversary* $\mathcal{A}$ *we have that*

$$\mathrm{Prob}\left[\mathsf{SessUnf}_{\mathcal{A}}^{\mathcal{TS}}(n) = 1\right] \approx 0$$

is negligible.

Note that we let the adversary $\mathcal{A}$ decide when to stop the execution and to start evaluating the predicate. Hence, if it is advantageous and the adversary already detects a winning situation, it may end the execution immediately (instead of messing up the winning state by, say, corrupting another party). In our case this is easy to spot since all the data required to evaluate the predicate are known to the adversary.

Predicate SessUnfPred on execution state

1 : $p \leftarrow$ **true**

2 :   // any accepting party must have honest partner with same tsid (or corrupt partner)

3 :   **foreach** $\ell \in \{\ell \mid \mathsf{ACC}(\ell) = \mathsf{true} \wedge \mathsf{ID}(\ell) \notin \mathsf{Corrupt}\}$ **do**

4 : $p \leftarrow p \wedge [\mathsf{PID}(\ell) \in \mathsf{Corrupt}$

5 : $\vee \, \exists \ell' \neq \ell : (\mathsf{TSID}(\ell') = \mathsf{TSID}(\ell) \neq \bot \wedge \mathsf{PID}(\ell) = \mathsf{ID}(\ell'))]$

6 :   **endforeach**

7 :   // Collisions among identifiers only between opposite partners

8 :   **foreach** $(\ell, \ell') \in \{(\ell, \ell') \mid \ell \neq \ell' \wedge \mathsf{ID}(\ell), \mathsf{ID}(\ell') \notin \mathsf{Corrupt}$

9 : $\wedge \mathsf{TSID}(\ell) = \mathsf{TSID}(\ell') \neq \bot\}$ **do**

10 : $p \leftarrow p \wedge [(\mathsf{ID}(\ell), \mathsf{ID}(\ell')) \in \mathcal{C} \times \mathcal{S} \cup \mathcal{S} \times \mathcal{C}]$

11 : **endforeach**

12 : **return** p // where we identify true = 1 and false = 0

Fig. 5. Security predicate SessUnfPred for session-definite unforgeability

3.2   Security of the eIDAS Transaction System

Before proving the eIDAS transaction system unforgeable we need to make some assumptions about the underlying cryptographic primitives. As in [11] we model the key derivation function $\mathsf{KDF}_{\mathcal{M}}$ as a random oracle. We furthermore assume that the H function used to hide the actual transaction is collision-resistance in the sense that the probability $\mathbf{Adv}_{\mathcal{B},\mathsf{H}}^{\mathrm{coll}}(n)$ of $\mathcal{B}$ outputting such a collision is negligible for every efficient adversary $\mathcal{B}$.

We also assume that forging signatures is infeasible, i.e., for any efficient adversary $\mathcal{B}$ the probability $\mathbf{Adv}_{\mathcal{B},\mathcal{SIG}}^{\mathrm{unf}}(n)$ of breaking the terminal's signature scheme given through $\mathcal{SIG} = (\mathsf{KG}_{\mathcal{S}}, \mathsf{Sig}, \mathsf{SVf})$ in an adaptive chosen-message attack (see [14] for a formal definition) is negligible. We analogously demand that forging MACs for the scheme given through $\mathcal{MAC} = (\mathsf{KDF}_{\mathcal{M}}, \mathsf{MAC}, \mathsf{MVf})$ is infeasible, i.e., $\mathbf{Adv}_{\mathcal{B},\mathcal{MAC}}^{\mathrm{unf}}(n)$ is negligible for any efficient adversary $\mathcal{B}$ against the MAC scheme.

Finally, as in [11] we assume that the Gap-Diffie-Hellman problem in the group specified by D_C is hard. That is, consider an efficient adversary $\mathcal{B}$ which receives (in multiplicative notation) g^a, g^b for generator g and hidden random a, b and which gets access to an oracle which for adversarially chosen group elements Y, Z verifies for the adversary whether $Y^a = Z$ or not. The adversary's task it to output $\mathrm{DH}(g^a, g^b) = g^{ab}$. We now require that for no efficient adversary the probability $\mathbf{Adv}_{\mathcal{B},D_C}^{\mathrm{GapDH}}(n)$ of computing that DH value is negligible.

Theorem 1 (Session-definite Unforgeability). *The eIDAS transaction system in Sect. 2 is session-definite unforgeable in the random oracle model, assuming collision resistance of* H, *unforgeability of the signature and MAC scheme, and the GapDH assumption. More precisely, for any efficient adversary* $\mathcal{A}$ *there exists efficient adversaries* $\mathcal{B}_1, \mathcal{B}_2, \mathcal{B}_3, \mathcal{B}_4$ *such that*

$$\text{Prob}\left[\text{SessUnf}_{\mathcal{A}}^{\mathcal{TS}}(n) = 1\right] \leq \binom{s}{2} \cdot \left(2^{-n} + \frac{R}{q}\right) + \boldsymbol{Adv}_{\mathcal{B}_1,\mathsf{H}}^{coll}(n) + S \cdot \boldsymbol{Adv}_{\mathcal{B}_2,\mathcal{SIG}}^{unf}(n)$$

$$+ S \cdot \boldsymbol{Adv}_{\mathcal{B}_3,\mathcal{MAC}}^{unf}(n) + C \cdot S \cdot \boldsymbol{Adv}_{\mathcal{B}_4,D_C}^{GapDH}(n)$$

where we assume that Compr is a R-regular function, q is the group size specified by D_C, *the adversary initiates at most s sessions, and there are at most C cards and S service providers.*

Moreover, adversaries $\mathcal{B}_1, \ldots, \mathcal{B}_4$ *have roughly the same running time* $\mathcal{A}$ *plus the time to carry out the other steps in the experiment.*

Proof (Sketch). We given the proof only for the case of a deterministic hash $\mathsf{H}(\mathsf{T})$ and single initializations through INIT; for probabilistic hashes and synchronous initializations the proof can be adapted easily.

Assume that an adversary $\mathcal{A}$ mounts an attack against session-definite unforgeability. In order to win the adversary must either create a collision in two honest card-holder sessions, or in two honest service-provider sessions, or make one of the two types of parties accept such that there is no matching session (with a party of the other type, either corrupt or not having the same tsid).

The idea of ruling out the above attack possibility is that: sessions among honest card holders or among honest service providers do not collide because each session identifier sid contains fresh random values r_C resp. cpk_T of both sides. The other property follows since the adversary, unless it forges signatures, cannot make a card holder accept without having an honest provider sign and output the session identifier sid. Since the session identifier includes the collision-resistant hash of transaction T this argument extends to the fully augmented identifiers tsid, as required by the security definition.

The final step is to note that, analogously to the signature case, an adversary making an honest provider accept without having an honest card-holder partner also requires the adversary to forge MACs. The latter argument is a bit more involved, but can be seen to follow from the proof that TA together CA is a secure key exchange protocol [11]. This is the step where we also use the Gap-Diffie-Hellman assumption. The full proof is omitted for space reasons.   □

4   Transaction Privacy

Analogous to the case of unforgeability we first describe the general security requirements and then discuss that the eIDAS transaction system meets these requirements.

Experiment $\mathsf{TPriv}_{\mathcal{A}}^{\mathcal{TS}}(n)$

---

1 : $b \leftarrow \{0,1\}$

2 : **foreach** $i \in \mathcal{C} \cup \mathcal{S}$ **do**

3 :   **if** $i \in \mathcal{C}$ **then** $(sk_i, pk_i, cert_i) \leftarrow \mathsf{KG}_\mathcal{C}(1^n)$ **fi**

4 :   **if** $i \in \mathcal{S}$ **then** $(sk_i, pk_i, cert_i) \leftarrow \mathsf{KG}_\mathcal{S}(1^n)$ **fi**

5 : **endforeach**

6 : $pks \leftarrow \{(pk_i, cert_i) \mid i \in \mathcal{C} \cup \mathcal{S}\}$

7 : $a \leftarrow \mathcal{A}^{\mathrm{INIT}(\cdot,\cdot),\mathrm{SEND}(\cdot,\cdot),\mathrm{CORRUPT}(\cdot),\mathrm{CHALL}(b,\cdots)}(1^n, pks)$

8 : **return** $a = b$

Fig. 6. Transaction privacy experiment

4.1   Defining Privacy

Transaction privacy refers to the inability for the eID service to determine the transaction, even though it operates on the hash value. We use an indistinguishability-based approach here in which a privacy-adversary can initiate (multiple) executions on a random choice of one of two adversarially-chosen transactions T_0, T_1. This of course assumes that transactions are augmented by sufficient entropy, or else the adversary can easily determine the choice of the transaction used in the hash value.

The attack model is as in case of unforgeability. The only difference is now that the adversary now also gets a challenge oracle CHALL, which is initialized with a secret bit $b \leftarrow \{0,1\}$. If called about identities id $\in \mathcal{C}$, id$' \in \mathcal{S}$, as well as two transactions T_0, T_1, then the challenge oracle executes $\ell \leftarrow$ INIT(id, id$'$, T_b) to initialize both parties, and it returns the session lables (ℓ, ℓ') to the adversary. From then on the adversary can communicate with the card-holder and service provider sessions via the SEND oracle for the corresponding label (and in particular learn the hashed transaction). The adversary eventually should predict the bit b.

We next define privacy with the experiment in Fig. 6.

Definition 2 (Transaction Privacy). *A transaction system $\mathcal{TS}$ is transaction private if for any efficient adversary $\mathcal{A}$ we have that*

$$\mathrm{Prob}\left[\mathsf{TPriv}_{\mathcal{A}}^{\mathcal{TS}}(n) = 1\right] \leq \tfrac{1}{2} + negl(n)$$

is negligibly close to $\tfrac{1}{2}$.

Conceivably, any transaction-private system needs to be preportioned.

4.2   Privacy of the eIDAS Transaction System

The privacy of the eIDAS transaction system now relies on the hiding property of the hash function, namely, that the probability of being able to distinguish

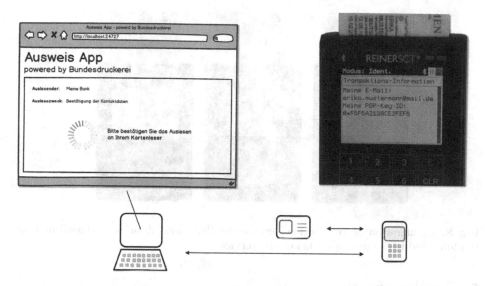

Fig. 7. Prototype implementation on a card reader. In this example the identity card has already been connected to the card reader, and the user is now asked via the (mockup) software on the computer to authenticate the e-mail address and PGP fingerprint on the reader.

$H(T_0, r_0)$ from $H(T_1, r_1)$ for chosen T_0, T_1 and random r_0, r_1 is infeasible for any efficient adversary $\mathcal{B}$. We note that this is straightforward to formalize in terms of the hiding property of commitment schemes (see again [14]), such that for the advantage $\mathbf{Adv}_{\mathcal{B},H}^{hide}(n)$ distinguishing the two cases it holds:

Theorem 2 (Transaction Privacy of the eIDAS Transaction System).
The eIDAS transaction system provides transaction privacy. More precisely, for any efficient adversary $\mathcal{A}$ making at most Q challenge queries there exists an efficient adversary $\mathcal{B}$ such that

$$\mathrm{Prob}\left[\mathsf{TPriv}_{\mathcal{A}}^{\mathcal{TS}}(n) = 1\right] \leq \tfrac{1}{2} + Q \cdot \mathbf{Adv}_{\mathcal{B},H}^{hide}(n).$$

Moreover, the running time of $\mathcal{B}$ is essentially the one of $\mathcal{A}$, plus the time to execute the other steps of the privacy experiment.

Proof. Each call of $\mathcal{A}$ to the CHALL oracle creates another fresh "commitment" of either the left or the right transaction. Then all parties work on the hashed value only. It follows that $\mathcal{A}$'s success probability is bounded by the probability of distinguishing at most Q left commitments from Q right commitments. Since a standard hybrid argument for commitments shows that such Q commitments (for adaptively chosen pairs) can only increase the distinguishing advantage compared to a single commitment by a factor Q, the claim now follows. □

Fig. 8. Immigration of transaction verification (left) into data access confirmation (middle) and PIN entering (right) of eID service.

5   Implementation

As mentioned before, the eIDAS transaction system has been successfully integrated in a test bed for the German identity card, involving the Reiner SCT cyberJack reader. Recall that the user places the card in (or near) the reader and initiates a service through the software on its computer. The software application then requests the user to verify the transaction data (see Fig. 7). The transaction data is encoded into an admissible format for the auxiliary data of the eID service under an unused object identifier such that the card, upon receiving the data, authenticates them through the protocol but ignores its semantics. In contrast, the reader has been modified to interpret these data accordingly.

From the user's perspective the steps to authenticate transaction data integrate smoothly with the other eID steps (see Fig. 8). In the first step, where the regular eID system and the transaction system differ slightly, the user now checks the transaction data on the card reader, e.g., the mobile phone number in Fig. 8. Then the user proceeds as for the regular eID service, confirming the card data the eID service can access (step 2 in Fig. 8), and finally entering the card's PIN (step 3).

Overall, implementing the eIDAS transaction system requires minimal changes to the underlying system—only the reader's software needs to be adapted slightly—and to provide corresponding software applications.

6   Conclusion

The eIDAS transaction system is an easy and practical method to authenticate transactions via the eIDAS infrastructure. The work here demonstrates that, cryptographically, it also provides strong unforgeability guarantees, thwarting for example replay attacks. Furthermore, it also allows to hide the actual transaction data from the underlying infrastructure, again in a very strong sense.

Acknowledgments. We thank the anonymous reviewers of WISTP 2016 for valuable comments.

References

1. Bundesamt für Sicherheit in der Informationstechnik (BSI, Federal Office for Information Security): Advanced Security Mechanism for Machine Readable Travel Documents - Extended Access Control (EAC), Password Authenticated Connection Establishment (PACE), and Restricted Identification (RI), BSI-TR-03110, Version 2.0 (2008)
2. Bundesamt für Sicherheit in der Informationstechnik (BSI, Federal Office for Information Security): Technical Guideline TR-03110-2: Advanced Security Mechanisms for Machine Readable Travel Documents and eIDAS Token, Part 2, Protocols for electronic IDentification, Authentication and trust Services (eIDAS). BSI-TR-03110, Version 2.2 (2015)
3. Morgner, F.: Transaktionsabsicherung mit der Online-Ausweisfunktion. Kryptographische Bindung von Transaktionsdaten an den Personalausweis. Presentation, CeBit 2014, March 2014
4. Bellare, M., Kohno, T., Namprempre, C.: Breaking and provably repairing the SSH authenticated encryption scheme: a case study of the encode-then-encrypt-and-MAC paradigm. ACM Trans. Inf. Syst. Secur. **7**(2), 206–241 (2004)
5. Bender, J., Dagdelen, Ö., Fischlin, M., Kügler, D.: The PACE|AA protocol for machine readable travel documents, and its security. In: Keromytis, A.D. (ed.) FC 2012. LNCS, vol. 7397, pp. 344–358. Springer, Heidelberg (2012)
6. Bender, J., Dagdelen, Ö., Fischlin, M., Kügler, D.: Domain-specific pseudonymous signatures for the german identity card. In: Gollmann, D., Freiling, F.C. (eds.) ISC 2012. LNCS, vol. 7483, pp. 104–119. Springer, Heidelberg (2012)
7. Bender, J., Fischlin, M., Kügler, D.: Security analysis of the PACE key-agreement protocol. In: Samarati, P., Yung, M., Martinelli, F., Ardagna, C.A. (eds.) ISC 2009. LNCS, vol. 5735, pp. 33–48. Springer, Heidelberg (2009)
8. Bender, J., Fischlin, M., Kügler, D.: The PACE|CA protocol for machine readable travel documents. In: Bloem, R., Lipp, P. (eds.) INTRUST 2013. LNCS, vol. 8292, pp. 17–35. Springer, Heidelberg (2013)
9. Canetti, R., Krawczyk, H.: Analysis of key-exchange protocols and their use for building secure channels. In: Pfitzmann, B. (ed.) EUROCRYPT 2001. LNCS, vol. 2045, pp. 453–474. Springer, Heidelberg (2001)
10. Coron, J.-S., Gouget, A., Icart, T., Paillier, P.: Supplemental access control (PACE v2): security analysis of PACE integrated mapping. In: Naccache, D. (ed.) Cryphtography and Security: From Theory to Applications. LNCS, vol. 6805, pp. 207–232. Springer, Heidelberg (2012)
11. Dagdelen, Ö., Fischlin, M.: Security analysis of the extended access control protocol for machine readable travel documents. In: Burmester, M., Tsudik, G., Magliveras, S., Ilić, I. (eds.) ISC 2010. LNCS, vol. 6531, pp. 54–68. Springer, Heidelberg (2011)
12. Hanzlik, L., Kutylowski, M.: Restricted identification secure in the extended Canetti-Krawczyk model. J. UCS **21**(3), 419–439 (2015)
13. Hanzlik, L., Krzywiecki, Ł., Kutyłowski, M.: Simplified PACE|AA protocol. In: Deng, R.H., Feng, T. (eds.) ISPEC 2013. LNCS, vol. 7863, pp. 218–232. Springer, Heidelberg (2013)
14. Jatz, J., Lindell, Y.: Introduction to Modern Cryptography. Chapman & Hall/CRC Cryptography and Network Security Series, 2nd edn (2015)

15. Kutyłowski, M., Krzywiecki, Ł., Kubiak, P., Koza, M.: Restricted identification scheme and diffie-hellman linking problem. In: Chen, L., Yung, M., Zhu, L. (eds.) INTRUST 2011. LNCS, vol. 7222, pp. 221–238. Springer, Heidelberg (2012)
16. Maurer, U., Tackmann, B.: On the soundness of authenticate-then-encrypt: formalizing the malleability of symmetric encryption. In: Al-Shaer, E., Keromytis, A.D., Shmatikov, V. (eds.) ACM CCS 2010, pp. 505–515. ACM Press, October 2010
17. Namprempre, C.: Secure channels based on authenticated encryption schemes: a simple characterization. In: Zheng, Y. (ed.) ASIACRYPT 2002. LNCS, vol. 2501, pp. 515–532. Springer, Heidelberg (2002)

Novel Lightweight Signcryption-Based Key Distribution Mechanisms for MIKEY

Kim Thuat Nguyen[1($\boxtimes$)], Nouha Oualha[1], and Maryline Laurent[2]

[1] CEA, LIST, Communicating Systems Laboratory,
91191 Gif-sur-yvette Cedex, France
{kimthuat.nguyen,nouha.oualha}@cea.fr
[2] Institut Mines-Telecom, Telecom SudParis,
UMR CNRS 5157 SAMOVAR, 9 Rue Charles Fourier, 91011 Evry, France
maryline.laurent@telecom-sudparis.eu

Abstract. Multimedia Internet KEYing (MIKEY) is a standard key management protocol, used to set up common secrets between any two parties for multiple scenarios of communications. As MIKEY becomes widely deployed, it becomes worthwhile to not confine its applications to real-time or other specific applications, but also to extend the standard to other scenarios as well. For instance, MIKEY can be used to secure key establishment in the Internet of Things. In this particular context, Elliptic Curve Cryptography-based (ECC) algorithms seem to be good candidate to be employed by MIKEY, since they can support equivalent security level when compared with other recommended cryptographic algorithms like RSA, and at the same time requiring smaller key sizes and offering better performance.

In this work, we propose novel lightweight ECC-based key distribution extensions for MIKEY that are built upon a previously proposed certificateless signcryption scheme. To our knowledge, these extensions are the first ECC-based MIKEY extensions that employ signcryption schemes. Our proposed extensions benefit from the lightness of the signcryption scheme, while being discharged from the burden of the public key infrastructure (PKI) thanks to its certificateless feature. To demonstrate their performance, we implemented our proposed extensions in the Openmote sensor platform and conducted a thorough performance assessment by measuring the energy consumption and execution time of each operation in the key establishment procedure. The experimental results prove that our new MIKEY extensions are perfectly suited for resource-constrained devices.

1 Introduction

Multimedia Internet KEYing (MIKEY) [5] is a key management protocol which is intended for use with real-time applications. MIKEY provides different methods to establish a session key with multiple parties, in addition to the authentication of parties if required. For example, MIKEY pre-shared key method permits

© IFIP International Federation for Information Processing 2016
Published by Springer International Publishing Switzerland 2016. All Rights Reserved
S. Foresti and J. Lopez (Eds.): WISTP 2016, LNCS 9895, pp. 19–34, 2016.
DOI: 10.1007/978-3-319-45931-8_2

any two parties with a pre-shared secret to set up a secure communication. However, this mechanism suffers from scalability issues since it is unpractical to pre-distribute a common key for any two parties in large networks, e.g. the Internet of Things (IoT). To be scalable, public key encryption-based methods, where any two parties can establish security communications without any *a priori* shared common keys, have been proposed to be employed by MIKEY.

These different key distribution mechanisms can be classified into two categories: (i) a key exchange mode and (ii) a key transport mode. The MIKEY key exchange modes, such as, MIKEY-DHSIGN [5], MIKEY-DHHMAC [13], are usually based on the Diffie-Hellman (DH) key exchange [20]. These modes provide the perfect forward secrecy property, i.e. the compromise of long-term keying materials does not reveal previously derived session keys. Additionally, both communicating parties participate in the session key generation process. As a result, DH-based modes require at least two message exchanges to set up a common secret key. As another disadvantage, these modes do not support the establishment of group keys.

In key transport modes, on the other hand, the initiating party is responsible for the key generation. The generated keys are then encrypted using the public key of the responding party. Even if key transport modes do not provide perfect forward secrecy, they are more efficient in terms of computation and communication than DH-based modes. Indeed, only a half roundtrip is needed to set up a common key between two parties. Existing key transport modes of MIKEY generally employ a public key encryption algorithm to protect transferred keys, such as RSA [18] or ECIES [15] and an additionally public key signature algorithm to sign MIKEY message. In this paper, we propose to use more lightweight key transport modes built upon a signcryption scheme defined in [21], which is an authenticated encryption algorithm that combines encryption and signature procedures in an optimized manner. The signcryption scheme is based on Elliptic Curve Cryptography (ECC), thus inheriting multiple advantages of ECC in terms of performance. As mentioned in [15], ECC-based schemes require smaller key sizes and offer better security per bit, when compared with known cryptographic algorithms like RSA. Moreover, the signcryption scheme in [21] offer the certificateless feature that allows to dispense the two parties with the provision of a digital certificate issued by a Public Key Infrastructure (PKI).

Our contribution: In this paper, we first introduce two novel key transport mechanisms for the standardized key management protocol MIKEY [5]. The main idea is to apply the certificateless elliptic curve Korean signature-based signcryption scheme, namely ECKSS, defined in [21] as the public key encryption algorithm to construct MIKEY messages. Then, we present experimental performance results of the two proposed key distribution methods by measuring the energy consumption and the execution time for each operation. Our solutions have been implemented and validated using the Openmote sensor platform [2]. The experimental results show that our proposed extentions to MIKEY are suited for resource-constrained devices.

Paper outline: The rest of this paper is organized as follows. Section 2 surveys several existing ECC-based key transport solutions proposed for MIKEY and presents briefly related work on signcryption schemes. Section 3 provides several notations and recalls our proposed signcryption scheme provided in [21]. We describe in details our proposed key transport mechanisms for MIKEY in Sect. 4. Section 5 discusses several security considerations needed for our proposals. The performance assessment of our proposals is given in Sect. 6, while Sect. 7 concludes our work.

2   Related Work

As MIKEY [5] becomes more deployed, extensions to the base protocol have emerged [4,6,15]. Several of these extensions brought additional key distributions methods to MIKEY, for instance based on Elliptic Curve Cryptography (ECC) [23]. Since ECC support requires smaller keys while keeping the same security level as other asymmetric algorithms like RSA, ECC usage is considered interesting for devices with limited performance and storage capabilities. ECC extensions to MIKEY offer new mechanisms for authentication, encryption and digital signature to provide secure key distribution. ECC-based mechanisms such as ECDH to extend the Diff-Hellman exchange [20], ECDSA or ECGDSA for digital signatures, Elliptic Curve Integrated Encryption Scheme (ECIES) and Elliptic Curve Menezes-Qu-Vanstone Scheme (ECMQV) to provide, respectively, integrated encryption and authenticated key exchange, have been defined in [23]. To the best of our knowledge, ECC-based signcryption mechanisms have not been proposed for MIKEY, even though these mechanisms have been present in the literature for many years, and many ECC-based signcryption mechanisms offer a good performance thanks to their optimized authenticated public key encryption besides the advantages of ECC.

Signcryption schemes allow to simultaneously perform the functions of both digital signature and encryption. Most of existing signcryption schemes are derived from popular signature schemes (refer to the survey in [27]). For examples, Zheng's scheme [28] is based on ElGamal encryption and signature schemes [12], and Shin et al.'s scheme [24], called SCDSA+, is based on DSA (Digital Signature Algorithm) signature scheme [14]. Zheng's scheme requires complex interactive zero-knowledge proof to validate the non-repudiation and does not provide insider confidentiality. On the other hand, the security of Shin et al.'s scheme has not been formally proven. KCDSA (Korean Certificate-based Digital Signature Algorithm) [19] is a variant of DSA, whose design allows to relieve the signature generation and verification procedures of modular inversions required in DSA. Two signcryption variants based on KCDSA have been proposed by Yum et al. in [26]. However, the first variant is confidentiality insecure in the insider model, while the second one is not semantically secure due to the disclosure of the hash of the message.

ECC-based signcryption schemes have also been proposed in several papers like [17,25], which are both based on ECDSA. In [21], we have proposed a new signcryption scheme based on ECKCDSA, and we have formally proven the security of this scheme in the random oracle model, thus providing outsider/insider confidentiality and unforgeability, in addition to non-repudiation, while being more efficient in terms of communication and computation costs than existing signcryption schemes. Moreover, our scheme offers the certificateless feature, so certificates are not needed to verify initiator/responder's public keys. In this paper, we propose to extend the MIKEY protocol with new key distribution methods based on our signcryption scheme [21], and we demonstrate the advantages and gains in terms of performance achieved by these methods.

3   Preliminaries

In this section, we introduce several notations and review briefly our elliptic curve-based signcryption scheme proposed in [21].

3.1   Abbreviations and Notations

The definitions and abbreviations, as described in Table 1, and used throughout the rest of this document are consistent with those used in the MIKEY standard [5].

Table 1. Abbreviations

$P + Q$	Addition of two elliptic curve points P and Q
$t.P$	Addition of P with itself t times
$s\|\|t$	Concatenation of two strings s and t
$\perp$	Error symbol
KMS	Key Management Server
I	Initiator
R	Responder
HMAC	Hash Message Authentication Code
MAC	Message Authentication Code
TEK	Trafic-Encrypting Key
TGK	TEK Generation Key

3.2   The Certificateless Elliptic Curve Korean Signature-Based Signcryption

In this subsection, we describe our certificateless signcryption scheme based on elliptic curve, named as ECKSS. The security of this scheme has been formally proved in the random oracle model [21].

Considered Actors. We consider three main actors in our scenario presented in the following.

- Two parties: an Initiator (I) and a Responder (R), which respectively initiates the communication and responds to incoming requests.
- A trusted Key Management Server (KMS), which is responsible for generating keying materials and that acts as the root of trust of the responder and initiator. The proposed solutions support also multiple KMSs i.e., the initiator or the responder may use a different KMS, but this multi-authority setting is considered as out of scope of the paper.

Security Parameter Generation Process. Depending on the security parameter as input, KMS first runs the Setup algorithm to define an elliptic curve E over finite field $\mathbb{F}_p$ with a generator G, where p is the prime modulus. Two hash functions are also defined: $H_1 : \{0,1\}^* \rightarrow \mathbb{Z}_p$ and $H_2 : \{0,1\}^* \rightarrow \{0,1\}^*$. (Enc, Dec) are the encryption and decryption algorithms of a symmetric cipher. Then, KMS executes the KeyGen algorithm to generate the keying material for I and R. KMS first chooses the master key as mk from $\mathbb{Z}_p$. Its public key is then calculated as $PK_{KMS} = mk.G$. For an entity A with the identifier id_A, KMS generates the public and private values of an entity A as follows.

- Compute $V_A = x_A.G$, where x_A is a random number on $\mathbb{Z}_p$
- Compute the private key for A: $priv_A = (mk + x_A.H_1(id_A||V_A||G||PK_{KMS}))^{-1}$
- Compute $P_A = priv_A^{-1}.G$
- Set the public key of A as $PK_A = (P_A, V_A)$

As we shall see, we can validate the public key of A by using the following equation:

$$P_A = PK_{KMS} + H_1(id_A||V_A||G||PK_{KMS}).V_A \tag{1}$$

ECKSS Description. The detailed procedure of ECKSS is described in the following:

- Signcrypt($priv_I, PK_I, PK_R, M$) → CT: To signcrypt a message M intended to R, I executes the following steps:

1. Choose randomly $x \leftarrow \mathbb{Z}_p$
2. Compute $K = x.P_R$
3. Generate a secret key: $\tau = H_2(PK_I||PK_R||K)$
4. Compute $r = H_1(PK_I||PK_R||K||M)$
5. Compute $s = priv_I.(x - r)$
6. Compute $c = \mathsf{Enc}_\tau(M)$
7. Send the ciphertext $CT = (r, s, c)$ to R

- Unsigncrypt($priv_R, PK_R, PK_I, CT$) → M: Upon receiving the ciphertext $CT = (r, s, c)$ from I, R has to perform the following procedure:

1. Compute $K = (s.priv_R^{-1}).P_I + (r.priv_R^{-1}).G$.
2. Get the secret keys: $\tau = H_2(PK_I||PK_R||K)$
3. Compute $\mathsf{Dec}_\tau(c) = M$
4. Verify that $r = H_1(PK_I||PK_R||K||M)$

Note that I and R can be sure about the public values of the other party by verifying the Eq. (1). This feature makes ECKSS *certificateless* since it does not require certificates to authenticate the public keys.

4 Novel Signcryption-Based Key Distribution Methods for MIKEY

In this section, we first present the payload and data type formats of a MIKEY key transport mechanism. Then, we clarify our design goals for proposing new key distribution methods for MIKEY. Finally, we give details on these extensions in respect to the original MIKEY payload formats.

4.1 Basic Payload and Message Formats of a MIKEY Key Transport Mechanism

Figure 1 describes the basic message composition of a MIKEY key transport method that uses a public-key encryption algorithm, for example, in the MIKEY-RSA [5] and MIKEY-ECIES [15] modes. The mechanisms contain two message exchanges: the I_MESSAGE and the R_MESSAGE. The main objective of the Initiator's message is to distribute one or more TGKs and a set of security parameters in a secure manner. We recall the payload notions as defined in [5], in the following:

- HDR: The MIKEY header, which contains related data and information mapping to the specific security protocol used.
- T: The timestamp, used to prevent replay attacks.
- RAND: The random byte-string, which is used as a value for the freshness of the session key generation process.
- IDx: The identity of the entity X (IDi: Identity of the Initiator, IDr: Identity of the Responder).
- SP: The security policies.
- KEMAC: The Key Data Transport Payload, which contains the encrypted TGKs and a MAC.
- CHASH: The Cert Hash Payload, which is the hashes of the used certificates (e.g. CERTi).
- PKE: The Envelope Data Payload, which contains the encrypted envelope key, env_key.
- SIGNx: The signature covering the entire MIKEY message, which is generated using the signature key of the entity X.
- V: The verification message payload containing the MAC calculated over the entire MIKEY message.

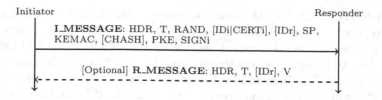

Fig. 1. Basic message format for a MIKEY public key encryption method

As described in Fig. 1, the MIKEY public key encryption method first chooses an envelope key env_key. This key is then to be encrypted using the public key PK_R of the Responder and conveyed in the PKE payload: PKE = $E(PK_R, \text{env\_key})$. Then, the encr_key and the auth_key are derived from the envelope key, env_key. These two keys are used to build the KEMAC payload where the encr_key is used to encrypt the TGKs. The encrypted part is then followed by a MAC calculated using auth_key over the entire KMAC payload. The whole MIKEY message is then integrity protected by the signature payload SIGNi.

4.2 Design Motivations

The novel key transport mechanisms for MIKEY are designed to put forwards the following motivations:

- **Performance and Efficiency**: Our proposed ECKSS signcryption scheme is able to transport secret data in a secure manner without intensive calculation. Thus, ECKSS-based methods for MIKEY is able to address the same scenario as the other key establishment methods in MIKEY [15]. In fact, existing MIKEY modes are intended for application-layer key management and multimedia applications. However, thanks to ECKSS lightweight computation requirements, the proposed methods can be considered in constrained environments such as IoT. We prove the feasibility of our proposed mechanisms in such environment in Sect. 6. Furthermore, the mechanisms are based on elliptic curve cryptography (ECC). Additionally, when compared with existing ECC-based asymmetric methods of MIKEY, our proposed mechanisms are the most efficient while offering equivalent security guarantees. More details are provided in Sect. 6.1.
- **PKI Independence**: ECKSS can be applied in the context where no access to a public-key infrastructure (PKI) is available. Indeed, the validation of entity's public keys is realized in equation (1) without certificates. Moreover, as pre-shared master secrets are not required, the proposed ECKSS-based schemes should be as scalable as other existing asymmetric mechanisms of MIKEY.

4.3 The MIKEY-ECKSS Mode Specification

Figure 2 defines the message exchanges for our first proposal MIKEY-ECKSS. Similarly to other MIKEY public key encryption methods such as MIKEY-RSA

[5] or MIKEY-ECIES [15], the main objective of the Initiator's message is to distribute one or more TGKs in a secure manner. This method reuses the defined payload in Sect. 4.1 except the payload ECKSSi in the I_MESSAGE. This payload transports actually the encrypted TGKs through the triple (r, s, c) as defined in Sect. 3.2. To guarantee the integrity protection, we employ the payload SIGNi, which is a signature covering the entire I_MESSAGE. As described in [5], the SIGNi payload will use either ECDSA or ECGDSA as the signature algorithm.

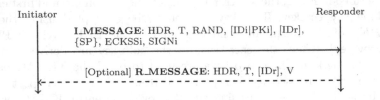

Fig. 2. Elliptic curve Korean signature-based signcryption key distribution method for MIKEY

Upon receiving the I_MESSAGE, R first approves the integrity of the message by verifying the appended signature payload SIGNi. If the verification holds, it then uses the Unsigncrypt algorithm to decrypt the payload ECKSSi in order to obtain the values of TGKs. In case mutual authentication is required, the verification message, V, is calculated by building a MAC over the concatenation of the header HDR (the same as the one that was used in the I_MESSAGE), the timestamps, the identities of the two parties, using the authentication key. The latter is derived from the received TGKs. Then, we append the V payload to the concatenation (HDR, T, [IDi, PKi], [IDr]) to form the R_MESSAGE. However, as depicted in Fig. 2, the R_MESSAGE is optional.

4.4 MIKEY-ECKSS-HMAC Mode Specification

In this subsection, we describe in detail our second key distribution extension for MIKEY. We call this mode MIKEY-ECKSS-HMAC, since this mode uses ECKSS to envelop the TGKs and HMAC to ensure the authentication of the messages exchanged. As we shall see, the use of the signature payload SIGNx still requires multiple exponentiations in the signature generation and verification processes, e.g. 3 modular exponentiations are needed if using ECDSA. As a result, MIKEY-ECKSS-HMAC is even more lightweight than MIKEY-ECKSS, which is suitable for constrained devices.

Figure 3 describes in detail the MIKEY-ECKSS-HMAC mode. We use the same notations for the payload names as defined in Sect. 4.1. In the I_MESSAGE, the ECKSSi payload contains the triple (r, s, c) as depicted in Sect. 3.2. The KEMAC payload conveys the Hash Message Authentication Code (HMAC) of

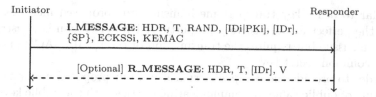

Fig. 3. HMAC-authenticated Elliptic Curve Korean signature-based signcryption key distribution method for MIKEY

the entire MIKEY message. This technique is also employed in the MIKEY-DHHMAC method [13]. The HMAC value is calculated using the secret key k_{auth}. This key is generated during the encryption of TGKs using the ECKSS algorithm. Indeed, we make modifications in step 4 of the Signcrypt algorithm and in step 2 of the Unsigncrypt algorithm (see Sect. 3.2 for more details). Another secret key k_{auth} in addition to τ is generated, as depicted in Table 2. This key is to be used in the creation of HMAC.

Table 2. Modifications made to the Signcrypt and Unsigncrypt algorithms

Signcrypt	Unsigncrypt
3) Generate a couple of secret keys: $\tau, k_{auth} = H_2(PK_I \| PK_R \| K)$	2) Get the secret keys: $\tau, k_{auth} = H_2(PK_I \| PK_R \| K)$

Upon receiving the I_MESSAGE, R first runs the Unsigncrypt algorithm to get the value of TGKs and k_{auth}. The authentication key k_{auth} is then used to verify that the I_MESSAGE has not been modified by an attacker. Indeed, a MAC is calculated over the entire I_MESSAGE using k_{auth}. This value is then compared with the hashed value extracted from the KEMAC payload. On the other hand, the R_MESSAGE's construction is optional as depicted in Fig. 3. This message is only needed when mutual authentication between parties is required.

5 Security Considerations

As this paper proposes two new methods for the MIKEY protocol, existing security considerations discussed in [5] apply here as well.

As mentioned in [5], one should select a secure symmetric cipher supporting at least 128 bits as a practical choice for the actual media protection. In our proposals, the payload ECKSSi carries the actual encrypted TGKs, the used encryption algorithm should also offer a security level of at least 128 bits. For the selection of hash functions, we recommend to work at least with SHA-256 [8] when constructing the ECKSSi payload and other payloads as well. This should be seriously taken into account in order to achieve the 128-bit level.

Similar to other key transport mechanisms, our proposed methods do not provide the perfect forward secrecy property. A Diffie-Hellman key distribution resolves this issue but requires the transmission of the R_MESSAGE in order to set up a common secret key.

In order to provide the *certificateless* feature, our proposed methods rely on the binding of public values of communicating parties with the public keys issued by KMS. Thus, after validating a provided public value using equation (1), we can be sure that only KMS is able to generate such value. It also means that the KMS can read all traffic between any parties administrated by the KMS. However, we assumed that the KMS is a fully trusted party.

6 Performance Assessment

In this section, we first quantify the performance of our schemes. Then, we describe our testing environment and the used methodology to achieve the experimental measurements. Finally, we provide in detail the performance results in terms of energy consumption and the time execution of our proposals including the ECKSS algorithm and the two proposed MIKEY modes.

6.1 Comparison with Related Work

Table 3 illustrates the performances of our two proposed methods and multiple ECC-based MIKEY modes in related work. The table first identifies if the scheme is a key exchange method or a key transport method. Then, it shows if the scheme is independent to the public key infrastructure or not. This property means that a PKI-independent scheme does not require standard digital certificates to provide authentication between communicating parties and hence the scheme is discharged from complex operations during certificate verification, revocation and management processes. Then, the efficiency of each scheme is evaluated with respect to the computational cost demonstrated in terms of the number of expensive operations needed to generate the I_MESSAGE and the R_MESSAGE. Here, we consider the three most expensive operations for an ECC-based scheme: modular point multiplication (PM), modular inversion (I) and pairing operation (e). Furthermore, we provided also the name of the payload that requires these expensive operations. For example, in a PM column, the line "2 (PKE) + 1 (SIGNi)" means that two point multiplications are executed to build the PKE (public key encryption) payload and 1 other point multiplication is calculated to build the SIGNi (signature) payload. For simpler comparison, if not explicitly specified in each mode, we assume that SIGNi payload carries an ECDSA signature and its related data.

As we shall see, the first two modes in Table 3: MIKEY-DHSIGN and MIKEY-ECQMV, are two ECC-based key exchange methods proposed for MIKEY. These methods are based on the Diffie-Hellman key exchange [20]. Hence, the R_MESSAGE is compulsory in order to setup a common secret key. On the other hand, in a key transport mechanism, I envelops and sends directly

Table 3. Performance comparison of our propositions and ECC-based MIKEY modes in related work

Mode	Type	PKI	I_MESSAGE			R_MESSAGE		
			PM	I	e	PM	I	e
MIKEY-DHSIGN [15]	KE	Yes	1 (DH) + 1 (SIGNi)	1(SIGNi)	0	1 (DH) + 2 (SIGNi)	1 (SIGNi)	0
MIKEY-ECQMV [15]		Yes	1(ECCPT)+1 (SIGNi)	1 (SIGNi)	0	1 (PKE)+2 (SIGNi)	1 (SIGNi)	0
MIKEY-SAKKE [16]	KT	No	3 (SAKKE)+1 (SIGNi)	1 (SIGNi)	0	2 (SAKKE)+4 (SIGNi)	0	1 (SAKKE)
MIKEY-ECIES [15]		Yes	2 (PKE)+1 (SIGNi)	1 (SIGNi)	0	1 (PKE)+2 (SIGNi)	1 (SIGNi)	0
MIKEY-ECKSS		No	1 (ECKSSi) + 1 (SIGNi)	0	0	2 (ECKSSi) + 2 (SIGNi)	0	0
MIKEY-ECKSS-HMAC		No	1 (ECKSSi)	0	0	2 (ECKSSi)	0	0

Meaning of abbreviations: PM: Modular point multiplication; I: Modular Inversion; e: Pairing operation; PKI: Public Key Infrastructure; KE: Key Exchange; KT: Key Transport

a secret key/message that can be used as a session key without the response from R.

As our proposed schemes are key transport mechanisms, we only make direct comparison with other key/message distribution mechanisms proposed for MIKEY. As depicted in Table 3, MIKEY-ECIES [15] seems to be our direct competitor in terms of performance since it is slightly more heavyweight than our first proposal MIKEY-ECKSS (with two more modular inversions to compute). In addition, MIKEY-ECKSS is more lightweight in the generation of the I_MESSAGE which can be beneficial for a very resource-constrained initiator. Our second proposal MIKEY-ECKSS-HMAC is even more efficient than our first one. As such, it requires only 1 point multiplication for generating the I_MESSAGE and 2 point multiplications for generating the R_MESSAGE. Furthermore, both proposals do not require certificates to validate the public values of communicating parties, which is not the case in MIKEY-ECIES mode. MIKEY-SAKKE [16] is also exempted from the use of PKI. However, this mode is much more expensive than our two methods since a pairing operation needs to be executed when receiving the R_MESSAGE.

6.2   Experimental Tools and Platforms

We implemented our assessment program in C for the operating system Contiki 3.0 [10]. Based on the Relic library version 0.4.0 [3], we evaluated our proposed MIKEY modes on the elliptic curves secg_k256. Its domain parameters have been recommended by SECG [22], which provides a security level of 128 bits. In addition, we opted for the sensor node Openmote to evaluate the required operations. Openmote [2] is a low power wireless sensor module featured with 32 MHz Cortex-M3 microcontroller, a CC2520-like radio transceiver, 32 kB of RAM, 512 kB of ROM and an IEEE 802.15.4 radio interface. This platform supports 32 bit addressing and sufficient RAM and ROM capacities. Such features are needed in order to use a cryptographic library along with an application on top of it.

In our testing scenario, we encrypted data using AES in CBC mode. For MAC and message verification function, we used SHA-256 as secure hash algorithm, which provides digests (hash values) that are 256 bits. Furthermore, we transported each time a TGK with the size of 32 bytes in our tests. In each case, the experimental measurements have been obtained by calculating the average of 100 executions for each operation.

6.3   Methodology

For measuring the processing time, we used two timers provided in the rtimer library of Contiki [10]. The first timer with 128 ticks per second was employed to measure the execution time of expensive operations. The second one is more powerful with 32768 ticks per second. It was used to measure the time duration of the mote running on a specific mode.

On the other hand, in order to assess the energy consumption, we employed a software-based online energy estimation mechanism described in [11]. In this model, we can calculate the energy consumption E in Joule of an operation on Contiki using the following equation:

$$E = U * \sum I_m * t_m \tag{2}$$

where U is the supply voltage, I_m is the hardware specific current draw, t_m is the time duration and m means a particular mode (e.g. active power mode, low power mode, transmit mode and receiver mode). In our scenario, the value of U is typically 3V, as with two new AA batteries. Besides, the current draw of the sensor node in each mode is extracted from its data sheet [1]. Concretely, we considered the following modes in our measurement: power mode 1 (cpu active mode), power mode 2 (low power mode), active-mode rx (receive mode) and active-mode tx (transmit mode). The consuming current draw for each mode are respectively: $I_{pm1} = 0.6\,mA$, $I_{pm2} = 1.3\,\mu A$, $I_{rx} = 20\,mA$ and $I_{tx} = 24\,mA$, as described in [1]. The time duration t_m that the mote is in mode m, is measured using Powertrace and Energest power profile [9]. These latters are pre-loaded tools in the Contiki OS, which provide an accuracy up to 94 % of the energy consumption of a device.

6.4   Experimental Results of ECKSS

In this subsection, we provide the experimental results of our signcryption scheme ECKSS.Table 4 shows the execution time and energy cost of ECKSS algorithms on the elliptic curve secg_k256 over the Openmote platform. The results reveal that even for a really lightweight signcrypt algorithm with only one point multiplication, it requires up to 2.6 s to compute and consumes 5.6 mJ. The resources required for an unsigncrypt are practically doubled since the algorithm has to compute 2 point multiplications. We provide also in Table 4 the resources consumed by an entity to validate other party's public values. As we shall see, this process consumed the same order of magnitude of time and energy

Table 4. Energy consumption and time execution of ECKSS algorithms on the Openmote platform

Algorithm	Time (s)	Energy (mJ)
ECKSS Signcrypt	2.64	5.6
ECKSS Unsigncrypt	5.8	12.4
Public key validation	3.12	6.6

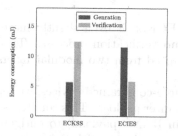 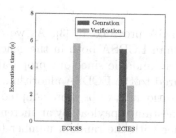

Fig. 4. Performance comparison of our proposal ECKSS with the algorithm ECIES

as the signcrypt algorithm. Such property is advantageous since the verification of certificates in a PKI-based scheme is usually complex and energy and time consuming.

In Fig. 4, we compare the performance of our ECKSS implementation with the standard algorithm ECIES, as specified in [7]. ECIES's implementation is provided in the Relic library [3]. We remark that the total work load required by our scheme ECKSS is practically identical to the one of ECIES. As we can see in Table 3, ECKSS is more rapid in the data encryption process but slower in the data decryption process.

6.5 Experimental Results of the Proposed MIKEY Modes

In this subsection, we describe the performance of our prototype implementations for the two proposed MIKEY modes.

In MIKEY-ECKSS's implementation, we use ECDSA as the signature algorithm. Table 5 provides the performance of ECDSA algorithms on the Openmote platform. These experimental results are measured based on the implementation

Table 5. Energy consumption and time execution of ECDSA algorithms on the Openmote platform

Algorithm	Time(s)	Energy (mJ)
ECDSA signature generation	2.75	6.3
ECDSA signature verification	5.83	13.6

Table 6. Energy consumption and time execution of our proposed MIKEY modes on openmote

Mode	I_MESSAGE		R_MESSAGE	
	Time (s)	Energy (mJ)	Time (s)	Energy (mJ)
MIKEY_ECKSS	5.6	11.9	11.4	24.3
MIKEY_ECKSS_HMAC	2.6	5.6	5.7	12.2

of ECDSA provided in [3]. As we can see, ECKSS is even slightly more efficient than ECDSA both in the generation and verification processes. This fact is understandable since our proposal is exempted from two modular inversions compared to the ECDSA algorithm.

Additionally, to be more adapted to resource-constrained devices, we replace the timestamps payload by an incremental counter payload. This counter is used together with the random number (carried in RAND payload) to mitigate the replay attacks. If it is the first time that I communicates with R, the counter is set to 0. It is increased by 1 after every successful key/data transportation.

Table 6 demonstrates the average time and energy consumption for generating the I_MESSAGE and R_MESSAGE, respectively. The measures show that the MIKEY-ECKSS-HMAC mode is approximately two times more efficient than the MIKEY-ECKSS mode. The performance gap between them lies in the cost of creating the SIGNi payload. As such, instead of certificates and signatures, MIKEY-ECKSS-HMAC uses a keyed hash message authentication code (carried by the KEMAC payload) to guarantee the integrity of the messages exchanged.

Figure 5 provides a graphical view of the performance of our proposals in comparison with the MIKEY-ECIES mode. The performance of the latter are roughly estimated by summing the experimental results of the two algorithms ECIES and ECDSA given in Fig. 4 and Table 5. As we shall see, the MIKEY-ECIES mode has a slightly higher computational cost in comparison with our proposed modes. However, it requires certificates to validate the public keys.

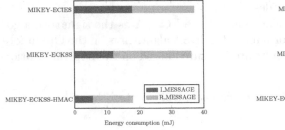
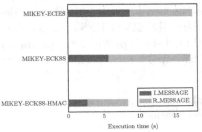

Fig. 5. Performance comparison of our proposed MIKEY modes and MIKEY-ECIES mode

This constraint could be very costly for a sensor node, since the verification of certificates is usually complex and consuming in time and energy.

7   Conclusion

In this paper, we proposed two novel signcryption-based key transport methods for MIKEY. Both methods are relieved from the dependance on a public key infrastructure thanks to their certificateless feature, and are more lightweight in terms of computation when compared with existing ECC-based key transport mechanisms proposed for MIKEY. The performance of the proposed methods have been demonstrated by experimental implementations on the Openmote sensor platform. The results confirmed that our proposed MIKEY extensions are feasible on resource-constrained devices. Hence, they can be used not only as key distribution mechanisms for real-time applications but also as lightweight key distribution solutions for the Internet of Things applications.

References

1. Cc2538 data sheet. http://www.ti.com/lit/ds/symlink/cc2538.pdf. Last accessed May 2016
2. Openmote platform. http://www.openmote.com/. Last accessed May 2016
3. Relic toolkit - an efficient library for cryptography. https://github.com/relic-toolkit/relic. Last accessed May 2016
4. Abdmeziem, M.R., Tandjaoui, D.: An end-to-end secure key management protocol for e-health applications. Comput. Electr. Eng. **44**, 184–197 (2015)
5. Arkko, J., Carrara, E., Lindholm, F., Naslund, M., Norrman, K.: Rfc 3830: Mikey: multimedia internet keying. Internet Engineering (2004)
6. Boudguiga, A., Olivereau, A., Oualha, N.: Server assisted key establishment for WSN: a mikey-ticket approach. In: Proceedings of the 12th IEEE International Conference on Trust, Security and Privacy in Computing and Communications, pp. 94–101 (2013)
7. Brown, D.: Standards for efficient cryptography, sec 1: elliptic curve cryptography. Released Standard Version 1 (2009)
8. Dang, Q.: Recommendation for applications using approved hash algorithms. US Department of Commerce, National Institute of Standards and Technology (2008)
9. Dunkels, A., Eriksson, J., Finne, N., Tsiftes, N.: Powertrace: Network-level power profiling for low-power wireless networks (2011)
10. Dunkels, A., Grönvall, B., Voigt, T.: Contiki-a lightweight and flexible operating system for tiny networked sensors. In: Proceedings of the 29th Annual IEEE International Conference on Local Computer Networks, pp. 455–462 (2004)
11. Dunkels, A., Osterlind, F., Tsiftes, N., He, Z.: Software-based on-line energy estimation for sensor nodes. In: Proceedings of the 4th workshop on Embedded networked sensors, pp. 28–32. ACM (2007)
12. El Gamal, T.: A public key cryptosystem and a signature scheme based on discrete logarithms. In: Blakely, G.R., Chaum, D. (eds.) CRYPTO 1984. LNCS, vol. 196, pp. 10–18. Springer, Heidelberg (1985)

13. Euchner, M.: Hmac-authenticated Diffie-Hellman for Multimedia Internet Keying (mikey) (2006)
14. Fips, P.: 186-2, Digital Signature Standard (DSS). National Institute of Standards and Technology (NIST) (2000)
15. Fries, S., Ignjatic, D.: On the applicability of various multimedia internet keying (mikey) modes and extensions. Technical report (2008)
16. Groves, M.: Mikey-sakke: Sakai-kasahara key encryption in multimedia internet keying (mikey) (2012)
17. Han, Y., Yang, X.-Y., Wei, P., Wang, Y., Hu, Y.: ECGSC: elliptic curve based generalized signcryption. In: Ma, J., Jin, H., Yang, L.T., Tsai, J.J.-P. (eds.) UIC 2006. LNCS, vol. 4159, pp. 956–965. Springer, Heidelberg (2006)
18. Ignjatic, D., Dondeti, L., Audet, F., Lin, P.: RFC4738 - MIKEY-RSA-R: an additional mode of key distribution in multimedia internet keying (2006)
19. Lim, C.H., Lee, P.J.: A study on the proposed korean digital signature algorithm. In: Ohta, K., Pei, D. (eds.) ASIACRYPT 1998. LNCS, vol. 1514, pp. 175–186. Springer, Heidelberg (1998)
20. Merkle, R.C.: Secure communications over insecure channels. Commun. ACM **21**(4), 294–299 (1978)
21. Nguyen, K.T., Oualha, N., Laurent, M.: Lightweight certificateless and provably-secure signcryptosystem for the internet of things. In: Proceedings of the 14th IEEE International Conference on Trust, Security and Privacy in Computing and Communications (IEEE TrustCom 2015) (2015)
22. Brown, D.R.L.: Sec 2: Recommended elliptic curve domain parameters (2010)
23. Brown, D.R.L., Chin, E., Tse, C.C.: Ecc algorithms for mikey. Work in Progress (2007)
24. Shin, J.-B., Lee, K.S., Shim, K.-A.: New DSA-verifiable signcryption schemes. In: Lee, P.J., Lim, C.H. (eds.) ICISC 2002. LNCS, vol. 2587, pp. 35–47. Springer, Heidelberg (2003)
25. Tso, R., Okamoto, T., Okamoto, E.: ECDSA-verifiable signcryption scheme with signature verification on the signcrypted message. In: Pei, D., Yung, M., Lin, D., Wu, C. (eds.) Inscrypt 2007. LNCS, vol. 4990, pp. 11–24. Springer, Heidelberg (2008)
26. Yum, D.H., Lee, P.J.: New signcryption schemes based on KCDSA. In: Kim, K. (ed.) ICISC 2001. LNCS, vol. 2288, pp. 305–317. Springer, Heidelberg (2002)
27. Yung, M., Dent, A.W., Zheng, Y.: Practical Signcryption. Springer Science & Business Media, Heidelberg (2010)
28. Zheng, Y.: Signcryption or how to achieve cost (signature & encryption) cost (signature)+ cost (encryption) (1999). http://www.pscit.monash.edu.au/yuliang/pubs/signcrypt.ps.Z

Codes v. People: A Comparative Usability Study of Two Password Recovery Mechanisms

Vlasta Stavova[1]([⊠]), Vashek Matyas[1], and Mike Just[2]

[1] Faculty of Informatics, Masaryk University, Brno, Czech Republic
vlasta.stavova@mail.muni.cz, matyas@fi.muni.cz
[2] School of Mathematical and Computer Sciences, Heriot-Watt University,
Edinburgh, UK
m.just@hw.ac.uk

Abstract. Password recovery is a critical, and often overlooked, requirement of account management. Currently popular solutions, such as security questions and out-of-band communications, have recognized security and usability issues. In this paper we evaluate two alternate recovery solutions considered by our industrial partner, using backup codes and trusted people, in order to determine their suitability as a viable password recovery solution. In this paper we focus on the usability evaluation of these two representative recovery methods, and not on the specifics of their design – while our evaluation results do indirectly point to general design enhancements. Our study determined that participants felt that backup codes (implemented as a QR-code in our solution) offer levels of usability and security that are acceptable to users for securing their "ordinary" accounts. For accounts perceived to require more security (e.g., online banking) more security was preferred by participants, resulting in a preference for trusted party recovery compared to backup codes. Our results also suggest that further research and deployment considerations should be given to options for other methods of password recovery, such as backup codes and trusted parties (Full details and paper supplementary materials can be found at http://crcs.cz/papers/wistp2016.).

1 Introduction

Nearly every website that enables users to create an account also provides a process to recover the account, in case of a forgotten password, for example. This process is referred to by many names, such as account recovery, password recovery, password reset, secondary authentication and last-resort authentication [8,16,22]. The recovery process should be usable, and as secure as the access to the account via the primary authentication.

Researchers have shown that passwords, as a primary form of authentication, are indeed forgotten or lost, so that some form of recovery is required [12,19]. Though current recovery solutions, such as the answers to *challenge questions*, are proven not to be reliable and secure enough [7]. Moreover, there are several

Published by Springer International Publishing Switzerland 2016. All Rights Reserved
S. Foresti and J. Lopez (Eds.): WISTP 2016, LNCS 9895, pp. 35–50, 2016.
DOI: 10.1007/978-3-319-45931-8_3

examples of attackers gaining access to an account due to weak password recovery [10, 15, 23].

There are several ways in which password or account recovery can be performed, including the use of *challenge questions, out-of-band communications* (using email or SMS), calling a *help-desk operator*, using *password hints* or *backup codes*, or *using a trusted person*. Research in 2010 indicated that *out-of-band communications* and *challenge questions* were the most frequent methods used [8]. For the most part, current password recovery processes have maintained this trend. For example, Dropbox's password recovery process consists of an out-of-band email with a link to reset user's password [3]. Google services use a recovery email address or recovery phone number [6]. If a user has no access to his recovery email, phone or any other option, the user's identity can be verified by answering several questions about his account [4].

Three security questions must be answered by a user to recover his password for Apple services (iCloud, the App Store, the iTunes Store and more) [5]. All previously mentioned web services also support two-factor authentication. Since this option usually requires the combination of a computer and a mobile phone, there must be an approach to when the mobile phone is lost, stolen, or out-of-order. One common approach involves an emergency *backup (QR) code*. For example, after enabling two factor authentication in Dropbox[1], a user receives a special 16-digit backup code. The user must write this key down and store it somewhere safe. In case of losing his phone, this code may be used for an emergency access to the system [2]. Google users who use two factor authentication may download a backup code too or may add a backup phone in addition to the standard one [6]. Very similarly, Apple users get a recovery key for two factor authentication to be used when the trusted device is lost [5]. As an alternative to a *backup code*, researchers have also investigated using *trusted people* to support recovery [22], and at least Facebook has deployed such a solution, referred to as "trusted contacts"[2].

In this paper, we evaluate two password recovery methods based on the above-mentioned techniques: *backup codes* and cooperation of a *trusted person*. Both recovery methods were shortlisted by a company SODATSW. that offers secure data solutions. This company wanted to evaluate both solutions and compare them in terms of usability. The company agreed to use students as participants with the condition that both IT and non IT oriented students would be involved into study.

Thus, our task was to evaluate the usability of these two methods in order to determine their suitability as a viable option for password recovery and discuss possible further research and deployment consideration for other methods of password recovery.

---

[1] Dropbox has recently added an option to use Universal 2nd Factor (U2F) security keys to partially mitigate against mobile phone issues, though this too requires possession of a USB, which might become lost, stolen, or out-of-order. See https://blogs.dropbox.com/dropbox/2015/08/u2f-security-keys/.

[2] https://www.facebook.com/notes/facebook-security/introducing-trusted-contacts/10151362774980766.

To achieve our goal, we conducted a study with 186 student participants in order to compare the two password recovery methods.

In Sect. 2 we describe the related work in the area of password recovery. Section 3 introduces our approach to the design of the two password recovery methods, while Sect. 4 specifies the experiment design. Section 5 explains the experiment analysis and we conclude in Sect. 6.

2 Related Research

In this section we highlight relevant research related to currently used techniques for the recovery (security questions, and out-of-band communications), as well as previous work on the two methods we investigate in this paper (backup codes and trusted people).

2.1 Current Recovery Techniques

A recent study by Google concluded that security questions are neither secure nor reliable enough to be used as a standalone account recovery mechanism [7]. As a major issue, security questions might get successfully guessed. High guessability may be caused by using publicly available answers (16 % of answer can be found in social network profiles [20]), using answers available to user's family and close friends (they can guess 17 % of answers correctly in less than five attempts [21]) or small answer spaces (more than 40 % security questions have small answer spaces [16,20]). The other disadvantage connected to security questions is that users tend to forget their own answers. Research [21] showed that participants forgot 20 % of their own answers within six months. Considering the fact that password recovery is often a last-resort option to regain access to a system, this is a very serious drawback leading to user frustration and potentially to more expensive forms of recovery, such as through a help desk. As a solution to this issue, researchers have tested an approach where questions were chosen by users themselves [16]. The approach was based on the idea that users will choose questions familiar to them, and thus they will not have a problem to recall answers. Contrary to expectations, the approach did not bring the anticipated improvement.

Out-of-band communications for password recovery (also used for secondary authentication) have risen in popularity, for example Google strongly prefers out-of-band password recovery (via SMS or email) over security questions [7].

Despite their importance for secondary authentication, and the fact that smart phones aggregate many potentially sensitive functions, more than 60 % of smart phone users do not lock their device [1]. This poses a threat for password recovery based on out-of-band communication (via email or SMS). Further, smart phone theft is a serious issue. About 3.1 million smart phones were stolen in USA in 2013. Moreover, 1.4 million smart phones were lost and never recovered in the same year [1]. When the smart phone is stolen, an attacker may initiate the password recovery based on the SMS or gain free access to an email account which can be also be misused for password recovery. When a user does not react quickly and does not change all his secondary authentications connected with the smart phone, his accounts may become compromised. Recent research on two-factor authentication demonstrates that given one compromised device, either a PC or a mobile phone, an attacker is able to compromise another one by launching a cross-platform infection attack [11].

In terms of usability, Bonneau et al. [7] compared the main account recovery methods (SMS reset code, email and security questions) used in a Google environment. While they showed that out-of-band communication channels like SMS and email have a higher success rate (respectively 80 % and 74 %) than security questions (ranges from 44 % to 60 %), the highest success rate still leaves a 20 % failure.

2.2   Existing Research on Codes and People

Recovery based on a *backup code* is used by several account providers, especially for the recovery process for two-factor authentication. However, it has received only limited attention in the research literature. The use of a backup code should reduce the instances of "being forgotten" or of a smart device becoming lost or not working properly, as the code is typically stored offline. The backup code may be provided to the user in a plain text or shown in a more sophisticated way, for example as a *QR code*.

Saving a code as a QR code instead of a written, alphanumeric code may have several benefits. For example, it might avoid errors when entering the code during recovery, as it may simply be more convenient to scan rather than type.

A QR code is a two-dimensional barcode that can include up to 4296 alphanumerical characters – a string long enough to store a strong password. All devices equipped with a camera and a QR code decoding application can serve as a QR code reader. Authentication using a QR code has been already presented in the literature [17,18], but it was mainly designed for primary authentication. One step of these authentication schemes is to send a QR code with encoded information from a service provider to a user. The user decodes information stored in the QR code and generates a one-time password. The use of the QR code serves as an alternative to a security card in both cases. Unfortunately, the approach from [18] relies on the fact that user's smart phone must be well protected since the smart phone stores a user's long-term secret key. Similarly, another approach [17] also relies on information stored in a user's smart phone. Thus, smart phone theft poses a danger for both approaches.

A more recent approach for password recovery is to use a *trusted party*. This method relies on a user's trusted person or people to help him recover an account access.

This method seems to be a good match to use with social networks where trusted people are selected by the user from his trustworthy friends. For example, this method is used at Facebook and was studied in Microsoft Live ID [22]. The tested approach was based on requesting recovery codes by user's trusted friends via specialized web interface. The user must collect from them at least three codes out of four to regain access to the system.

When a Facebook user forgets his password, he must contact his trusted friends to send a recovery request to the provider and obtain the security code. The user must collect at least three codes from three to five selected trusted friends [13]. The trusted party based method is prone to Forest fire attack [13], which misuses the fact that the user and his trusted friends are all members of one single system. If a small subset of users are compromised, all friends who trust them can be compromised too. As the number of compromised accounts rises, even more users may be compromised. In other words, it spreads like a forest fire.

3   Our Password Recovery Approaches

When designing password recovery processes, we discussed all of our approaches with SODATSW company designing a new secure data storage solution. The company insisted on a balance between usability, security and resistance to a smart phone theft. Based on SODATSW requirements, a Master thesis [14] reviewing possible approaches to password recovery was written, also suggesting some new ones. After a final round of discussions with the company, we agreed to test the approach based on a QR code and the other based on a trusted person.

3.1   Password Recovery via One-Time Password Stored in a QR Code

We designed a simple password recovery process using the backup code in the form of the QR code. The steps of this process are as follows:

1. A user receives a QR code via a registered letter (or any other service that guaranteed delivery to the receiver) and hides it in a secret place. The QR code contains a backup code.
2. If the user forgets his password, the recovery process can be initiated.
3. To start the recovery, the user scans the QR code.
4. The user inserts his user name into a system and retypes the code from the QR code reader into the system. When the user has a smart phone with the QR code reader and Internet access, he may open the system in the smart phone and copy and paste the code directly.
5. The system requires setting a new password.
6. After setting a new password, the user gains access to the system.

The QR code is not bound to a specific device, so when a user's own smart phone is stolen, the user can utilize any other QR code reader. It is also a disadvantage, because any QR code reader can read the QR code with the backup code. This increases requirements for the secret distribution and storage of the QR code. The user is instructed to securely store the QR code together with his important contracts. It is also strictly forbidden for the user to scan the QR code in an advance and store it in the smart phone (though this might be difficult to enforce).

Unlike a one-time password stored as text on a piece of paper, a one-time password stored as a QR code enables a user to copy a decoded password directly from a smart phone application to the system which can be opened in the smart phone. Of course, when the user has only a QR reader without an access to the Internet, password retyping is unavoidable. A possible drawback is when the recovery password from a QR code is used, a new QR code must be securely distributed to the user. Company SODATSW is aware of it and plans to use this solution only in countries that have necessary infrastructure. As far as costs are concerned, QR codes are not expensive to produce, but the price of secure distribution must be taken into account.

3.2   Trusted Party Based Password Recovery

Unlike the use of a QR backup code, the use of a trusted party is based on shared inter-personal trust. To balance usability and also take into account a potential problem with low willingness to provide a phone number of a user's friends, we decided to require only one trusted person for each user (and the user himself also actively participates in the recovery). The trusted person may or may not be another system user. The user is expected to set family members or co-workers as a trusted person to decrease the probability of a Forest fire attack [13].

A step-by-step password recovery process (see also Fig. 1) was designed as follows:

1. During the registration process, a user registers his phone number and also the phone number of the person he trusts.
2. When a password is lost or forgotten, the user will call the client center.
3. If the phone number he used for a call matches with the phone number registered in the system, a client center operator sends him a first half of a backup code via SMS.
4. The user must instruct his trusted person to call the client center and ask for a second half of the password.
5. The trusted person who recognizes the user's voice or appearance will do the task. If the trusted person's phone number matches with the phone number registered in the system, the operator sends the other half of the code to the user.
6. The user inserts his user name and both codes into the system.
7. The system requires setting a new password.
8. After setting a new password, the user gains an access to the system.

If an attacker steals a user's mobile phone, he does not know which of his friends is the trusted person. Even if the attacker knows this information, he must convince the trusted person to call the client center. To increase overall security and to decrease the probability of impersonating the user by an attacker, users are encouraged to instruct their trusted party to proceed with a call to the client

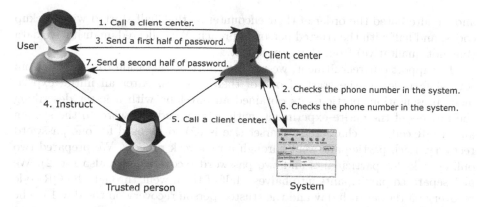

Fig. 1. Trusted party based recovery

center only after proper identification. For example, the user should instruct the trusted party to call a client center only during a face-to-face meeting or a phone call.

One disadvantage of this process is that during registration users may not fully think about the prospect of a password recovery and might be less likely to submit the phone number of an appropriately reliable and trusted person. Further, this person may change during a user's life and it would be important to keep this information up-to-date. Also, it is not the most efficient recovery process due to the fact that the trusted person may be away (for example on business trip, on holiday) when his call is necessary. This recovery method is also based on the user's phone number being registered into the system. If a user loses his number and in the same time forgets his password, this password recovery can not be successfully processed. The other issue may be that people might forget which person they designated. But similarly, they can forget the response for a security question (as we mentioned in the previous section). Recovery costs are higher, because the client center must be available, but the interaction may be automated.

4 Experiment Design

To compare both approaches, an experiment in cooperation of Faculty of Social Studies and Faculty of Informatics was designed. The experiment design was undertaken in accordance with experimental and ethical regulations of our university.

The experiment ran in May and June 2015 and the main aim of the experiment was to compare both approaches. There were 186 participants in total (of the original 203 who underwent full registration), half of them from the Faculty of Informatics, the other half together from other faculties (mainly from Faculty of Social Studies, Faculty of Law and Faculty of Arts). We used a within-subject experiment design – all participants went through both recovery approaches, and we alternated the order of their encounter so that half started with backup codes, and half with the trusted person approach. We collected quantitative data (but not qualitative) from this experiment.

To support our recruitment, we made a short presentation to students from several faculties at the start of one of their lectures. After an initial experiment presentation, participants obtained an envelope with a letter describing the process of the entire experiment, with a login and password to the system and a QR code (14 characters, charset size is 62) to be used for one password recovery. Each participant went through a two-week process. We prepared two online tasks for participants and two password recoveries (see also Fig. 2). We also separated participants into halves. Half of them went through the QR code recovery on the seventh day and the trusted person recovery on the day 15. The other half of participants used a an opposite recovery order. The experiment length was two weeks for each participant. We estimated that the time spent in the experiment would be 45 min for each participant.

- When participants first logged into the system, they filled an initial questionnaire, provided their demographics and information necessary for both recoveries (their phone number, their trusted person's phone number). We only mentioned that it should be a person of trust, for example, a good friend or a family member.
- On the fourth day after the first login, participants were encouraged to log into the system and to execute a short task of computing a number of characters in an attached PDF file. The purpose of this step was to attempt to maintain an active, realistic environment for participants.
- On the seventh day of the experiment, participants were asked to process a first recovery. Half of the participants went through a recovery using their QR code, and the other half used the trusted party based recovery. After completing the recovery, participants filled a questionnaire to evaluate it.

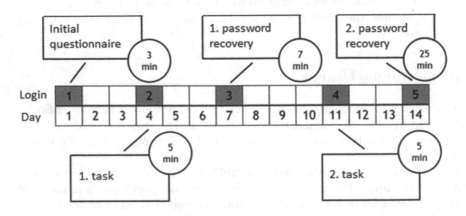

Fig. 2. Experiment process

- On the eleventh day participants were asked to complete a second task. The task was to find a concrete paper, read through it, find one particular piece of information and insert it into the system.
- Fifteen days after the experiment started, participants completed their second password recovery and filled in a final, longer questionnaire where they evaluated and compared both recovery processes.

We sent email reminders to participants to remind them to perform the above tasks. As a motivation to join the experiment, we offered $400 and 25 32 GB MicroSD cards to 26 randomly chosen participants who went through all experiment steps.

5 Experiment Results and Analyses

5.1 Participants

There were 186 participants in total (of the 203 undergoing full registration). All participants were students of our university (for a detailed breakdown see Table 1). All of them have at least secondary education.

Table 1. Experiment participants overview

Faculty	Males	Females	Participants in total
Faculty of Informatics	75	17	98
Faculty of Social Studies	23	41	67
Faculty of Law	8	9	17
Faculty of Arts	1	5	10
Other faculties	2	5	9

The experiment had 5 phases, and participants went through the initial questionnaire, two tasks and two password recoveries. 132 participants out of 186 finished all phases. Half of the 132 participants went through the QR code recovery first followed by the trusted party. The other half (also 66) went through the process in an alternate order.

The majority (117) of participants were aged 19–22 years, while 69 participants were between 23 and 26 years. For a detailed view of when participants decided to leave the experiment, see Table 2. The fact that all participants were students is a limitation, though participants were recruited from both IT and non IT related programs. Since all participants are young people, we expect that they are more technically skilled than older generation.

Table 2. Experiment phases and dropped out participants. The table shows the number of participants who dropped before proceeding with each experiment phase. Group 1 has the QR code as 1st recovery and trusted party based recovery as 2nd recovery. Group 2 has alternate order of recoveries

Group	Initial questionnaire	1st task	1st recovery	2nd task	2nd recovery
Group 1	5	4	3	15	–
Group 2	4		21	0	2	–

5.2   Recovery Method Evaluation

Participants went through two password recoveries in the experiment. After each recovery, participants evaluated the recovery in four categories. There were 132 participants who performed these evaluations (we involved only those who went through both recoveries). We did not observe any significant difference in answers between participants who had started with one recovery method versus the other.

- **Difficulty:** How difficult was it for you to use the recovery? The Likert scale was used for responses from 1 (totally easy) to 6 (totally difficult). We conducted a paired t-test analysis and it proved that the QR code password recovery is considered by participants to be less difficult (mean $= 1.72$, SD $= 1.1$) than the trusted party based recovery (mean $= 2.79$, SD $= 1.56$) ($t(132) = 7.37$, $p < 0.001$).
  We did not observe any significant difference between men (mean $= 2.57$, SD $= 1.49$) and women (mean $= 3.067$, SD $= 1.60$) in evaluating difficulty of the trusted party recovery ($t(133) = -1.92$, $p = 0.057$) and also no significant difference between men (mean $= 1.71$, SD $= 0.12$) and women (mean $= 1.72$, SD $= 0.14$) in evaluating difficulty of the QR code recovery ($t(148) = -0.054$, $p = 0.957$).
  We observed significant difference between IT (trusted party, mean $= 2.32$, SD $= 1.40$), (QR code recovery, mean $= 1.48$, SD $= 0.931$) and non IT participants (trusted party, mean $= 3.25$, SD $= 1.56$), (QR code recovery, mean $= 1.98$, SD $= 1.22$) in both the trusted party ($t(133) = 3.59$, p<0.001) and the QR code recovery ($t(148) = 2.85$, $p = 0.005$). IT participants considered both recoveries as less difficult than non IT participants.
  Correlation of age and the trusted party recovery difficulty is significant ($r = 0.22$, $p = 0.011$), similarly correlation of age and the QR code recovery difficulty ($r = 0.21$, $p = 0.007$). The older user is, the more difficult recovery is.
- **Security:** How secure do you consider the recovery? The Likert scale was used for responses from 1 (totally secure) to 6 (totally insecure). The paired t-test proved that participants in this scale consider the QR code based recovery less secure (mean $= 3$, SD $= 1.15$) than the trusted party based recovery (mean $= 2.38$, SD $= 1.17$) ($t(129) = -5.25$, $p < 0.001$).
  Men (mean $= 3.2$, SD $= 1.22$) and women (mean $= 2.7$, SD $= 0.96$) had significant difference in evaluating security of the QR code based password recovery ($t(144) = 2.94$, p<0.004). Men considered the QR code based recovery

significantly less secure than women. On the other hand, there is no significant difference observed in security of the trusted party based recovery ($t(121) = 0.24$, $p = 0.8$) between men (mean $= 2.41$, SD $= 1.27$) and women (mean $= 2.36$, SD $= 1.07$).

Very similar results are obtained when comparing IT and non IT participants. Non IT participants (mean $= 2.74$, SD $= 1.00$) considered the QR code based recovery significantly more secure ($t(144) = -2.94$, $p = 0.004$) than IT participants (mean $= 3.29$, SD $= 1.22$). There is no difference in IT (mean $= 2.53$, SD $= 1.18$) and non IT participants (mean $= 2.25$, SD $= 1.18$) in evaluating security of the trusted party based recovery ($t(131) = -1.34$, $p = 0.18$).

Correlation of age and the trusted party recovery security is not significant ($r = 0.14$, $p = 0.1$), similarly correlation of age and the QR code recovery security ($r = 0.128$, $p = 0.123$).

- **Advanced security:** How secure do you consider to use this recovery for online banking? The Likert scale was used for responses from 1 (totally secure) to 6 (totally insecure). When considering a password recovery for a system with sensitive data, based on the paired t-test, the QR code based recovery is considered as less sufficient for online banking (mean $= 3.92$, SD $= 1.34$) than the trusted party based recovery (mean $= 2.89$, SD $= 1.38$) ($t(132) = -7.62$, $p < 0.001$). However, the trusted party based recovery still only received a mean score between 2 and 3, and hence was not viewed as "totally secure".

Men (mean $= 4.17$, SD $- 1.38$) and women (mean $= 3.62$, SD $= 1.24$) evaluated differently advanced security of the QR code based password recovery ($t(147) = 2.46$, $p = 0.015$), but saw no difference in advanced security of the trusted party based recovery ($t(133) = 0.53$, $p = 0.594$, men:(mean $= 2.97$, SD $= 1.39$), women:(mean $= 2.84$, SD $= 1.38$)).

IT and non IT participants had no difference in evaluating advanced security of both the QR code based recovery ($t(147) = -1.61$, $p = 0.108$) and the trusted party based recovery ($t(133) = -1.17$, $p = 0.24$).

There is no significant correlation for age and advanced security of the QR code based recovery ($r = -0.007$, $p = 0.929$) and the trusted party based recovery ($r = 0.125$, $p = 0.14$).

- **User friendliness:** How user friendly do you consider the recovery? The Likert scale was from 1 (totally user friendly) to 6 (totally user unfriendly). The paired t-test proved that the QR based password recovery is considered to be more user friendly (mean $= 2$, SD $= 1.2$) than the trusted party based recovery (mean $= 3.58$, SD $= 1.57$), ($t(132) = 9.83$, $p < 0.001$).

There is no significant difference in user friendliness of both recoveries for men and women (QR code recovery: ($t(148) = 0.00$, $p = 1$), trusted party based recovery ($t(133) = 0.44$, $p = 0.65$)). We observed significant difference in evaluating user friendliness of IT and non IT respondents in the QR code based recovery ($t(148) = 2.41$, $p = 0.017$), but no difference in the trusted party based recovery ($t(133) = -0.628$, $p = 0.531$). IT participants (mean $= 1.77$, SD $= 1.107$) evaluated the QR code based recovery more user friendly than non IT participants (mean $= 2.25$, SD $= 1.35$).

There is also a significant but weak correlation between age and user friend-liness for the trusted party based recovery ($r = 0.176$, $p = 0.041$) and the QR code based recovery ($r = 0.16$, $p = 0.42$).

5.3   Overall Views

At the end of the experiment, participants were asked about their opinion of the two recovery methods using categories similar to those above. We also asked for their overall recovery method preference. The questions they were asked were "Which recovery do you consider more easy to use/secure/user friendly?" and "Which recovery do you overall prefer more?" The possible responses were "QR code recovery", "Trusted party based recovery" and "Both similarly". We used answers only from those 132 participants who went through both recoveries.

- **Ease to use:** 113 (86%) participants considered the QR code recovery eas-ier to use than the trusted party based recovery. Only 6 (4%) participants thought the opposite and 13 (10%) participants considered both methods similarly easy.
- **Security:** 90 (68%) participants considered the trusted party based recovery more secure than the QR code based recovery. Only 14 (10%) participants had an opposite opinion and 28 (21%) did not see a difference between both methods.
- **User friendly:** 100 (76%) participants considered the QR code based recov-ery more user friendly over the trusted party based recovery. Only 6 (5%) participants thought the opposite and 26 (20%) considered both recoveries to be equally user friendly.
- **Overall recovery preferences:** When participants were ask to choose one recovery that they prefer, 76 (58%) participants preferred the QR based recov-ery whereas 35 (25%) participants preferred the trusted party based recovery. 21 (16%) participants preferred both recoveries equally.

We also conducted a χ^2 [9] test and Fisher's exact test (when some crosstab cells remained empty) and we did not find (at the significance level $\alpha = 0.05$) any statistically significant differences in perceptions of security, user friendliness and overall preferences of these recovery methods between men and women or IT and non IT participants. The only statistically significant difference ($p = 0.03$) is in easiness to use recoveries between IT and non IT participants. IT participants had higher tendency to choose "Both options were similarly easy to use" over "Trusted party based recovery was easiest to use" in comparison with non IT participants.

5.4   Other Observations

In terms of the *effectiveness of both recovery methods*, we can report that we observed some unsuccessful trials. 79% participants succeeded with a QR code based recovery at the first try. Moreover, 89% participants did a QR code based recovery with zero or one unsuccessful trial. Recovery with a trusted party had similar results. 75 % of participants succeeded on their first attempt. In addition, 88 % of the users processed a trusted party based recovery with zero or one unsuccessful trial. In comparison to earlier studies on currently used recovery techniques such as challenge questions where 20 % of participants forget their answers after 6 months [21], our studied recovery methods show an improvement. We observed no significant difference in number of trials of men and women or IT and non IT participants.

The success rate (ratio between the number of successful attempts and the total number of attempts) of a trusted party based recovery is approximately 48 %. The success rate for QR code based recovery is approximately 49 %. This shows that both methods seem to be similarly prone to error. We had no limits in attempts to insert a code in the recovery. The ratios are particularly low due to few outliers who tried to insert a recovery code 10, 11, 12 or 13 times before they succeeded.

The time between system request to start recovery and finishing the recovery was on average nearly 53 min for the trusted party based recovery, and 9 min for the QR code based recovery. From the user's point of view *trusted party based recovery is slower than the other recovery method.*

We also included a couple of additional questions related to the difficulty of carrying out the recovery processes. The first was related to the difficulty of finding a QR code reader. We used the Likert scale from 1 (totally easy) to 6 (totally difficult) for responses. In general, participants found it very easy to locate their QR code reader (mean $= 1.64$, SD $= 1.17$). We conducted a t-test and observed statistical significant differences (at the statistical significance level $\alpha = 0.05$, $t(130) = 2.86$, $p < 0.05$) between participants from the Faculty of Informatics (mean $= 1.36$, SD $= 0.92$) and participants from other faculties (mean $= 1.92$, SD $= 1.33$). Statistically significant differences ($\alpha = 0.05$, $t(130) = -2.21$, $p < 0.05$) in this question were also observed between men (mean $= 1.49$, SD $= 0.99$) and women (mean $= 1.89$, SD $= 1.33$). To sum up, even with these relative differences, all participants found it easy (with mean scores less than 2).

The second question related to the difficulty of QR code scanning. We used the Likert scale from 1 (totally easy) to 6 (totally difficult) for responses. Generally speaking, participants considered this process easy (mean $= 1.35$, SD $= 0.95$), but we observed a significant difference (at the statistical significance level $\alpha = 0.05$, $t(130) = 3.72$, $p < 0.001$) between participants from the Faculty of Informatics (mean $= 1.06$ SD $= 0.24$) and participants from other faculties (mean $= 1.65$, SD $= 1.27$). Participants from the Faculty of Informatics considered the QR code scanning even easier than their colleagues from different faculties. Very similarly, participants considered it to be very easy to call a client center (mean $= 1.84$, SD $= 1.19$), and we did not observe any statistically significant difference between IT and non IT students or men and women. On the other hand, we must take into account that if a participant had a serious problem to find the QR code reader or had a problem to call the client center, he may have stopped the experiment without completing the questionnaire.

Related to the use of the client center, there were several issues connected with password recoveries. The major flaw connected with the QR code recovery was that several QR code reading applications do not distinguish characters "l" and "I", "O" and "0". One participant also reported that his QR reading application showed the whole text in lower case. One solution may be to recommend a particular QR code reading application that would work correctly to avoid above mentioned issues. Another solution may be also to remove problematic characters out of the backup code. Of course, it could mean that codes would be lengthened.

The client center similarly observed issues connected with the trusted party based recovery. We have observed several difficulties in retyping SMS codes from a phone to the system. For participants was hard to recognize several problematic characters. For example "0" instead "O". The solution can be same as in the previous case.

6   Conclusion

We evaluated two alternate recovery solutions, using backup codes and trusted people. Despite the fact that both methods have expectable drawbacks, our research set out to confirm these issues to support our goal of promoting a discussion on other types of recovery processes. Despite the fact that the *trusted party based recovery was considered by 90 (68 %) participants to be more secure than the QR code based recovery* (14 participants (11 %)), the majority of participants gave their *overall preferences to the solution that they consider easier to use and more user friendly: the QR code based recovery.* 100 participants out of 132 considered the QR code based recovery more user friendly and 113 participants considered it easier to use than the trusted party based recovery. We observed that for the trusted party based recovery participants spent more time to perform the recovery (53 minutes for trusted party and 9 min for QR code) whereas the number of unsuccessful trials were nearly equal – 89 % participants processed the QR code recovery with one or zero unsuccessful trial and 88 % did the same with the trusted party based recovery. We observed several interesting points such as that IT participants considered both recoveries as less difficult than non IT participants. Men (and IT participants) considered the QR code based recovery significantly less secure than women (and non IT participants).

We also observed that participants perceived a strong difference between an "ordinary" website level of security and the security good enough to be used for their online banking. When comparing both recovery methods, results for the "standard security" were nearly the same, but for security good enough for online banking there were significant differences in answers so that the trusted party based recovery was considered to be more secure. Our participants, who are university students, seemed to be well aware of possible secure drawbacks of our solutions.

As for the perception of password recovery difficulty, both recoveries scored similarly. *We did not find (at the statistical significance level $\alpha = 0.05$) that there would be any difference in recovery preferences (security, user friendliness or in overall recovery preference) between men and women or the IT and non IT participants.* The only significant difference was between IT and non IT participants in ease of use. IT participants tended to choose "Both recovery methods are similarly easy to use" more than non IT participants who slightly more preferred the trusted party recovery as easier to use.

We recommended to the company to offer the QR code solution as a default for all users. The trusted party based recovery should be suggested only to users who demand a higher level of security. The trusted party based recovery can be then used either instead or even in combination with the QR code based recovery.

Acknowledgments. The authors acknowledge the support of the Masaryk University (MUNI/M/1052/ 2013). Authors would like to thank Department of social studies for a help with a data analysis.

References

1. Smart phone thefts rose to 3.1 million in 2013 (2014). http://www.consumer reports.org/cro/news/2014/04/smart-phone-thefts-rose-to-3-million-last-year. Accessed 15 Jun 2016
2. How do i enable two-step verification on my account? (2015). https://www.dropbox.com/en/help/363. Accessed 15 Jun 2016
3. I forgot my password. How do i reset it? (2015). https://www.dropbox.com/help/168. Accessed 15 Jun 2016
4. I'm having trouble resetting my password (2015). https://support.google.com/accounts/answer/1723426?hl=en. Accessed 15 Jun 2016
5. Security and your Apple ID (2015). https://support.apple.com/en-us/HT201303. Accessed 15 Jun 2016
6. Set up a recovery phone number or email address (2015). https://support.google.com/accounts/answer/183723?hl=en. Accessed 15 Jun 2016
7. Bonneau, J., Bursztein, E., Caron, I., Jackson, R., Williamson, M.: Secrets, lies, and account recovery: lessons from the use of personal knowledge questions at google. In: Proceedings of the 24th International Conference on World Wide Web, pp. 141–150. International World Wide Web Conferences Steering Committee (2015)
8. Bonneau, J., Preibusch, S.: The password thicket: technical and market failures in human authentication on the web. In: WEIS (2010)
9. Corder, G., Foreman, D.: Nonparametric Statistics: A Step-by-Step Approach. Wiley, New York (2014)
10. Cubrilovic, N.: The Anatomy of the Twitter Attack (2009). http://techcrunch.com/2009/07/19/the-anatomy-of-the-twitter-attack/. Accessed 15 Jun 2016
11. Dmitrienko, A., Liebchen, C., Rossow, C., Sadeghi, A.-R.: On the (in)security of mobile two-factor authentication. In: Christin, N., Safavi-Naini, R. (eds.) FC 2014. LNCS, vol. 8437, pp. 365–383. Springer, Heidelberg (2014)
12. Florencio, D., Herley, C.: A large-scale study of web password habits. In: Proceedings of the 16th International Conference on World Wide Web, pp. 657–666. ACM (2007)

13. Gong, N.Z., Wang, D.: On the security of trustee-based social authentications. IEEE Trans. Inf. Forensics Secur. **9**(8), 1251–1263 (2014)
14. Hamerník, J.: Autentizační metody používané k obnově přihlašovacího hesla, Master thesis (in Czech), Masaryk University (2014). Accessed 15 Jun 2016
15. Honan, M.: How Apple and Amazon Security Flaws Led to My Epic Hacking (2012). http://www.wired.com/2012/08/apple-amazon-mat-honan-hacking/all/. Accessed 15 Jun 2016
16. Just, M., Aspinall, D.: Personal choice and challenge questions: a security and usability assessment. In: Proceedings of the 5th Symposium on Usable Privacy and Security, p. 8. ACM (2009)
17. Lee, Y.S., Kim, N.H., Lim, H., Jo, H., Lee, H.J.: Online banking authentication system using mobile-OTP with QR-code. In: 2010 5th International Conference on Computer Sciences and Convergence Information Technology (ICCIT), pp. 644–648. IEEE (2010)
18. Liao, K.C., Lee, W.H.: A novel user authentication scheme based on QR-code. J. Netw. **5**(8), 937–941 (2010)
19. Moallem, A.: Did you forget your password? In: Marcus, A. (ed.) HCII 2011 and DUXU 2011, Part II. LNCS, vol. 6770, pp. 29–39. Springer, Heidelberg (2011)
20. Rabkin, A.: Personal knowledge questions for fallback authentication: security questions in the era of Facebook. In: Proceedings of the 4th Symposium on Usable Privacy and Security, pp. 13–23. ACM (2008)
21. Schechter, S., Brush, A.B., Egelman, S.: It's no secret. Measuring the security and reliability of authentication via secret questions. In: 2009 30th IEEE Symposium on Security and Privacy, pp. 375–390. IEEE (2009)
22. Schechter, S., Egelman, S., Reeder, R.W.: It's not what you know, but who you know: a social approach to last-resort authentication. In: Proceedings of the SIGCHI Conference on Human Factors in Computing Systems, pp. 1983–1992. ACM (2009)
23. Wikipedia: Sarah Palin email hack — Wikipedia, The Free Encyclopedia (2015). https://en.wikipedia.org/w/index.php?title=Sarah_Palin_email_hack&direction=next&oldid=667446959. Accessed 15 Jun 2016

Secure Hardware Systems

An Implementation of a High Assurance Smart Meter Using Protected Module Architectures

Jan Tobias Mühlberg[1]($\boxtimes$), Sara Cleemput[2], Mustafa A. Mustafa[2],
Jo Van Bulck[1], Bart Preneel[2], and Frank Piessens[1]

[1] iMinds-DistriNet, KU Leuven, Celestijnenlaan 200A, 3001 Leuven, Belgium
jantobias.muehlberg@cs.kuleuven.be
[2] ESAT-COSIC and iMinds, KU Leuven, Kasteelpark Arenberg 10,
3001 Leuven-Heverlee, Belgium

Abstract. Due to ongoing changes in the power grid towards decentralised and highly volatile energy production, smart electricity meters are required to provide fine-grained measurement and timely remote access to consumption and production data. This enables flexible tariffing and dynamic load optimisation. As the power grid forms part of the critical infrastructure of our society, increasing the resilience of the grid's software components against failures and attacks is vitally important.

In this paper we explore the use of Protected Module Architectures (PMAs) to securely implement and deploy software for smart electricity meters. Outlining security challenges and an architectural solution in the light of security features provided by PMAs, we evaluate a proof-of-concept implementation of a security-focused smart metering scenario. Our implementation is based on Sancus, an embedded PMA for low-power microcontrollers. The evaluation of our prototype provides strong indication for the feasibility of implementing a PMA-based high assurance smart meter with a very small software Trusted Computing Base, which would be suitable for security certification and formal verification.

Keywords: Smart meter security · Smart grid · Protected module architectures · Distributed embedded computing · Sancus

1 Introduction

The smart grid is an extension of the traditional electricity grid. It includes smart appliances, renewable energy resources and smart electricity meters, facilitating bidirectional communication between these components and stakeholders, e.g., between a smart meter and the grid operator [9]. This is needed to deal with the volatility of renewable energy sources and new appliances such as electric vehicles, and to increase the reliability and sustainability of electricity delivery – one of the most critical resources of our time.

Electricity Smart Metering Equipment (ESME), i.e., smart meters, have three main responsibilities. Firstly, ESME measure the consumption of electricity and essential grid parameters, such as voltage or frequency, and timely

© IFIP International Federation for Information Processing 2016
Published by Springer International Publishing Switzerland 2016. All Rights Reserved
S. Foresti and J. Lopez (Eds.): WISTP 2016, LNCS 9895, pp. 53–69, 2016.
DOI: 10.1007/978-3-319-45931-8_4

provide this data to the grid operator. Secondly, they operate a Load Switch, which can disconnect a premise from the electricity grid. The grid operator may use this in emergency cases to avoid a black-out. Finally, ESME communicate consumption data to smart appliances or an In-Home Display (IHD) present at the premise for local inspection and micro-management by the client. Relying on ESME involves security risks that range from privacy infringements to full-scale black-outs [12,29]. Physically isolating an ESME's critical software components, e.g., by using multiple microprocessors, can mitigate attacks against the grid's digital infrastructure. However, this can be prohibitively expensive and the use of trusted computing to achieve logical separation has been proposed [16,29]. An architecture based on trusted computing to implement High Assurance Smart Meters (HASMs) – smart meters with high security guarantees, certification and verification as design goals – poses a potential solution [4].

In this paper we implement a simplified scenario for smart meter deployment and evaluate its security aspects. We refer to components from the British Department of Energy & Climate Change's "Smart Metering Implementation Programme (SMIP)" [6]. However, our implementation may divert substantially with respect to details specified in the SMIP documents. We simplify communication protocols and we adopt architectural changes suggested in [4], relying on Protected Module Architectures (PMAs) [24] to implement security features. Our choice of technologies suggests a number of architectural changes relative to [4,6], which we discuss in detail. Importantly, the goal of this paper is *not* to accurately implement the SMIP specification but to provide a security-focused reference implementation that illustrates the use of embedded PMAs to achieve a notion of *high assurance smart metering* by means of logical component isolation, mutual authentication and by minimising the software Trusted Computing Base (TCB).

Our scenario contains software components that implement a HASM to be installed at a client's premises, and a Load Switch that can enable or disable power supply to the premises. We further implement components to represent the grid operator's Central System and an IHD. The HASM and the Load Switch communicate with the Central System via a Wide Area Network (WAN) Interface. In our case, the WAN Interface supports periodic access to the HASM's operational data, as well as control of the Load Switch. The HASM and the IHD communicate via the Home Area Network (HAN) Interface. Only consumption data is periodically sent from the HASM to the IHD via this interface. All components are implemented in software only and are meant to be deployed as PMs on microcontrollers or larger systems that facilitate software component isolation and authenticated and secure communication between PMs. Essentially, we model a smart metering scenario as a distributed reactive system, relying on security features provided by modern PMAs.

In the remainder of this paper we describe the basic architecture of a smart metering environment according to the SMIP documents [6]. We outline security challenges and an architectural solution as described in [4], in the light of security features provided by PMAs. The key contribution of this paper is to provide a proof-of-concept implementation of a security-focused smart metering scenario, based on Sancus [19], an embedded PMA for low-power TI-MSP430 microcontrollers. We discuss the security objectives and architectural considerations of our implementation and evaluate its performance and the impact on the size of the system's deployed and trusted code base. Our prototype and evaluation provide a strong indication for the feasibility of implementing a secure, high assurance ESME and communicating controllers for smart home appliances, based on our architecture. The Sancus core, infrastructure software and our implementation are available at https://distrinet.cs.kuleuven.be/software/sancus/wistp16/.

2 High Assurance Smart Metering

Smart Electricity Metering. The British SMIP working documents [5,6] specify the physical requirements, functional requirements, interface and data requirements of an ESME. According to [6], an ESME minimally includes the following physical components: a clock, data storage, an electricity meter (i.e., metrology component), a Load Switch, a random number generator, a display, a HAN Interface, and a physical interface to connect to an independent Communication Hub [5], which is responsible for communicating with the grid operator's Central System over a dedicated WAN Interface. The ESME can communicate with the Communication Hub via its HAN Interface, which is furthermore used to connect to two types of local devices. *Type 1* devices store security credentials and can exchange authenticated and encrypted commands and data with the ESME, whereas *Type 2* devices do not store any security credentials and can only receive commands or data from the ESME.

As for the ESME's functional requirements, three main categories can be distinguished. First, an ESME should be capable of establishing and maintaining confidentiality- and integrity-preserving communication channels to receive command from and send data to the Central System (via the Communication Hub) and pre-defined local devices. Second, the ESME should be able to calculate bills, based on up-to-date tariffs, in credit as well as in prepayment mode. Finally, the ESME should be able to disconnect the household from the electricity grid by operating a Load Switch.

In addition, the ESME should store the following types of data: constant data (e.g., identifiers, model type, variant), internal data (e.g., installation credentials), configuration data (e.g., billing calendar, device log, security credentials, electricity quality thresholds), and operational data (e.g., import/export energy registers, cumulative and historical consumption data, power event log, security log).

Smart Metering Using Trusted Computing. However, ESME might be insufficiently secure, since *(1)* there is little isolation between the different modules that run on it, *(2)* it is possible to influence the ESME via the HAN Interface, and *(3)* it is easy to fill up the security log with non-critical events. Also, it might be impractical to have the Communication Hub physically separated from the ESME. In fact, the ESME should be a high assurance system, since the safety and security requirements are critical, due to the potentially huge physical impact of an attack. The German BSI has decided to introduce a specific component, the smart meter gateway, to their smart metering architecture [2]. This gateway, which is installed at a client's premise, acts as communication unit between the client's local devices (including the ESME) and the Central System, and provides the necessary security properties by deploying several layers of protection using a PKI. Although this solution provides a sufficient level of security, as also pointed out by von Oheimb [20], it is prohibitively expensive in terms of computational costs (mainly due to the use of PKI). Yan et al. [29], as well as Metke and Ekl [16] proposed using trusted computing in the smart grid to provide system, process and data integrity. However, they gave no details on how to implement this. Petrlic [22] proposed that each ESME must have a trusted platform module which acts as a tamper-resistant device and calculates users' bills based on the metering data measured at the ESME and the pricing data provided by the Central System. Jawurek et al. [11] proposed to use a plug-in component – placed between the ESME and the Central System – to calculate users' bills. LeMay et al. [14] described an implementation of a smart meter using Trusted Platform Modules and Virtual Machine Monitors. Unlike our work however, they did not give details on the internal architecture of the smart meter.

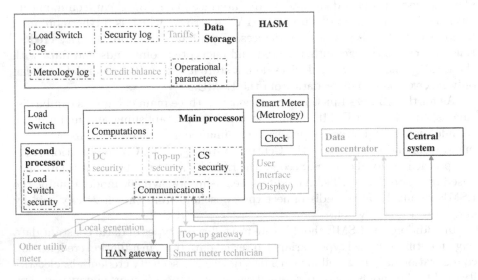

Fig. 1. Simplified version of a HASM according to [4]

The HASM proposed by Cleemput et al. (shown in Fig. 1) [4] contains roughly the same physically separate components as the ESME: data storage, the Load Switch, the main processor, the metrology component, the display, and the clock. However, it also features a second processor for the Load Switch security module. The HASM has six different communication interfaces: an interface to the other-utility meter, an interface to the local generation, the HAN Interface, an interface to the top-up gateway, a local maintenance interface and an interface to a data concentrator.

There are several differences between this HASM and the standard ESME:

- A HASM contains an additional processor which houses a dedicated security module with exclusive access to the Load Switch. This is the most critical module in the smart meter, since hacking this module allows an attacker to disconnect households from the electricity grid.
- A separation kernel is used to logically isolate the rest of the modules on the main processor. These modules are: security modules, a computations module and a communications module. The latter corresponding to the Communication Hub in the ESME architecture. However, rather than being a separate component, we consider it as a part of the HASM.
- The log files are divided into three different logs: a metrology log, a security log and a Load Switch log. This ensures that the attacker cannot flush an event out of the Load Switch log by generating less critical security events.
- The three security modules implement separate communication components, one for the Data Concentrator, one for the Top-Up component, and one for the Central System.
- All incoming communication must first go through the communications module and from there on directly to one of the security modules.
- The HAN Interface must be a one-way interface, such that only communication from the HASM to the HAN gateway is possible. This is important, since the smart appliances and the IHD are considered untrusted components, so they should not be able to influence the HASM. Note that this means, we only consider *Type 2* devices. We believe this is a practical assumption, since the in-home devices are not under the control of the grid operator, thus it is difficult to have pre-established keys between these devices and the HASM. Furthermore, we cannot think of convincing use cases where communication from the in-home devices to the HASM is strictly necessary. The main difference between the HAN Interface and the WAN Interface is that the latter is an interface to a trusted entity. Thus, the WAN Interface is a bidirectional interface, where all data is authenticated and encrypted.

Our Scenario. In this paper we present a simplified version of a HASM, as illustrated in Fig. 1. We do not consider the display present on the smart meter itself, and we only consider two communication interfaces: a WAN Interface to the Central System and a HAN Interface to the HAN gateway. Moreover, we implement only the following representative subset of ESME use cases.

Billing. For our implementation we only consider non-prepaid billing in Credit-Mode. Prepaid billing is an interesting use case in itself that exhibits security and privacy aspects different from non-prepaid billing. We are confident that our prototype could easily be extended to support prepaid billing. There are two main threats to the billing process: fraud and privacy infringements.

Load switching. As mentioned above, the Load Switch can be used to remotely enable or disable power supply at the client's premises. The main threat for this use case consists of an adversary who manages to cause a large-scale black-out by triggering the Load Switch. This is the most critical threat to our architecture, since concurrently disconnecting many consumers may cause a cascading instability, eventually bringing down large parts of the electricity grid. Ultimately, even public facilities that rely on the electricity grid, such as sewer operations, traffic lights and the telephone network, will be affected.

Consumer feedback. The goal of providing the user with fine-grained consumption data through the HAN Interface is to realise energy savings, as well as to allow them to connect smart appliances. The main threat in this use case is an adversary influencing the smart meter via the HAN Interface.

3   Authentic Execution with PMAs

PMAs [24] are a new brand of hardware security architectures, the main objective of which is to support the secure and isolated execution of critical software components with a minimal, hardware-only TCB. Implementations of PMAs for higher-end systems – Intel's Software Guard Extensions (SGX) [15] or ARM's TrustZone [1] – as well as several prototypes for embedded application domains [8,13,19] have been proposed. Software components that are specifically designed and implemented to leverage PMA features are provided with strong confidentiality and integrity guarantees regarding their internal state, and can mutually authenticate each other. More specifically, modern PMAs offer a number of security primitives to (1) configure memory protection domains, (2) enable or disable software module protection, and (3) facilitate key management for secure local or remote inter-module communication and attestation.

A Notion of Authentic Execution. PMAs allow us to securely implement authentic execution of distributed event-driven applications that execute on a heterogeneous shared infrastructure with a small TCB. These applications are characterised by consisting of multiple components that execute on different computing nodes and for which program flow is determined by events such as sensor inputs or external requests. As an example, consider the HASM with its sensors (electricity measuring element), communication interfaces (WAN and HAN), and actuators (Load Switch).

Roughly speaking, our notion of authentic execution is the following: if the application produces a physical output event (e.g., disabling supply via the Load Switch), then there must have happened a sequence of physical input events such that that sequence, when processed by the application (as specified by the application's source code), produces the output event.

This notion of authentic execution does provide strong integrity guarantees: it rules out both spoofed events as well as tampering with the execution of the program. Informally, if the executing program produces an output event, it could also have produced that same event if no attacker was present.

Any physical output event can be explained by means of the untampered code of the application, and the actual physical input events that have happened.

Building Blocks. Authentic execution relies on well-defined application components that are encapsulated as PMs and that are protected by the PMA. PM software components consist of a contiguous code and data section in the shared address space. Hardware-level PMAs such as Sancus [19] rely on a lightweight program counter based access control mechanism [26] to enforce that a PM's private data section is exclusively managed via its corresponding code section, which can only be entered via a few predefined entry points. The latter impedes code abuse attacks (e.g., Return Oriented Programming [3]) against PMs.

In distributed event-driven applications, each PM consumes *input events* and produces *output events*. The types of these events and communication channels are to be defined at compile-time. Components that directly interact with sensors or actuators are further able to claim *exclusive access* to interrupt vectors or device registers that are accessed through memory-mapped I/O on low-end microcontrollers [19]. Program code and access permissions form the identity of a PM, which can be *attested* cryptographically by remote parties, including other components of the distributed application. Intuitively, successful attestation implies that a software component is deployed with no modifications on a specific computing node, obtained exclusive access over its desired hardware resources, and that protection has been enabled through the PMA.

Trusted Computing Base. A key strength of hardware-level PMAs such as Sancus is that they reduce the TCB up to the point where a remote stakeholder only has to trust the Sancus-enabled microcontroller, and the implementation of his own modules to be guaranteed authentic execution. Only the software components that implement the actual application logic of a distributed application have to be deployed as PMs. Of course, the compilation and deployment processes, running on the remote stakeholder's infrastructure, still need to be trusted. Yet, supporting software such as (embedded) Operating Systems (OSs), network stacks, module loaders, and even components implementing event management and distribution are explicitly untrusted as to authentic execution security guarantees. However, as we outline further on, such infrastructure software components may be trusted with regard to *availability* guarantees.

4   Implementation

In this section we present and discuss our proof-of-concept implementation of a HASM's software stack. Relying on Sancus [19] as the underlying architecture and the approach to authentic execution outlined in Sect. 3, we implement a representative subset of the HASM architecture as a reactive system, which is illustrated in Fig. 2: The core of our implementation is formed by three distributed PMs that realise the ESME's metering component, the Load Switch, and

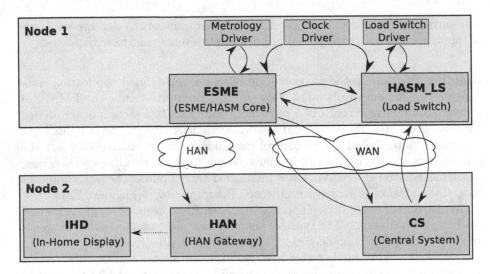

Fig. 2. Our implementation of a HASM's software stack using distributed PMs. Boxes shaded in red represent PMs and continuous arrows denote secure communication channels between these PMs. The IHD executes without PMA protection and must rely on alternative mechanisms to secure its communication with the HAN Interface

the grid operator's Central System. These PMs communicate bidirectionally over the untrusted WAN interface, where authenticated encryption is used to guarantee confidentiality and authenticity of messages, and to attest module integrity. A fourth PM implements the HAN Gateway, which acts as a unidirectional security gateway to relay consumption data to in-house appliances such as the IHD. For completeness we add such an IHD as an untrusted software component. The PMs are deployed and configured according to a Deployment Descriptor that defines which modules are to be loaded on which computing nodes and which module outputs are to be linked to which inputs. A section of the Deployment Descriptor, focusing on the Load Switch PM is given in Listing 1.

Our implementation runs on two TI MSP430 microcontrollers that implement the Sancus extensions; we rely on the Contiki OS [7] for untrusted supporting software such as the scheduler and the network stack. Figure 2 mentions three driver PMs that are meant to securely produce low-level I/O events (i.e., clock ticks and electricity consumption readings) and to operate actuators (the Load Switch). As we do not have all these hardware components available, we have left the implementation of these driver PMs for future work. Key features of Sancus and other PMAs are hardware-based isolation and integrity protection of PMs, and the built-in mechanisms for deriving, storing and managing cryptographic keys. These features naturally lead to a number of changes in the overall design of a HASM, specifically with respect to the system's communication infrastructure. We discuss these design choices below

```
 1  {                                      24        "to_input": "cs_in"
 2      "nodes": [                         25      },
 3          {                              26      {
 4              "type": "sancus",          27        "from_module": "HASM_LS",
 5              "name": "node1",           28        "from_output": "cs_out",
 6              "ip_address": "...",       29        "to_module": "CS",
 7              "vendor_id": 4660,         30        "to_input": "ls_in"
 8              "vendor_key": "..."        31      },
 9          }                              32      {
10      ],                                 33        "from_module": "ESME",
11      "modules" : [                      34        "from_output": "ls_out",
12          {                              35        "to_module": "HASM_LS",
13              "type": "sancus",          36        "to_input": "esme_in"
14              "name": "HASM_LS",         37      },
15              "files": ["hasm_ls.c"],    38      {
16              "node": "node1"            39        "from_module": "HASM_LS",
17          }                              40        "from_output": "esme_out",
18      ],                                 41        "to_module": "ESME",
19      "connections": [                   42        "to_input": "ls_in"
20          {                              43      }
21            "from_module": "CS",         44      ]
22            "from_output": "ls_out",     45  }
23            "to_module": "HASM_LS",      46
```

Listing 1: Deployment descriptor for the Load Switch PM: HASM_LS

Communications. In our implementation, the *Communications* component described in Sect. 2 is represented by an Event Manager which is an untrusted software component running on every node that is responsible for routing events from a PM's outputs to (another) PM's inputs. The Event Manager cannot decrypt and inspect these events. Instead, PMs themselves maintain keys for each communication channel. Decrypting events and verifying authenticity and freshness is implemented by each module, based on the cryptographic primitives provided by the PMA hardware. In consequence, PMs such as our Load Switch component and the Central System are easier and more securely implemented by defining bidirectional communication channels that use communication media and the Event Manager transparently, relying on purpose-specific keys.

In Listing 1 we present the section of the Deployment Descriptor that is relevant for deploying and configuring the Load Switch PM. As can be seen, the Deployment Descriptor specifies which node the PM is to be deployed on, and how input and output channels are to be linked together. Intuitively, a connections entry defines a unidirectional channel between a from_module PM and a to_module PM. The entries from_output and to_input correspond with module-specific handles for the connection that can be referred to in the source code of each PM. At deployment time, when configuring the channel, a symmetric key is securely transferred to each of the two PM endpoints, using hardware-level module keys provided by the PMA implementation.

We illustrate the use of module-specific channel handles in Listing 2. The Sancus compiler ensures that only successfully authenticated and decrypted events will ever be received at the input handles, and the PM's source code defines how to react upon these events. E.g., the Load Switch PM implements an access control policy by defining that only the Central System may issue commands to

```
1   #include <sancus/reactive.h>        18      if (data[2] & DISABLE_SPLY) {
2                                        19        sply_state = SPLY_DISABLED;
3   #include "commands.h"                20        cs_out(DISABLE_SPLY, 1);
4                                        21      }
5   SM_OUTPUT(HASM_LS, cs_out);          22      if (data[2] & GET_SPLY_STAT) {
6   SM_OUTPUT(HASM_LS, esme_out);        23        cs_out(sply_state, 1);
7                                        24      }
8   static uint8_t SM_DATA(HASM_LS)      25   }
9     sply_state;                        26
10                                       27   SM_INPUT(HASM_LS, esme_in, data,
11  SM_INPUT(HASM_LS, cs_in, data,       28      len)
12    len)                               29   {
13  {                                    30      if (data[2] & GET_SPLY_STAT) {
14    if (data[2] & ENABLE_SPLY) {       31        esme_out(sply_state, 1);
15      sply_state = SPLY_ENABLED;       32      }
16      cs_out(ENABLE_SPLY, 1);          33   }
17    }                                  34
```

Listing 2: Simplified C source code of the Load Switch PM: hasm_ls.c

change the system's supply state. The ESME PM may only query the supply state. In a more realistic implementation, changing the supply state must then result in using a driver PM to operate an actual load switch peripheral (i.e., an electrical relay).

Use of Separate CPUs. Another important aspect of using a PMA is that strong isolation and integrity protection of PMs guarantee that a PM's code and data can only be accessed through well-defined entry point functions. This effectively rules out attacks from the OS or any other software on a computing node. As a result, two PMs can securely co-exist on the same computing node without risking interactions that lead to manipulation of a PM's state in a way that is not defined by the source code of the PM, which is why we decided to deploy the Load Switch on the same node as the ESME. However, as we discuss in Sect. 5 guaranteeing availability and system progress may require further changes to the configuration. That is, availability and real-time requirements must be reflected by the hardware configuration. As evident from our deployment mechanism, module configurations and deployment details are easily adapted to different hardware configurations.

Persistent Storage. Strong component isolation further weakens the requirement for implementing a dedicated data storage component. Instead individual PMs can securely store operational data in the modules' secret data section and manage access to this data directly. This is particularly true in the case of size-bounded circular log buffers as specified in [6]. Methods to persist this operational data can be implemented with hardware support by the PMA [25]. Alternatively, secure resource sharing for persistent storage can be implemented as described in [27], via an intermediate PM that implements an access control policy for the module that "owns" the data.

5   Evaluation

In this section we evaluate the TCB and security properties of our HASM implementation. Our prototypic implementation is based on a developmental version of Contiki 3.x running on a Sancus-enabled openMSP430 [10,19] that is programmed on a Xilinx Spartan-6 FPGA. We do not provide a detailed performance evaluation as this does not yield interesting results beyond what is published in related work [18,19,27]: module loading, enabling protection, initial attestation and key deployment is relatively slow and may prolong startup of a HASM by a few milliseconds. The performance of cryptographic operations at run-time does not incur prohibitive overheads and the relatively relaxed real-time constraints specified in [6] (in the order of tens of seconds or minutes) can easily be met by our implementation. These results are in-line with a previous implementation of a smart meter for the MSP430 [17], where cryptography is implemented in software. A discussion of availability and real-time guarantees of our approach in the presence of adversaries concludes this section.

Table 1. Size of the software for running the evaluation scenario. The shaded components are part of the TCB

Component	Source LOC	Binary Size (B)	Deployed
Contiki	38386	16316	per node
Event manager	598	1730	per node
Module loader	906	1959	per node
ESME/HASM Core	119	2573	once
Load Switch	79	2377	once
HAN Gateway	30	1599	once
Central System	63	2069	once
Deployment Descriptor	90	n/a	n/a

TCB Size and Implications. Table 1 shows the sizes of the different software components deployed on nodes. As can be seen, the majority of the code running on a node – about 40 kLOC – is untrusted in our model. A total of only 291 LOC comprising of the actual application code is compiled to PMs and needs to be trusted, together with 90 LOC of the deployment descriptor. That is, only 1 % of the deployed code base is part of the software TCB. When looking at the binary sizes of the these software components, the difference between infrastructure components (19.5 KiB) versus TCB (8.4 KiB, 43.1 %) appears less prominent, which is due to a large number of conditionally compiled statements in Contiki as well as compiler generated entry points and stub code in the PMs.

For a full implementation of a HASM that provides trusted paths from sensors to the Central System, one also has to consider driver code. Without having the actual physical components for building a smart meter available, we conjecture that the sizes of such driver PMs are probably on par with our HASM implementation. Nevertheless, the reduction of the TCB when using our approach is substantial in comparison with other implementations that focus on security and attestation [14], which leads to a reduced attack surface on each node. The application owner, i.e., the grid operator, does not have to trust *any* infrastructure software but the driver modules that his application uses. As shown in related work, embedded programs of the size of our HASM PMs can be formally verified at acceptable efforts [23] and are more manageable in safety and security certification than the entire deployed code base. Of course, the TCB of our scenario also includes compilers and hardware. We aim to address the security of these parts of the TCB by means of secure compilation [21].

Security Evaluation. As explained in Sect. 3, the security property offered by our approach is that any physical output event can be explained by means of the untampered code of the application, and the actual physical input events that have happened. For the operator of a smart grid, this is a valuable property: it means that the response to a request to disable supply at a client's premises implies that the request was received and processed, down to the level of the Load Switch driver. To give another example, the guarantee also means that received consumption data is indeed based on the measurement of a specific metering element and the chain of untampered PMs that process the measurement. Together with the use of timestamps and nonces (at application level) and the built-in cryptographic communication primitives, our approach provides further confidentiality and freshness guarantees for the system's outputs.

From our discussion of design choices it can be seen that the use of PMAs must be considered early in the software development cycle since component isolation will affect the way in which components interact with one another. In particular, different protection domains cannot easily communicate through shared memory but must rely on cryptography and authenticated method invocation. Software developers will require tool support to isolate security critical code in protected modules, to design communication mechanisms and to to assess the reliability, performance and security characteristics of the resulting software system.

Software that is executing in a PM can still be subject to low-level attacks that exploit implementation details. Such attacks can cause memory corruption within the module and may even allow the attacker to control the internal execution of the module. This is because a software component encapsulated in a PM may offer a richer API than just input and output of primitive values. Methods or functions callable from the malicious context might also accept references to mutable objects or function pointers as parameters, or produce those as return values. Ongoing research addresses this by means of secure compilation, formal verification and the use of safe programming languages.

Furthermore, while our approach and the use of PMAs in general offer strong confidentiality and integrity guarantees for software modules, they offer no availability, let alone real-time guarantees, which we discuss below.

Availability and Real-Time Guarantees. The HASM/ESME reference implementation presented and evaluated above shows the feasibility of encapsulating high assurance smart metering functionality in isolated PM software components. Such an approach provides a grid operator with strong guarantees regarding the internal state of the smart meter and the authenticity of its measurements, while the underlying infrastructure software remains explicitly untrusted. However, as the timely execution of the smart metering PMs cannot be ensured, these guarantees do not extend to *availability*. Consider for example the scenario where an adversary exploits a remote vulnerability in the network stack or dynamic software loader. Our approach prevents such an attacker from operating the Load Switch peripheral or altering the security logs, but currently does not protect against various denial-of-service attacks where a malicious or buggy application for example overwrites crucial OS data structures or monopolises CPU time.

In the context of high assurance smart metering architectures availability properties cannot be considered out of scope. From the SMIP requirements document [6], we identified at least the following three real-time properties:

1. The HAN gateway shall receive information updates from the ESME at least every 10 s, and send them out to the IHD for visualisation purposes.
2. When operating in prepaid mode, the ESME shall be capable of monitoring the leftover credit balance, and disabling the power supply when a certain "disablement threshold" has been exceeded.
3. The ESME shall include measures to prevent physical tampering with the device. Upon detection of an unauthorised physical break-in event, the ESME shall establish a "locked state" whereby the power supply is disabled.

A challenging aspect of our proposed architecture is how to incorporate such hard real-time constraints. While non-trivial, we believe our reference implementation can serve as a base for an enhanced architecture that preserves the timely execution of security- and safety-critical functionality, even on a partially compromised smart meter. In the following, we outline several required extensions that allow the above real-time criteria to be met, without enlarging the TCB for the grid operator's security guarantees.

Secure Interrupt Handling. In a real-time computing system interrupts are commonly used to notify the processor of some asynchronous outside world event that requires immediate action. As an example, to meet requirement 3 above, a push button connected to the smart meter's case could raise an Interrupt Request (IRQ) when detecting physical tampering with the device. In response to such an IRQ, the PM operating the Load Switch should be activated so as to establish the locked state and disable the power supply.

Importantly, while the SMIP smart meter specifications document [6] does not provide a specific timing constraint for establishing the locked state, this real-time deadline can be considered *hard*. That is, severe system damage (e.g., damage to the grid or critical infrastructure, large-scale fraud) may occur when an adversary succeeds in physically accessing the smart meter's internals without the locked state being established.

The idea to enable secure interrupt handling in our ESME reference implementation is to register the entry point of the Load Switch PM as the interrupt handler for the intrusion detection IRQ. There are multiple ways in which an adversary, after having gained code execution on the smart meter, can prevent the IRQ handler from being (timely) executed. First, an attacker may overwrite the system-wide Interrupt Vector Table (IVT) that records interrupt handler addresses. This can be prevented by mapping the IVT memory addresses into the immutable text section of a dedicated PM. Second, an adversary may hold on to the CPU by disabling interrupts for arbitrary long times. To prevent such a scenario, and to establish a deterministic interrupt latency, running applications should not be allowed to unconditionally disable interrupts. For this, a hardware/software co-design has been proposed [28] to make PMs fully interruptible and reentrant, without introducing a privileged software layer that enlarges their software TCB, and while preserving secure compilation guarantees [21] via limited-length atomic code sections in a preemptive environment.

Preemptive Multitasking. Requirements 1 and 2 above necessitate the periodic execution of the ESME PM to monitor the client's power consumption and outstanding prepaid credit. In our current event-driven prototype, the Event Manager might schedule a periodic event that updates power consumption measurements in the ESME PM. However, when all input and output events have run-to-completion semantics, the Event Manager cannot be guaranteed to be timely executed, if at all. We will therefore explore *preemptive* scheduling of event handlers where a lightweight protected scheduler PM configures a timer interrupt before passing control to the untrusted event handler thread. Such an approach enables the protected scheduler (or Event Manager for that matter) to multiplex CPU time between multiple mutually distrusting application threads, while remaining responsive to asynchronous external events.

Importantly, in line with the notion of authentic execution introduced in Sect. 3, the protected scheduler should solely encapsulate the scheduling policy. A compromised scheduler PM should affect CPU availability only, and should not change the property that a grid operator can explain all physical output events by means of the observed physical input events and the application's source code. However, after successful attestation of the scheduler PM, the grid operator will be provided with additional availability guarantees, as defined by the scheduling policy. This ensures that, even in the case of a network failure or compromised infrastructure software, the smart meter's vital functionality will continue to execute as expected: power consumption will be monitored, and the supply will be disabled when the accumulated debt exceeds the pre-set threshold.

6   Conclusions

We have implemented and discussed a proof-of-concept prototype of a security-focused software stack for a smart metering scenario. Our implementation includes a High Assurance Smart Meter, a Load Switch, a HAN Gateway with In-Home Display, and a simplified Central System. Relying on the security guarantees of an embedded Protected Module Architecture, our approach and prototype guarantee that all outputs of the software system can be explained by the system's source code and the actual physical input events. We further guarantee integrity and confidentiality of messages while relying on a very small software Trusted Computing Base. For scenarios that involve critical infrastructure, such as the smart grid, we believe that our approach has the strategic advantage of enabling formal verification and security certification of small, isolated software components while maintaining the strong security guarantees of the distributed system that is formed by the interaction of these components.

In future work we will extend the prototype to support real electricity metering hardware and work towards providing strong real-time and availability guarantees in distributed event-driven smart sensing scenarios. We believe that our approach for implementing the smart meter can be reused to implement similar applications in the Internet of Things or in sensor networks.

Acknowledgments. The authors would like to thank B. Defend, K. Kursawe and C. Peters from ENCS for their many useful suggestions and help. This work has been supported in part by the Research Fund KU Leuven, by the Research Council KU Leuven: C16/15/058i, by the Research Foundation – Flanders (FWO), through KIC Innovation Project SAGA supported by KIC InnoEnergy SE and by the EU FP7/2007-2013 programme under grant 610535 – AMADEOS.

References

1. Alves, T., Felton, D.: Trustzone: integrated hardware and software security. ARM White Paper **3**(4), 18–24 (2004)
2. BSI: Protection profile for the gateway of a smart metering system (smart meter gateway PP) (2014). https://www.commoncriteriaportal.org/files/ppfiles/pp0073b_pdf.pdf
3. Checkoway, S., Davi, L., Dmitrienko, A., Sadeghi, A.R., Shacham, H., Winandy, M.: Return-oriented programming without returns. In: 17th Conference on Computer and Communications Security (CCS 2010), pp. 559–572. ACM (2010)
4. Cleemput, S., Mustafa, M.A., Preneel, B.: High assurance smart metering. In: 17th International Symposium on High Assurance Systems Engineering (HASE 2016), pp. 294–297. IEEE (2016)
5. Department of Energy, Climate Change: Smart metering implementation programme - communications hub technical specifications; version 1.46 (2014). https://www.gov.uk/government/uploads/system/uploads/attachment_data/file/381536/SMIP_E2E_CHTS.pdf
6. Department of Energy, Climate Change: Smart metering implementation programme - smart metering equipment technical specifications; version 1.58 (2014). https://www.gov.uk/government/uploads/system/uploads/attachment_data/file/381535/SMIP_E2E_SMETS2.pdf
7. Dunkels, A., Gronvall, B., Voigt, T.: Contiki - a lightweight and flexible operating system for tiny networked sensors. In: 29th Annual International Conference on Local Computer Networks, pp. 455–462. IEEE (2004). http://www.contiki-os.org/

8. Eldefrawy, K., Francillon, A., Perito, D., Tsudik, G.: SMART: secure and minimal architecture for (establishing a dynamic) root of trust. In: 19th Annual Network and Distributed System Security Symposium (NDSS 2012), (2012)

9. Farhangi, H.: The path of the smart grid. IEEE Power Energy Mag. 8(1), 18–28 (2010)

10. Girard, O.: openMSP 430 (2009). http://opencores.org

11. Jawurek, M., Johns, M., Kerschbaum, F.: Plug-in privacy for smart metering billing. In: Fischer-Hübner, S., Hopper, N. (eds.) PETS 2011. LNCS, vol. 6794, pp. 192–210. Springer, Heidelberg (2011)

12. Kalogridis, G., Sooriyabandara, M., Fan, Z., Mustafa, M.A.: Toward unified security and privacy protection for smart meter networks. IEEE Syst. J. 8(2), 641–654 (2014)

13. Koeberl, P., Schulz, S., Sadeghi, A.R., Varadharajan, V.: TrustLite: a security architecture for tiny embedded devices. In: EuroSys 2014, 14 pages. ACM (2014)

14. LeMay, M., Gross, G., Gunter, C.A., Garg, S.: Unified architecture for large-scale attested metering. In: HICSS 2007. IEEE (2007)

15. McKeen, F., Alexandrovich, I., Berenzon, A., Rozas, C.V., Shafi, H., Shanbhogue, V., Savagaonkar, U.R.: Innovative instructions and software model for isolated execution. In: HASP 2013, 8 pages. ACM (2013)

16. Metke, A.R., Ekl, R.L.: Security technology for smart grid networks. IEEE Trans. Smart Grid 1(1), 99–107 (2010)

17. Molina-Markham, A., Danezis, G., Fu, K., Shenoy, P., Irwin, D.: Designing privacy-preserving smart meters with low-cost microcontrollers. In: Keromytis, A.D. (ed.) FC 2012. LNCS, vol. 7397, pp. 239–253. Springer, Heidelberg (2012)

18. Mühlberg, J.T., Noorman, J., Piessens, F.: Lightweight and flexible trust assessment modules for the internet of things. In: Pernul, G., Ryan, P.Y.A., Weippl, E. (eds.) ESORICS. LNCS, vol. 9326, pp. 503–520. Springer, Heidelberg (2015). doi:10.1007/978-3-319-24174-6_26

19. Noorman, J., Agten, P., Daniels, W., Strackx, R., Herrewege, A.V., Huygens, C., Preneel, B., Verbauwhede, I., Piessens, F.: Sancus: Low-cost trustworthy extensible networked devices with a zero-software trusted computing base. In: 22nd USENIX Security Symposium, pp. 479–498. USENIX (2013)

20. von Oheimb, D.: IT security architecture approaches for smart metering and smart grid. In: Cuellar, J. (ed.) SmartGridSec 2012. LNCS, vol. 7823, pp. 1–25. Springer, Heidelberg (2013)

21. Patrignani, M., Agten, P., Strackx, R., Jacobs, B., Clarke, D., Piessens, F.: Secure compilation to protected module architectures. ACM Trans. Program. Lang. Syst. 37(2), 6:1–6:50 (2015)

22. Petrlic, R.: A privacy-preserving concept for smart grids. In: Sicherheit in vernetzten Systemen. DFN Workshop, pp. 1–14. Books on Demand GmbH (2010)

23. Philippaerts, P., Mühlberg, J.T., Penninckx, W., Smans, J., Jacobs, B., Piessens, F.: Software verification with VeriFast: industrial case studies. Sci. Comput. Program. (SCP) 82, 77–97 (2014)

24. Strackx, R., Noorman, J., Verbauwhede, I., Preneel, B., Piessens, F.: Protected software module architectures. In: Reimer, H., Pohlmann, N., Schneider, W. (eds.) ISSE 2013 Securing Electronic Business Processes, pp. 241–251. Springer, Wiesbaden (2013)

25. Strackx, R., Piessens, F.: Ariadne: a minimal approach to state continuity. In: 25th USENIX Security Symposium. USENIX (to appear, 2016)

26. Strackx, R., Piessens, F., Preneel, B.: Efficient isolation of trusted subsystems in embedded systems. In: Jajodia, S., Zhou, J. (eds.) SecureComm 2010. LNICST, vol. 50, pp. 344–361. Springer, Heidelberg (2010)
27. Van Bulck, J., Noorman, J., Mühlberg, J.T., Piessens, F.: Secure resource sharing for embedded protected module architectures. In: Akram, R., Jajodia, S. (eds.) WISTP 2015. LNCS, vol. 9311, pp. 71–87. Springer, Heidelberg (2015). doi:10. 1007/978-3-319-24018-3_5
28. Van Bulck, J., Noorman, J., Mühlberg, J.T., Piessens, F.: Towards availability and real-time guarantees for protected module architectures. In: 15th International Conference on Modularity, pp. 146–151. ACM (2016)
29. Yan, Y., Qian, Y., Sharif, H., Tipper, D.: A survey on cyber security for smart grid communications. IEEE Commun. Surv. Tutorials **14**(4), 998–1010 (2012)

Security Challenges of Small Cell as a Service in Virtualized Mobile Edge Computing Environments

Vassilios Vassilakis[1]([✉]), Emmanouil Panaousis[2], and Haralambos Mouratidis[2]

[1] School of Computing and Engineering, University of West London, London, UK
vasileios.vassilakis@uwl.ac.uk
[2] Secure and Dependable Software Systems Research Cluster,
School of Computing, Engineering, and Mathematics,
University of Brighton, Brighton, UK
{e.panaousis,h.mouratidis}@brighton.ac.uk

Abstract. Research on next-generation 5G wireless networks is currently attracting a lot of attention in both academia and industry. While 5G development and standardization activities are still at their early stage, it is widely acknowledged that 5G systems are going to extensively rely on *dense small cell deployments*, which would exploit *infrastructure and network functions virtualization* (NFV), and push the network intelligence towards network edges by embracing the concept of *mobile edge computing* (MEC). As security will be a fundamental enabling factor of *small cell as a service* (SCaaS) in 5G networks, we present the most prominent *threats* and *vulnerabilities* against a broad range of *targets*. As far as the related work is concerned, to the best of our knowledge, this paper is the first to investigate security challenges at the intersection of SCaaS, NFV, and MEC. It is also the first paper that proposes a set of criteria to facilitate a clear and effective taxonomy of security challenges of main elements of 5G networks. Our analysis can serve as a staring point towards the development of appropriate 5G security solutions. These will have crucial effect on legal and regulatory frameworks as well as on decisions of businesses, governments, and end-users.

Keywords: Security · Small cell as a service · Network functions virtualization · Mobile edge computing · 5G

1 Introduction

Rapid advances in the industry of handheld devices and mobile applications has fuelled the penetration of interactive and ubiquitous web-based services into almost every aspect of our lives. At the same time, users expect almost *zero-delay* and *infinite-capacity* experience. However, current 4G technologies reveal their

© IFIP International Federation for Information Processing 2016
Published by Springer International Publishing Switzerland 2016. All Rights Reserved
S. Foresti and J. Lopez (Eds.): WISTP 2016, LNCS 9895, pp. 70–84, 2016.
DOI: 10.1007/978-3-319-45931-8_5

inherent limitations, as discussed in [1]. This is true, for both human-to-human and machine-to-machine (M2M) communications [2,3]. Both will require radically different architectural design, network protocols, and business models. To achieve that, researchers are working towards the next-generation 5G wireless networks aiming to offer high-speed and personalized services to both humans and machines, when and where needed [4].

To support highly dense areas where a vast number of users want to access the network infrastructure, deployment of *small cells* (SCs) is envisioned. These can co-operate with traditional macro cells, to provide high levels of user experience [5,6]. SCs will play a significant role in 5G networks, which are expected to be highly heterogeneous. That is, future 5G networks will comprise a variety of *collocated resources*, such as indoor and outdoor SCs, macro cell sites, and WiFi access points. Another driving force in 5G will be the advances in *hardware virtualization* technologies, which can facilitate the realization of the *small cell as a service* (SCaaS) concept [7].

The primary benefit that comes with SCaaS is that independent actors own and lease their cellular infrastructure to multiple *mobile network operators* (MNOs); therefore SCaaS provides a natural *multi-tenant* support, by allowing each MNO to be a tenant of the infrastructure and getting a "slice" of the physical SC infrastructure [8]. This is not the only advantage that SCaaS can offer to 5G. We can leverage SCaaS to provide high-speed, low-latency communications, and to offload the mobile core network traffic and computation to the network edge, giving life to the concept of *mobile edge computing* (MEC) and *fog computing*, which has recently attained attention [9–11].

Finally, another important technology of 5G is *network function virtualization* (NFV), which: decouples network functions from their physical location; offers flexible function migration; and distributes functions across different network components [12,13]. It is worth mentioning that NFV can be further enhanced with the concept of *software-defined networking* (SDN) decoupling the control plane from the data plane [14,15].

Although 5G network technologies are still taking shape, and standardization activities are still ongoing, it is expected that SCaaS, MEC, NFV, and SDN are going to be *integral parts* of 5G networks. For example, the recently started EU 5G-PPP project SESAME (Small cEllS coordinAtion for Multi-tenancy and Edge services) aims to provide solutions in the field [16]. Another, EU 5G-PPP project called 5G-ENSURE aims at defining the security architecture and developing security enablers for 5G [17].

1.1   Contribution

In order to investigate the security challenges of 5G networks, one must look into the security issues of its elements and their interaction. In this paper, we identify the security *threats* and *vulnerabilities* of SCaaS, NFV, and MEC, as a first step towards a more comprehensive 5G security analysis that we intend to undertake in future work. Our analysis is focused on SC infrastructure, whose security is a very crucial issue because SCs are expected to support both MNOs and end-users, who cannot tolerate financial losses or data privacy violations, and therefore they seek the highest possible security guarantees. Having a comprehensive view and taxonomy of security threats and vulnerabilities in SCs, is prerequisite for architecting optimal security solutions.

1.2   State-of-the-Art

The state-of-the-art within the field of 5G security is in its infancy. Mantas *et al.* [18] investigated some of the potential threats and attacks against the main components of 5G systems. The authors mainly focus on security issues related to the user equipment, and although they briefly go beyond that, they do not present security issues that open up as a result of SCaaS, NFV, and MEC. Apart from this, they lack a clear list of criteria that facilitate the creation of a taxonomy of threats and vulnerabilities. In an even less depth, in terms of threats and vulnerabilities investigation, Fang *et al.* [19] propose a high level security framework for 5G networks, without paying particular attention in the technologies we consider in our paper, here.

Within the realm of physical layer security for 5G networks, Yang *et al.* [20] investigate the security challenges that open up when considering the technologies of heterogeneous networks, massive multiple-input multiple-output (MIMO), and millimeter wave, which are likely to be important parts of 5G networks. Furthermore, Duan and Wang [21] investigated the security challenges, focusing mainly on authentication handover and privacy protection in 5G. The contribution of these papers is not directly comparable to ours, here, and we only referred to them for completeness.

1.3   Outline

This paper is structured as follows. In Sect. 2, we describe a generic, high-level architecture for SCaaS. We also present our assumptions regarding the SCaaS security and the adversarial model. Section 3 discusses the security challenges of SCaaS and reveals major security threats that arise due to (i) network resources and functions being virtualized, (ii) the adoption of MEC, and (iii) the incorporation of NFV and SDN concepts. We also present a set of criteria to facilitate the taxonomy of security challenges and discuss their mutual dependencies. Finally, Sect. 4 concludes this paper by summarizing its contributions and presenting our plans for future work.

2   Prerequisites

2.1   System Architecture

Our considered high-level system architecture for SCaaS is in line with [22] and has been illustrated in Fig. 1. The main elements of this architecture include: infrastructure virtualization; NFV; SDN, and MEC. According to the

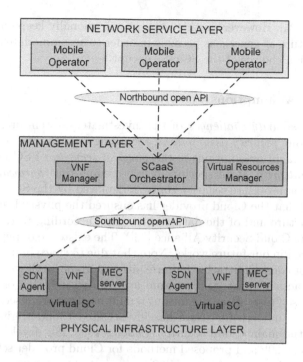

Fig. 1. High-level system architecture for small cell as a service.

SC infrastructure virtualization principle, the *physical SC* is sliced into a number of *virtual SCs* (VSCs). To enable MEC services, each VSC is equipped with a MEC server, which has the ability to communicate with the Cloud and to execute some of the functions that are traditionally hosted in the Cloud. Furthermore, multiple MEC servers can be clustered to provide enhanced services in the form of a *light data centre* (Light DC) and managed by the *virtual resources manager* (VRM). Each VSC also accommodates a number of *virtual network functions* (VNFs) and it is managed by the *SCaaS Orchestrator* via an SDN agent. Above the *management layer* there is the *service layer*, in which multiple tenants (i.e., MNOs) are accommodated.

The network service layer accommodates MNOs who are benefited from having *on-demand access* to SC resources without owing the physical infrastructure. MNOs communicate with the SCaaS Orchestrator, located in the management layer, who orchestrates the allocation of virtual resources to MNOs. The SCaaS Orchestrator closely collaborates with the VRM, which is responsible for the management of virtual resources of MEC servers in the physical infrastructure layer. The control of VSCs is performed via SDN agents using some appropriate SDN protocol, such as the MobileFlow [23]. Finally, various network functions, such as *firewalling* and *deep packet inspection* (DPI), are virtualized using the NFV technology and managed by the VNF Manager. A specific realization of the architecture of Fig. 1 could be, for example, the SESAME architecture [16,24]. However, in this work we intentionally keep our considered system architecture as generic as possible in order to accommodate a wide range of implementation choices of the SCaaS concept.

2.2   Security Assumptions

To identify the *security challenges* of the investigated system architecture, we first introduce our *security assumptions*, regarding the baseline security of the system. One of main assumptions is the *physical security* of SC infrastructure and *hardware integrity*. More specifically, we assume that *hardware tampering* is prevented by appropriate security controls deployed by the SC infrastructure owner [25], and that the Cloud provider has ensured the physical security of the Cloud infrastructure and of the data centres (e.g., according to the recommendations from the Cloud Security Alliance [26]). The existence of physical attacks will be considered in our future works. Note that due to space limitations, in this paper, we do not consider attacks that are initiated from the Cloud side. Instead, we focus on attacks originated either from *user equipment* (UE) or from the SC infrastructure itself (e.g., from a malicious tenant or a compromised system component). Besides, modern literature has investigated Cloud-originated attacks and identified the main Cloud security challenges [27,28]; developed adequate security solutions [29]; and proposed methods for Cloud provider selection based on security and privacy requirements [30].

2.3   Adversarial Model

Our analysis adopts the widely-used Dolev-Yao adversarial model [31]. According to this model, the cellular network is represented as a *set of abstract entities* that exchange messages and the adversary is capable of overhearing, intercepting, and synthesizing any message and they are only limited by the constraints of the deployed cryptographic methods. For example, the adversary neither is able to forge the message authentication code (MAC) nor has the means to obtain the plaintext of encrypted messages.

Apart from the above, we enrich the adversarial model by considering *compromised nodes*. The adversary per se could be a *legitimate tenant* interacting with network entities by using valid credentials and having *privileged access* to virtualized resources. Yet the adversary might run any management application in their VSC or specify various policies within its virtual domain, which is defined as a cluster of VSCs allocated to the same tenant.

3   Security Challenges

In this section we discuss the security challenges that emerge from the adoption of the SCaaS concept, using as a reference the architecture of Fig. 1. We adopt the widely-used threat taxonomy proposed in [32] and identify the security challenges that arise due to specific architectural characteristics and interaction of various components and layers of SCaaS. The different security challenges can be classified according to five categories.

- **Precondition**: What are the necessary conditions to be met before the adversary is able to launch the attack? For example, if the attack requires a particular service running on the victim side, the existence of an open interface is a precondition; another case is when the adversary has some particular access rights.
- **Vulnerability**: What are the vulnerabilities of the system components or the network interfaces, which can be exploited by the adversary? For example, some components could be implemented in software with flaws or non-adequate cryptographic mechanisms could be in place [33].
- **Target**: Which components or interfaces are the potential attack targets? Other considerations include the communication layer the adversary targets and whether he aims to compromise the control or the data plane or both.
- **Method**: What are the various attack methods, tools and techniques that the adversary might use? In the same category we examine whether the adversary follows an active (e.g., replay attack) or passive strategy (e.g., passive reconnaissance).
- **Effect**: What is the impact of a successful attack on the victimized system component or network interface? Impact might be, for instance, unavailability of some services, financial costs, and leakage of sensitive data.

Below, we identify specific security challenges for each of the aforementioned five categories.

3.1   Precondition

Regarding precondition, the following types of requirements might be valid for the adversary.

Specific configuration: In some cases, to launch an attack against a component, the adversary requires that this component has specific exploitable configuration or runs a specific software. For example, a precondition for a *denial-of-service* (DoS) attack [34,35] can be specific configuration of the VRM with regard to the allocation of resources to tenants. Yet, some flaws in the resource allocation algorithm can allow the adversary to prevent a tenant from accessing its portion of virtual resources. Also, other types of DoS attacks may exploit the broadband nature of the wireless medium. For example, malicious interference at the physical layer, even using off-the-shelf hardware, can cause packet collisions at the media access control (MAC) layer [36].

Ubiquitous connectivity: If a network component or function can be accessed via the public Internet, this may be exploited by a *remote adversary*. The adversary will require a way of discovering the vulnerable component and sending messages via control or data plane. By moving the network intelligence to the network edge, as with the Light DC, a pool of MEC servers is usually available for UEs to be connected via the Internet using conventional methods. Also, the *physical location* and *distributed or centralised nature* of the SCaaS Orchestrator could be an important factor influencing its security. For example, one way to realise the SCaaS Orchestrator is as a distributed function with its instances located across multiple SCs (e.g., in the form of a VNF). In such case, if public Internet is used to remotely configure various SCaaS policies, this can be exploited by the adversary.

Privileged access: The adversary has privileged access to some parts of the network components or functions. The privileged access can be either at the administrator level or at the user level. For example, the adversary may be a legitimate UE receiving service from its MNO, with the latter being a legitimate tenant of the SC network infrastructure. Also, the emerging *bring your own device* (BYOD) trend in modern enterprises, constitutes many conventional security solutions incapable of protecting the private network [37]. For example, a Trojan horse that infected an employee's device, can bypass the security of the corporate firewall.

3.2 Vulnerabilitiy

SDN controller weaknesses: Some vulnerabilities are caused by flaws in software and programming errors. This may lead, for example, to control flow attacks [38] and buffer overflow attacks [39]. This issue is particularly important in the context of next-generation wireless networks, where the trend is to implement the control plane in software and to virtualize network functions [40, 41].

Flaws of NFV platforms: The virtualised environment itself could introduce many potential security problems [42]. In particular, flaws of the virtualisation platform in place, may constitute the guest operating system (OS) vulnerable to side-channel attacks. For example, weak isolation between host and guest OSs may lead to a side-channel attack based on cache leakage [43].

Cloud based management: Some vulnerabilities stem from the Cloud based management nature of certain network components. The Cloud based interface used for configuration and updates could be used as a potential attack channel.

Weak access control and authentication: Use of weak or default passwords could be easily exploited by an adversary and should be avoided. Also, some components may have hard-coded passwords, which can be exploited by the adversary towards the establishment of backdoor access; stealthy or not.

Weak cryptographic mechanisms: Weaknesses or improper use of cryptographic mechanisms may lead to security breaches in authentication processes and data confidentiality. Also, the generation of cryptographic keys shouldn't rely on weak random number generators. Other security problems may arise due to communication protocols that use weak cryptographic primitives. Hence, it should be ensured that the cryptographic security controls are in place [44]. This is to say that any adopted public-key scheme that enables the encryption of the communications among SC, UE, and the Cloud, should be sufficiently secure.

3.3   Target

Physical small cell infrastructure: Attacks on the specific piece of hardware that is used in the cellular network [45]. For example the physical SC infrastructure can be a target of hardware attacks. While it is a common practice for the users to authenticate themselves to mobile devices before using them, the devices usually do not do the same to users. This means that there is a risk for the authentication secret to be revealed to a non-authenticated device. Hence, an attacker may try to obtain the secret, by replacing the device with a malicious one [46].

NFV-based management system: Some attacks initiated inside virtualised environments may aim at taking control of the Hypervisor [47]. Also, the SCaaS Orchestrator is an attractive attack target due to being in the "middle" of the system model architecture, as well as other components of the *management layer*, such as the VNF Manager. Finally, impersonation by the adversary of one of the VNFs or the MEC server when communicating with the management layer could be a potential threat.

VM-hosted operating system: Both host and guest OS may be targeted [48], and to alleviate the impact of such an attack, adequate isolation must be enforced between guest virtual machines (VMs), as well as between the host and guest VMs. The adversary could attempt to break the isolation by exploiting, e.g., some flaws of the virtualisation platform in use [49].

Mobility management entity: In some cases, the attack does not target a specific layer in the system architecture, but it rather aims to *take control* of a specific network entity, either physical or virtual, such as the mobility management entity (MME). Protecting against such kind of attacks will be even more difficult when a distributed MME is introduced in 5G networks [50].

MEC-based application: A certain application that runs, for instance, on a MEC server is a potential attack target. This does not affect only the SC that hosts the compromised MEC server. Due to clustering of MEC servers into the Light DC, as discussed in Sect. 2, and their communication with the Cloud, a compromised MEC server can be used as a door to attack other network entities and components. Also, the adversary may attempt to attack the network service isolation. This may result in the violations of limits for virtual resources or unauthorized use of other tenants' resources. We assume that the adversary can attempt to impersonate another tenant or another network entity. Also, it may attempt to decrypt the intercepted messages.

MobileFlow protocol: A usual attack target is the protocol used for communication, management or control purposes, such as the MobileFlow protocol [23]. For example, the southbound and northbound interfaces, shown in Fig. 1, are potential attack targets when attempting to hijack the communication of the SCaaS Orchestrator with VSCs and MNOs. Also, the communication within the SC infrastructure could be targeted; for example, between the management and the physical infrastructure layer. This may enable an adversary to alter the network

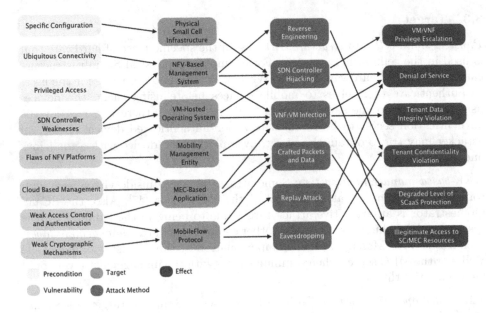

Fig. 2. Dependencies among security challenges of Small Cell as a Service in virtualised MEC environments.

policies and create attack channels. In particular, possible attack targets are (i) communication of the VNF Manager with VNFs in a SC; and (ii) communication of the VRM with MEC servers. Hence, the adversary may try to alter or disable legitimate policies and cause attacks such as DoS and privilege escalation or to violate the privacy of other tenants data.

3.4 Method

Reverse engineering: The adversary collects and analyses sensitive information about the network and its functionality. She may also try to decompile the software to retrieve the source code. This may enable the adversary to identify vulnerabilities in the software or network interfaces. In some cases, the adversary may exploit weaknesses in the implemented access control mechanisms and exploit a device through normal usage, i.e., as a legitimate user. Other reverse-engineering techniques may target users' sensitive personal information. For example, the increasing popularity of mobile crowdsourcing and mobile sensing projects [51] may enable an attacker to exploit various personal data such as the user location, mobility patterns or web browsing habits [52].

SDN controller hijacking: By exploiting the SDN controller implementation weaknesses, the adversary tries to divert the control flows to a controlled device [53]. Then the captured messages can be *discarded* preventing the data plane entities from proper operation. In a more advanced case, the captured messages may be manipulated with a special purpose code and sent into the network.

VNF/VM infection: The adversary infects a virtual network component, such as a VM or a VNF, with a malicious code. In this way, an unwanted and potentially harmful functionality can be added to the affected system and can modify its behaviour. The future trends in *network softwarization* and *programmability* [54, 55] make this attack method particularly important. Furthermore, in a typical virtualised environment, guest VMs are expected to run in complete isolation. This means that a VM is not able to interact with the host and other VMs nor is able to monitor or control them in any way. This isolation is typically enforced by the Hypervisor. However, such virtualised environments may be vulnerable to the so-called *VM escape attack* [56], which is a process of breaking out the aforementioned VM isolation. This can be achieved for example by installing malware on the Hypervisor [57].

Crafted packets and data: The adversary can attack communication and control protocols by injecting crafted packets or crafted input data. These actions may exploit, for example, the parsing vulnerabilities of protocol implementations [58].

Replay attack: The adversary captures packets or packet fragments and replays them at appropriate times aiming to cause protocol failures or other types of disruption and confusion.

Eavesdropping: The adversary observes messages exchanged between various network components or functions. In this way, sensitive information can be obtained, especially if this information is weakly protected by cryptographic mechanisms or not protected at all.

3.5   Effect

VM/VNF privilege escalation: The adversary, who has already some level of limited access privilege (e.g., to a VM or a VNF), manages to gain more privilege. This may have very serious negative effects for SDN-based mobile networks [59] as well as for the emerging *Internet of things* (IoT) technologies [60].

Denial of service: A potential outcome of attacks can be DoS leading to switched off or malfunctioning SC, or unavailable MEC servers. Also, a DoS attack against the SCaaS Orchestrator can cause service disruption and data loss. Yet, in a multi-tenant environment, security implications that may arise due weak isolation between tenants may allow adversaries to compromise more than one tenants upon compromising one of the other tenants. Furthermore, a DoS attack may be launched from within the SC [11].

Tenant data integrity violation: Some data or code, including various configuration settings and security policies, can be altered. This is a particularly important issue in a virtualised multi-tenant environment. It must be taken into account that some tenants could be malicious. Hence, adequate data isolation for different tenants must be ensured. This could be done, for example at the database level or at the hardware level.

Tenant confidentiality violation: In some cases sensitive information of a tenant may be leaked and made available to the adversary or to a malicious tenant.

Degraded level of SCaaS protection: A possible effect can be the degradation of SCaaS infrastructure protection. This can be achieved, for example, by altering the security policies or switching to weaker cryptographic mechanisms.

Illegitimate access to SC/MEC resources: The adversary gains illegitimate access to the SC resources (physical or virtual) or MEC environment. Given the increasing trend of outsourcing data and applications, an adequate security solution must ensure that only authorised entities gain access. Also, the insider threat should be considered and appropriate mechanisms must be put in place for preventing service providers form misusing tenants' data.

In Fig. 2, we show, in the form of a directed graph, an example of possible dependencies of these categories. For instance, to cause DoS, the adversary could select VM/VNF infection as an attack method. To achieve that, malware could be injected in the management system (e.g., to the VRM or the VNF Manager in Fig. 1), a VM-hosted OS, or a MEC-based application (i.e., by compromising a MEC server), which constitute the potential attack targets. To target, e.g., the VM-hosted OS, the adversary could possibly exploit the SDN controller weaknesses or flaws of NFV platforms, and take advantage of any privileged access rights.

4 Conclusion

In this paper, we have identified the most important security challenges of SCaaS in virtualized environments of 5G networks. We envision that novel technologies, such as NFV, SDN, and MEC will be adopted in the future and will play an important role in the SCaaS realization. We have summarized the main security challenges that (i) open up with these technologies and (ii) arise due to the interoperability among them, which enables SCaaS. We have highlighted the necessary conditions for the adversary to be able to launch an attack; the vulnerabilities of various system components and network interfaces that can be exploited by the adversary; potential targets of attacks, such as management systems and applications; various methods and techniques that can be used by the adversary; and finally, the impact of the attacks on an SCaaS provider and its tenants. In future work, we intend to study and evaluate prominent security solutions developed for protecting virtualized SC networks and systems per se, focusing on NFV, SDN, and MEC. This security assessment will use this paper, here, as a basis.

Acknowledgements. The present work has been performed in the scope of the SESAME (*"Small cEllS coordinAtion for Multi-tenancy and Edge services"*) European Research Project and has been supported by the Commission of the European Communities (*5G-PPP/H2020, Grant Agreement No. 671596*).

References

1. Boccardi, F., Heath, R.W., Lozano, A., Marzetta, T.L., Popovski, P.: Five disruptive technology directions for 5G. IEEE Commun. Mag. **52**(2), 74–80 (2014)
2. Andreev, S., et al.: Understanding the IoT connectivity landscape: a contemporary M2M radio technology roadmap. IEEE Commun. Mag. **53**(9), 32–40 (2015)
3. Vardakas, J.S., Zorba, N., Skianis, C., Verikoukis, C.V.: Performance analysis of M2M communication networks for QoS-differentiated smart grid applications. In: IEEE Globecom Workshops (GC Wkshps), pp. 1–6 (2015)
4. Patel, S., Malhar, C., Kapadiya, K.: 5G: Future mobile technology - vision 2020. Int. J. Comput. Appl. **54**(17), 6–10 (2012)
5. Andrews, J.G.: Seven ways that HetNets are a cellular paradigm shift. IEEE Commun. Mag. **51**(3), 136–144 (2013)
6. Osseiran, A., et al.: Scenarios for 5G mobile and wireless communications: the vision of the METIS project. IEEE Commun. Mag. **52**(5), 26–35 (2014)
7. Trakas, P., Adelantado, F., Verikoukis, C.: A novel learning mechanism for traffic offloading with small cell as a service. In: IEEE International Conference on Communications (ICC), London, U.K. (2015)
8. Giannoulakis, I., et al.: System architecture and aspects of SESAME: Small cEllS coordinAtion for Multi-tenancy and Edge services. In: 2nd IEEE Conference on Network Softwarization (NetSoft), Workshop on Software Defined 5G Networks (Soft5G), Seoul, Korea (2016)
9. Soldani, D., Manzalini, A.: A 5G infrastructure for anything-as-a-service. J. Telecommun. Syst. Manag. **3**(2), 1–10 (2014)
10. Vaquero, L.M., Rodero-Merino, L.: Finding your way in the fog: towards a comprehensive definition of fog computing. ACM SIGCOMM Comput. Commun. Rev. **44**(5), 27–32 (2014)
11. Roman, R., Lopez, J., Mambo, M.: Mobile edge computing, fog et al.: A survey and analysis of security threats and challenges. arXiv preprint arxiv:1602.00484 (2016)
12. Han, B., Gopalakrishnan, V., Ji, L., Lee, S.: Network function virtualization: challenges and opportunities for innovations. IEEE Commun. Mag. **53**(2), 90–97 (2015)
13. Yu, R., Xue, G., Kilari, V., Zhang, X.: Network function virtualization in the multi-tenant cloud. IEEE Netw. **29**(3), 42–47 (2015)
14. Ameigeiras, P., et al.: Link-level access cloud architecture design based on SDN for 5G networks. IEEE Netw. **29**(2), 24–31 (2015)
15. Sun, S., Kadoch, M., Gong, L., Rong, B.: Integrating network function virtualization with SDR and SDN for 4G/5G networks. IEEE Netw. **29**(3), 54–59 (2015)
16. EC H2020 Small sEllS coordinAtion for Multi-tenancy and Edge services (SESAME) Project, July 2016. https://5g-ppp.eu/sesame/
17. EC H2020 5G-ENSURE, July 2016. https://5g-ppp.eu/5g-ensure/
18. Mantas, G., et al.: Security for 5G Communications. Fundamentals of 5G Mobile Netw. John Wiley & Sons Ltd. (2015)
19. Fang, Q., Weijie, Z., Guojun, W., Hui, F.: Unified security architecture research for 5G wireless system. In: 11th Web Information System and Application Conference, Tianjin, China (2014)
20. Yang, N., et al.: Safeguarding 5G wireless communication networks using physical layer security. IEEE Commun. Mag. **53**(4), 20–27 (2015)
21. Duan, X., Wang, X.: Authentication handover and privacy protection in 5G HetNets using software-defined networking. IEEE Commun. Mag. **53**(4), 28–35 (2015)

22. Vassilakis, V.G., Moscholios, I.D., Alzahrani, B.A., Logothetis, M.D.: A software-defined architecture for next-generation cellular networks. In: IEEE International Conference on Communications (ICC), Kuala Lumpur, Malaysia (2016)

23. Pentikousis, K., Wang, Y., Hu, W.: Mobileflow: toward software-defined mobile networks. IEEE Commun. Mag. **51**(7), 44–53 (2013)

24. Fajardo, J.O., et al.: Introducing mobile edge computing capabilities through distributed 5G cloud enabled small cells. Mobile Netw. Appl., 1–11 (2016). Springer, US

25. Skorobogatov, S.: Physical attacks and tamper resistance. In: Tehranipoor, M., Wang, C. (eds.) Introduction to Hardware Security and Trust, pp. 143–173. Springer, New York (2012)

26. Cloud Security Alliance, Security Guidance for Critical Areas of Focus in Cloud Computing V2.1, December 2009

27. Subashini, S., Kavitha, V.: A survey on security issues in service delivery models of cloud computing. J. Netw. Comput. Appl. **34**(1), 1–11 (2011)

28. Ryan, M.D.: Cloud computing security: the scientific challenge, and a survey of solutions. J. Syst. Softw. **86**(9), 2263–2268 (2013)

29. Zissis, D., Lekkas, D.: Addressing cloud computing security issues. Future Gener. Comput. Syst. **28**(3), 583–592 (2012)

30. Mouratidis, H., Islam, S., Kalloniatis, C., Gritzalis, S.: A framework to support selection of cloud providers based on security and privacy requirements. J. Syst. Softw. **86**(9), 2276–2293 (2013)

31. Dolev, D., Yao, A.C.: On the security of public key protocols. IEEE Trans. Inf. Theory **29**(2), 198–208 (1983)

32. Papp, D., Ma, Z., Buttyan, L.: Embedded systems security: threats, vulnerabilities, and attack taxonomy. In: 13th Annual Conference on Privacy, Security and Trust, Izmir, Turkey (2015)

33. Mihaljevic, M.J., Gangopadhyay, S., Paul, G., Imai, H.: Generic cryptographic weakness of k-normal Boolean functions in certain stream ciphers and cryptanalysis of grain-128. Periodica Math. Hungarica **65**(2), 205–227 (2012)

34. Gobbo, N., Merlo, A., Migliardi, M.: A denial of service attack to GSM networks via attach procedure. In: Cuzzocrea, A., Kittl, C., Simos, D.E., Weippl, E., Xu, L. (eds.) CD-ARES Workshops 2013. LNCS, vol. 8128, pp. 361–376. Springer, Heidelberg (2013)

35. Merlo, A., Migliardi, M., Gobbo, N., Palmieri, F., Castiglione, A.: A denial of service attack to UMTS networks using SIM-less devices. IEEE Trans. Depend. Secure Comput. **11**(3), 280–291 (2014)

36. Fragkiadakis, A., Askoxylakis, I., Chatziadam, P.: Denial-of-service attacks in wireless networks using off-the-shelf hardware. In: Streitz, N., Markopoulos, P. (eds.) DAPI 2014. LNCS, vol. 8530, pp. 427–438. Springer, Heidelberg (2014)

37. Armando, A., Costa, G., Merlo, A.: Bring your own device, securely. In: 28th ACM Symposium on Applied Computing, Coimbra, Portugal (2013)

38. Davi, L., et al.: MoCFI: a framework to mitigate control-flow attacks on smartphones. In: 19th Annual Network & Distributed System Security Symposium, San Diego, USA (2012)

39. Wang, L.B., Wei, G.H., Li, Z.: Research of defense scheme against buffer overflow attack in embedded system. J. Comput. Appl. 12 (2012)

40. Wang, H., Chen, S., Xu, H., Ai, M., Shi, Y.: SoftNet: a software defined decentralized mobile network architecture toward 5G. IEEE Netw. **29**(2), 16–22 (2015)

41. Vassilakis, V.G., Moscholios, I.D., Alzahrani, B.A., Logothetis, M.D.: On the security of software-defined next-generation cellular networks. In: IEICE Information and Communication Technology Forum (ICTF), Patras, Greece (2016)
42. Kotsovinos, E.: Virtualization: Blessing or curse? Commun. ACM **54**(1), 61–65 (2011)
43. Barthe, G., Betarte, G., Campo, J.D., Luna, C.: Cache-leakage resilient OS isolation in an idealized model of virtualization. In: IEEE 25th Computer Security Foundations Symposium, Cambridge, USA (2012)
44. Bhargavan, K., Fournet, C., Kohlweiss, M., Pironti, A., Strub, P.: Implementing TLS with verified cryptographic security. In: 34th IEEE Symposium on Security and Privacy, San Francisco, USA (2013)
45. Rostami, M., Koushanfar, F., Rajendran, J., Karri, R.: Hardware security: threat models and metrics. In: 32nd IEEE/ACM International Conference on Computer-Aided Design, San Jose, CA (2013)
46. Findling, R.D., Mayrhofer, R.: Towards device-to-user authentication: protecting against phishing hardware by ensuring mobile device authenticity using vibration patterns. In: 14th ACM International Conference on Mobile and Ubiquitous Multimedia, pp. 131–135 (2015)
47. Perez-Botero, D., Szefer, J., Lee, R.B.: Characterizing hypervisor vulnerabilities in cloud computing servers. In: 8th ACM International Workshop on Security in Cloud Computing, Hangzhou, China, pp. 3–10 (2013)
48. Suzaki, K., Iijima, K., Yagi, T., Artho, C.: Memory deduplication as a threat to the guest OS. In: 4th ACM European Workshop on System Security, Salzburg, Austria (2011)
49. Hoesing, M.T.: Virtualization security assessment. Inf. Secur. J.: A Global Perspect. **18**(3), 124–130 (2009)
50. Giust, F., Cominardi, L., Bernardos, C.: Distributed mobility management for future 5G networks: overview and analysis of existing approaches. IEEE Commun. Mag. **53**(1), 142–149 (2015)
51. Chen, P.Y., Cheng, S.M., Ting, P.S., Lien, C.W., Chu, F.J.: When crowdsourcing meets mobile sensing: a social network perspective. IEEE Commun. Mag. **53**(10), 157–163 (2015)
52. Han, Q., Liang, S., Zhang, H.: Mobile cloud sensing, big data, and 5G networks make an intelligent and smart world. IEEE Netw. **29**(2), 40–45 (2015)
53. Goktas, E., Athanasopoulos, E., Bos, H., Portokalidis, G.: Out of control: overcoming control-flow integrity. In: 35th IEEE Symposium on Security and Privacy, San Jose, CA (2014)
54. Nikaein, N., et al.: Network store: exploring slicing in future 5G networks. In: 10th International ACM Workshop on Mobility in the Evolving Internet Architecture, Paris, France (2015)
55. Chin, W.H., Fan, Z., Haines, R.: Emerging technologies and research challenges for 5G wireless networks. IEEE Wirel. Commun. **21**(2), 106–112 (2014)
56. Luo, S., Lin, Z., Chen, X., Yang, Z., Chen, J.: Virtualization security for cloud computing service. In: 4th International Conference on Cloud and Service Computing (CSC), 174–179 (2011)
57. Oyama, Y., Giang, T.T., Chubachi, Y., Shinagawa, T., Kato, K.: Detecting malware signatures in a thin hypervisor. In: 27th Annual ACM Symposium on Applied Computing, Trento, Italy (2012)
58. Hu, C., Li, Z., Ma, J., Guo, T., Shi, Z.: File parsing vulnerability detection with symbolic execution. In: IEEE 6th International Symposium on Theoretical Aspects of Software Engineering, Beijing, China (2012)

59. Chen, M., Qian, Y., Mao, S., Tang, W., Yang, X.: Software-defined mobile networks security. Mob. Netw. Appl., 1–15 (2015)
60. Roy, S., Manoj, B.S.: IoT enablers and their security and privacy issues. In: Mavromoustakis, C.X., Mastorakis, G., Batalla, J.M. (eds.) Internet of Things (IoT) in 5G Mobile Technologies. Modeling and Optimization in Science and Technologies, vol. 8, pp. 449–482. Springer International Publishing, Switzerland (2016)

An HMM-Based Anomaly Detection Approach
for SCADA Systems

Kyriakos Stefanidis[1] and Artemios G. Voyiatzis[2]([⊠])

[1] Industrial Systems Institute/RC 'Athena', Patras, Greece
stefanidis@isi.gr
[2] SBA Research, Vienna, Austria
avoyiatzis@sba-research.org

Abstract. We describe the architecture of an anomaly detection system based on the Hidden Markov Model (HMM) for intrusion detection in Industrial Control Systems (ICS) and especially in SCADA systems interconnected using TCP/IP. The proposed system exploits the unique characteristics of ICS networks and protocols to efficiently detect multiple attack vectors. We evaluate the proposed system in terms of detection accuracy using as reference datasets made available by other researchers. These datasets refer to real industrial networks and contain a variety of identified attack vectors. We benchmark our findings against a large set of machine learning algorithms and demonstrate that our proposal exhibits superior performance characteristics.

1 Introduction

The continuous interconnection of Industrial Control Systems (ICS) to public and corporate networks exposes them to the common Information Technology (IT) vulnerabilities and attacks. The security mechanisms that are traditionally used in the ICS environment cover the basic needs for authentication, authorization and (sometimes) communication confidentiality. However, they leave the Operations Technology (OT) networks open to more elaborate IT-based network attacks.

The rise of security incidents involving malicious network activity in critical infrastructures drives the need for intrusion detection technologies and mechanisms to be adapted for the OT environment. Several methodologies have been proposed recently that attempt to solve the problem of designing an efficient Network Intrusion Detection System (NIDS) specifically for the integrated IT–OT environment [21].

There are many approaches proposed in the literature, especially using anomaly detection techniques. These approaches use a combination of the known machine learning algorithms in order to determine the normal behavior of the network and detect any abnormal network traffic. The unique characteristics of network traffic in OT environments, including stable connectivity, periodicity in

S. Foresti and J. Lopez (Eds.): WISTP 2016, LNCS 9895, pp. 85–99, 2016.
DOI: 10.1007/978-3-319-45931-8_6

traffic patterns, use of standard application level protocols, are discussed in [5]. These characteristics render network-based anomaly detection a useful approach.

The main issue discussed in the literature for NIDS is the need to correlate a high enough amount of traffic (i.e., network packets) so as to decide on the abnormality of the sampled traffic. To support real-time detection of abnormal traffic, it is interesting to explore the efficiency of an approach that relies only on individual packets. Towards this direction, the use of Hidden Markov Model (HMM) approaches is limited within the literature. This despite that HMM is among the most promising approaches for this problem [19].

In this paper, we design and evaluate an HMM-based Network Intrusion Detection System (NIDS) for the OT environment. The system exploits the unique traffic characteristics of an ICS, and especially of SCADA systems communicating over TCP/IP technologies. Our aim is achieve a high-rate of detection of a wide range of attack vectors. The evaluation of the system is based on freely-available datasets that represent the operation of real industrial networks and have already been used to test several machine learning algorithms. This allows a fair comparison of our HMM-based approach with other machine learning approaches that are proposed in the literature.

The rest of the paper is organized in four sections. Section 2 provides a survey of approaches for anomaly detection in the ICS environment. Section 3 describes the proposed system architecture. Section 4 describes the experimental setup and the datasets used for evaluating the accuracy of the system. Section 5 presents and discusses our findings. Finally, Sect. 6 provides our conclusions and the future directions of work.

2   Literature Review

Many researchers tackled the problem of efficient anomaly detection in ICS environments using a wide range of machine learning techniques and targeting different application scenarios. A recent comprehensive account of such IDS, including a taxonomy of attacks is available in [21]. We revisit some representative works in the following paragraphs.

Ali *et al.* focused on the advanced metering infrastructure (AMI) [2]. The authors used a fourth-order Markov chain to model the AMI behavior via the event logs of the network. They proposed a configuration randomization mechanism in order to make the system more robust against evasion attempts.

Caselli *et al.* dealt with semantic attacks that involve sequences of permitted events and how they elude a normal NIDS [7]. The authors used discrete-time Markov chains to describe the normal operations and calculated the weighted distance between the states for the detection mechanism.

Erez *et al.* considered the Modbus/TCP protocol and focused only on the values of the control registers [9]. They classified the control registers in three classes and constructed three different behavior models, one for each class. Yoon *et al.* also considered the Modbus/TCP protocol [20]. They used Dynamic Bayesian Networks and Probabilistic Suffix Trees for traffic modeling. They also incorporates a mechanism that checks whether a detected anomaly is based on missing messages instead of an attack.

Ntalampiras *et al.* used an HMM to model the relationship between data streams from two network nodes [14]. They used a combination of emulated network components and simulated physical devices for the experimental framework. They considered only two types of attacks, namely denial of service and replay attacks, for the evaluation of the system's efficiency.

Marti *et al.* combined a segmentation algorithm with a one-class support vector machine (SVM) [12]. They constructed an anomaly detection system specifically for petroleum industry applications. Schuster *et al.* also evaluated the efficiency on one class SVMs [17].

Almalawi *et al.* explored a two-step methodology based on unsupervised learning [3]. They performed an automatic classification of normal and abnormal operation states as a first step. Then, they automatically extracted proximity detection rules for those states. The detection step is based on the kNN algorithm, raising the computational complexity to impractical levels.

Hadziosmanovic *et al.* followed the path of integrating the operational parameters of the network and its devices [10]. They extracted these parameters and used auto-regression and control limits in order to map the changes in the time domain. An alert was raised if the data did not fit the model or were outside the control limits.

Raciti *et al.* tackled the problem of designing a real-time detection system that can be implemented insider a smart metering system [16]. They used a basic clustering algorithm for this and they were more concerned on the deployment issues of such a system on a massive scale.

3   System Architecture

The proposed system is an anomaly detection system. Its underlying detection algorithm is based on Hidden Markov Model (HMM). The merits of an HMM-based approach for anomaly detection in ICS environments are discussed in [19]. This approach assumes that a model emits sequences of symbols. This model is a Markov process and its states are hidden from the observer. The model has a probability of transitioning from one state to another one and each state has a probability of emitting a symbol. An HMM is characterized by the following parameters:

- N: The number of states.
- M: The number of symbols (vocabulary).
- A: The probability distribution between stages ($N \times N$).
- B: The probability distribution to emit a symbol ($N \times M$).
- p: The probability vector on the starting state.

The overall system architecture is depicted in Fig. 1.

The system operates in two distinct phases: the *training phase* and the *detection (evaluation) phase*. In the training phase, the parameters (A, B, p) of the

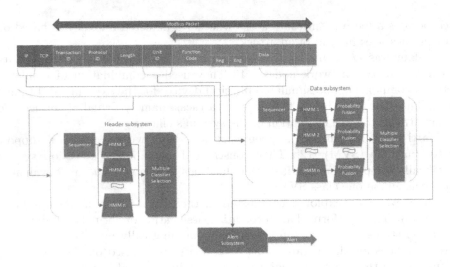

Fig. 1. System architecture

model are estimated, using a training set of sequences. The Baum-Welch algorithm is used in order to maximize the probability that the model emits the training sequences. In the detection phase, the Forward-Backward algorithm is used to calculate the probability that a received (captured) sequence is emitted by the model.

The core design problem is the selection of the sequences that are used to construct the model(s). We opted for two distinct models that are implemented in two subsystems, namely *header* and *data*. The subsystems collect different segments from each traversing network packet. The byte sequences of the segments are the sequences used at each subsystem's HMM. The exact choice of segments depends on the network and application protocols used in the SCADA system.

In general, an NIDS that targets all major ICS protocols must provide a configuration for each protocol. In the following, we will discuss the subsystems' design for the case of a Modbus/TCP protocol.

3.1 The Modbus Protocol

Modbus is the *de facto* standard for connecting industrial electronic devices in ICS. Modbus is a simple and robust protocol, with two roles (master and slave) and stateless communication of request/response frame pairs. Modbus frames can be carried over serial links or TCP/IP. The Modbus slave device is modelled as a set of four memories, namely *coils*, *discrete inputs*, *holding registers*, and *input registers*. The control loops and the reporting can be modeled as a series of *reads* and *writes* of these memories.

The format of a Modbus frame when transmitted over TCP/IP is depicted in Fig. 2. The Modbus/TCP Application Data Unit (ADU) consists of a 7-byte

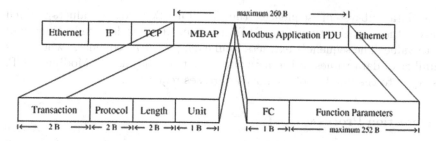

Fig. 2. Modbus frame encapsulation in TCP segments

header (Modbus Application Header, MBAP) and a Modbus Protocol Data Unit (PDU) of up to 253 bytes.

The MBAP consists of a 2-byte transaction identifier; a 2-byte protocol identifier (set to 0x0000 for Modbus); a 2-byte length field, indicating the number of the following bytes; and a 1-byte unit identifier (set to 0xFF, equivalent to the slave address in the serial version of Modbus).

The Modbus PDU carries requests that are defined in *function codes* (FC), ranging from 0 to 127, while negative responses range from 128 to 255. Each function code can be followed by *function parameters*, passing request parameters to the slave. For example, a *read coil* function code is followed by the address (number) of the specific coil to be read. Modbus is a simple protocol and its implementation should be straightforward and bug-free; however this is not the case [18].

3.2 Header Subsystem

The first subsystem is the "Header subsystem". This subsystem is responsible for detecting anomalies on the network traffic from attacks that manipulate the header information. Example attacks of this type include denial of service, fake devices, sending data to third parties, and Modbus response or command injection.

The header subsystem sequences the Modbus Function Code, the Modbus/TCP header, and selected parts of the TCP and IP headers. One sequence is extracted from each captured packet. The output of the subsystem is one probability.

3.3 Data Subsystem

The second subsystem is the "Data subsystem". This subsystem outputs n distinct probabilities for each packet. The mean value of those is the final output of the subsystem for this packet. This subsystem is responsible for detecting attacks that manipulate the data that are produced by all the devices participating in the network. Such attacks are usually malicious device tampering or could be side-effects of a network attack.

The data subsystem sequences the Modbus/TCP data value(s). Each sequence is the concatenation of the IP address, the Modbus device identifier, and one data value. The sequencer extracts from each packet n sequences, where n is the number of data values in the network packet. In the case of Modbus/TCP, this is equal to the number of memory addresses requested.

3.4 Detection Process

Each subsystem contains multiple HMMs and each sequence is routed through all the contained models. The use of multiple classifiers can help reach better accuracy, as shown in [15]. The resulting probabilities from each classifier are fused together, as described in [4]. The final outcome is an overall probability for each packet. We note that all the HMMs are trained with the same training data but with different (random) starting parameters.

The last part of the detection process is the classification. Each subsystem has a certain threshold under which the packet is classified as being part of an attack. The threshold is necessary because the result of an HMM is an unweighted probability (i.e., a "log-likelihood"), which can only be evaluated in conjunction with the log-likelihoods that the HMM outputs for normal traffic.

Finally, if one of the subsystems issues an alert, the system routes this alert to the SCADA or another part of the IDS, depending on the system deployment.

4 Datasets and Experimental Setup

In order to evaluate the efficiency of the proposed system, we need a set of data from either a simulated or a real environment. This dataset should have a mix of normal traffic and attack traffic from various attacks. We opted for freely-available datasets that have already been used for the evaluation of existing systems, in order to be able to compare our approach with known solutions and algorithms.

4.1 Description of Datasets

The datasets that are originally chosen are the three datasets of [13]. These datasets contain measurements from a laboratory-scale gas pipeline, a laboratory-scale water tower, and a laboratory-scale electric transmission system. All three datasets contain pre-processed network transaction data but the lower communication layers (Ethernet, IP, and TCP) are stripped. The range on the number of entries on each dataset varies from 100,000 to 5,000,000.

Due to the vast amount of data in the given datasets, the time needed for each experiment grew prohibitively long. We resorted on using the limited versions (offered from the same source) that contain 10 % random samples from the original datasets. The effectiveness of various tested machine learning algorithms remains mostly unchanged, regardless on the version of datasets that is used for the experiment [11].

The value of these datasets for the evaluation of our system lies on the fact that these datasets contain real measurements and both the network protocol headers and the payload of each entry (measurement) are available. Furthermore, these datasets include both normal traffic and a variety of simulated attacks. Each entry is categorized in one of seven (7) attack vectors (including the normal traffic) as follows:

0. Normal (Normal)
1. Naïve Malicious Response Injection (NMRI)
2. Complex Malicious Response Injection (CMRI)
3. Malicious State Command Injection (MSCI)
4. Malicious Parameter Command Injection (MPCI)
5. Malicious Function Code Injection (MFCI)
6. Denial of Service (DoS)
7. Reconnaissance (Recon)

The attack vectors contain both header and payload manipulation patterns. We consider them sufficient for the purpose of the evaluation of our system.

One last limitation is the absence of TCP/IP data on each packet. Since our system combines the payload data, the IP address and the unit (device) identifier (id), we had to simplify the data sequencing subsystem and assume that the pairs (unit id, measurement) define each a distinct sensor measurement.

4.2 Training Dataset

For the construction of the training dataset, we used a subset of the entries that are classified as "normal". We excluded the entries that contain apparent erroneous measurements, in order to keep the HMM training process as accurate as possible. The erroneous measurements are probably the result of a sensor malfunction or network error. Also, it is commonly-acceptable that the training process is not performed in real time but rather off-line and based on pre-processed data. Hence, the training dataset should not contain apparently faulty packets. We also performed quantization (rounding) of the measurements in order to further enhance the accuracy of the training process for the data subsystem. The exact rounding of each value is dependent on the range of the readings for each device.

We used only a subset of the normal traffic as a training dataset, in order to measure the efficiency of our system in classifying normal data as such and evaluate the false positive probability. This traffic was not used afterwards during the detection phase.

4.3 Experimental Setup

For the experiment implementation, we used the machine learning framework Accord [1]. Accord provides a well-tested and documented library for constructing various types of HMMs, training them using the Baum-Welch learning algorithm and evaluating the log-likelihood that they generate a given sequence, using the Forward-Backward algorithm. Since the datasets were already available in text format, there was no need for actual packet capture and manipulation for the purposes of this experiment.

We note that a complete implementation of our system requires the use of an established NIDS (e.g., snort! [8]) and the implementation of the subsystems as a preprocessor that runs before the normal detection engine but once the packet is decoded.

Our initial experiments showed that the water and the gas datasets produce similar results. Therefore, we will present in the next Section only the results from the water pipeline. On the other hand, the electric data lacks information about the header values on each entry and gives only the measurements from the 132 sensors. Since our system relies on both the header and the payload data, we opted not to use this dataset in the evaluation.

5   Results and Discussion

In this section, we will present the experimental results and provide some insights regarding the use of HMMs in detecting network attacks in ICS environments. We first showcase the operation of the two subsystems and then present the overall evaluation of the system in terms of detection efficiency. Then, we present a comparison of the results against already established algorithms that have been tried on the same dataset.

5.1   Operation Scenarios

Figure 3 depicts a time window during which an NMRI attack takes place. One of the outcomes of this attack is that the sensor measurements are skewed to the extent that they cross the boundaries of a normal operation. In the first part of the Figure, the sensor measurements as taken from the dataset are shown; the effect of the attack is clearly identifiable between the samples 36 and 67. In the second part of the Figure, the estimations by the data subsystem are depicted as a series of likelihoods for each entry (the exponent of the log-likelihood that the subsystem outputs). The likelihood becomes zero during the attack. This piece of information can be used as an alert signal from the data subsystem, as it correctly identifies one of the outcomes of the attack.

It might be the case that the effect of this NMRI-type attack, i.e., the skewing of the measurements, is an unintended consequence of the way the dataset was compiled in first place. We note that (i) only few of the attacks in the dataset have any effect on the actual sensor measurements and (ii) we evaluate the effectiveness of *both* the subsystems in our system. Thus, we include this data skewness as an attack indicator for the purpose of the experiments. Such manipulations of the readings are common in attack scenarios where an outsider tampers the information in-transit rather than directly in the sending system.

Figure 4 depicts a time window during which a Recon attack takes place. While this attack is active, various header fields deviate from their "normal" values, as the attacker tries to derive useful information. The first part of the Figure

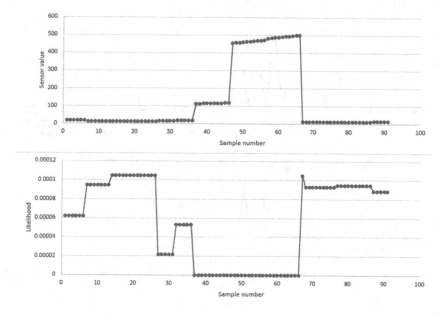

Fig. 3. Attack and detection under an NMRI attack

depicts five different header fields that should either stay constant or change in a predictable way (e.g., `command_address` and `response_address` should change together). During the attack, they get abnormal values. In the second part of the Figure, the estimations by the header subsystem are provided. During attack (samples 11–16; 18; 20; and 34–48), the likelihood drops to zero in almost all cases. Again, we use this piece of information as an alert signal from the header subsystem.

We note that for the case of the header values, the likelihoods during normal operation are more or less stable, while for the case of the data values (e.g., those shown in Fig. 3), the likelihoods exhibit a wider distribution. However, in both cases the likelihood drops to almost zero during the attacks in both cases. Still, there are scenarios where the likelihood does fall a few orders of magnitude compared to normal traffic but does not reach zero. These facts affect the selection of a threshold value for denoting an abnormal behavior. The threshold for the data subsystem needs to be set after the training procedure and upon careful examination of the system's output (likelihoods) during normal operation.

5.2 Results

Classification Efficiency. The efficiency of the system in correctly classifying normal and attack traffic for the whole dataset is summarized in Table 1. Line one and two depict the actual number of entries for each attack vector (0–7) and the number of entries that are correctly classified. Line three depicts the classification efficiency as a percentage for each attack vector. The "All" column contains the

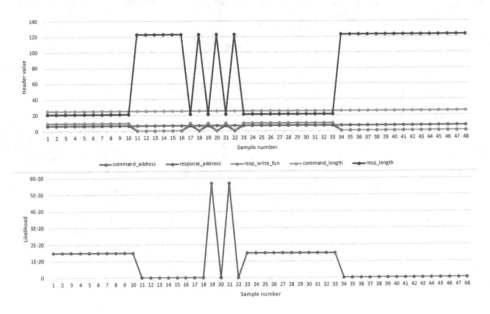

Fig. 4. The attack and detection graph under a Reconnaissance attack

overall classification efficiency for all the entries (normal and attacks), while the "Attacks" column contains the classification only for the attack entries.

The classification efficiency is more than 95 % for most of the attacks and the normal traffic. The classification does not succeed in identifying the CMRI and MSCI attacks. Upon further inspection, it appeared that this can be attributed to some flaws in the training dataset that allowed the HMMs to be trained to recognize such attacks as normal traffic. However, these flaws were identified by the header subsystem; the data subsystem could not identify them as the attack forced data values that are predictable but yet within the "normal" boundaries for the specific sensor they came from. Further details as well as the ramifications of this behavior are discussed in the next section.

There are only a few false positives, i.e., normal traffic classified as attack traffic, less than 1 %. The false positives consist almost entirely of erroneous sensor readings or network packets. This is an expected outcome, given the preprocessing of the training dataset. It can be considered as a trade-off between raising the probability of correctly identifying actual attacks and raising the probability of generating false positives.

Comparisons. The dataset we used for the evaluation of our system has been used extensively as a reference dataset for evaluating a wide range of machine learning algorithms [11]. The applicability of these algorithms for anomaly detection in the ICS environment is studied in [6]. We compare the efficiency of our approach with the published study in Table 2. While not all the algorithms are

Table 1. Detection accuracy

Classification	Normal	NMRI	CMRI	MSCI	MPCI	MFCI	DoS	Recon	All	Attacks
Actual	19,503	1,198	1,457	209	410	155	135	4,132	27,199	7,696
Detected	19,424	1,159	0	0	389	155	134	4,132	25,393	5,969
Percentage (%)	99.6	96.7	0.00	0.00	94.9	100	99.3	100	93.4	77.6

directly comparable with our approach, the efficiency of the latter is directly comparable to most of them.

In the case of a DoS attack, 16 out of the 34 algorithms have less than 90 % accuracy, while our approach reaches 99 %. During Recon, MPCI, and MFCI attacks, almost all algorithms produce nearly perfect results. The case of CMRI and MSCI is an area of future improvement for our system, while they can be handled by most the evaluated algorithms. In contrast, the NMRI attack is a hard case for 14 algorithms, while it can be easily detected by our approach. All the algorithms and our approach as well exhibit a very low number of false positives in all cases.

It is clear that our approach gives comparable results to the most effective machine learning algorithms while using only the information on each individual sample without the need of correlation of multiple samples of the same traffic flow. It is also clear that it is unable to detect all the attack vectors within the dataset. A discussion on why those attack vectors eluded detection and how this can be remedied is found in the next section.

5.3 Discussion

The approach we propose exploits the unique characteristics of an ICS environment and is able to identify most of the attacks presented in the reference datasets. The detection rate is comparable to already-tested machine learning algorithms and through careful adjustment of the training data and the HMM parameters, this rate can be further enhanced. As an example, the detection rate for the NMRI attack has doubled by eliminating easily identifiable erroneous data from the training set. Also, system design parameters, such as the number of parallel HMMs and the number of hidden states can affect the efficiency of the overall system.

We highlight that our proposed approach relies only on per-packet information and needs not to correlate multiple packets on the same network stream. This makes the system suitable for real-time applications, where correlation of multiple packets can adversely effect the speed of detection. It also allows it to be deployed in data storage constrained environments due to non existent storage requirements. Considering also the case of low rate (or stealthy) attacks, the system is able to detect such an attack without the need of a large number of packets that are part of the attack.

On the topic of the training data, we see that the proposed system exhibits increased sensitivity to errors or malicious activities during the preparation of

Table 2. Comparisons with known machine learning algorithms (as reported in [11])

Algorithm	Normal (0)	NMRI (1)	CMRI (2)	MSCI (3)	MPCI (4)	MFCI (5)	DOS (6)	Recon (7)
Proposed and Evaluated system	100 %	97 %	0 %	0 %	95 %	100 %	99 %	100 %
Best First Decision Tree (BFTree)	100 %	97 %	99 %	87 %	99 %	95 %	95 %	100 %
Decision Stump	99 %	0 %	0 %	0 %	0 %	0 %	0 %	100 %
FaultTree (FT)	100 %	94 %	100 %	93 %	99 %	95 %	96 %	100 %
J48 Decision Tree	100 %	95 %	100 %	90 %	99 %	73 %	91 %	100 %
J48Graft Decision Tree	100 %	95 %	100 %	89 %	99 %	68 %	88 %	100 %
Logiboost Alternating Decision Tree (LADTree)	100 %	94 %	99 %	93 %	99 %	0 %	73 %	100 %
Logistic Model Tree (LMT)	100 %	86 %	100 %	93 %	99 %	95 %	93 %	100 %
Logistic Regression	100 %	4 %	99 %	93 %	99 %	95 %	67 %	100 %
Multilayer Perceptron	98 %	2 %	99 %	93 %	99 %	95 %	68 %	100 %
Nave Bayes Tree (NBTree)	100 %	96 %	99 %	93 %	98 %	95 %	95 %	100 %
Radial Basis Function Network (RBFNetwork)	98 %	1 %	99 %	93 %	99 %	95 %	88 %	100 %
RandomErrorPruning Tree (REPTree)	100 %	95 %	100 %	90 %	99 %	95 %	95 %	100 %
RandomForrest	100 %	96 %	100 %	90 %	99 %	93 %	93 %	100 %
RandomTree	99 %	96 %	100 %	90 %	98 %	81 %	91 %	100 %
SimpleCart	100 %	96 %	100 %	88 %	99 %	95 %	94 %	100 %
SimpleLogistic	98 %	36 %	99 %	93 %	99 %	95 %	68 %	100 %
Sequential Minimal Optimization (SMO)	98 %	1 %	99 %	93 %	99 %	73 %	44 %	100 %
BayesNet	98 %	98 %	95 %	97 %	100 %	100 %	99 %	100 %
ComplementNaiveBayes	100 %	0 %	0 %	0 %	29 %	100 %	0 %	100 %
DMNBtext	100 %	0 %	0 %	0 %	44 %	100 %	0 %	100 %
NaiveBayes	43 %	0 %	99 %	97 %	99 %	100 %	96 %	100 %
NavieBayesMultinomial	100 %	0 %	0 %	97 %	81 %	100 %	39 %	100 %
NaiveBayesMultinomial Updateable	100 %	0 %	0 %	97 %	81 %	100 %	39 %	100 %
NaiveBayesSimple	0 %	95 %	98 %	56 %	62 %	0 %	0 %	2 %
NaiveBayesUpdateable	43 %	0 %	99 %	97 %	99 %	100 %	96 %	100 %
ConjunctiveRule	100 %	0 %	0 %	0 %	0 %	0 %	0 %	100 %
DecisionTable	98 %	98 %	95 %	94 %	98 %	95 %	91 %	100 %
DTNB	98 %	98 %	95 %	97 %	99 %	100 %	100 %	100 %
Jrip	99 %	98 %	94 %	97 %	99 %	100 %	100 %	100 %
Nnge	97 %	97 %	75 %	97 %	99 %	100 %	97 %	100 %
OneR	97 %	98 %	95 %	0 %	0 %	0 %	0 %	100 %
PART	99 %	98 %	95 %	97 %	99 %	100 %	100 %	100 %
Ridor	99 %	98 %	94 %	97 %	99 %	100 %	100 %	100 %
ZeroR	0 %	0 %	0 %	0 %	0 %	0 %	0 %	0 %

the training data. As an example, our system was unable to detect the CMRI attack; this can be mostly credited to the fact that a limited amount of normal data exhibited the same pattern, probably due to some network error. This fact remained unnoticed during the preparation phase of the training set, which in turn resulted in the less-optimal training of the system's parameters. Hence, we highlight the importance of having access to carefully-inspected and validated reference datasets.

The reference datasets we used for our evaluation exhibit some limitations that might affect the applicability of our approach in real-world scenarios. Such limitations include the lack of information for the lower-than-IP network layers and that the measurements come from only one sensor node. We hope that more detailed datasets become publicly available for the benefit of the research community and the industry practice alike. We consider as an interesting enhancement for the detection itself to incorporate information regarding the actions performed by the SCADA operators themselves; such information can be utilized to detect suspicious traffic, which is a result of a malicious operators' actions.

As it has been raised many time in the research literature already, an anomaly-based NIDS *cannot* effectively capture the whole picture of the complex ICS system under attack. It is better to integrate it in a defense-in-depth strategy, combined with a signature-based IDS for known attacks; this would speed up more the detection capabilities and provide more fine-grained information under specific attacks. Furthermore, this integration could significantly reduce the number of fake alerts (false positives) for the SCADA operator and contribute towards a more comprehensive reporting system that can present the alerts in a meaningful for the SCADA operator context.

6 Conclusions and Future Work

In this paper, we presented a novel approach for an HMM-based NIDS. Our approach exploits the unique characteristics of the ICS environment. We evaluate the efficiency of our approach using reference datasets taken from a real-world industrial system. These datasets contain a diverse set of attack vectors allowing for the evaluation of our approach under realistic operation scenarios.

The proposed system succeeds in detecting most of the attack vectors, both targeting application logic via payload information (i.e., the sensor measurements) and network logic via header information. We evaluated the detection rate and compared the efficiency of our approach with a large set of algorithms available in the literature. The detection rate is directly comparable with the latter and can further improved by tuning the system parameters and the quality of the training set.

More importantly, the proposed system, in contrast to other approaches, can produce the results on a per-packet basis, without needing to correlate samples with historical traffic information. This makes it more suitable for real-time applications and high-speed or large-scale environments (high traffic volumes). Also, for detecting low-rate, stealthy attacks, that are often used as part of advanced persistent threats (APTs) against critical systems and infrastructures.

An interesting direction for future work includes the integration, if possible, of information related to actions performed by SCADA operators that can result unexpected (anomalous) traffic. Also, the integration of our approach with a signature-based IDS. Also, a study on the impact of the basic design parameters (number of parallel HMMs, number of hidden states, etc.) on the overall performance of the system is a mandatory step towards its adoption and deployment in real-time critical ICS. Last but not least, we consider necessary to extend the scope of the experiments using more diverse datasets, if they become publicly-available, which should incorporate a larger ICS environment, including more network segments, ICS devices, and sensors.

Acknowledgements. This work was partially supported by the GSRT Action "KRIPIS" of Greece with national and EU funds in the context of the research project "ISRTDI" and the COMET K1-Centres programme line of the Austrian Research Promotion Agency (FFG).

References

1. Accord.NET: Accord.NET Machine Learning Framework (2016). http://accord-framework.net/
2. Ali, M.Q., Al-Shaer, E.: Randomization-based intrusion detection system for advanced metering infrastructure. ACM Trans. Inf. Syst. Secur. **18**(2), 7:1–7:30 (2015). http://doi.acm.org/10.1145/2814936
3. Almalawi, A., Yu, X., Tari, Z., Fahad, A., Khalil, I.: An unsupervised anomaly-based detection approach for integrity attacks on SCADA systems. Comput. Secur. **46**, 94–110 (2014). http://dx.doi.org/10.1016/j.cose.2014.07.005
4. Ariu, D., Tronci, R., Giacinto, G.: HMMPayl: An intrusion detection system based on Hidden Markov Models. Comput. Secur. **30**(4), 221–241 (2011). http://dx.doi.org/10.1016/j.cose.2010.12.004
5. Barbosa, R.R.R.: Anomaly detection in SCADA systems: a network based approach. Ph.D. thesis, University of Twente, Enschede, April 2014. http://doc.utwente.nl/90271/
6. Beaver, J.M., Borges-Hink, R.C., Buckner, M.A.: An evaluation of machine learning methods to detect malicious SCADA communications. In: 2013 12th International Conference on Machine Learning and Applications, vol. 2, pp. 54–59 (2013). http://ieeexplore.ieee.org/lpdocs/epic03/wrapper.htm?arnumber=6786081
7. Caselli, M., Kargl, F.: Sequence-aware intrusion detection in industrial control systems. In: Proceedings of the 1st ACM Workshop on Cyber-Physical System Security, CPSS 2015, pp. 13–24 (2015)
8. Cisco: Snort (2015). https://www.snort.org/
9. Erez, N., Wool, A.: Control variable classification, modeling and anomaly detection in Modbus/TCP SCADA systems. Int. J. Crit. Infrastruct. Prot. **10**, 59–70 (2015). http://linkinghub.elsevier.com/retrieve/pii/S1874548215000396
10. Hadžiosmanović, D., Sommer, R., Zambon, E., Hartel, P.H.: Through the eye of the PLC: semantic security monitoring for industrial processes. In: Proceedings of the 30th Annual Computer Security Applications Conference, ACSAC 2014, pp. 126–135 (2014). http://dl.acm.org/citation.cfm?id=2664243.2664277

11. Hsu, J., Mudd, D., Thornton, Z.: Mississippi state university project report - SCADA anomaly detection project summary. Technical report, Mississippi State University (2014). http://www.ece.uah.edu/thm0009/icsdatasets/MSU_SCADA_Final_Report.pdf
12. Martí, L., Sanchez-Pi, N., Molina, J., Garcia, A.: Anomaly detection based on sensor data in petroleum industry applications. Sensors **15**, 2774–2797 (2015). http://www.mdpi.com/1424-8220/15/2/2774/
13. Morris, T., Srivastava, A., Reaves, B., Gao, W., Pavurapu, K., Reddi, R.: A control system testbed to validate critical infrastructure protection concepts. Int. J. Crit. Infrastruct. Prot. **4**(2), 88–103 (2011). http://www.sciencedirect.com/science/article/pii/S1874548211000266
14. Ntalampiras, S., Soupionis, Y., Giannopoulos, G.: A fault diagnosis system for interdependent critical infrastructures based on HMMs. Reliab. Eng. Syst. Saf. **138**, 73–81 (2015). http://dx.doi.org/10.1016/j.ress.2015.01.024
15. Perdisci, R., Ariu, D., Fogla, P., Giacinto, G., Lee, W.: McPAD: a multiple classifier system for accurate payload-based anomaly detection. Comput. Netw. **53**(6), 864–881 (2009). http://dx.doi.org/10.1016/j.comnet.2008.11.011
16. Raciti, M., Nadjm-Tehrani, S.: Embedded cyber-physical anomaly detection in smart meters. In: Hämmerli, B.M., Kalstad Svendsen, N., Lopez, J. (eds.) CRITIS 2012. LNCS, vol. 7722, pp. 34–45. Springer, Heidelberg (2013)
17. Schuster, F., Paul, A.: Potentials of using one-class SVM for detecting protocol-specific anomalies in industrial networks. In: 2015 IEEE Symposium Series on Computational Intelligence, pp. 83–90 (2015)
18. Voyiatzis, A., Katsigiannis, K., Koubias, S.: A Modbus/TCP fuzzer for testing internetworked industrial systems. In: 20th IEEE International Conference on Emerging Technologies and Factory Automation (ETFA 2015), Luxembourg, 8–11 September 2015
19. Yasakethu, S., Jiang, J.: Intrusion detection via machine learning for SCADA system protection. In: The 1st International Symposium for ICS & SCADA Cyber Security Research, pp. 101–105 (2013)
20. Yoon, M.k., Ciocarlie, G.F.: Communication pattern monitoring: improving the utility of anomaly detection for industrial control systems. In: NDSS Workshop on Security of Emerging Networking Technologies (SENT) (2014)
21. Zhu, B.X.: Resilient control and intrusion detection for SCADA systems. Ph.D. thesis, EECS Department, University of California, Berkeley, May 2014. http://www.eecs.berkeley.edu/Pubs/TechRpts/2014/EECS-2014-34.html

Attacks to Software and Network Systems

Attacking and Defending Dynamic Analysis System-Calls Based IDS

Ishai Rosenberg[1]([⊠]) and Ehud Gudes[1,2]

[1] The Open University of Israel, Raanana, Israel
ishai.msc@gmail.com
[2] Ben-Gurion University, Beer-Sheva, Israel

Abstract. Machine-learning augments today's IDS capability to cope with unknown malware. However, if an attacker gains partial knowledge about the IDS's classifier, he can create a modified version of his malware, which can evade detection. In this article we present an IDS based on various classifiers using system calls executed by the inspected code as features. We then present a camouflage algorithm that is used to modify malicious code to be classified as benign, while preserving the code's functionality, for decision tree and random forest classifiers. We also present transformations to the classifier's input, to prevent this camouflage - and a modified camouflage algorithm that overcomes those transformations. Our research shows that it is not enough to provide a decision tree based classifier with a large training set to counter malware. One must also be aware of the possibility that the classifier would be fooled by a camouflage algorithm, and try to counter such an attempt with techniques such as input transformation or training set updates.

Keywords: Malware detection · Malware obfuscation · Decision trees · Behavior analysis · Camouflage algorithm · Machine learning

1 Introduction

Past intrusion detection systems (IDS) generally used two methods of malware detection: (1) Signature-based detection, i.e., searching for known patterns of data within the executable code. A malware, however, can modify itself to prevent a signature match, for example by using encryption. Thus, this method can be used to identify only known malware. (2) Heuristic-based detection is composed of generic signatures, including wild-cards, which can identify a malware family. This method can identify only variants of known malware.

Machine-learning can be used in-order to extend the IDS capabilities to classify software unseen before as malicious or benign by using static or dynamic features. However, our research shows that malware code can be transformed to render machine learning classifiers almost useless, without losing the original functionality of the modified code. We call such a generic transformation, based on the classifier type and the features used, a *camouflage algorithm*.

© IFIP International Federation for Information Processing 2016
Published by Springer International Publishing Switzerland 2016. All Rights Reserved
S. Foresti and J. Lopez (Eds.): WISTP 2016, LNCS 9895, pp. 103–119, 2016.
DOI: 10.1007/978-3-319-45931-8_7

In this paper, we present a camouflage algorithm for decision tree and random forest based classifiers whose input features are sequences of system calls executed by the code at run-time. Our research has three main contributions:

1. Developing an automatic algorithm to decide which system calls to add to a malware code to make this code being classified as benign by our IDS, without losing its functionality. We then alleviate the assumption of full knowledge of the classifier by the attacker, showing that partial training set information might be enough.
2. Evaluating the algorithm against a large subset of malware samples, while previous work evaluated specific examples only.
3. Investigating possible transformations of the IDS input in-order to counter the camouflage algorithm - as-well-as a modified camouflage algorithm to evade those transformations.

While the above contributions are shown for specific classifier types (decision tree and random forest) and for specific features as input (system calls sequences), we believe the ideas are more general, and can be applied also to different classifiers with different features. The rest of the paper is structured as follows: Sect. 2 discusses the related work. Section 3 presents the problem definition and the evaluation criteria for the camouflage algorithm. Section 4 describes the IDS in detail and Sect. 5 discusses the camouflage algorithm implementation. Section 6 presents the experimental evaluation and Sect. 7 concludes the paper and outlines future research.

2   Background and Related Work

2.1   Machine Learning Binary Classifiers

The use of system calls to detect abnormal software behavior was shown in [4,15]. System call pairs (n-grams of size 2) from test traces were compared against those in the normal profile. Any system call pair not present in the normal profile is called a mismatch. If the number of system calls with mismatches within their window in any given time frame exceeded a certain threshold, an intrusion was reported.

Various machine learning classifiers, such as decision trees, SVM, boosted trees, Bayesian Networks and Artificial Neural Networks have been compared to find the most accurate classification algorithm; with varying results (e.g.: [3] chose decision trees, [8] chose boosted decision trees, etc.). The different results were affected, e.g., by the training set and the type of the feature set used.

There are two ways to extract the classifier features. They can be extracted statically (i.e., without running the inspected code), e.g.: byte-sequence (n-gram) in the inspected code [8]. The features can also be extracted dynamically (i.e., by running the inspected code), including: CPU overhead, time to execute, memory and disk consumption [12] or executed system calls sequences, either consecutive [15] or not [14]. A survey of system calls monitors and the attacks against them was conducted in [5], stating that in-spite of their disadvantages, they are commonly used by IDS machine learning classifiers.

While using static analysis has a performance advantage, it has a main disadvantage: Since the code isn't being run, it might not reveal its "true features". For example, if one looks for byte-sequence (or signatures) in the inspected code [8], one might not be able to catch polymorphic malware, in which those signatures are either encrypted or packed and decrypted only during run-time, by a specific bootstrap code. Other limitations of static analysis and techniques to counter it appear in [11]. Obviously, a malware can still try to hide if some other application (the IDS) is monitoring its features dynamically. However, in the end, in-order to operate its malicious functionality, a malware must reveal its true features during run-time.

Since a dynamic analysis IDS must run the inspected code, it might harm the hosting computer. In-order to prevent that, it's common to run the code in a sandbox; a controlled environment, which isolates between the malicious code to the rest of the system, preventing damage to the latter. This isolation can be done: (1) At the application-level, meaning that the malicious code is running on the same operating system as the rest of the system, but its system calls affect only a quarantined area of the system, e.g., Sandboxie[1]. (2) At the operating system level (e.g., VMWare Workstation), meaning the operating system is isolated but the processor is the same. (3) At the processor level, meaning all machine instruction are generated by an emulator like Qemu (e.g. TTAnalyze). While an emulator-based sand-boxing technique might be harder to detect, it can be done, e.g., using timing attacks due-to the emulator performance degradation, as shown in [13]. Therefore, we have used the VM sandbox mechanism to implement our IDS.

2.2 The Camouflage Algorithms

Modification of the input to a decision-tree classifier based on static analysis features (binary n-grams) was presented in [7]. A simulation of the IDS classifier of the installed anti-virus program was constructed by submitting a collection of malicious and benign binaries to the classifier via a COM (Component Object Model) interface, which runs the installed anti-virus on a file path argument and returns the classifier's decision for this file. Then, a feature-set similar to the attacker' s code that would be classified as benign was found manually in the simulated decision tree. Finally, the authors appended the feature bytes to positions ignored by the system loader in the attacker's code, manually transforming its feature set to the benign one. In contrast, we encountered a dynamic analysis classifier, which is harder to fool [11].

Suggested ways to modify system call sequences were presented in [18]. It deals with *mimicry attacks*, where an attacker is able to code a malicious exploit that mimics the system calls trace of benign code, thus evading detection. [18] presents several methods: (1) Make benign system calls generate malicious

---

[1] http://www.sandboxie.com/.

behavior by modifying the system calls parameters. This works since most IDSs ignore the system call parameters. (2) Adding semantic *no-ops* - system calls with no effect, or whose effect is irrelevant, e.g.: opening a non-existent file. The authors showed that almost every system call can be no-op-ed and thus the attacker can add any needed no-op system call to achieve a benign system call sequence. (3) Equivalent attacks – Using a different system call sequence to achieve the same (malicious) effect.

In our work, we also use the second technique, since it's the most flexible. Using it, we can add no-op system calls that would modify the decision path of the inspected code in the decision tree, as desired. Main differences: (1) We have created an automatic algorithm and tested it on a large group of malware to verify that it can be applied to any malware, not only specific samples. (2) We verified that the modified malicious code functions properly and evade by executing it after its camouflage. (3) We refer to partial knowledge of the attacker. The authors mentioned several other limitations of their technique in [5] due-to the usage of code injection, which don't apply to our paper. One may claim that the IDS should consider only successful system calls to counter this method. However, every system call in a benign code may return either successfully or not, depending on the system's state and therefore may cause such IDS to falsely classify this code.

A similar method to ours was presented in [10]. The authors used system calls dependence graph (SCDG) with graph edit distance and Jaccard index as clustering parameters of different malware variants and used several SCDG transformations on the malware source code to "move" it to a different cluster. Our approach is different in the following ways: (1) Our classification method is different, and handles cases which are not covered by their clustering mechanism. (2) [10] showed a transformation that can cause similar malware variants to be classified at a different cluster - but not that it can cause a malware to be classified (or clustered) as a benign program, as shown in this paper. (3) Their transformations are limited to certain APIs only - and would not be effective for malware code that doesn't have them.

[16] presented an algorithm for automated mimicry attack on FSA (or overlapping graph) classifier using system call n-grams. However, this algorithm limits the malware code that can be camouflaged using it, to one that can be assembled from benign trace n-grams.

In [1,2], attacker-generated samples were added to the training set of the classifier, in-order for it to subvert the classification of malware code to benign, due-to its similarity to the added samples. However, it requires the attacker to have access to the classifier's DB, which is secured. In contrast, our method, which does not modify the classifier, is more feasible to implement.

3   Problem Description

We deal with two separated issues: (1) Classification of the inspected code, which was not encountered before, by the IDS as benign or malicious, using its system calls sequences. (2) Developing an algorithm to transform the inspected code, in-order to change the classification of the inspected code by the IDS from malicious to benign, without losing its functionality. The general problem can be defined formally as follows:

Given the traced sequence of system calls as the array sys_call, where the cell: $sys\_call[i]$ is the i-th system call being executed by the inspected code ($sys\_call[1]$ is the first system call executed by the code).

Define the IDS classifier as:

$classify(benign\_training\_set, malic\_training\_set, inspected\_code\_sys\_calls)$,

where $inspected\_code\_sys\_calls$ is the inspected code's system calls array, $benign\_training\_set$ is a set of system calls arrays used to train the classifier with a known benign classification and $malic\_training\_set$ is a set of system calls arrays used to train the classifier with a known malicious classification. $classify()$ returns the classification of the inspected code: either benign or malicious.

Given that an inspected code generates the array: $malic\_inspected\_code\_$ sys_calls, define the camouflage algorithm as a transformation on this array, resulting with the array: $C(malic\_inspected\_code\_sys\_calls)$. The success of the camouflage algorithm is defined as follows: Given that:

$classify(benign\_training\_set, malic\_training\_set, malic\_inspected\_code\_sys\_calls)$
= malicious, the camouflage algorithm result is:

$classify(benign\_training\_set, malic\_training\_set, C(malic\_inspected\_code\_sys\_calls))$
= benign and:

$malic\_behavior(C(malic\_inspected\_code\_sys\_calls))=$
$malic\_behaviour(malic\_inspected\_code\_sys\_calls)$.

While in Sect. 6.3 we would show that partial knowledge of the training set is enough to generate a probabilistic camouflage, we initially assume that the attacker has access to the IDS and to the decision tree model it is based upon. Such knowledge can be gained by reverse engineering the IDS on the attacker's computer, without the need to gain access to the attacked system - just to have access to IDS. As shown in [7], an IDS decision tree can be recovered this way by exploiting public interfaces of an IDS and building the decision tree by feeding it with many samples and examining their classifications. Reconstruction attacks such as the one described in [6] for a C4.5 decision tree could also be used for this purpose. This assumption, that the IDS classifier, can be reconstructed, is common in several papers on this subject (e.g.: [2,5,10,16,18], etc.), as-well-as in cryptography (Kerckhoffs's principle). We further assume the attacker knows the system calls trace that would be produced by the malware on the inspected system. While the system calls trace might be affected by, e.g., files' existence and environment variables' values on the target system, it is highly unlikely, since the IDS should be generic enough to work effectively on all the clients' systems, making system-dependent flows rare.

The effectiveness of our IDS is determined by two factors (P is the probability):

1. We would like to minimize the false negative rate of the IDS, i.e. to minimize P(*classify(benign_training_set, malic_training_set, malic_inspected_code_sys_calls) =* benign).
2. We would like to minimize the false positive rate of the IDS, i.e. to minimize P(*classify(benign_training_set, malic_training_set, benign_inspected_code_sys_calls) =* malicious).

The overall effectiveness of the camouflage algorithm will be measured by the increased number of false negatives, i.e. we would like that:

$$P(\textit{classify(benign\_training\_set, malic\_training\_set,}$$
$$C(\textit{malic\_inspected\_code\_sys\_calls})) = \text{benign}) \geq$$
$$P(\textit{classify(benign\_training\_set, malic\_training\_set,}$$
$$\textit{malic\_inspected\_code\_sys\_calls}) = \text{benign}).$$

Therefore, the effectiveness of the camouflage algorithm is defined as the difference between the two probabilities (which are computed by the respective frequencies). The higher the difference between those frequencies, the more effective is the camouflage algorithm.

One way to fight the camouflage algorithm is to apply transformations on the input sequences of system calls and apply the classifier on the transformed sequences. The assumption is that the transformed sequences would reduce the effectiveness of the camouflage algorithm. We define a transformation of the system calls trace of the inspected code as *T(malic_inspected_code_sys_calls)*. We define the transformation *T* to be *effective* iff:

1. It would not reduce the malware detection rate, i.e.:
   P(*classify(T(benign_training_set), T(malic_training_set), T(malic_inspected_code_sys_calls))=* malicious) ≥ P(*classify(benign_training_set, malic_training_set, malic_inspected_code_sys_calls) =* malicious)
2. It would not reduce the benign software detection rate, i.e.:
   P(*classify(T(benign_training_set), T(malic_training_set), T(benign_inspected_code_sys_calls))=* benign) ≥ P(*classify(benign_training_set, malic_training_set, benign_inspected_code_sys_calls) =* benign)
3. It would reduce the camouflage algorithm effectiveness:
   P(*classify(benign_training_set, malic_training_set, C(malic_inspected_code_sys_calls))=* benign) ≥ P(*classify(T(benign_training_set), T(malic_training_set), T(C(malic_inspected_code_sys_calls)))=*benign).

In the next two sections we describe in detail the IDS and camouflage algorithm implementations.

4   IDS Implementation

In-order to implement a dynamic analysis IDS that would sandbox the inspected code effects, we have used VMWare Workstation, where changes made by a malicious code can be reverted. We used a Windows XP[2]. SP3 OS without an internet connection (to prevent the possibility of infecting other machines). The inspected executables were run for a period of 10 s (and then forcefully terminated), which resulted in about 10,000 recorded system calls per executable on average (the maximum number recorded per executable was about 60,000).[3]

The system calls recorder we have used for Windows records the Nt* system-calls. The usage of this low layer of system calls was done in-order to prevent malware from bypassing Win32API (e.g. *CreateFile()*) recording by calling those lower-level, Nt* APIs (e.g. *NtCreateFile()*). We have recorded 445 different system calls, such-as *NtClose()*, etc.

We have implemented the classifier using scikit-learn[4]. We selected the CART decision tree algorithm, similar to C4.5 (J48) decision tree, which was already proven to be a superior algorithm for malware classification [3]).

The training set for the binary classifier contains malicious and benign executables. The malicious executables were taken from VX Heaven[5]. They were selected from the 'Win32 Virus' type. Focusing on this specific mode of action of the malicious code reduce the chance of infection of other computers caused by using, e.g., worm samples. The number of malicious and benign samples in the set was similar (521 malicious samples and 661 benign samples) to prevent a bias towards classification with the same value as the majority of the training samples.

As features for the decision tree we used the position and the type of the system call, e.g.: $sys\_call[3] = NtCreateFile$. Thus, the number of available feature values was very large (about 850,000). Therefore, we performed a feature selection of the 10,000 (best) features with the highest values for the χ^2 (chi-square) statistic of the training set, and created the decision tree based only on the selected features. This choice was made to ease the explanation of our algorithm in the next section. In Sect. 6.2 we would use more robust features and show that our algorithm works in this case either.

5   The Camouflage Algorithm Implementation

The goal of the camouflage algorithm is to modify the sequence of system calls of the inspected code in a way that would cause the classifier to change its classification decision from malicious to benign without harming its functionality.

---

[2] We used Windows XP and not newer versions, in-order to allow computer viri that use exploits found on this OS but patched afterward to run on our IDS either, thus detecting both new and old (but still used) malware.

[3] Tracing only the first seconds of a program execution might not detect certain malware types, like "logic bombs" that commence their malicious behavior only after the program has been running some time. However, this can be mitigated both by classifying the suspension mechanism as malicious or by tracing the code operation throughout the program execution life-time, not just when the program starts.

[4] http://scikit-learn.org/.

[5] http://vxheaven.org/.

This is done by finding a benign decision path (i.e., a path that starts from the tree root and ends in a leaf with benign classification) in the decision tree with the minimal edit distance [9] from the decision path of the malware (or the minimal Levenshtein distance between the paths' string representations). Then we add (not remove or modify, to prevent harming the malware functionality) system calls to change the decision path of the modified malware code to that of the benign path. Selecting the minimal edit distance means less malware code modifications.

In-order to modify the system calls sequence without affecting the code's functionality, we add the required system calls with invalid parameters. This can be done for most system calls with arguments. Others can be called and ignored. For example: opening a (non-existent) file, reading (0 bytes) from a file, closing an (invalid) handle, etc. One may claim that the IDS should consider only successful system calls. However, it is difficult for it to determine whether a system call is invoked with invalid parameters just to fool it, since even system calls of legitimate programs are sometimes being called with arguments that seem to be invalid, e.g., non-exiting registry key. In addition, IDSs that verify the arguments tend to be much slower (4–10 times slower, as mentioned in [17]).

In the basic version of our classifier, an internal node in the decision tree contains a decision condition of the form: $system\_call[i] =? system\_call\_type[k]$. Assume without loss of generality that if the answer is yes (i.e., $system\_call[i] = system\_call\_type[k]$), the branch is to the right (R child), and if the answer is no, the branch is to the left (L child). An example of a decision tree is presented in Fig. 1. In this decision tree, if the malware code trace contains: {$sys\_call[1]=NtQueryInformationFile$, $sys\_call[2]=NtOpenFile$, $sys\_call[3]=NtAddAtom$, $sys\_call[4]=NtWriteFile$} (decision path: $M'=RRRR$, classified as a malicious) and if the algorithm will insert as the fourth system call a system call with a type different than $NtWriteFile$, the classifier will declare this malware code as benign, since the decision path would change from M' to $P1$.

While there is no guarantee that the algorithm would converge (step 3 in Algorithm 1 exists in-order to prevent an infinite loop by switching back and forth between the same paths), it did converge successfully for all the tested samples, as shown in Sect. 6. The reason for this is the rationale behind the decision tree based on system calls: The behavior of malware (and thus the system calls sequences used by it) is inherently different from that of benign software. Because-of that, and since the decision tree is trying to reduce the entropy of its nodes, the malicious and benign software do not spread uniformly at the leaf nodes of the decision tree but tend to be clustered at certain areas. Our path modifications direct the decision path to the desired cluster.

The general algorithm is depicted in Algorithm 1. Before explaining the details of the algorithm, let's discuss the possible edit operations when modifying a malware decision path. We will demonstrate the edit operations using the decision tree depicted in Fig. 1:

1. *Substitution*: There can be two types of substitutions: Sub_L - a substitution $L{\rightarrow}R$ (e.g., from $P{=}RRRL$ to $P'{=}RRRR$) and Sub_R - a substitution $R{\rightarrow}L$ (e.g., from $M{=}RRL$ to $P3{=}LRL$ in Fig. 1).
2. *Addition:* Add_R - an addition of R (e.g., from $M{=}RRL$ to $P1{=}RRRL$ in Fig. 1) or Add_L - an addition of L (e.g., from $P{=}RRL$ to $P'{=}LRRL$).
3. *Deletion:* Del_L - A deletion of L (e.g., from $P{=}LRL$ to $P'{=}RL$) or Del_R - a deletion of R (e.g., from $P{=}RRL$ to $P'{=}RL$).

Since the only allowed modification is an insertion of a dummy system call, the algorithm handles the above 6 edit operations as follows:

- If the edit_op is Sub_L, *or* Add_R, or Del_L: Given that the condition (in the parent node of the modified\added node) is: $sys\_call[i] {=}?\ sys\_call\_type[k]$, add $sys\_call[i]{=}sys\_call\_type[k]$. Note that the equivalent of Del_L is Sub_L followed by a tree re-evaluation, since this is the only edit op allowing you to remove the L without actually deleting a system call, which might harm the code's functionality.
- If the edit_op is Sub_R, or Add_L or Del_R: Given that the condition: $sys\_call[i] {=}?\ sys\_call\_type[k]$, add $sys\_call[i]{=}sys\_call\_type[m]$ s.t. $m\ != k$. The above note about deletion applies here too.

After each edit operation, the malware trace changes: The dummy system call addition might have affected every condition on the tree in the form of: $sys\_call[j] {=}?\ sys\_call\_type[k]\, s.t.\ j{\geq}i$. Therefore, we need to re-evaluate the entire decision path and find again the benign paths which are closest to it. Step 2(a) exists in-order to minimize the effects of the current edit operation on the path after re-evaluating it. The system calls insertion would ideally be done automatically, e.g., by usage of tools such-as *LLVM*, as done in [10], However, as mentioned by the authors, such tools are currently lack support for dealing with the Windows CRT and Platform SDK API calls, which are used by most Windows malware. Thus we assume that the attacker would manually insert the system calls, added by the camouflage algorithm, to the malware source code. This is demonstrated for the "Beetle" virus, in the next section.

Example 1. We demonstrate Algorithm 1 using the decision tree in Fig. 1:
Given the malware code:
$$\{sys\_call[1]{=}NtQueryInformationFile,\ sys\_call[2] = NtOpenFile,$$
$$sys\_call[3]{=}NtWriteFile,\ sys\_call[4]{=}NtClose\},$$

Its path in the IDS's decision tree is: $M{=}RRL$ (=Right-Right-Left), and the benign paths in the decision tree are: $P1{=}RRRL$, $P2{=}LLL$ and $P3{=}LRL$, the edit distances are $d(M, P1){=}1$, $d(M, P2){=}2$, $d(M, P3){=}1$. The tuples to check are: $\{(M, P1),\ (M, P2),\ (M, P3)\}$. We have two paths with a minimal edit distance: $edit\_sequence(M, P1){=}\{Add_R\ (at\ position\ 3)\}$ and $edit\_sequence(M, P3) = \{Sub_R(at\ position\ 1)\}$. The condition for-which we need to add R in $P1$ is: $system\_call[3] = NtAddAtom$. Thus: $i{=}3$. The condition for-which the edit operation applies in $P3$ is: $system\_call[2] = NtOpenFile$. Thus: $i{=}2$. Therefore, we start from $P1$ and not from $P3$, since its index is larger.

Algorithm 1. System-Calls Based Decision Tree's Camouflage Algorithm

---

1. Given the decision tree of the IDS and a specific malware trace (i.e. its sequence of system calls as recorded) with the decision tree's path M, find all the IDS's decision tree's benign paths, $P1..Pm$, and create a list l of m tuples to check: $l=\{(M, P1)..(M, Pm)\}$. Set $path\_count[M] = 0$

2. For each tuple (dec_path, Pj) in l, find the minimum edit distance between dec_path and Pj, $d(dec\_path, Pj)$. Select the tuple with the minimal such edit distance and find the minimal sequence of edit operations needed to change dec_path to Pj, ordered from the root of the tree to the leaf\classification node (i.e. by position in the decision path). If l is empty: Report failure.

   (a) If there is more than a single path with the same minimal edit distance, look at the first edit operation in each such path. Assuming the condition is of the form: $system\_call[i] =? system\_call\_type[k]$, select the path that maximizes i.

3. Set $path\_count[des\_path] += 1$. If $path\_count[des\_path] \geq max\_decision\_path\_count$: Remove all tuples that contain dec_path from l and go to step 2.

4. Assuming the benign path to fit is Pj, modify the malware code based on the first edit operation in the edit sequence, as was explained above:

   (a) If the edit_op is Sub_L, Add_R, or Del_L then: Add $sys\_call[i]=sys\_call\_type[k]$. Else: Add $sys\_call[i]=sys\_call\_type[m]$ s.t. $m \mathrel{!=} k$.

5. $system\_call[i..n]$ from before the modification now become $system\_call[i+1..n+1]$. Re-evaluate the new system calls sequence and generate a new decision path M'.

6. If M' ends with a benign leaf: Report success. Else: Remove (dec_path, Pj) from l, and add all the tuples with the modified malware code $\{(M', P1)..(M', Pm)\}$ to l. Set $path\_count[M'] = 0$

7. Go to step 2.

In-order to modify M to $P1$, we add: $sys\_call[3] = NtAddAtom(NULL, 0, NULL)$ (the edit_op is Add_R). Notice that we add the system call with invalid parameters. The new malware code is:

   $\{sys\_call[1]=NtQueryInformationFile, sys\_call[2] = NtOpenFile, sys\_call[3]= NtAddAtom, sys\_call[4]= NtWriteFile, sys\_call[5]=NtClose\}$.

Its decision path is $M'=RRRR$. M' is not classified as benign – so we remove $(M, P1)$, and add all the tuples with the modified code M'. Thus, we need to examine:

   $\{\{M, P2), (M, P3), (M', P1), (M', P2), (M', P3)\}$.

The tuple we would inspect in the next iteration is $(M', P1)$: $d(M', P1)=1$ and $i=4$ (which is larger than 2 for $(M, P3)$). The algorithm would converge after the next iteration, in which we would add $sys\_call[4] \mathrel{!=} NtWriteFile$, and the modified malware code would be classified as benign $(P1)$.

5.1 Random Forest Camouflage Algorithm

In Sect. 6.2, the classifier with the best performance was random forest. Since a random forest is actually a collection of decision trees, if we extend the same

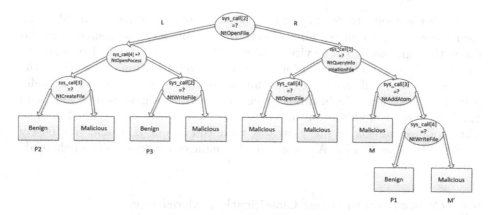

Fig. 1. A system calls based decision tree

assumptions made in Sect. 3, that-is: we know all the trees in the random forest, we can create a camouflage algorithm for random forest.

The rationale of the algorithm is simple: Since all decision trees in the random forest actually represents parts of the same code flow, we can modify each of them in turn, using Algorithm 1, and keep using the modified system calls trace, until we can fool the majority of them, thus fooling the entire random forest.

6   Experimental Evaluation

In-order to test the detection rate of our IDS, we used benign files collection from the Program Files folder of Windows XP SP3 and from our collection of third party benign programs and malware of Win32 Virus type, from VX Heaven's collection. The test set contained about 650 benign programs and 500 malware, which were different from the ones used to train the IDS in Sect. 4. The malware detection rate and the benign detection rate (as computed by the definitions specified in Sect. 3), were 84.3 % and 88.9 % respectively, as shown in the first line of Table 2.

In-order to test our camouflage algorithm, we have selected all the malware samples from our test set, which were correctly classified (i.e., as malicious) by our IDS (436 samples). We applied the camouflage algorithm on them: *None* of the camouflaged system calls sequences of those samples were identified by our IDS (effectiveness of 100 %, by the definition in Sect. 3).

We have applied the random forest camouflage algorithm on all the malware code that were detected by the random forest: 445 different samples. While there is no guarantee that the algorithm would converge, all modified section traces were classified as benign by our IDS, i.e., camouflage algorithm effectiveness of 100 %. This is due-to the same rationale mentioned in Sect. 5.

To test a complete "end-to-end" application of our system in real-life, we used the source code of the virus "Beetle"[6]. We compiled the source code and ran it through our IDS. The virus system calls trace was classified correctly as malicious by our IDS. After using our camouflage algorithm, we received the modified system calls sequence, classified as benign by our IDS. We manually matched the system calls in this sequence to the virus original source code, and applied the same modifications to it - and then recompiled the modified version. The modified version of the virus was then run in our IDS, and was falsely classified by it as benign. As expected, the malicious functionality of the code remained intact.

6.1   Comparison to Other Classification Algorithms

We've implemented and compared the effectiveness of different classification algorithms, using the same features, training set and test set. In-order to take into account true and false positives and negatives, we tried to maximize the Matthews correlation coefficient (MCC), which is used in machine learning as a measure of the quality of binary classifications [1].

The results appear in Table 1.

Table 1. Detection rate of the IDS by classifier type

Classifier type	Malware detection rate (TPR)	Benign software detection rate (TNR)	MCC
Decision tree	84.3	88.9	0.76
Random forest	86.1	89.5	0.77
k-Nearest Neighbors	89.4	86.0	0.77
Naïve Bayes (Gaussian)	87.0	54.5	0.50
Naïve Bayes (Bernoulli)	97.9	59.9	0.64
Ada-Boost	87.4	84.8	0.74
Support vector machine (Linear)	87.5	86.4	0.76
Support vector machine (RBF)	96.3	74.9	0.74
Linear discriminant analysis	82.6	82.6	0.68

The Random Forest classifier and k-Nearest Neighbors classifier were the best overall, taking into account both malware and benign software detection rate (by maximizing the MCC).

---

[6] The description and the source code of this virus are available at: http://vxheaven. org/lib/vpe01.html.

6.2 Countering the Camouflage: Section-Based Transformations

The basic form of decision tree node condition is: $system\_call[i] = ?system\_call\_type[k]$. However, using this kind of input makes the IDS classification fragile: It's enough that we add a single system call in the middle of the sequence or switch the positions of two system calls, to change the entire decision path.

Therefore, we want to transform the input data (the system calls array) in a way that would make a modification of the inspected code harder to impact the decision tree path of the modified code, thus counter the camouflage algorithm. In-order to define those transformations, we first divide the system calls sequence to small sections of consecutive system calls. Each system calls section would have a fixed length, m. Thus, $section[i] = (sys\_call[(i-1)*m+1],..,sys\_call[i*m])$.

In an *order-preserving without duplicates removal section-based transformation*, we define the discrete values of the the decision nodes in the tree to be: $section[i] = ? (sys\_call[(i-1)*m+1], sys\_call[(i-1)*m+2],.., sys\_call[i*m])$. However, this transformation is more specific than the basic model - so it would be easier to fool - and thus we didn't use it. This changes when adding *duplicates removal*: If there is more than a single system call of the same type in a section - only the first instance (which represent all other instances) appears in the section. This transformation prevents the possibility to split a system call into separate system calls (e.g. two *NtWriteFile()* calls, each writing 100 bytes, instead of a single call writing 200 bytes). Therefore, this was the first transformation we used.

The second transformation we examined is *non-order-preserving without duplicates removal*. This transformation is identical to the *order-preserving without duplicates removal transformation*, except for the fact that the system calls in each section are ordered in a predetermined order (lexicographically), regardless of their order of appearance in the trace. Using this transformation makes the probability of affecting the decision tree path by switching the places of two arbitrary system calls much smaller. Only the switching of two system calls from different sections might affect the decision path.

The last transformation we considered is *non-order-preserving with duplicates removal*. It is identical to the former, except for the fact that if there is more than a single system call of the same type in a section - only one instance (which represent all other instances) would appear in the section. This transformation handles both system calls switching and splitting. Notice that this transformation makes a section similar to a set of system calls: Each value can appear at most once, without position significance.

In-order to test the detection rate of our modified IDS, we used the same test set used for the basic model. A section size of $m=10$ was chosen. The detection rate, computed by the definitions specified in Sect. 3, appear in Table 2.

As can be seen from this table, section-based transformations are effective, by the definition in Sect. 3.

In-order to test our camouflage algorithm effectiveness vs. the modified IDS, we have used the camouflage algorithm shown in Algorithm 1 to modify the system calls trace. Then we have applied the input transformation on the

Table 2. Detection rate of the IDS by input transformation type

Input type	Malware detection rate	Benign software detection rate
No transformation (original DB)	84.3	88.9
Non order-preserving, without duplicates removal	87.4	90.7
Non order-preserving, with duplicates removal	86.5	88.1
Order-preserving, with duplicates removal	87.6	91.3
No transformation (updated DB)	86.5	88.7

modified system calls trace - and then we fed it to the input-transformed IDS variant. Without transformation we got a false-negative rate of 100 %. With section-based transformation, non order-preserving, without duplicates removal - we got 18.8 %. With section-based transformation, non order-preserving, with duplicates removal we got 17.2 %. With section-based transformation, order-preserving, with duplicates removal - we got 17.4 %.

We see that each input transformation reduces the effectiveness of the camouflage dramatically, since the camouflage we applied was designed against individual system calls and not against input transformations.

Countering the Input Transformations with Custom-Fit Camouflage Algorithm

One might argue that camouflaging a system calls trace in our basic IDS (without the transformations suggested in Sect. 6.2) is an easy task. One needs to add only a single system call at the beginning to change all following system calls positions, thus affecting the decision path in the tree. Can we apply our camouflage algorithm on our section-based IDS with the same effectiveness?

In-order to fit our camouflage algorithm to section-based transformations, we have used Algorithm 1, except that in each iteration we added an entire system calls section, instead of a single system call. This is done in step 4: Assuming the condition is:

$section[i] =? (sys\_call[(i-1)*m+1], sys\_call[(i-1)*m+2], .., sys\_call[i*m])$,

if the edit_op is Sub_L, Add_R, or Del_L then:

Add $section[i] = (sys\_call[(i-1)*m+1], sys\_call[(i-1)*m+2], .., sys\_call[i*m])$

(add the same section).

Else: Add $section[i] = (sys\_call'[(i-1)*m+1], sys\_call[(i-1)*m+2], .., sys\_call[i*m])$

s.t. $sys\_call'[(i-1)*m+1] \; != \; sys\_call[(i-1)*m+1]$

(add a section with a different first system call).

The section is added with the same transformation type as the IDS: either *order preserving* or not, and either with or without *duplicates removal*.

We have applied this algorithm on all section-based transformations described in Sect. 6.2. Like Algorithm 1, there is no guarantee that the algorithm would converge. However, all 436 modified section traces were classified as benign by our IDS, with all input transformations, i.e., camouflage algorithm effectiveness of 100 %. This is due-to the same rationale mentioned in Sect. 5. This was also the case when modifying the random forest camouflage algorithm mentioned in Sect. 5.1 to counter input transformations by replacing Algorithm 1 used by it with this variant.

6.3 Partial Knowledge of the IDS

So far, we assumed that the attacker has full knowledge of both the classifier type, the training set used to create it and its features, in-order to generate the exact same classifier and then use it to camouflage the malicious code. We can alleviate this assumption: If the attacker can gain partial knowledge about the training set, he can construct the simulated classifier using *only* the training set he knows about and use it in Algorithm 1. Such partial knowledge is easy to gather, e.g., using the VirusTotal[7] samples closest to the IDS release date, which are very probable to be used by the IDS. We have trained the attacker classifier using a part of the training set which is used by the IDS classifier, as mentioned in Sect. 6. We then camouflaged the entire test set using Algorithm 1, based on the attacker partial knowledge based classifier.

We discovered that a knowledge of 86.4 % of the IDS training set is enough to create a camouflage that is 56.6 % effective. A knowledge of 77.7 % of the training set provides camouflage effectiveness of 31.3 % and 69.1 % of it provides effectiveness of 25.4 %. We also tested a full knowledge of the training set, with different features being selected (in case of chi-square equality). In this case, the camouflage is 64 % effective. Finally, we tested a full knowledge of the attacker on the training set and features, followed by an update of the IDS training set size by 1.7 %, without the attacker knowledge. In this case, the generated camouflage was 75.5 % effective. This means that training set updates can decrease the camouflage algorithm effectiveness, which was supported by our results, which are not shown due to space limitation.

From all the experiments, it is clear that the camouflage algorithm is useful to an attacker even with partial knowledge of the classifier.

7 Conclusions

In this article, we have shown that malware code which has been identified by a specific machine learning classifiers (decision tree or random forest) can be camouflaged in-order to be falsely classified as benign. We have done so

---

[7] https://www.virustotal.com/.

by modifying the actual code being executed, without harming its malicious functionality. We then applied a defense mechanism to the camouflage algorithm, called input transformations, making it more robust, and showed that it can also be evaded.

This suggests that it is not enough to use a machine learning classifier with a large DB of benign and malicious samples to detect malware - one must also be aware of the possibility that such classifier would be fooled by a camouflage algorithm - and try to counter it with techniques such as continuous updating of the classifier's training set or application of the input transformation that we discussed. However, as we have shown, even such transformations are susceptible to camouflage algorithms designed against them.

Our future work in this area would examine the effectiveness of our camouflage algorithm on other machine-learning classifiers (e.g. SVM, boosted trees, etc.) and find other algorithms to cope with such classifiers.

References

1. Baldi, P., Brunak, S., Chauvin, Y., Andersen, C.A., Nielsen, H.: Assessing the accuracy of prediction algorithms for classification: an overview. Bioinformatics 16(5), 412–424 (2000)
2. Biggio, B., Rieck, K., Ariu, D., Wressnegger, C., Corona, I., Giacinto, G., Rol., F.: Poisoning behavioral malware clustering. In: Proceedings of the 7th ACM Workshop on Artificial Intelligence and Security (2014)
3. Firdausi, I., Lim, C., Erwin, A.: Analysis of machine learning techniques used in behavior based malware detection. In: Proceedings of 2nd International Conference on Advances in Computing, Control and Telecommunication Technologies, pp. 201–203 (2010)
4. Forrest, S., Hofmeyr, S., Somayaji, A., Longsta, T.: A sense of self for unix processes. In: IEEE Symposium on Security and Privacy, pp. 120–128. IEEE Press, USA (1996)
5. Forrest, S., Hofmeyr, S., Somayaji, A.: The evolution of system-call monitoring. In: Proceedings of the Annual Computer Security Applications Conference, pp. 418–430 (2008)
6. Gambs, S., Gmati, A., Hurfin, M.: Reconstruction attack through classifier analysis. In: Cuppens-Boulahia, N., Cuppens, F., Garcia-Alfaro, J. (eds.) DBSec 2012. LNCS, vol. 7371, pp. 274–281. Springer, Heidelberg (2012)
7. Hamlen, K.W., Mohan, V., Masud, M.M., Khan, L., Thuraisingham, B.: Exploiting an Antivirus Interface. Comput. Stand. Interfaces 31(6), 1182–1189 (2009)
8. Kolter, J.Z., Maloof, M.A.: Learning to detect malicious executables in the wild. In: Proceedings of the 10th International Conference on Knowledge Discovery and Data Mining, pp. 470–478 (2004)
9. Navarro, G.: A guided tour to approximate string matching. ACM Comput. Surv. 33(1), 31–88 (2001)
10. Ming, J., Xin, Z., Lan, P., Wu, D., Liu, P., Mao, B.: Replacement attacks: automatically impeding behavior-based malware specifications. In: Malkin, T., Kolesnikov, V., Lewko, A.B., Polychronakis, M. (eds.) ACNS 2015. LNCS, vol. 9092, pp. 497–517. Springer, Switzerland (2015)

11. Moser, A., Kruegel, C., Kirda, E.: Limits of static analysis for malware detection. In: 23rd Annual Computer Security Applications Conference, pp. 421–430 (2007)
12. Moskovitch, R., Gus, I., Pluderman, S., Stopel, D., Fermat, Y., Shahar, Y., Elovici, Y.: Host based intrusion detection using machine learning. In: Proceedings of Intelligence and Security Informatics, pp. 107–114 (2007)
13. Raffetseder, T., Kruegel, C., Kirda, E.: Detecting system emulators. In: Garay, J.A., Lenstra, A.K., Mambo, M., Peralta, R. (eds.) ISC 2007. LNCS, vol. 4779, pp. 1–18. Springer, Heidelberg (2007)
14. Rozenberg, B., Gudes, E., Elovici, Y., Fledel, Y.: Method for detecting unknown malicious executables. In: Kirda, E., Jha, S., Balzarotti, D. (eds.) RAID 2009. LNCS, vol. 5758, pp. 378–379. Springer, Heidelberg (2009)
15. Somayaji, A., Forrest, S.: Automated response using system-call delays. In: Proceedings of the 9th USENIX Security Symposium, pp. 185–198 (2000)
16. Sufatrio, Yap, R.H.C.: Improving host-based IDS with argument abstraction to prevent mimicry attacks. In: Valdes, A., Zamboni, D. (eds.) RAID 2005. LNCS, vol. 3858, pp. 146–164. Springer, Heidelberg (2006)
17. Tandon, G., Chan, P.: On the learning of system call attributes for host-based anomaly detection. Int. J. Artif. Intell. Tools 15(6), 875–892 (2006)
18. Wagner, D., Soto, P.: Mimicry attacks on host-based intrusion detection systems. In: Proceedings of the 9th ACM Conference on Computer and Communications Security, pp. 255–264 (2002)

Towards Automatic Risk Analysis
and Mitigation of Software Applications

Leonardo Regano, Daniele Canavese$^{(\boxtimes)}$, Cataldo Basile, Alessio Viticchié,
and Antonio Lioy

Dip. di Automatica e Informatica, Politecnico di Torino, Torino, Italy
{leonardo.regano,daniele.canavese,cataldo.basile,
alessio.viticchie,lioy}@polito.it

Abstract. This paper proposes a novel semi-automatic risk analysis
approach that not only identifies the threats against the assets in a software application, but it is also able to quantify their risks and to suggests
the software protections to mitigate them. Built on a formal model of
the software, attacks, protections and their relationships, our implementation has shown promising performance on real world applications. This
work represents a first step towards a user-friendly expert system for the
protection of software applications.

Keywords: Software protection · Software risk analysis · Software
attacks

1 Introduction

Software is pervasive in our life. We rely on software applications for our leisure
and to ease our work, regardless of our fields of activity. In addition, software
is one of the pillars of the world economy that moves billions to trillions of dol-
lars. Developers have to protect their applications from tampering and avoid
that confidential data in their software are disclosed. In short, companies have
to protect the assets in their software, assets that are exposed to very powerful attacks, known as Man-at-the-End (MatE) attacks, from crackers that fully
control the execution environment of the software to protect.

When the software must be protected, the human experience is the leading factor and almost the only one. While big companies have ad hoc teams to
decide how to protect their applications or they can pay specialized companies,
small and medium enterprises cannot afford the costs for properly protecting
their software. By remaining vulnerable, it can damage the companies themselves, generating monetary losses, and all of us, becoming a vector for various
kind of malware. Automatic or assisted techniques are needed to help software
developers in protecting their applications.

In this paper we propose a novel risk analysis approach to (1) identify the
threats against the assets in target applications, (2) quantify their risks against
them and (3) suggest potential mitigations. In this context, the *mitigations* are

S. Foresti and J. Lopez (Eds.): WISTP 2016, LNCS 9895, pp. 120–135, 2016.
DOI: 10.1007/978-3-319-45931-8_8

the protections applied to each asset in order to reduce their exposure to the identified risks. This work represents a first step towards an expert system that can drive the software developers in all the delicate phases of software protection. While the ambition is to make software protection another standard, almost push-button activity like the compilation, in the short term, our approach can be an interesting solution for small and medium enterprises.

A preliminary version of this work has been already published [1], focusing only on the automatic threats identification. With respect to our previous approach, the main improvements in this paper are the risk quantification and the proposal of mitigations. In addition, we greatly improved the expressivity of our model, thus leading to an increased accuracy of the attacks identification phase. A formal modelling of attacker purposes, strategies, and approaches to tampering, allows a more sophisticated analysis that also associates discovered attacks to the protections that would reduce their likelihood and consequences. Together with the formalization of a more sophisticated vulnerability identification system, building and validating our novel risk analysis model has required the impact's assessment of both attacks and protections on the software assets. For a better validation of our model, we have collected assessment information by means of questionnaires proposed to experts in software protection.

This paper is structured as follows. Section 2 presents our approach, its inputs, outputs and work-flow. Section 3 introduces a reference application that we will use to practically describe our achievements. Section 4 describes our formal model for describing an application for risk analysis purposes. Section 5 introduces the threats and mitigation identification engines whose performance is detailed in Sect. 6. Section 7 presents previous works in the field. Finally, Sect. 8 draws conclusions and sketches future research directions.

2   Approach

This section presents a general overview of our approach, whose work-flow is sketched in Fig. 1.

The input to our system is the set of the source files of the application to protect. Currently, only the C and C++ languages are supported, but the

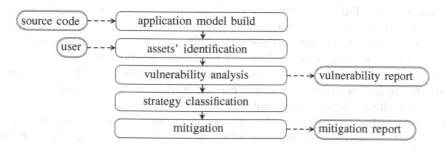

Fig. 1. General work-flow of our approach.

same core ideas can be easily extended to any other programming language. The first phase, **application model build**, consists of a static analysis of the source code, which is parsed and analyzed to create an abstract model of the application. We named *application part* a generic piece of code of the application under analysis. The application parts are either *data*, that include (global and local) variables, class fields and function/method parameters, and *code areas*, which consist of functions, methods, classes or a particular code region in a function/method. Code areas have a hierarchical structure that allow them to contain other application parts. For instance, a class (a code area) can contain a method (another code area) that, in turn, encloses a local variable (a datum). Apart the containment association, application parts are also linked together via a set of other relationships, such as the call graph information. More information about these relationships is available in Sect. 4.

Once the initial application model has been automatically constructed, the user must finalize it by selecting which application parts actually need to be protected and the security properties that need to be guaranteed on them. Application parts that are associated to at least one security property are named *assets*. This is performed during the **assets' identification** phase. Identifying assets is pivotal in our approach as they are both the elements to protect (developers' perspective) and the targets of the attacks (attackers' perspective). We focus on four security properties in this work: integrity and confidentiality, which were already modelled in our previous paper, execution correctness and weak confidentiality, which are novel contributions.

For instance, some application parts can be marked with the *integrity* property, when they must be preserved from modifications. In this case, either the parts must be hard to modify or any modification must be detected. In other cases, the developers may want to guarantee the *execution correctness*, a stronger form of integrity that in addition requires that a code area must be called as expected. For instance, application parts marked with the execution correctness cannot be skipped, like authentication/license checks. Parts marked with the *confidentiality* property must be unintelligible for an attacker, such as keys to decrypt media streams or patented algorithms. Some data may be also tagged with the *weak confidentiality* property. This property is breached when the attacker is able to retrieve the datum at every moment of the application execution (thus for hard-coded data the weak confidentiality is the same as the normal confidentiality). This is mostly interesting for attacks that target the assets of a victim's application (i.e., not the attacker's copy) by means of a distributed approach aiming at continuously obtaining the data values. For instance, in case of an OTP (One-Time Password) generator[1] that generates the next password by hashing the value of a fixed seed and a counter modified at each generation, the variable storing the counter can be marked with weak confidentiality. To predict the next passwords (not only the next one), it does not suffice that the attacker obtains once the value of victim's counter, he has to obtain it just before every generation. Therefore, either he is able to access every time the

---

[1] See the example in [1] for more details on the OTP generator application.

victim's application to read the counter value, or he has to obtain one counter, understand the counter update function, and reproduce it on his copy.

During the assets' identification, the user is also given the opportunity to override the relationships that were previously automatically deduced or refine them with more precise associations. In addition, some important information may not be extracted by means of automatic tools as its correct identification would require knowledge that is not inferrable from the source code. For instance, correctly deducing that a function encrypts or decrypts some data is complex, especially if the code makes use of ad-hoc cryptographic libraries. Furthermore, some inferred relationships can be transformed into more accurate ones by means of a manual user intervention. As an example, a license verification function can invoke another function if and only if a previous license check is passed. These functions are automatically related by the automatic analysis with a simple *call* relationship. However our model supports a more expressive association, the *enables* one, used to indicate that a function can be only executed if another one has been "successfully" executed. To simplify this phase, we developed a simple yet effective domain specific language presented in Sect. 4. With this language, manually added data can be saved on disk, avoiding to ask the users to input them again at each analysis.

Once a valid and accurate application model has been constructed and validated by the user, during the **vulnerability analysis** phase, our system identifies all the attacks that can disrupt the security properties of the assets and produce a vulnerability report for the user. Attacks are sequences of simpler actions that an attacker must perform to mount it, the *attack steps*. Therefore, in our case, an attack is an ordered list of attack steps and will be thus called *attack path*. This simplification does not influence the accuracy of our analysis since we are interested in the effects of the attacks, regardless of their steps' order. For instance, two attack paths $(step_1, step_2, step_3)$ and $(step_1, step_3, step_2)$ are produced when both $step_2$ and $step_3$ can be executed at the same time or when their relative ordering does not matter. When producing the report to the user our approach will present only one of the two previous attack paths, by eliminating the clones. These sample attack paths are known as *unique attack paths*.

After having detected the attack paths, the **strategy identification** phase is performed. This phase consists in the classification of all the attack steps of the inferred attack paths in order to understand their purpose towards the goal. In our work, we classify attack steps in seven *strategy* types: static and dynamic code analysis, static and dynamic tampering, sniffing and spoofing, and compromission attacks. Note that, sniffing and spoofing also consider traditional network Man-in-the-Middle (MitM) attack steps while the compromission type includes code injection and attempts to control the application victim's copy[2].

---

[2] We have distinguished compromission from tampering as their purpose is different. When tampering with an application the attacker modifies the application code to achieve a goal or remove a protection on his own copy, compromission includes the cases where the attackers inject code to remotely control a pool of victims' applications.

Finally, the **mitigation** phase produces a mitigation report that lists all the protection techniques that can be used to mitigate (either block or render more difficult) all the attack paths. A *protection*, in our approach, is able to mitigate a set of attack step types with a particular level of efficacy (low, medium or high). We assume that an attack path is mitigated by a protection if it is able to mitigate at least one of its steps. This phase considers the following protections:

- *anti-debugging*, which makes more difficult to perform dynamic analysis by attaching a trusted debugger, preventing attackers from using their own [2];
- *algorithm hiding*, a set of obfuscation techniques against the reverse engineering, protecting a code's confidentiality and understandability [3];
- call stack checks, which verifies the execution correctness by checking that functions are called in the right order [4];
- *barrier slicing*, which enforces the integrity of data and code areas by moving them to a trusted server where they will be executed [5];
- *code guards*, which are checks added in an application to detect and react to integrity breaches [6];
- *code mobility*, which protects application parts from reverse engineering and analysis by removing them from the application to be installed at run time when they need to be executed [7];
- *data hiding*, which involves altering the data structures and the functions' data flow for ensuring data confidentiality [8];
- *remote attestation*, which protects application integrity by forcing the application to periodically send integrity proofs to a verification server [9].

After having revised the protection proposed by the mitigation report, the suggested protections can be applied on the assets. This stage has been implemented within the ASPIRE project by tagging all the variables and code areas with some special annotations that are later processed by the custom ASPIRE protection tool-chain.

3   Reference Example

We introduce here one of the applications we used to test our approach, the Linux Memory Game[3], an open source video game written in C based on the popular card game Memory. The game is played with a set of cards' pairs placed face down on a table. The player's goal is to find all the matching pairs with the minimum number of card turns. The game provides five skill levels: little one, beginner, skilled, master and daemon. When playing at the little one difficulty, all the cards are face up and visible (it is for children). On the other hand, in the highest difficulty level the cards are moved in different (and increasingly difficult) ways after every flip.

   In our reference example, the main goal of the attacker is to win with the lowest number of flipped cards. On the other hand, the software developer must

---

[3] The source code is available at https://packages.debian.org/stretch/lmemory.

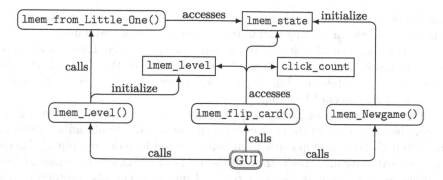

Fig. 2. Diagram showing the application parts relationships.

preserve the correctness of the game and the validity of the best scores, e.g., to keep the interest on it, as it happened for World of Warcraft.

Figure 2 depicts a diagram showing the relationships (function calls, accesses and initializations of variables) between the most important application parts in the game. The card values are stored in the global variable lmem_state, a vector of integers whose elements are the cells in the card matrix, an asset. Its weak confidentiality must be safeguarded, as the attacker can play with all the cards visible, but also its integrity, since he can force a known card arrangement.

lmem_state is set by the lmem_Newgame() function, executed when a new game starts. lmem_Newgame() is also an asset, whose integrity must be preserved.

A critical datum is also click_count, an integer variable that counts the number of cards flipped. The developer must guarantee its integrity to avoid unwanted modifications (as an attacker can lower it to increase its final score).

The function lmem_flip_card() is executed every time a card is flipped and its logic can be summarized in the following steps: (1) when the user has clicked on a new card, turn its face up; (2) increase the click count; (3) if there are already two cards face up, then turn them face down; (4) if there is already a card face up and it matches with new card, remove both cards from the table; (5) rearrange all the face down cards according to the selected skill level.

The lmem_from_Little_One() function flips back all the cards and it is invoked by the lmem_Level() function, which in turn is called when the user changes the difficulty level from the little one level to a higher one. These three functions must be preserved from modifications since a plethora of attacks can be mounted against them, that is, their execution correctness must be guaranteed.

In the following sections, we will identify a set of attacks that can be used to alter the normal work-flow of the application. We will start our discussion by informally introduce some of them here.

The attacker might start by trying to discover the position of all the cards, even if they are face down, or to force a known card configuration. An attacker can locate lmem_state by debugging a function that writes this vector, such as lmem_Newgame(), executed when a new game starts, thus easily recognizable via dynamic or static analysis. He can force some card values in `lmem_Newgame()` by using a known card configuration from a previously played game.

The attacker can also statically or dynamically change `lmem_Level()` to avoid the invocation of `lmem_from_Little_One()`. In this way the attacker can start with the little one difficulty level then switch to a higher one to be able to play with all the card faced up.

Finally, every step of `lmem_flip_card()` is vulnerable. The attacker can tamper the code to avoid the click count increase in order to obtain a reasonable score (step 2). He can stop cards from being turned face down (step 3). He can skip the card matching check, thus all the pairs of cards will be removed from the table, allowing an easy victory (step 4). Finally, he can also pretend to play at a higher skill level, whilst having a game at a lower difficulty (step 5).

4   Application Modeling

Our approach aims at automatically inferring attacks and protections that mitigate them by means of a Knowledge Base (KB). In this context, the starting knowledge is the application itself. The application code is theoretically the best source of information, since it models the complete application behavior. However, it also contains low level details that are not interesting for our kind of analysis. Therefore, a more abstract form is better suited for our purposes, that is the application meta-model.

Figure 3 sketches the UML class diagram of the meta-model describing a generic application in our approach.

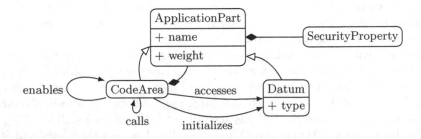

Fig. 3. UML class diagram of the application meta-model.

In our meta-model, an application is essentially a container of several application parts that can be either a datum or a code area. A code area can recursively contain one or more other application parts.

Every application part has a name (e.g., the variable or function name) and a *weight*, a non-negative real number used to explicitly indicate its importance (the greater the weight the more important the part). Weights are only meaningful for the assets and are used to compute the risk values during the risk assessment phases. Application parts are associated to a non-empty list of *security properties* to ensure, which are also considered as the targets of the attacker.

The Data class stores an additional *type* attribute stating their data type (e.g., integer or string). This field is used to discard the unsuitable protections since some techniques might be applicable only to some kind of instances (e.g., data obfuscation for integer variables only).

Code areas are complex types with the following relationships:

- a code area *accesses* a datum when it reads or writes its content;
- a code area *initializes* a datum with a value (it represents the first writing of a value in a variable);
- a code area *calls* another code area;
- a code area *enables* another area if its execution depends on the (successful) execution of another area.

Our meta-model is simple and could be constructed by hand, but this task can be very time consuming as real applications might have hundreds or thousands of application parts. For this reason, the application model build phase in our approach automatically extract the application model from its source code and instantiates its components accordingly. As anticipated in Sect. 2, static analysis can lead to inaccurate or incomplete results that need to be complemented by the user input for validation and refinement purposes. To help users store this additional information, we developed a Domain Specific Language, the Application Description Language (ADL), which expresses the same concepts as the application meta-model, but in a more human readable form. Its Backus-Naur syntax rules are shown in Fig. 4.

The terminal symbols **ID** and **FLOAT** respectively represents a valid C/C++ identifier and a sign-less floating point value.

As an example, Fig. 5 reports the description in ADL of the `lmem_flip_card()`, `lmem_Newgame()` and `lmem_state` assets for the Memory game.

Application ::= *ApplicationPart**;
ApplicationPart ::= *Datum* | *CodeArea*;
Datum ::= *DatumType* ID("{"
    ("properties" *SecurityProperty* ("," *SecurityProperty*)*
    "weight" FLOAT)? "}" | ";");
CodeArea ::= "codeArea" ID (("{"
    ("properties" *SecurityProperty* ("," *SecurityProperty*)*
    "weight" FLOAT)?
    (*Relation* ID ("," ID)*)* "}") | ";");
Relation ::= "accesses" | "initializes" | "calls" | "enables";
DatumType ::= "integer" | "integerArray" | ...;
SecurityProperty ::= "confidentiality" | "weakConfidentiality" | "integrity" |
    "executionCorrectness";

Fig. 4. Grammar of the Application Description Language (ADL).

```
code lmem_flip_card {
        properties integrity
        accesses lmem_level, click_count, lmem_state }
code lmem_Newgame {
        properties integrity
        initializes lmem_state }
```

Fig. 5. Assets description in ADL.

5   Vulnerability Analysis and Mitigation

In this section we present the vulnerability analysis and mitigation reporting steps of our approach. A preliminary work of the vulnerability analysis is available in a previously published paper [1], whose main ideas are summarized below:

- Facts are stored into a Knowledge Base (KB), initially populated with information concerning the application obtained from the application model.
- Breaching the assets properties becomes the goal of the attackers. Goals are modelled as properties. In this paper, the properties are: confidentiality, weak confidentiality, integrity and execution correctness.
- Attack step are modelled as rules of inference $P \rightarrow C\,(id)$, where id is an *identifier* of the attack step, that is its name, P is a set of *premises*, that is a set of facts in the KB that must be true in order to trigger the step, C is a set of *conclusions*, that is a set of additional facts that hold after the attack step is performed. Note that some attack steps (e.g. setting up a remote server) do not breach any security property, they are just preliminary actions needed to breach some properties (like the confidentiality of some data).
- Some inferences are not attack steps, relating different steps/facts and application parts (i.e., if x is in the KB do not perform the attack step y).

Once the Knowledge Base has been populated, all the attack paths are obtained by means of backward programming, which starts from the attack steps that breach the goals and progressively adduces facts that make the premises of attack steps true until the axioms are reached (i.e., attack steps or facts that have no premises). Attack paths can be extracted in an automatic way with any inferential engine of choice.

The previous attack path discovery model has been improved by adding new inference types that allow the detection of a larger set of attacks. The most important improvement consists in making the model more expressive by introducing the concept of attack strategy. Strategies are formal ways to determine the behavior of an attacker and they are modelled by changing the way the backward reasoning process work. In some cases, strategies enable a different set of attack steps. For instance, if the attacker has to tamper with the victim's copy, he has to perform several network-oriented attack steps (e.g. creating fake servers, tampering with the victim's OS, injecting malware). More strategies can be enabled at the same time. Moreover, certain facts are derived only if certain attack strategies are applied and certain premises are enabled or disabled based on the strategy. Enabling more sophisticated strategies (that may include more attack steps and render premises more sophisticated require) may have a significant impact on the performance.

As a first instance of strategy, together with MatE attacks, we have modeled attack strategies depicting distributed scenarios, where an attacker tries to gain access to data of an application running on a victim PC. As an example, we have introduced an attack step modeling a code injection attack, where the attacker modifies a code of the victim application to send to him all the data accessed by the code. We also added strategies to breach the weak confidentiality. As anticipated, to breach this property, the attacker must know the value of the datum on the victim application at every moment of the application execution. In our internal model, we modelled additional preconditions: the attacker must not only obtain the value of the datum (e.g., with the code injection attack step described before), but he must also retrieve, either with static or dynamic attacks, all the code areas that access (and therefore potentially modify) the datum. Referring to the example application in Sect. 3, we have marked lmem_state, which contains the position of the cards, with the weak confidentiality. To breach it, the attacker must not only locate the datum in memory, but he must also execute the lmem_Newgame code before reading the datum value, because, as we can see in Fig. 2, lmem_Newgame initializes lmem_state. We also take into account the call graph of the application, thanks to the calls relationships: in particular, if a code has been executed, i.e., if the execute code step is present in the attack path, all the codes called by the first one are considered as executed.

We can also model indirect attack strategies, when the attacker has to start tampering with other parts of the application to achieve his goal. For instance, some code areas are executed only if first enabled by the execution of other code areas. An example may be an application that contains a license check function that, if performed successfully, enables the execution of the rest of the application. In our internal model a code area is enabled not only if the enabler code area has been executed before, but also if it have been changed, covering cases such as the license check in which the attacker, instead of using a working license, modifies the license check code to bypass it.

Another strategy has been defined to represent attacks against the execution correctness: an attacker can breach the execution correctness of a code not only modifying the latter, but also avoiding all the calls to it.

Finally, we greatly improved the accuracy of the attack path inference rules, which now leverage a greater number of relationships between the application parts, such as the ones described in Sect. 4. Furthermore, we added several new kind of attack steps, such as a new one representing the execution of a single code area, needed to better handle the relationships such as the initializes association and the dynamic attacks in general.

As as example, the attack where the attacker can play at higher level of difficulty with open cards by avoiding the call by lmem_Level() to lmem_from_Little_One (Sect. 3) can be automatically obtained by the attack deduction phase if lmem_from_Little_One is marked with the execution correctness property. In this case if the corresponding strategy is enabled it produces the different attack steps in Fig. 6. Attack paths are represented as rectangles, while attack facts are drawn with rounded rectangles. Links between attack steps are represented as thick arrows, while links between attack steps and the produced facts are draw with normal arrows. Facts deduced by other facts are linked with dashed arrows.

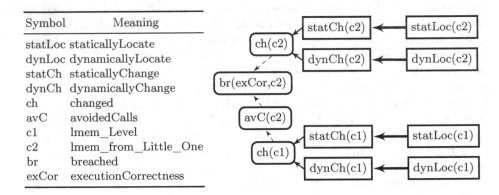

Symbol	Meaning
statLoc	staticallyLocate
dynLoc	dynamicallyLocate
statCh	staticallyChange
dynCh	dynamicallyChange
ch	changed
avC	avoidedCalls
c1	lmem_Level
c2	lmem_from_Little_One
br	breached
exCor	executionCorrectness

Fig. 6. Diagram showing the attack paths breaching the execution correcteness of the `lmem_from_Little_One` function.

To help security engineers to select the most vulnerable assets and properly decide what to protect in their applications, we also provide a measure about how dangerous is an attack path. Of course, custom formulas can be used in alternative to adapt to target applications and their business models.

Given all the deduced attack paths AP_i, all their attack steps $AS_{i,j}$, and all the assets a_k, we define the *risk* $\Omega^\epsilon_{AP_i}$ of an attack path AP_i against attackers with expertise ϵ as:

$$\Omega^\epsilon_{AP_i} = \pi(AP_i, \epsilon)\, \Gamma_{AP_i} \tag{1}$$

The $\pi(AP_i, \epsilon)$ in Eq. 1 is the probability that an attacker with expertise ϵ is able to successfully complete of the attack path. Note that, in estimating the probability to successfully mount an attack path, we consider the probabilities that an attacker with expertise ϵ is able to successfully execute all the attack steps needed to complete it, that is, $\pi(AP_i, \epsilon) = f(\pi(AS_{i,j}, \epsilon))$. The idea behind this formula is that an attacker, to successfully complete an attack path, must correctly undertake all the steps constituting it. We have tested our approach with $f = \min$ (the one that gave us best results), with an unrealistic but very conservative $f = \max$, and with $f = \cdot$.

Γ_{AP_i} is a quantitative measure of the damage resulting from a successful attack path, calculated as the sum of the damage $\Gamma_{AS_{i,j}}$ from each attack step:

$$\Gamma_{AP_i} = \sum_j \Gamma_{AS_{i,j}} = \sum_j \sum_k (W_{a_k} b(a_k, AS_{i,j}))$$

where W_{a_k} is the user-defined asset weight, and $b(a_k, \mathrm{AS}_j)$ is a function, deduced by our inference system, that returns the fraction of the security properties of the asset a_k that are breached by the attack step AS_j, that is, it returns 1 if all the security properties are compromised and 0 if none[4]. Finally, the values obtained with the risk formulas are mapped on a three values score (low, medium, high) with an ad hoc mapping.

Our inference system also suggests a list of protections that can be implemented to mitigate the risk of an attack. Protections can be applied to code areas and data, and are associated to a mitigation level, which is a measure of how much they reduce the probability of success of a particular attack step. To assess the mitigation of the risk associated to an attack path against application assets after the application of a set of protections selected by the user from the proposed ones, we recalculate the risk by using an updated value of the probability to successfully perform every attack step in the presence of the selected protections. To this purpose, we override the function $\pi(\mathrm{AS}_{i,j}, \epsilon)$ into $\pi(\mathrm{AS}_{i,j}, \epsilon, \{p_l\}_l)$ that also considers that $\{p_l\}_l$ protections are deployed to protect the asset.

The values of the expertise levels needed by the attacker to undertake an attack step, and the mitigation levels of the protections (and corresponding probabilities) that we have used in our experiments have been obtained by means of questionnaires proposed to 20 software protection experts in the ASPIRE project (https://aspire-fp7.eu/) consortium and advisory board.

6   Experimental Results

We have implemented our approach in Java 8 as a set of plug-ins for the Eclipse Mars platform. In addition we used XText 2.9.0 for developing the ADL parser and SWI-Prolog 7.2.3 for the attack path engine. In order to speed up the computation, the inference engine is implemented as a multi-threaded Prolog program so that multiple assets can be evaluated in parallel.

We tested our framework on the Linux Memory Game application described in Sect. 3. It is written in C and contains 53 application parts (10 global variables and 43 functions). We have marked 6 application parts as assets. The tests have been performed on an Intel i7-4980HQ 2.80 GHz with 16 GB of memory under Linux Debian 4.5.0, allocating 4 CPU cores for the vulnerability analysis phase. Table 1 summarizes our results on the application where $\mathcal{C}^{\mathrm{W}}$ stands for weak confidentiality, $\mathcal{I}$ for integrity and $\mathcal{E}$ for execution correctness.

The whole analysis process completed in 344.1s (less than 6 minutes) with all the attack strategies enabled. Note that the computation time is heavily influenced by the indegree and outdegree of the code areas in the call graph. A higher number of relationships surrounding an application part leads to a higher number of search combinations, which the vulnerability analysis has to try and take into account. For instance, `click_count` is directly used by only 2

---

[4] In practice, we assume that the whole asset weight assigned by the user is gained by the attacker when all the security properties are compromised.

Table 1. Memory game attack statistics

Assets		Attacks		risks		Chosen
Part	Property	Total	Uniques	Initial	Mitigated	protection
click_count	$\mathcal{I}$	2	2	medium	low	anti-debugging
lmem_from_Little_One()	$\mathcal{E}$	12	6	high	low	code guards
lmem_flip_card()	$\mathcal{E}$	37	16	high	low	remote attestation
lmem_level	$\mathcal{I}$	3	3	medium	low	code mobility
lmem_state	$\mathcal{C}^W$	20	8	high	low	code guards
lmem_state	$\mathcal{I}$	4	4	high	low	anti-debugging
lmem_Newgame()	$\mathcal{E}$	32	14	high	low	remote attestation
TOTAL		110	53	–	–	

application parts and its analysis takes only 1.4s, while `lmem_flip_card()` is related to 16 application parts and its analysis takes 322.4s.

The framework found 110 attacks on the assets, which reduces to only 53 unique attacks if we discard the attack step order (see Sect. 2). For the risk analysis we opted to use an 'amateur' expertise level due to the type of the example application. The risks columns in the table respectively list the risk of the most dangerous attack than can be mounted against an asset and the mitigated risk by using the strongest protection technique supported by our approach (also shown in the table).

Most of the attacks have a high risk to be performed even by an amateur attacker, but using the techniques suggested by our framework all of them can be nearly avoided reducing their risks to low. For instance, the attack path $(statLoc(c2), statCh(c2), ch(c2), br(exCor, c2))$ (Fig. 6) against the execution correctness of `lmem_from_Little_One()` has a high risk to be executed. However, our implementation has detected that using the code guards technique will lower the risk to low since the attack step $statCh(c2)$ will be severely hindered.

7   Related Works

The vulnerability assessment is a common issue for different and interdisciplinary fields of research. In the same way, knowledge base decision support systems are employed in several fields that need to take a decision based on a large amount of pre-collected information. For this reason, several projects have been proposed in literature. However, to our knowledge there are no works that completely matches what we have discussed so far. In this section we present some of the works that are relevant to our discussion. Works can be categorized as ontology-based, Petri net and graph based, and web-based systems.

7.1   Ontology-Based Systems

Applied to risk management, Ekelhart *et al.* presented a ontology-based system that aims at acting as a decision support system [10]. The work proposed by the authors relies on a methodology, called AURUM (*AUtomated Risk and Utility Management*), which is used to perform risk estimation, risk reduction and defense cost estimation. The expert system proposed by the authors is able to support decisions in risk analysis, mitigation and safeguard evaluation.

Fenz *et al.* have proposed an expert system aiming at semi-automatically inferring the needed controls to protect a system using an ontology. The expert system, named FORISK [11], is the result of an extension of two their previous works [12,13]. It is a formal representation of information security standards, risk determination and automated identification of countermeasures.

7.2   Petri Nets

Dalton *et al.* have shown that it is possible to model and probabilistically analyse attack trees by using Petri nets [14]. This method aims at automatically simulate the system behavior and, alongside the attack tree methodology, identify the proper countermeasures.

Dahl *et al.* introduced an interval timed coloured Petri net based mechanism that is able to analyse multi-agent and multi-stage attacks [15]. The proposed method automatically identifies vulnerabilities in network-based systems.

Coloured Petri nets have been also used by Wu *et al.* to model hierarchical attacks. Attacks are subdivided into high level and low level attacks. The former ones represent all the paths and the system vulnerabilities exploited to perform the attack. Based on this modelling it is possible to deduce attack cost estimation and risk measurements. The latter ones use separated coloured Petri nets to describe the details of the attack transitions. This level enhance the attack understanding and the effective countermeasure identification.

Yao *et al.* have recently proposed a Petri net based mechanism to analyse SDN threats [16]. In the proposed mechanism they use Petri nets to model the SDN structure and data flow. Then, they employs attack trees to model the attacks. Anyway, they only proposed a method for modelling attacks without delivering any mechanism to deduce countermeasures or cost evaluations.

7.3   Web-Based and Bayesian Network

Xie *et al.* based their network security analysis under uncertainty on Bayesian networks [17]. This approach aims at improving the enterprise security analysis. They built the Bayesian network on the security graph model. They tested and validated the approach using attack semantics and experimental studies. They also demonstrated that the system does not suffer parameter perturbation.

A Bayesian network based risk management framework have been proposed by Poolsappasit *et al.* [18]. The framework allows system administrators to evaluate the chance of network compromises, foreseeing how to mitigate and managing them. The system relies on a genetic algorithm that can perform single and multiple objective optimization of security administrator objectives.

A comparison of common methods for security information sharing has been performed by Steffan et al. [19]. They evaluated the capabilities of the systems in supporting avoidance and discovering of vulnerabilities. Finally, they suggested a method based on collaborative attack modelling. The proposed methodology combines graph-based attack modelling with a collaborative web-based tool.

Basset et al. developed a method to analyse network security based on probabilistic graphs [20] modeling actors, events and attributes of a network as nodes. Then, an estimate is associate to each node; it represents the ease of realizing the event, condition or attribute of the node. Attacks are modelled as paths in the graph that reach compromising conditions. They finally associate a probability to each edge in the attack paths thus allowing the final attack chance.

8   Conclusions and Future Work

In this paper we have extended the work initially proposed in [1]. Our approach semi-automatically constructs a representation of an application source code, searches the attacks against software assets and identifies the protections that can mitigate them, performing a risk analysis and protection evaluation cycle.

We have shown that our implementation is able to infer a great number of attacks that could be probably be identified by manual inspection of the code in a very long time. Based on this information, it assesses the risks against the application assets. Furthermore, our inference engine suggests if a protection can mitigate an attack, hence it is able to propose how to protect an application in an automatic way and estimates the residue risk, with minimal user intervention.

For the future, we aim to boost the performance of our approach and support more complex inference rules. We are planning to add the support to suggest an optimal sequence of protections that can be applied to an application, taking into account their synergies (protections that are known to work well when applied on the same assets) and their suggested order of application of the protections.

Acknowledgements. The research leading to these results has received funding from the European Union Seventh Framework Programme (FP7/2007-2013) under grant agreement number 609734.

References

1. Basile, C., Canavese, D., D'Annoville, J., De Sutter, B., Valenza, F.: Automatic discovery of software attacks via backward reasoning. In: Proceedings of SPRO 2015: The 1st International Workshop on Software Protection, pp. 52–58 (2015)
2. Shields, T.: Anti-debugging - a developers view. Technical report, Veracode (2009)
3. Anckaert, B., Madou, M., De Sutter, B., Bus, B.D., Bosschere, K., Preneel, B.: Program obfuscation: a quantitative approach. In: Proceedings of QOP 2007: The 3rd Workshop on Quality of Protection, pp. 15–20 (2007)

4. De Sutter, B.: D2.08 ASPIRE Offline Code Protection Report (2015)
5. Ceccato, M., Preda, M.D., Nagra, J., Collberg, C., Tonella, P.: Barrier slicing for remote software trusting. In: Proceedings of 7th IEEE International Working Conference on Source Code Analysis and Manipulation, pp. 27–36 (2007)
6. Chang, H., Atallah, M.J.: Protecting software code by guards. In: Sander, T. (ed.) DRM 2001. LNCS, vol. 2320, pp. 160–175. Springer, Heidelberg (2002)
7. Falcarin, P., Carlo, S.D., Cabutto, A., Garazzino, N., Barberis, D.: Exploiting code mobility for dynamic binary obfuscation. In: Proceedings of the WorldCIS 2011: 1st World Congress on Internet Security, pp. 114–120 (2011)
8. Collberg, C., Thomborson, C., Low, D.: A taxonomy of obfuscating transformation. Technical report, University of Auckland (1997)
9. Coker, G., Guttman, J., Loscocco, P., Herzog, A., Millen, J., O'Hanlon, B., Ramsdell, J., Segall, A., Sheehy, J., Sniffen, B.: Principles of remote attestation. Int. J. Inf. Secur. **10**, 63–81 (2011)
10. Ekelhart, A., Fenz, S., Neubauer, T.: Ontology-based decision support for information security risk management. In: Proceedings of ICONS 2009: The 4th International Conference on Systems, pp. 80–85 (2009)
11. Fenz, S., Neubauer, T., Accorsi, R., Koslowski, T.: Forisk: formalizing information security risk and compliance management. In: Proceedings of DSN-W 2013: The 3D Conference on Dependable Systems and Networks Workshop, pp. 1–4 (2013)
12. Ekelhart, S.F.A.: Formalizing information security knowledge. In: Proceedings of CCS 2009: The 4th International Symposium on Information, Computer, and Communications Security, pp. 183–194 (2009)
13. Fenz, S., Ekelhart, A., Neubauer, T.: Information security risk management: in which security solutions is it worth investing? Commun. Assoc. Inf. Syst. **28**, 329–356 (2011)
14. Dalton, G.C., Mills, R.F., Colombi, J.M., Raines, R.A.: Analyzing attack trees using generalized stochastic Petri nets. In: Proceedings of IAW 2006: The 4th Information Assurance Workshop, pp. 116–123 (2006)
15. Dahl, O.M., Wolthusen, S.D.: Modeling and execution of complex attack scenarios using interval timed colored Petri nets. In: Proceedings of IWIA 2006: The 4th International Workshop on Information Assurance, pp. 157–168 (2006)
16. Yao, L., Dong, P., Zheng, T., Zhang, H., Du, X., Guizani, M.: Network security analyzing and modeling based on Petri net and attack tree for SDN. In: Proceedings of ICNC 2016: The 5th International Conference on Computing, Networking and Communications, pp. 1–5 (2016)
17. Xie, P., Li, J.H., Ou, X., Liu, P., Levy, R.: Using Bayesian networks for cyber security analysis. In: Proceedings of DSN 2010: The 40th International Conference on Dependable Systems and Networks, pp. 211–220 (2010)
18. Poolsappasit, N., Dewri, R., Ray, I.: Dynamic security risk management using Bayesian attack graphs. IEEE Trans. Dependable Secure Comput. **9**, 61–74 (2012)
19. Steffan, J., Schumacher, M.: Collaborative attack modeling. In: Proceedings of SAC 2002: The 17th ACM Symposium on Applied Computing, pp. 253–259 (2002)
20. Bassett, G.: System and method for cyber security analysis and human behavior prediction Patent US 9292695 (2016)

Runtime Code Polymorphism as a Protection Against Side Channel Attacks

Damien Coroussé[1,2]([✉]), Thierno Barry[1,2], Bruno Robisson[3], Philippe Jaillon[4], Olivier Potin[4], and Jean-Louis Lanet[5]

[1] Univ. Grenoble Alpes, 38000 Grenoble, France
[2] CEA, IST, MINATEC Campus, 38054 Grenoble, France
damien.courousse@cea.fr
[3] CEA-Tech DPACA, Gardanne, France
[4] École Nationale Suprieure des Mines de Saint-Etienne, Saint-Étienne, France
[5] Inria de Rennes, Rennes, France

Abstract. We present a generic framework for runtime code polymorphism, applicable to a broad range of computing platforms including embedded systems with low computing resources (e.g. microcontrollers with few kilo-bytes of memory). Code polymorphism is defined as the ability to change the observable behaviour of a software component without changing its functional properties. In this paper we present the implementation of code polymorphism with runtime code generation, which offers many code transformation possibilities: we describe the use of random register allocation, random instruction selection, instruction shuffling and insertion of noise instructions. We evaluate the effectiveness of our framework against correlation power analysis: as compared to an unprotected implementation of AES where the secret key could be recovered in less than 50 traces in average, in our protected implementation, we increased the number of traces necessary to achieve the same attack by more than $20000\times$. With regards to the state of the art, our implementation shows a moderate impact in terms of performance overhead.

1 Introduction

Side channel attacks are an effective means to recover a secret, by the observation of physical phenomena related to the secured activity. From the knowledge of the program under attack (e.g. the AES cipher), the attacker will try to establish a correlation between the observation traces and hypothesis about the intermediate values used during the secret computation (e.g. the output of the first SBOX computation). The hypothesis that provides the best correlation value is then used to recover the secret (e.g. the value of the AES key). Usually, a few points in the observation traces exhibit good correlation values with the hypothesis, which correspond to the *leakage point*, i.e. the time when the secret is observable during the computation.

© IFIP International Federation for Information Processing 2016
Published by Springer International Publishing Switzerland 2016. All Rights Reserved
S. Foresti and J. Lopez (Eds.): WISTP 2016, LNCS 9895, pp. 136–152, 2016.
DOI: 10.1007/978-3-319-45931-8_9

Two main protection schemes are effective against side channel attacks: *hiding* and *masking*. The key idea of masking is to split the sensitive values of the secured computation in several shares, in order to break the correlation between the observations and the hypothetical intermediate values. To recover the secret key from a masked implementation, and provided that the shares are computed at different times, an attacker needs correlation analysis of higher orders, i.e. analysis involving several observation points simultaneously. However, higher order attacks present a computational complexity that grows exponentially with the order of the attack; they are therefore more difficult to use in practice. Hiding consists in moving the point of information leakage both in time (during the secured activity) and in space (location of the activity on the chip), and in reducing the amplitude of the observable leakage. Indeed, side channel correlation analysis relies on precise spatial and temporal control of the target, and the effectiveness of the attack is strongly correlated to the amount of spatial and temporal variation in the observation signal [13]. Spreading the point of leakage over different times or places over many executions will drastically reduce the effectiveness of the attack, requiring more observation traces and/or more powerful analyses to recover the secret. In practice, robustness against side channel attacks is provided by a combination of hiding and masking countermeasures.

We define polymorphism as the capability to regularly change the behaviour of a secured component at runtime without altering its functional properties. By modifying the temporal and spatial properties of the observations of the attacked target, polymorphism increases the difficulty to perform the correlation analysis used in side channel attacks. Hence, it can be understood as a hiding countermeasure.

Non-deterministic processors [15] achieve what we call *polymorphic execution*, i.e. the shuffled execution of a program from a static binary input residing in program memory. May et al. achieve dynamic instruction shuffling [15] and random register renaming [14]. Bayrak et al. [6] describe an instruction shuffler: a dedicated IP inserted between the processor and the program memory (instruction cache). Nowadays, many Secure Elements integrate similar features in order to de-synchronise observation traces and to decrease the signal to noise ratio. Dedicated hardware designs offer a better security to performance ratio, at the expense of a higher cost. With the fast growing market of the Internet of Things, software-only solutions are appealing since they could be more easily adapted to the wide range of product architectures available, and are upgradeable.

By software means only, [1,10] propose to compile a program that contains several functionally equivalent execution paths, where one of the execution paths is randomly selected at runtime. This approach reduces the overhead on execution time at the expense of an increased program size. Amarilli et al. [3] were the first of our knowledge to exploit compilation of code variants against side channel attacks. A new program version is generated before each execution thanks to a modified static compiler, in order to shuffle instructions and basic blocks at runtime. Their approach is shown to increase the number of traces of DPA on AES by a factor of 20. The work of Agosta et al. [2] is the closest of our work. They present a code morphing runtime framework that involves register renaming, instruction shuffling and the production of semantically equivalent code fragments.

In this paper, polymorphism is implemented with runtime code generation driven by random data. The key idea is to regularly generate new versions of the secured binary code on the target. Each program version is functionally equivalent but has a different implementation, so that each execution would lead to a different observation. The polymorphic code generator is produced by a framework for runtime code generation adapted to the constraints of embedded systems (Sect. 2). We detail the mechanisms used to bring variability in the generated code by selecting random registers, randomly selecting semantically equivalent instructions, reordering instructions, and inserting noise instructions. We provide an experimental evaluation of the effectiveness of our approach against Correlation Power Analysis (CPA) on a software implementation of AES, and show that execution time and code size overheads are compatible with the memory and computation capabilities of constrained embedded targets (Sect. 3). We present related works of our knowledge in Sect. 4, and conclude in Sect. 5.

2   Runtime Code Polymorphism for Embedded Systems

2.1   Overview of deGoal

deGoal is a framework for runtime code generation. Its initial motivation is the use of runtime code specialisation to improve program performance, e.g. execution time, energy consumption or memory footprint. In this section, we first sketch the characteristics of deGoal and then present how we extended it for the purpose of security.

In classical frameworks for runtime code generation such as interpreters and dynamic compilers, the aim is to provide a generic infrastructure for code generation, bounded by the syntactic and semantic definition of a programming language. The generality of such solutions comes at the expense of an important overhead in runtime code generation, both in terms of memory footprint and computing time and computing energy. In deGoal, a different approach is used: code segments (thereafter called *kernels*) are generated and tuned at runtime by ad hoc runtime code generators, called *compilettes*. Each compilette is specialised to produce the machine code of one kernel. Syntactic and semantic analyses are performed at the time of static compilation, and compilettes embed only the processing knowledge that is required for the runtime optimisations selected. As a consequence, compilettes offer very fast code generation (10 to 100 times faster than typical frameworks for runtime code interpretation or dynamic compilation), present a low memory footprint, can run on small microcontroller architectures such as 8/16-bit microcontrollers [5], and are portable [8].

The building and the execution of an application using deGoal consist in the following steps as illustrated in Fig. 1: writing the source code using a mix of

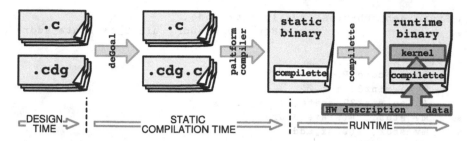

Fig. 1. deGoal workflow: from the writing of application's source code to the execution of a kernel generated at runtime

C source code and of our dedicated cdg language; compiling the binary code of the application and the binary code of compilettes; at runtime, generating the binary code of kernels by compilettes and in the end running the kernels.

Cdg is an assembly-like DSL. From the programmer's perspective, it represents a major paradigm shift: Cdg expressions describe machine code that will be *generated* at runtime instead of instructions to be executed. Compilettes are implemented by using a mix of ANSI C and Cdg expressions. The C language is used to describe the control part of the compilette that will drive code generation, while Cdg expressions perform code generation. The Cdg instruction set includes a variable-length register set, extensible by the programmer. From this high-level instruction set, compilettes map the Cdg expressions to machine code according to (1) the characteristics of the data to process, (2) the characteristics of the execution context at the time of code generation, (3) the hardware capabilities of the target processor, (4) execution time and/or energy consumption performance criteria. In all cases, code generation is fast, produces efficient code, and is applicable to low-resource embedded systems such as micro-controllers [5].

2.2 A Polymorphic SubBytes Function

We introduce in this section the implementation of the SubBytes function of AES as a tutorial introduction to deGoal, before presenting in greater details the internals of runtime code generation. It is also the protected implementation used in our experiment (Sect. 3).

The code generator is implemented with Cdg like any other code generator designed in deGoal. At this stage, polymorphic code generation is a feature provided by the code generation framework but has no need to be explicitly controlled by the programmer. In Listing 1.1, the function gen_subBytes is a standard C function, its implementation being translated from Cdg to plain C source code before the static compilation.

```
1   void gen_subBytes (cdg_insn_t* code,
2                      uint8_t* sbox_addr, uint8_t* state_addr)
3   {
4   #[
5     Begin code Prelude
6     Type uint32 int 32
7     Alloc uint32 state, sbox, i, x, y
8     mv state, #(state_addr)
9     mv sbox, #(sbox_addr)
10    mv i, #(0)
11    loop:
12      lb x, @(state+i)   //  x := state[i]
13      lb y, @(sbox+x)    //  y := sbox[x]
14      sb @(state+i), y   //  state[i] := y
15      add i, i, #(1)
16      bneq loop, i, #(16)
17    rtn
18    End
19  ]#;
20  }
```

deGoal allows to mix Cdg expressions for code generation, enclosed between the delimiters #[and]#, and C code. Moreover, C expressions, enclosed in #( ), can be inserted inside Cdg expressions; they will be evaluated at the time of code generation, i.e. at the time the compilette is executed. The program code of the SubBytes routine is written in a memory buffer at the address contained in the variable code (lines 1 and 5). Lines 6–7 declare the instantiation of typed variables that will be mapped at the time of runtime code generation to physical registers. The variables state and sbox store respectively the address of the AES state and the address of the Sbox (C variables state_addr and sbox_addr line 2). A label (loop, line 11) defines the starting location the loop over the 16 state bytes. The variable i stores the loop index. It is initialised at line 10 and used as an offset value for the load and store instructions, respectively at lines 12 and 14, where the notation @(a+k) (lines 12 to 14) denotes an indirect memory access to the address stored in the variable a, offseted by an address variable k. The Sbox substitution is produced at line 14, where the temporary variable y is loaded with the memory contents at address sbox offseted by x. The Cdg instruction rtn (line 17) generates the termination code of the SubBytes routine, and the Cdg instruction End (line 18) terminates the code generation: it flushes the live instructions remaining in the instruction scheduler (Sect. 2.3), and emits the machine code of backward branches for which the branch destination address cannot be calculated during the first code generation pass (not detailed in this paper).

2.3 Implementation of Code Polymorphism with deGoal

In this work, we re-target the original purpose of deGoal in order to focus on security aspects: we exploit the flexibility provided by deGoal for runtime code

Input: the list of available registers *free*
Output: the updated list of available registers *free*
Output: the id of the physical register allocated *reg*
▷ Get a random register among the list of available registers
$l \leftarrow$ Length$(free)$
$i \leftarrow$ Rand$(0, l - 1)$
$reg \leftarrow free[i]$
▷ Remove register i from the list of free registers
$free \leftarrow$ Delete$(free, i)$
Algorithm 1. Random Register Allocation

generation to achieve runtime code polymorphism. A program code produced by the polymorphic code generator is thereafter called *polymorphic instance*.

Register Allocation. In dynamic compilers, instruction selection and instruction scheduling are usually performed before register allocation [12]. Despite allocation techniques used in dynamic compilers, such as linear scan [17], provide a reduced computational cost as compared to graph colouring usually used in static compilers, they are still out of reach of the computational power available in the platforms that we target. Hence, in a compilette, register allocation is done first, before instruction scheduling, by using a greedy algorithm (Algorithm 1). Our purpose is to lighten the pressure on instruction selection and instruction scheduling: if register allocation is done first, it becomes possible to perform instruction scheduling from a much simpler intermediate representation: our allocator simply needs to maintain a list of the free registers available.

Instruction Selection. Instruction selection is performed after register allocation for the motivations detailed previously. Instruction selection is done at the level of Cdg expressions: each expression can be mapped to one or more machine instructions depending on the target processor architecture and code generation options (e.g. favour code compactness or code execution time). Instruction selection is implemented with switch ... case segments driven by random values. For the purpose of achieving code polymorphism, we introduce supplementary variants to provide more opportunities for polymorphism. The semantic equivalences used in the context of the experiment presented in this paper, that are possibly selected by instruction selection are described below (r denotes a random value):

```
c := a xor b <=> c := ((a xor r) xor b) xor r
c := a xor b <=> c := (a or b) xor (a and b)
c := a - b   <=> k := 1 ; c:= (a + k) + (not b)
c := a - b   <=> c := ((a + r) - b) - r
```

We emphasize on the fact that, despite the number of semantic variants introduced for random instruction selection is low in the current experiment, adding

Input: the instruction buffer B (a circular buffer)
Input: the instruction to insert I
Output: B

▷ look for insertion slots, from the last buffer instruction
$pos \leftarrow \text{Tail}(B)$
while I *has no data dependence with* $B[pos]$ **do**
| $pos \leftarrow \text{Prev}(B[pos])$
end
▷ randomly insert the new instruction
$i \leftarrow \text{Rand}(pos, \text{Tail}(B))$
$B \leftarrow$ insert I at position i in B
▷ flush the first instruction if B is full
if $\text{Prev}(\text{Head}(B))$ *is equal to* $\text{Tail}(B)$ **then**
| emit instruction at $\text{Head}(B)$
| $\text{Head}(B) \leftarrow \text{Next}(\text{Head}(B))$
end

Algorithm 2. Instruction Shuffling

new instruction variants will only have an impact on the memory footprint of the code generation library embedded onto the target but not on the execution time of code generation. In other words, adding more selection variants will grow the size of the `switch ... case` segments used in instruction selection, but does not impact the performance of branching to one of the cases from the `switch` expression.

Instruction Scheduling. The process of instruction selection, presented above, produces instructions in a bounded ordered instruction buffer that behaves like a FIFO. At this stage, the instruction buffer contains the machine instruction encodings, and the description of *defs* and *uses* registers (i.e. modified and read registers, respectively). The instruction buffer is implemented with doubled-chained lists. This clearly has a strong impact on the manipulation cost of the data structure, but we have chosen this implementation to maximise the number of insertion opportunities versus execution efficiency. The experimental section shows that the performance of polymorphic code generation remains good.

In traditional compilers, instruction scheduling aims at improving the performance of code execution: machine instructions are ordered in program memory in order to minimise execution time, in particular the number of processor idle cycles. The difficulty of scheduling lies in finding a possibly optimal ordering of machine instructions without breaking the semantics of the original source program. To achieve this, resource constraints, control-dependence and data-dependence need to be considered.

In the case of code polymorphism, our aim is to exploit scheduling opportunities to generate many variants of the same source program, all functionally equivalent and semantically correct. Hence, code performance is only a secondary matter, and we consider resource constraints that impact code correctness, but not those that only impact program performance. Instruction scheduling is performed in one pass (Algorithm 2): each time a new instruction is inserted in the instruction buffer, first the list of possible insertion slots is computed, by comparing the defs and uses of the inserted instruction and of the instructions already stored in the buffer. Next, the insertion position is randomly selected among the list of insertion slots previously identified. If no insertion slot was found, the new instruction is appended at the end of the instruction buffer. If the instruction buffer is full, its first instruction is emitted in program memory to free one instruction slot.

Pipeline hazards [16], which only affect program performance but not program correctness, are considered in our scheduling policy. Our main purpose is to lighten the computational cost of scheduling, but this choice has an other interesting effect: processor stalls, which are an observable effect of pipeline hazards on the execution of a program, are likely to add a supplementary source of temporal variation in the observation of program execution. Still in the aim of fast code generation, control-dependence constraints are simply handled by considering control instructions as scheduling barriers: when a control instruction is met, the whole instruction buffer is flushed.

Insertion of Noise Instructions. Noise instructions are appended to the end of the instruction buffer *before* the insertion of a new instruction (Sect. 2.3). n noise instructions are inserted with probability p, where n is in a configurable uniform discrete distribution $[1; N]$. If needed, extra registers are randomly selected in the list of free registers. If no register is available, registers are randomly selected, pushed and popped on the stack before and after use. Several kinds of instructions can be inserted: core arithmetic instructions that execute in one processor cycle (e.g. integer operations add or sub) or in several processor cycles (e.g. multiply and accumulate mla on ARM Cortex-M cores) and memory accesses to a data table possibly provided by the user (e.g. the SBOX lookup table).

Code Generation Interval. It is related to the generation frequency of new polymorphic instances relatively to the number of executions (Eq. 1). ω is a value with no unit in $[1; +\infty[$. When $\omega = 1$, a new polymorphic instance is generated before each execution; if $\omega \to +\infty$, a polymorphic instance is generated only once at startup, which is equivalent to the use of statically generated code. Our hypothesis is that, the closer ω is to 1, the more difficult a physical attack should be, because of the lower probability that the observation of two executions will appear correlated. On the other hand, the overhead incurred by code generation is more important as ω is smaller.

$$\omega = \frac{\text{nb. executions}}{\text{nb. code generations}} \tag{1}$$

3   Experimental Evaluation

3.1   Experimental Setup

We used the STM32VLDISCOVERY evaluation kit from STMicroelectronics. The board is fitted with a Cortex-M3 core running at 24 MHz, provides only 128 kB of flash memory and 8 kB of RAM, and is not equipped with hardware security protections. All the binary programs are produced from the arm-none-eabi GNU/gcc toolchain in version 4.8.1 provided by Code Sourcery, using the compilation options -O3 -static -mthumb -mcpu=cortex-m3. Therefore, we compare our implementation with the fastest reference implementation that we could obtain from the target compiler.

The side-channel traces were obtained with a 2208A PicoScope, which features a 200 MHz bandwidth and a vertical resolution of 8 bits. We use an EM probe RF-B 3-2 from Langer, and a PA 303 preamplifier from Langer. The sampling acquisition is performed at 500 Msample/s over a window of 10000 samples.

Our reference implementation is an unprotected 8-bit implementation of AES that follows the NIST specification, and all the round functions are generated at runtime, in RAM, by a polymorphic code generator specialised for this implementation of AES, as introduced in Sect. 2. All the polymorphic mechanisms presented above are activated in the code generator. The probability of inserting noise instructions is set to $p = 1/8$, and the number of inserted instructions n is selected in the uniform discrete distribution $[1; 8]$. A new polymorphic instance can be generated every $\omega = \{1, 10, 100, 1000, 10000\}$ executions of AES, but for the side channel attack we use the shortest code generation interval, $\omega = 1$.

3.2   Model of Attack

We perform the attack on the output of the SubBytes function in the first AES round. On the contrary to most first order CPA analysis where the synchronisation point is put at the beginning of the AES encryption, we consider the case where the attacker is able to create a synchronisation point at the beginning of the SubBytes function. To ease the temporal alignment of the measurement traces, a trigger signal is generated via a GPIO pin on the board, held high during the execution of the SubBytes function. Using this setup, the security evaluation is performed with stricter conditions since the execution variability of the polymorphic AddRoundKey function does not contribute to the variations in the observation traces.

The code generator itself could be also the target of attacks even it does not access to the value of the secret key. Such attacks are however out of the scope of this paper and are left for future works.

3.3   Correlation Power Analysis

We perform a first order CPA against both unprotected and protected implementations. We model the electromagnetic emission with the Hamming weight

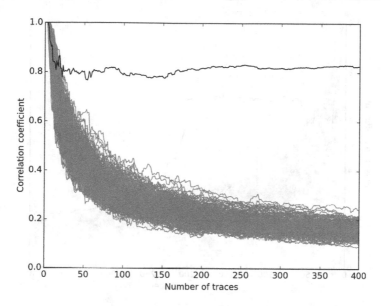

Fig. 2. Correlation values from the CPA attack on the unprotected AES

of one byte of the output of the first SubBytes function. The analysis computes the sample estimation r of Pearson's correlation coefficient ρ between each trace and the model, for each possible hypothetical value of the involved key part.

Figure 2 presents the results of our CPA attack on the unprotected implementation. The correct key distinguishes from all the other hypothetical key values as soon as 35 traces with correlation values above 0.8. This result validates the experimental setup and the choice of the Hamming weight model used in the correlation analysis. As an illustration example of the impact of polymorphism, we show in Fig. 3 the results of a CPA attack on our polymorphic implementation, for a code generation interval of $\omega = 200$, i.e. far above the number of traces necessary to recover the AES key on the unprotected implementation. In this case, the first 200 traces are obtained from the execution of the same polymorphic instance of AES, which explains why the correlation value of the correct key clearly distinguishes from the other key hypotheses. After 200 executions, a new polymorphic instance is generated and executed for the next 200 executions. The impact of polymorphism on the correlation traces is clearly visible: the correlation of the correct key hypothesis suddenly decreases after 200 traces. After 300 traces, the correct key hypothesis is no longer distinguishable from the other key hypothesis because the correlation analysis merges the execution traces from two AES instances that behave differently. This also illustrates the fact that, in practice, the code generation interval ω must have a value strictly below the number of traces required to recover the key from an unprotected implementation. This setting is however strongly depending on the nature of the target and the practicability of the attack on an unprotected implementation.

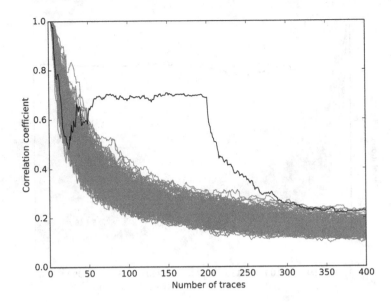

Fig. 3. Correlation values from the CPA attack on the polymorphic AES, $\omega = 200$

When a new polymorphic instance is generated after each execution ($\omega = 1$), 100000 traces are necessary to recover the key with a success rate of 50 % (Fig. 4). A success rate of 100 % is reached after 120000 traces.

3.4 Execution Time Overhead

To estimate the cost added by our protection to a reference implementation, we measure the execution time overhead k (Eq. 2), where t_{ref}, t_{gen} and t_{poly} respectively denote the average execution time of the unprotected reference implementation, the average execution time of the polymorphic runtime code generation and the average execution time of the polymorphic instance. Our measure of the execution time overhead takes into account the increase of the execution time due to the execution of the polymorphic instance (which has a suboptimal code as compared to the reference unprotected implementation) and due to runtime code generation. In this measurement, we consider that the overhead incurred by code generation is distributed over ω runs.

$$k = \frac{t_{gen} + \omega \times t_{poly}}{\omega \times t_{ref}} \qquad (2)$$

Table 1 compares the execution times of the unprotected AES and several variants of the polymorphic AES. In this section, we name the *full polymorphic AES* our implementation where all the round functions are protected with polymorphism. The unprotected version executes in 5320 processor cycles. We observe the execution time of the polymorphic versions over 1024 runs. The full polymorphic AES executes in 10487 to 13696 processor cycles (average

12211 cycles). Table 1 also illustrates the fact that, if only one round function is protected with polymorphism (AddRoundKey or SubBytes), the execution time overhead is reduced. The execution time of the unprotected version is perfectly stable over measurements because of the relative simplicity of the microarchitecture of our experiment target. However, in contrast, the execution time of the polymorphic versions presents important variations. Considering the stability of the execution time of the unprotected version, this variability can only be accounted to implementation variations in each polymorphic instance.

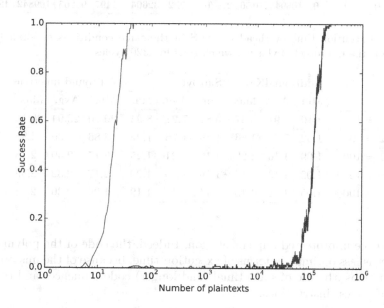

Fig. 4. Success rate of the CPA attack on the unprotected (green, leftmost) and the full polymorphic implementation (blue, rightmost), $\omega = 1$. (Color figure online)

Table 2 presents the overheads k computed for the execution time measurements detailed in Table 1, for different values of the code generation interval ω. For a full polymorphic AES, in the case a new polymorphic instance is generated before *each* execution of AES ($\omega = 1$), we measure an average overhead of 20.10 (worst case 26.16). However, the overhead quickly decreases when the code generation interval is increased, because the cost of runtime code generation is distributed over several executions of the same polymorphic instance. Considering the number of traces required to recover the key from the unprotected AES, a code generation interval of $\omega = 10$ could be an exploitable version. In this case, the execution time overhead is only of 4.36 in average (worst case 4.85).

Table 2 also illustrates the cost incurred by the polymorphic instances *only*. For large code generation intervals (e.g. $\omega = 10000$), the contribution of runtime code generation becomes negligible in the overall overhead, i.e. the overhead only represents the cost of executing the polymorphic instances as compared to

Table 1. Execution times (in cycles, measured for 1024 executions of each configuration) of the AES function (t_{exe}) and of the code generator (t_{gen}) for the unprotected version (Unprotected), the AES with a polymorphic AddRoundKey function only (AddRoundKey), the AES with a polymorphic SubBytes function only (SubBytes), and all four round functions polymorphic (All round functions).

	Unprotected			AddRoundKey			SubBytes			All round functions		
	Min.	Avg.	Max.	Min.	Avg.	Max.	Min.	Avg.	Max.	Min.	Avg.	Max.
t_{exe}	5320	5320	5320	5565	5977	6269	5850	6090	6340	10487	12211	13696
t_{gen}	0	0	0	10894	20166	27970	24922	32604	41497	95265	109842	127269

Table 2. Execution time overhead for AES in the same conditions as Table 1. The reference is the unprotected version, which runs in 5320 cycles.

	AddRoundKey			SubBytes			All round functions		
	Min.	Avg.	Max.	Min.	Avg.	Max.	Min.	Avg.	Max.
$\omega = 1$	3.16	4.91	6.37	5.81	7.27	8.94	20.10	22.94	26.16
$\omega = 10$	1.32	1.50	1.66	1.59	1.76	1.92	3.86	4.36	4.85
$\omega = 100$	1.09	1.16	1.22	1.16	1.21	1.25	2.17	2.50	2.78
$\omega = 1000$	1.09	1.13	1.18	1.16	1.15	1.20	2.17	2.32	2.59
$\omega = 10000$	1.05	1.12	1.18	1.11	1.15	1.19	1.99	2.30	2.58

the reference unprotected implementation. Indeed, the code of the polymorphic instances is less optimal, in terms of execution time, because of the mis-ordering of instructions, the use of suboptimal (and longer) code sequences and the execution of useless instructions.

3.5 Memory Footprint

Table 3 reports the memory footprint of our work, including the size of the code generators and the memory size reserved for code generation. The full polymorphic implementation presents an extra overhead of 16 KB of program size, but it is possible to reduce the memory footprint by partially applying polymorphism to AES: if only AddRoundKey and SubBytes are polymorphic, the memory overhead is of 8 KB only.

4   Related Works

The work of Agosta et al. [2] is the closest of our work: they were the first to gather in a same runtime code transformation framework the use of semantically equivalent code sequences, random register allocation, instruction shuffling and array permutations as a protection against side channel attacks. The code transformations are applied to the 64 xor instructions of a 32-bit implementation of AES based on OpenSSL. Due to the higher number of traces required to extract the key from an unprotected implementation (11600), the exploitable code generation intervals are higher (between 100 and 3000) than in our work. The execution times of the polymorphic code instance and of the code generator are respectively 1.07× and 392.5× the execution time of the unprotected AES, and they report an overhead of 5× for $\omega = 100$. In our work, all the instructions all the AES program are protected with polymorphism, where the overhead is only of 2.50× in average for $\omega = 100$; in the worst case $\omega = 1$, code generation is 23.9× the execution time of the reference unprotected AES.

Table 3. Memory footprint (in bytes) of complete programs running the unprotected AES and the polymorphic AES in the same variants as presented in Table 1

	Text	Data	Bss	Total
Unprotected	6144	40	772	6956
AddRoundKey only	8128	56	2948	11132
SubBytes only	7540	56	2948	10544
AddRoundKey + SubBytes	10964	88	3980	15032
Full polymorphic AES	16984	88	6028	23100

Other works present the design of polymorphic programs without intervention of runtime code generation, by random selection of functionally equivalent execution paths. Boulet et al. [7] describe the protection of Java Cards against side channel reverse engineering. The method applies to interpreters in virtual machines; it describes the random association and selection of functionally equivalent codes in the interpreter of the virtual machine. As compared to our work, this work does not use random register allocation, and instruction shuffling between code sections. Similarly, Crane et al. [10] propose to randomly switch the execution between different copies of program fragments to protect programs against cache side-channel attacks. The fragment variants are generated offline by a modified compiler, involving the insertion of nop instructions and random memory accesses. During program execution, the fragments are dynamically selected by trampolines with table-based random indirect branches. Their implementation targets a general-purpose multi-core desktop computer. Agosta et al. use a modified LLVM toolchain compiler to target ARM Cortex-M4 based microcontrollers [1]. Each instruction of the secured program section is replaced with several functionally equivalent instruction sequences. In addition, a masking scheme is applied for memory accesses and register spills. They report a performance overhead of 11× for the same cipher AES-S than in our study, however with code size overhead of 9×.

The execution of noise instructions (also called dummy instructions) is another known technique to introduce random time delays in order to mitigate side-channel attacks. In software, the execution of dummy instructions is achieved either by branching to a dedicated routine from predefined locations in the program (e.g. before, during and after the part of the code to protect) or by the triggering of a random delay interrupt. The routine for example executes a loop that decrements to zero the value of a randomly initialised register [9]. Hidden Markov models [11] or pattern matching [18] are effective techniques to remove in the observation traces the parts corresponding to the execution or dummy instructions, or to create synchronisation points in the traces to cancel the misalignment created by random delays. However, these analyses rely on the fact that the inserted temporal noise presents a distinctive signature (for example the header of the interrupt handler). Ambrose et al. [4] propose to randomly insert a limited set of predefined instructions, similar to regular code instructions, that could also use a randomly selected register. They argue that such instructions, which modify the internal state of the processor, are of the same nature than the rest of the program instructions, hence causing higher power variations due to bit flips in registers. One of the contributions of our work is to extend this idea one step further: the noise instructions inserted in the program are of the same nature than real program instructions (arithmetic operations, memory operations, etc.), and can target one or several free registers randomly selected. Furthermore, thanks to runtime code generation, we are able to better weave the noise instructions with the rest of the program as compared to the state-of-the art technique for dummy instructions.

5   Conclusion

We have presented a framework that achieves runtime code polymorphism as a generic protection against side channel attacks. Our implementation relies on a lightweight runtime code generation framework suitable for embedded systems, which usually out of reach of runtime code generation tools such as Just-In-Time compilers because of their low computing and memory resources. To the best of our knowledge, it is the first time that polymorphic runtime code generation could be achieved with such limited computing resources (8 kB of RAM and 128 kB of flash memory), with acceptable runtime overheads. Nevertheless, our implementation is applicable to cryptosystems and also to other software components that require some protections against physical attacks (e.g. pincode management, bootloaders, etc.), on a large range of computing platforms [8].

On our experimentation platform, we observed that the key can be recovered in less than 50 traces on an unprotected AES. However, on many real-life platforms, a side channel attack may require more traces to successfully extract a cipher key, even on an unprotected implementation: often than 10000 or 100000 traces. This means that, in practice, polymorphism can be effectively used with greater code generation intervals, so that the overhead of our approach becomes more tractable. Other design parameters, such as the parameters that control the insertion of noise instructions, will have an important impact both on the security margin and on the execution time and code size overheads.

Finally, we emphasise on the fact that polymorphism is not an end *per se*, but instead that it should be combined with other state of the art protections (e.g. masking). Provided the genericness of our approach and the lightness of our implementation, we consider that its integration in a more global security scheme is practical.

Acknowledgements. This work was partially funded by the COGITO project, funded by the French National Research Agency (ANR) as part of the program Digital Engineering and Security (INS-2013), under grant agreement ANR-13-INSE-0006-01.

References

1. Agosta, G., Barenghi, A., Pelosi, G., Scandale, M.: The MEET approach: Securing cryptographic embedded software against side channel attacks. IEEE TCAD **34**(8), 1320–1333 (2015)
2. Agosta, G., Barenghi, A., Pelosi, G.: A code morphing methodology to automate power analysis countermeasures. In: DAC, pp. 77–82. ACM (2012)
3. Amarilli, A., Müller, S., Naccache, D., Page, D., Rauzy, P., Tunstall, M.: Can code polymorphism limit information leakage? In: Ardagna, C.A., Zhou, J. (eds.) WISTP 2011. LNCS, vol. 6633, pp. 1–21. Springer, Heidelberg (2011)
4. Ambrose, J., Ragel, R., Parameswaran, S.: Rijid: random code injection to mask power analysis based side channel attacks. In: DAC, pp. 489–492 (2007)
5. Aracil, C., Couroussé, D.: Software acceleration of floating-point multiplication using runtime code generation. In: ICEAC, pp. 18–23 (2013)
6. Bayrak, A.G., Velickovic, N., Ienne, P., Burleson, W.: An architecture-independent instruction shuffler to protect against side-channel attacks. TACO **8**(4), 1–19 (2012)
7. Boulet, F., Barthe, M., Le, T.H.: Protection of applets against hidden-channel analysis, WO/2012/085482 (2013)
8. Charles, H.P., Couroussé, D., Lomller, V., Endo, F., Gauguey, R.: deGoal a tool to embed dynamic code generators into applications. In: Cohen, A. (ed.) CC 2014. LNCS, vol. 8409, pp. 107–112. Springer, Heidelberg (2014)
9. Coron, J.-S., Kizhvatov, I.: Analysis and improvement of the random delay countermeasure of CHES 2009. In: Mangard, S., Standaert, F.-X. (eds.) CHES 2010. LNCS, vol. 6225, pp. 95–109. Springer, Heidelberg (2010)
10. Crane, S., Homescu, A., Brunthaler, S., Larsen, P., Franz, M.: Thwarting cache side-channel attacks through dynamic software diversity. In: Network And Distributed System Security Symposium, NDSS. vol. 15 (2015)
11. Durvaux, F., Renauld, M., Standaert, F.-X., van Oldeneel tot Oldenzeel, L., Veyrat-Charvillon, N.: Efficient removal of random delays from embedded software implementations using hidden markov models. In: Mangard, S. (ed.) CARDIS 2012. LNCS, vol. 7771, pp. 123–140. Springer, Heidelberg (2013)
12. Kotzmann, T., Wimmer, C., Mössenböck, H., Rodriguez, T., Russell, K., Cox, D.: Design of the Java Hotspot client compiler for Java 6. TACO **5**(1), 7: 1–7: 32 (2008)
13. Mangard, S., Oswald, E., Popp, T.: Power Analysis Attacks: Revealing the Secrets of Smart Cards. Springer, Heidelberg (2007)
14. May, D., Muller, H.L., Smart, N.P.: Random register renaming to foil DPA. In: Koç, Ç.K., Naccache, D., Paar, C. (eds.) CHES 2001. LNCS, vol. 2162, p. 28. Springer, Heidelberg (2001)
15. May, D., Muller, H.L., Smart, N.P.: Non-deterministic processors. In: Varadharajan, V., Mu, Y. (eds.) ACISP 2001. LNCS, vol. 2119, p. 115. Springer, Heidelberg (2001)

16. Patterson, D.A., Hennessy, J.L.: Computer Organization and Design: The Hardware/Software Interface, 4th edn. Morgan Kaufmann (2011)
17. Poletto, M., Sarkar, V.: Linear scan register allocation. ACM Trans. Program. Lang. Syst. **21**(5), 895–913 (1999)
18. Strobel, D., Paar, C.: An efficient method for eliminating random delays in power traces of embedded software. In: Kim, H. (ed.) ICISC 2011. LNCS, vol. 7259, pp. 48–60. Springer, Heidelberg (2012)

Analysis of a Code-Based Countermeasure Against Side-Channel and Fault Attacks

Guillaume Barbu and Alberto Battistello[(✉)]

Oberthur Technologies, Security Group, Cité Photonique, Batiment ELNATH,
1er étage 1, allée des Lumières, 33600 Pessac, France
{g.barbu,a.battistello}@oberthur.com

Abstract. The design of robust countermeasures against Side-Channel Analysis or Fault Attacks is always a challenging task. At WISTP'14, a single countermeasure designed to thwart in the same effort both kinds of attacks was presented. This countermeasure is based on coding theory and consists in a specific encoding of the manipulated data acting in the same time as a random masking and an error detector. In this paper, we prove that this countermeasure does not meet the ambitious objectives claimed by its authors. Indeed, we exhibit a bias in the distribution of the masked values that can be exploited to retrieve the sensitive data from the observed side-channel leakage. Going further, we show that this bias is inherent to the nature of the encoding and that randomizing the code itself can be useful to reduce the bias but cannot completely fix the scheme.

Keywords: Side-channel analysis · Fault attacks · Coding theory · Countermeasure · AES

1 Introduction

Since the introduction of side-channel analysis and fault attacks against cryptographic implementations in the late 90s, the scientific community, both academic and industrial, has engaged a great effort in designing robust and efficient countermeasures to counteract these attacks. Usually, each countermeasure is designed to tackle only one of these two kinds of attacks. For instance, boolean masking [1] of key-dependent data is meant to avoid information leakage through a side-channel medium. On the other hand, time-redundant or data-redundant computations are implemented to detect fault injections during the execution of the algorithm.

Following the idea first introduced in [2] the authors of [3] proposed at WISTP'14 a new countermeasure named ODSM (for Orthogonal Direct Sum Masking) based on coding theory and showed how it could be applied to protect an AES implementation. Besides the application of code-based techniques, one of the novelty of ODSM is that the same countermeasure aims at defeating both side-channel analysis (SCA) and fault attacks (FA) at once.

Published by Springer International Publishing Switzerland 2016. All Rights Reserved
S. Foresti and J. Lopez (Eds.): WISTP 2016, LNCS 9895, pp. 153–168, 2016.
DOI: 10.1007/978-3-319-45931-8_10

By introducing a random mask in the encoding of a sensitive data, ODSM aims at decorrelating the side-channel leakage from the value of the sensitive variable. At the same time, by taking advantage of the error detection capability of the code, the scheme also allows to control the integrity of the manipulated data and eventually to detect induced faults.

Although the proposed countermeasure is pretty elegant from a theoretic point of view and that a proof of security is presented in the original article, we demonstrate in the following that such a proposal fails at ensuring resistance against SCA.

This article is organized as follows. Section 2 recalls some basic concepts of coding theory and defines some notions regarding side-channel attacks. Section 3 introduces the ODSM countermeasure described in [3] and its application to the AES. Section 4 gives the result of our analysis of the masking scheme with regard to SCA. In Section 5 we provide further evidence of the insecurity of the scheme by mounting a template attack against a real device. Section 6 proposes some improvements of the countermeasure to achieve a better resistance against SCA while preserving the FA resistance. Finally Sect. 7 presents concluding remarks and future works.

2   Preliminaries

This section gives the elementary notions required to both apprehend the potential of an attacker and follow the masking scheme design of [3].

2.1   Passive Side-Channel Analysis

Previously used by several intelligence agencies, but formally introduced to the academic community by Kocher *et al.* only in 1996, Side-Channel Attacks have revolutionized the world of cryptography [4,5]. In particular it is now common knowledge that the observation of physical interactions between a hardware executing a cryptographic algorithm and the surrounding environment may allow retrieving values of internally manipulated sensitive variables. Simple Power Analysis, consists in retrieving a secret value by simple observation of the power consumption of the device during a process depending on this secret value. As an example, on naive RSA implementations, the execution time may leak critical information on the value of secret key bits.

More complex attacks like Differential Power Analysis (DPA) make use of the statistical dependency between the observed interactions and the sensitive values. Concretely, in order to retrieve the secret key of an embedded AES, an attacker asks the ciphering of several known messages and observes the power consumption of the processor during the execution of the algorithm. After collecting enough observations, by correlating the messages and the power consumptions the attacker can retrieve the secret AES key on unprotected implementations.

Finally, Higher-Order Side-Channel Analysis (HO-SCA) consists in the higher order statistics analysis of several leakages in order to retrieve the corresponding key. SPA, DPA and all their variants have been used to break the security of many algorithms [6,7], the obvious effect was the design of efficient and effective countermeasures. While many ideas have been found [1,8,9], it remains hard and very costly to provide efficient countermeasures that guarantee security versus high-order attacks.

In the following we present the countermeasure of [3] which aims at thwarting both faults and side-channel analysis at once. The countermeasure makes use of results from coding theory which we recall in the next section.

2.2   Notions of Coding Theory

The following gives the few definitions and notations necessary to ease the reading and understanding of the masking scheme presented in Sect. 3.

Definition 1 (Binary Linear Code). *A binary linear code C of length n and dimension k is a linear subspace of dimension k of the vector space $\mathbb{F}_2^n$.*

A word of the code C is then a vector w such that $w \in C$.

Definition 2 (Supplement of vector space). *The supplement of the vector space C in $\mathbb{F}_2^n$ is the set of vectors D such that $C \oplus D = \mathbb{F}_2^n$, where $\oplus$ denotes the direct sum of two vector spaces.*

An element z in $\mathbb{F}_2^n$ can thus be decomposed uniquely as the sum of two elements c and d, respectively in C and D:

$$z = c \oplus d \tag{1}$$

Definition 3 (Generating matrix). *The vectors of the basis of a linear code C forms the generating matrix of C.*

In the following we will denote respectively by G and H the generating matrices of C and D. Then every element of C (resp. D) can be written uniquely as xG (resp. yH) for some x (resp. y) in $\mathbb{F}_2^{dim(C)}$ (resp. $\mathbb{F}_2^{dim(D)}$) and (1) can be rewritten as:

$$z = xG \oplus yH \tag{2}$$

Definition 4 (Dual code). *The dual code of C is the linear code $C^\perp = \{w \in \mathbb{F}_2^n | \forall c \in C,\ c \cdot w = 0\}$.*

Definition 5 (Parity matrix). *The parity matrix of C is the generating matrix of $C^\perp$.*

In the case where $C^\perp = D$, it comes straightforwardly that the dimension of D is $n - k$ if the dimension of C is k. Also the parity matrix of C is H.

Finally, we recall the proposition from [3] stating a necessary and sufficient condition to have C and $C^\perp$ supplementary in $\mathbb{F}_2^n$:

Proposition 1. *Without loss of generality (a permutation of coordinates might be necessary), we can assume that the generating matrix of C is systematic, and thus takes the form $[I_k \| M]$, where I_k is the $k \times k$ identity matrix. The supplementary D of C is equal to $C^\perp$ iff the matrix $I_k \oplus M M^T$ is invertible.*

This proposition is necessary for the construction of the masking scheme, as will be explained in the following section.

3   Orthogonal Direct Sum Masking and Its Application to AES

In this section, we introduce the Orthogonal Direct Sum Masking (ODSM) countermeasure as it was defined in [3]. Then we detail how the authors apply it in the case of an AES implementation.

3.1   Related Works

In [2], Bringer *et al.* introduced a masking scheme based on a specific encoding of the sensitive data and the corresponding mask. Following this scheme, the masking of sensitive data x with the random quantity m is obtained by computing $z = xF \oplus mG$, where:

- G is a generator matrix of the binary linear code C of length n, dimension k and minimum distance d
- F is a $k \times n$ matrix with k rows in $\{0,1\}^n$ all linearly independent of each other and not belonging to the binary linear code C.

Recovering x from the encoded word z can be achieved by multiplying z by the parity matrix of C: $zH^T = xFH^T \oplus mGH^T = xFH^T$. The authors then describe an application of this scheme to the AES.

However, as pointed out by Moradi in [10] certain limitations exist when choosing the matrix F in order to retrieve the sensitive value x from xFH^T. Namely, one should ensure that the application $x \mapsto xKH^T$ is bijective, *ie.* $(KH^T)^{-1}$ shall exist.

In addition, the author stresses that the application of the scheme to the AES requires a mask correction at each round of the cipher algorithm.

Finally, the work of Azzi *et al.* in [11] adapts the ODSM scheme to enhance the fault detection capability through non-linear functions. However this comes at the cost of additional computations with regards to the side-channel resistance property.

3.2   Orthogonal Direct Sum Masking

As previously stated, the construction of the ODSM lies on the fact that for the considered code C, we have $C^\perp \oplus C = \mathbb{F}_2^n$. Indeed, in this case we have $G \cdot H^T = 0$

and H is the parity matrix of $\mathcal{C}$. Consequently, in (2) we can recover x and y from z:

$$x = zG^T(GG^T)^{-1} \qquad (3)$$
$$y = zH^T(HH^T)^{-1} \qquad (4)$$

The principle of the masking scheme consists in representing a sensitive k-bit data x by a n-bit data z according to (2), where y is an $(n-k)$-bit random mask.

The sensitive value x can be easily recovered from z by using (3). In addition, the integrity of the manipulated data z can be verified as often as required by checking the integrity of the mask y thanks to (4), which provides the security against fault injection.

Based on this principle, the authors suggest to perform computation within the encoded/masked representation. Actually they show how applying operations on the sensitive value x can be achieved by applying associated operations on the encoded value z. To reach this goal, they split the different operations required into three categories and show how to proceed in each one:

2-operand Operations. In this case, they focus their attention on the xor operation. Actually this case is quite straightforward since it is only necessary to encode the operand and perform the xor. For instance, supposing we need to xor a round key k_i to x, we would have to compute $z' = z \oplus k_i G$. And we can check that $x \oplus k_i$ is computed within the masking scheme:

$$z' = z \oplus k_i G = (x \oplus k_i)G \oplus yH \qquad (5)$$

Binary Linear Operations. Let L be the matrix corresponding to the desired binary linear operation, then they suggest to construct a so-called *masked* binary linear operation whose corresponding matrix L' is constructed as follows:

$$L' = G^T(GG^T)^{-1}LG \oplus H^T(HH^T)^{-1}H \qquad (6)$$

And we can check again that xL is correctly computed within the masking scheme when zL' is computed.

Nonlinear Transformations. In this case, a *masked* version S' of the transformation S can be computed:

$$\forall z \in \mathbb{F}_2^n, \ S'(z) = S(zG^T(GG^T)^{-1})G \oplus zH^T(HH^T)^{-1}H \qquad (7)$$

$S(x)$ is correctly obtained within the masking scheme when computing $S'(z)$.

Following these guidelines, the authors claim that various computations can be carried out within the coset $\mathcal{C} \oplus d$ of the linear code $\mathcal{C}$, with d a mask randomly chosen in $\mathcal{D} = \mathcal{C}^\perp$.

3.3   ODSM in Practice: Application to the AES

The ODSM can be applied, in particular, to an implementation of the AES. For that purpose, the authors consider the 128-bit version of the cipher and propose to use the binary linear code of parameters [16,8,5] (meaning $n = 16$ and $k = 8$) which has a supplementary dual in $\mathbb{F}_2^{16}$.[1] Indeed, once the initial state has been encoded, the different operations of the AES can be straightfordwarly constructed as previously described.

AddRoundKey. The round key bytes only need to be encoded before being added to the encoded state: $z = z \oplus kG$.

ShiftRows. The ShiftRows operation remains unchanged. It only processes 16-bit words instead of 8-bit.

MixColumns. MixColumns can be computed by using the linear application generated from the matrix of the XTIME application by (6).

SubBytes. For the SubBytes operation, two approaches were proposed in [3]. The first one is a look-up table approach which requires to precompute the 16-bit output $S'(z)$ for all z as per (7). We note that this method implies a quite heavy memory overhead as a 128 kB-table needs to be stored (2^{16} 16-bit values). The second approach actually performs the SubBytes outside of the code and thus involves the recomputation of a new masked S' transformation for each encryption to ensure a proper masking. It is then necessary to compute for all x in $\mathbb{F}_2^k$:

$$S'_{recomp}(x) = S(x \oplus x') \oplus x'', \quad \text{with } x' \text{ and } x'' \text{ randomly chosen in } \mathbb{F}_2^k \quad (8)$$

The SubBytes is then performed as described in Algorithm 1. Our analysis is actually independent on the choice of either of the two approaches.

Algorithm 1. Masked SubBytes transformation on $z = xG \oplus yH$

$z = z \oplus x'G$;
$x = zG^T(GG^T)^{-1}$;
$x = S'_{recomp}(x)$;
$z' = xG \oplus yH$;
$z' = z' \oplus x''G$;
    return z';

---

[1] For the generating and parity matrices G and H and for L and L' corresponding to the standard and *masked* versions of the XTIME linear application of this code, we refer the reader to [3].

4 Side-Channel Analysis of the Masking Scheme

In this section we provide a deep analysis of the side-channel resistance of the masking scheme suggested in [3]. We demonstrate that it is possible to mount a first-order side-channel attack versus the countermeasure meant to be resistant to high-order attacks.

4.1 Striking Differences

The authors of [3] proved the security of the ODSM scheme versus d-th order side-channel analysis, where $d + 1$ is the distance of the dual code $\mathcal{C}^\perp$. Thus, with respect to the parameters of [3], the code is proved to be secure versus 4-th order attacks, 5 being the minimal distance of the dual code. The proof of security relies on the observation that the expected value of the leakage is independent on the sensitive value x (up to the 4th order statistical moments), after the encoding $xG \oplus yH$ with mask y.

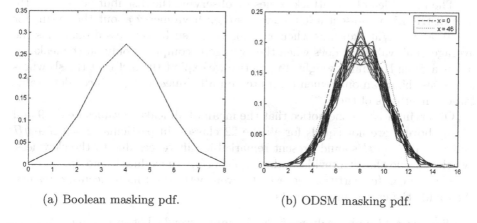

(a) Boolean masking pdf. (b) ODSM masking pdf.

Fig. 1. Pdf of the Hamming weights of the Boolean masking scheme vs ODSM masking scheme.

Figure 7 shows the expected probability density functions (pdf) of the Hamming weight (HW) of masked values for both boolean masking and the ODSM scheme. The results are obtained by collecting the distribution of the HW of $z = x \oplus y$ for Boolean masking (Fig. 1a), and $z = xG \oplus yH$ for ODSM, where x is fixed, and y takes all values in $\mathbb{F}_2^k$ (Fig. 1b).

As expected, in the boolean masking scheme the distributions are independent on the sensitive values, such that all distributions are superposed and only one curve is visible. On the other hand, in the ODSM scheme the distributions depend on the sensitive values and we can distinguish 22 different distributions, each one related to a particular set of sensitive values. In particular the distributions of the sensitive value $x = 0$ and $x = 46$ show striking differences.

We remark that an encoded value with HW of 0 can only be produced by encoding the sensitive value $x = 0$ with a mask $y = 0$. Similarly a HW of 16 can only be obtained when the encoded sensitive value equals 46. From Fig. 1b we thus observe that the extremum HW value 0 (resp. 16) is only present on the distribution of $x = 0$ (resp. $x = 46$). We further remark that for a sensitive encoded value equal to $x = 0$ (resp. $x = 46$), the HW of the encoded value can never be 4,3,2 or 1 (resp. 12, 13, 14, 15).

We show in the following that it is possible to exploit such striking differences by using 1st-order statistics in order to retrieve the sensitive values.

4.2   Means-only Attack on the ODSM Distribution

We have noticed that the difference between the leakage distributions of the ODSM masking scheme and that of classical boolean masking scheme may lead to weaknesses that have not been taken into account in [3]. In this section we exhibit an actual attack that exploits these very differences to retrieve the key value by using only 1st-order statistics on carefully selected leakages.

The basic idea of our attack comes by observing the distributions of Fig. 1b. The distributions present a left skewness (i.e.: asymmetry about the mean) for $x = 0$, and a right skewness when $x = 46$. While such skewness do not bias the average of all values, it does when the average is computed only on the leakages below a given Hamming weight. In practice we exploit the fact that the skewness preserves the mean only when computed on all values, but produces detectable biases on subsets of them.

Observing Fig. 1b one notice that the mean of all leakage values below 9 and those above 9 are not equals for all the 22 classes, in particular $z = 0G \oplus yH$ and $z = 46G \oplus yH$ should present remarkable differences due to the skewness. We thus argue that it provides a distinguisher for the values 0 and 46.

A more careful partitioning leads to even better and more accurate results. We divide the curves into two sets:

– a first set containing leakages with Hamming weight between 4 and 11,
– a second set for the remaining leakages.

The absolute difference of the two sets on theoretical distributions is depicted in Fig. 2, for each message, for all masks.

We further remark that this choice for the two sets allows to retrieve only the value corresponding to 46, as the skewness on 0 is not captured by such partitioning.

4.3   Simulations

In this section we show the results of the application of our attack described in Sect. 4.2 to simulated leakages of the ODSM scheme. For our simulations we computed the value $z = \text{Sbox}(m \oplus k_i)G \oplus yH$, where y is in $\mathbb{F}_{2^k}$ freshly regenerated at each execution. For each value z we computed the corresponding

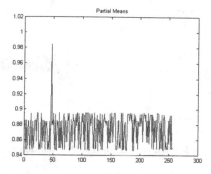

Fig. 2. Difference of the number of leakages between 4 and 11 and the rest.

leakage $\ell = HW(z) + B$, where B is a Gaussian noise with standard deviation σ. In order to evaluate the success rate of our attack with different noise levels, we have performed different campaigns where σ varies from 0 to 2. For each campaign we have simulated the leakage of 10, 000 computations for each byte value.

We start our attack by computing the minimum and the maximum values among all leakages. Then define the range s of all leakages as the difference between the maximum and minimum values, divided by 16. We then use this value to split the leakages into the two sets, the first containing those leakages whose value falls between $s * 4$ and $s * 11$ and the second with the remaining

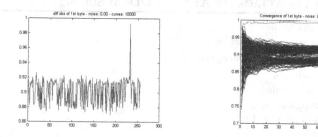

Fig. 3. Result of the attack with $\sigma = 0$ for 10, 000 leakages. (Color figure online)

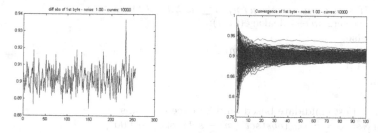

Fig. 4. Result of the attack with $\sigma = 1$ for 10, 000 leakages. (Color figure online)

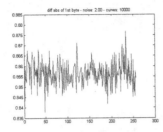 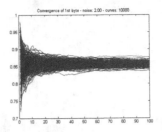

Fig. 5. Result of the attack with $\sigma = 2$ for $10,000$ leakages. (Color figure online)

leakages. We finally analyze the absolute difference of the two sets for each message. As observed in Fig. 2, only the message m which gives $\text{Sbox}(m \oplus k_i) = 46$ should produce a peak on the difference of means. Thus the peak found for a particular message m reveals $\text{Sbox}(m \oplus k_i) = 46$, so the attacker can retrieve the secret key byte $k_i = \text{Sbox}(46)^{-1} \oplus m$.

The key byte value used for our simulations is 43, thus we expect to obtain peaks for the message of value $233 = \text{Sbox}(46)^{-1} \oplus 43$. Figures 3, 4, 5 show the results obtained by using $10,000$ noisy executions for each message m. The left part corresponds to the value of the absolute differences for each message (thus for each of the 256 values we depict the value of the difference of means). The right part depicts the maximum value of the absolute difference for each

---

Algorithm 2. MEANS ATTACK ON AES-128 ODSM SCHEME.

// Find min and max values
l_max $= \max_{m \in \mathbb{F}_2^k, 0 \le i < \sharp curves}(\text{leakage}(m, i))$;
l_min $= \min_{m \in \mathbb{F}_2^k, 0 \le i < \sharp curves}(\text{leakage}(m, i))$;
// Derive HW boundaries
leakage_size=(l_max - l_min) / 16;
set1_limit $=$ leakage_size $\times$ 4;
set2_limit $=$ leakage_size $\times$ 11;
// Separate curves
for *m from 0 to 255* **do**
    for *i from 0 to 10,000* **do**
        if *set1_limit $\le$ leakage(m, i) $\le$ set2_limit* **then**
        | set2(m)+= leakage(m, i);
        else
        | set1(m)+= leakage(m, i);
        end
    end
end
// Select best candidate based on difference of means
best_message $= \max_m(abs(set2(m) - set1(m))/10,000)$;
return $k = Sbox(46)^{-1} \oplus$ *best_message*

---

key, sampled after each 100 curves. For right-side figures, the correct message hypothesis (233) is depicted in red.

We present the pseudocode of our attack in Algorithm 2.

We notice that our attack needs a huge number of curves to retrieve the key value even for relatively low noise simulations. For example, for $\sigma = 1$, we need about 384, 000 curves (1500 * 256) in order to retrieve the correct key hypothesis. The need for a considerable number of curves can be interpreted as a consequence of the masked values living in $\mathbb{F}_{2^{16}}^2$, and thus far more samples are required to obtain a representative sample of the underlying distribution. However, we remark that as soon as there is no noise, very few hundred traces are necessary to retrieve the correct key.

We want to stress the fact that despite the security proof given in [3], our attack shows that it is possible to retrieve the secret values protected with the ODSM scheme by using a first-order statistic on carefully selected leakages.

We finally insist on the fact that despite our attack applies here to the ODSM scheme with the parameters of [3], most choices of the code would succumb to such an attack.

5   Maximum Likelihood Attack

In this section we present a further attack to the countermeasure. As we have remarked in Section 4, the leakage corresponding to an HW of 0 can only be produced if both the sensitive value x and the mask y equal to 0. We thus suggest that it is possible to use a maximum likelihood (template) attack to distinguish the curves manipulating a variable z whose HW equals 0 from the others.

Template attacks are generally divided into two phases. In the first phase (profiling) the sensitive data is known to the attacker, for example she may employ an open sample, while in the second phase (attack) she tries to recover some unknown sensitive data by using new observations and the information collected during the profiling phase.

More formally, let us assume that the attacker retrieves a set of observations of the random variable z, where each observation has the form $\ell = \varphi(z) + B$, where φ is an unknown function and B a Gaussian noise with standard deviation σ. She can estimate the expectation μ_0 and covariance Σ_0 of ℓ when $z = 0$ and μ_1, Σ_1 when $z \neq 0$.

For a Gaussian distribution of expectation μ and covariance matrix Σ, the probability density function (pdf) of $\ell \in \mathbb{R}^t$ is defined as:

$$f(\ell) = \frac{1}{\sqrt{(2\pi)^t \det(\Sigma)}} \exp\left(-\frac{1}{2}(\ell - \mu)' \cdot \Sigma^{-1} \cdot (\ell - \mu) \right) . \qquad (9)$$

So by evaluating $f_{\ell|z=0}$ and $f_{\ell|z\neq0}$ she obtains the likelihood that $z = 0$ was the manipulated value.

Experiments. We have tested the template attack against a real device and we provide in this section the results of our experiments.

The target of our experiment is an ATMega328P device. We have by-passed the decoupling capacitors of the device which may filter out useful signals. We have then connected the oscilloscope to the device and measured the difference of potential at the ends of a resistor placed between the ground pin of the ATMega328P and the ground of the device. We have finally pre-filtered the input of the oscilloscope at 20 Mhz and sampled the data at 100 Mhz. Our settings allow to obtain small curves while keeping as much information as possible.

We have then collected 250, 000 leakages where we controlled the value of the mask. A random bit was used to select if $z = 0$ or $z \neq 0$ was used by the implementation. Knowledge of the random bit allowed us to split the set of acquisition between those with $z = 0$ and those with $z \neq 0$ to build templates. We also used this knowledge to verify the confidence of the likelihood distinguisher.

We show in Fig. 6 the differences between the expectation of the two sets. It is possible to distinguish important differences between them, in particular around points 250 and 300.

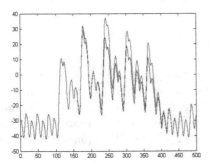 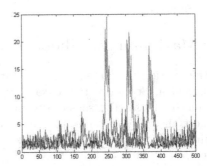

Fig. 6. Expectation and variance of real leakages when $z = 0$ and $z \neq 0$.

During attack phase we have acquired 250, 000 more curves and tried to separate them into two sets. The knowledge of the value of the random bit allowed us to verify the success rate of the distinguisher. We have used 80 points to estimate the pdfs of Eq. 9. These points were chosen as those providing the highest variance between the expectations of the two sets. In this settings we obtained 99.84 % of correct detection rate.

Our attack thus demonstrates that even for real devices it is possible to break the countermeasure by using only first and second order statistical attacks.

6   Possible Fix-Ups and Residual Issues

As shown in Sects. 4 and 5 the differences between the distributions of the Hamming weight of masked values for different inputs can be exploited by an attacker to recover manipulated secrets. In this section we propose a method to improve the resistance of the scheme to the attacks that we have presented in this work while preserving the fault detection capability.

6.1   Conservative Shuffling

In this section we suggest how to add algorithmic noise to the ODSM scheme in order to defeat the attack introduced previously. We show that our countermeasure preserves the fault detection capability and the possibility to perform computation within the masking scheme.

Our method relies on shuffling the generating matrices G and H of the code $\mathcal{C}$ and $\mathcal{D}$, losing the systematic form of $\mathcal{C}$'s generating matrix. Successively applying permutations on the columns of these matrices allows to randomize the mappings between elements of $\mathbb{F}_2^k$ and $\mathcal{C}$ (resp. $\mathbb{F}_2^{n-k}$ and $\mathcal{D}$) by randomizing the codewords of $\mathcal{C}$ (resp. $\mathcal{D}$) itself. We can note that the properties of the associated codes remain unchanged as we only reorder the columns of the generating matrices. In particular the duality between $\mathcal{C}$ and $\mathcal{D}$ is preserved since we apply the same permutation on both matrices G and H. This can be seen by recalling that any permutation of n columns of a $k \times n$ matrix can be realized by multiplying from the right this matrix by a permutation matrix P. Further recalling that P is orthogonal ($PP^T = \mathbb{I}$), it comes straightforwardly that:

$$GP(HP)^T = GP(P^T H^T) = G(PP^T)H^T = GH^T = 0 \qquad (10)$$

Such a process can be easily achieved at the cost of up to 12 bits of random used to select two columns to permute and an amount of circular shift. For the XOR operation, the permutation can be straightforwardly applied to the encoding of the operand: $z' = z \oplus k_i GP$. For the linear operation, the permutation needs to be reflected on the L' matrix of (6):

$$L'' = (GP)^T(GP(GP)^T)^{-1}LGP \oplus (HP)^T(HP(HP)^T)^{-1}HP \qquad (11)$$
$$= P^T(G^T(GG^T)^{-1}LG)P \oplus P^T(H^T(HH^T)^{-1}H)P \qquad (12)$$
$$= P^T(G^T(GG^T)^{-1}LG \oplus H^T(HH^T)^{-1}H)P \qquad (13)$$
$$= P^T L' P \qquad (14)$$

For the non-linear operation, only the table recomputation approach seems to be achievable with reasonable overhead as the look-up table approach would require to recompute the S' table for all z. Algorithm 1 should then be adapted as exposed in Algorithm 3.

Algorithm 3. Masked SubBytes transformation on $z = xGP \oplus yHP$

$z = z \oplus x'GP$;
$x = z(GP)^T(GG^T)^{-1}$;
$x = S'_{recomp}(x)$;
$z' = xGP \oplus yHP$;
$z' = z' \oplus x''GP$;
return z';

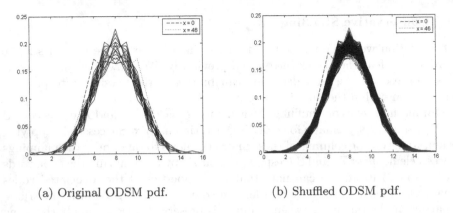

(a) Original ODSM pdf.   (b) Shuffled ODSM pdf.

Fig. 7. Hamming weights' pdf of encoded values for ODSM Vs Shuffled ODSM.

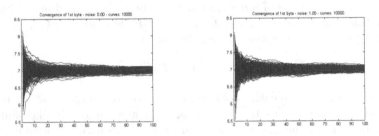

Fig. 8. Result of the attack with $\sigma = 0$ and $\sigma = 1$ for $10,000$ leakages.

Using such shuffled matrices for each encryption, we obtain the distribution depicted in Fig. 7b. Figure 7a is recalled for comparison purpose.

We can see that the distribution gives a much less explicit hint on the manipulated value compared to the original one. However we can still observe differences in the distributions for each value, supporting a residual weakness. Nevertheless, the attack described in Sect. 4 now fails even with a low noise level as can be seen in Fig. 8.

6.2   Residual Issue: Encoding 0

From the observation of Figs. 7a and b we can see that one potential weakness of the original scheme is not taken care of by our method. Indeed, we observe that the value $xG \oplus yH = 0\text{x}0000$ can only be obtained when $x = 0\text{x}00$.

By assuming that the attacker can detect the manipulation of the value $0\text{x}0000$ then she directly knows the corresponding value $0\text{x}00$ of the internal AES state. Such a weakness is not present in traditional boolean masking, where all masked values can be produced by all secret values.

Such an attack may not be merely theoretical since the hypothesis of retrieving the Hamming weight of internal values of more than one byte by SPA has been exploited in recent publications [12,13] in order to retrieve the operands of a 128-bit scalar multiplication.

We further remark that a similar SPA weakness would affect the ODSM scheme for any choice of code. Indeed, since the codes $\mathcal{C}$ and $\mathcal{D}$ are complementary duals and from the definition of $\mathcal{C}$ and $\mathcal{D}$ we know that:

$$\forall\, z \in \mathbb{F}_2^n,\ \exists!\ (x,y) \in \mathbb{F}_2^k \times \mathbb{F}_2^{n-k} \text{ such that } z = xG \oplus yH$$

This holds in particular when $z = 0$, which is thus equivalent to $xG = yH$ and to $x = y = 0$. Consequently even when randomizing G and H, we can only observe a value of null Hamming weight when the sensitive value x *and* the mask y are null. Unfortunately, as we have shown in Sect. 5 such weakness may be exploited by using template attacks. We can nevertheless stress that in case the attacker cannot control the value of the mask she may not be able to build the templates and consequently the attack should not work.

7 Conclusion

The definition of new countermeasures tackling in the same effort side-channel analysis and fault attacks is definitely a challenging task. The ODSM scheme succeeds in providing both a way to detect errors and ensuring the independency of the mean and the variance of the Hamming weight of masked data. However in this work we demonstrate that the distributions of Hamming weights of the ODSM encoded data are actually dependent on the sensitive values being manipulated, which renders the scheme helpless against a side-channel attack considering only 1st-order statistical moment of the observed leakage. Furthermore we have shown that some measures can be taken in order to reduce the leakage exposed when observing the Hamming weight distributions for a given sensitive value, although it turns out that the scheme cannot be made totally SCA-resistant. Still, countermeasures based on coding theory appear as promising candidates to improve the resistance of cryptographic implementations against both side-channel and fault attacks. In particular, the definition of methods allowing to perform the complete execution of an algorithm under the protection of the code is an interesting line of research for future works.

References

1. Coron, J.-S., Goubin, L.: On boolean and arithmetic masking against differential power analysis. In: Paar, C., Koç, Ç.K. (eds.) CHES 2000. LNCS, vol. 1965, pp. 231–237. Springer, Heidelberg (2000)
2. Bringer, J., Chabanne, H., Le, T.H.: Protecting aes against side-channel analysis using wire-tap codes. J. Cryptographic Eng. **2**, 129–141 (2012)
3. Bringer, J., Carlet, C., Chabanne, H., Guilley, S., Maghrebi, H.: Orthogonal direct sum masking. In: Naccache, D., Sauveron, D. (eds.) WISTP 2014. LNCS, vol. 8501, pp. 40–56. Springer, Heidelberg (2014)

4. Kocher, P.C.: Timing attacks on implementations of Diffie-Hellman, RSA, DSS, and other systems. In: Koblitz, N. (ed.) CRYPTO 1996. LNCS, vol. 1109, pp. 104–113. Springer, Heidelberg (1996)
5. Kocher, P., Jaffe, J., Jun, B.: Introduction to differential power analysis and related attacks. Technical report, Cryptography Research Inc. (1998)
6. Messerges, T.: Poweranalysis attacks and countermeasures for cryptographic algorithms. Ph.D. thesis, University of Illinois (2000)
7. Messerges, T.S., Dabbish, E.A., Sloan, R.H.: Power analysis attacks of modular exponentiation in smartcards. In: Koç, Ç.K., Paar, C. (eds.) CHES 1999. LNCS, vol. 1717, pp. 144–157. Springer, Heidelberg (1999)
8. Coron, J.-S.: Resistance against differential power analysis for elliptic curve cryptosystems. In: Koç, Ç.K., Paar, C. (eds.) CHES 1999. LNCS, vol. 1717, pp. 292–302. Springer, Heidelberg (1999)
9. Rivain, M., Prouff, E.: Provably secure higher-order masking of AES. In: Mangard, S., Standaert, F.-X. (eds.) CHES 2010. LNCS, vol. 6225, pp. 413–427. Springer, Heidelberg (2010)
10. Moradi, A.: Wire-tap codes as side-channel countermeasure - an FPGA-based experiment. In: Meier, W., Mukhopadhyay, D. (eds.) INDOCRYPT 2014. LNCS, vol. 8885, pp. 341–359. Springer, Heidelberg (2014)
11. Azzi, S., Barras, B., Christofi, M., Vigilant, D.: Using linear codes as a fault countermeasure for nonlinear operations: application to AES and formal verification. In: PROOFS: Security Proofs for Embedded Systems (2015)
12. Belaïd, S., Fouque, P.-A., Gérard, B.: Side-channel analysis of multiplications in $GF(2^{128})$. In: Sarkar, P., Iwata, T. (eds.) ASIACRYPT 2014, Part II. LNCS, vol. 8874, pp. 306–325. Springer, Heidelberg (2014)
13. Belad, S., Coron, J.S., Fouque, P.A., Grard, B., Kammerer, J.G., Prouff, E.: Improved side-channel analysis of finite-field multiplication. Cryptology ePrint Archive, Report 2015/542 (2015). http://eprint.iacr.org/

Access Control and Data Protection

LAMP - Label-Based Access-Control for More Privacy in Online Social Networks

Leila Bahri$^{(\boxtimes)}$, Barbara Carminati, Elena Ferrari, and William Lucia

DiSTA, Insubria University, Varese, Italy
{leila.bahri,barbara.carminati,elena.ferrari,william.lucia}@uninsubria.it

Abstract. Access control in Online Social Networks (OSNs) is generally approached with a relationship-based model. This limits the options in expressing privacy preferences to only the types of relationships users establish in the OSN. Moreover, current proposals do not address the privacy of *dependent* information types, such as comments or likes, at their atomic levels of ownership. Rather, the privacy of these data elements is holistically dependent on the aggregate object they belong to. To overcome this, we propose LAMP, a model that deploys fine grained label-based access control for information sharing in OSNs. Users in LAMP assign customized labels to their friends and to all types of their information; whereas access requests are evaluated by security properties carefully designed to establish orders between requestor's and information's labels. We prove the correctness of the suggested model, and we perform performance experiments based on different access scenarios simulated on a real OSN graph. We also performed a preliminary usability study that compared LAMP to Facebook privacy settings.

1 Introduction

Online Social Networks (OSNs) enable users to have more freedom and proximity in keeping in touch with their friends and in expanding their social contacts. However, they also create serious privacy concerns given the personal nature of information users share over them on almost a daily basis [3,7]. Users publish their personal stories and updates, as they might also express their opinion by interacting on information shared by others, but, in most cases, they are not fully aware of the size of the audience that gets access to their information.[1] Moreover, privacy settings currently available in OSNs remain both complicated to use, and not flexible enough to model all the privacy preferences that users may require [10].

This limitation seems to come, fundamentally, from relying solely on a relationship based model for access control (ReBAC), as mostly adopted by nowadays OSNs and research proposals. ReBAC is characterized by the explicit tracking of interpersonal relationships among users, and the expression of access control policies in terms of these relationships [5]. These relationships could refer to

---

[1] http://www.americanbar.org/publications/blt/2014/01/03a_claypoole.html.

© IFIP International Federation for Information Processing 2016
Published by Springer International Publishing Switzerland 2016. All Rights Reserved
S. Foresti and J. Lopez (Eds.): WISTP 2016, LNCS 9895, pp. 171–186, 2016.
DOI: 10.1007/978-3-319-45931-8_11

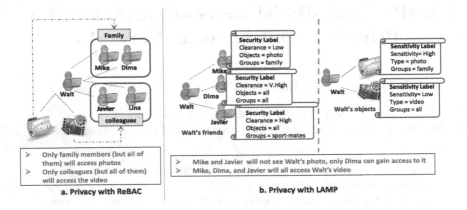

Fig. 1. Privacy management with ReBAC vs. LAMP

explicit friendship links established by users [2,6], or they could be inferred from relationships created between users through the resources they share [4] (e.g., connecting users who are tagged in the same photo), or by linking other public information, such as considering attendance to the same school, or originating from the same country as a basis for relationships between users (e.g., the work in [14]).

However, this type of access control limits, by design, the options for privacy settings. For instance, *defining privacy settings based only on the social relationships implicitly enforces that all the friends of a user who belong to the same relationship type are equal and, hence, will enjoy the same access and interaction rights.* For example, referring to Fig. 1a, if Walt categorizes Mike and Dima as *family*, and Javier and Lina as *colleagues*, then all the information Walt shares with the *family* group will be accessible by both Mike and Dima and the same goes for information shared with the *colleagues* one. In case Walt needs to share an item only with Mike and Javier, he is required to create a new group or categorization under which he declares both of them.

Additionally, the information that users create in OSNs is subject to interactions from their friends, resulting in the creation of intermingled nets of objects with multiple co-owners. For example, Walt shares a photo, and one of his friends tags Dima in it, or Dima shares a status update and Walt comments on it. Such scenarios exemplify the creation of aggregate content that is co-owned by multiple users in the system, who might have conflictual privacy preferences over it. Thus far, this problem has been approached mostly from a multiple ownership perspective. That is, the aggregate co-created content is considered as one single object over which multiple access preferences could be specified by its stakeholders, but only one is selected as dominant using different strategies, such as game theory, and majority voting [8,9,11,15,16]. This may limit the right of the co-owners in guarantying the enforcement of their individual privacy preferences over the specific content they have contributed with.

In contrast, our idea is that of looking at this co-owned content in terms of the relationships between its components. Thus, allowing us to model it as *separate pieces of data that are dependent on each other, but that are uniquely owned and for which unique privacy preferences could be specified by their owners.* Taking this approach simplifies the co-ownership problem and empowers users to be in full control over data they create at a fine granularity level. For example, if Walt is allowed to comment on Dima's status update, he may have the right to limit the audience of his comment and not to have it subject to the one set by Dima for the corresponding status update. Unfortunately, privacy settings available in today's OSNs do not allow the granularity of managing privacy for pieces of data that are dependent on others, such as comments or likes. Moreover, the available related research provides complex solutions that mostly rely on managing multi-ownership at an object's aggregate level, as mentioned above.

To overcome these limitations, in this paper, we propose a new model, LAMP (Label-based Access-control for More Privacy in OSNs), that introduces a new and more flexible way for users to express finer granularity levels of privacy for all information types, respecting the relationships and connections between objects as well. LAMP achieves this by exploiting the security principles of Mandatory Access Control (MAC), according to which a data administrator assigns ordered security levels (that is, labels) to subjects, and ordered sensitivity levels to objects [5]. However, differently from the centralized assignment of labels by a single data administrator as in MAC, LAMP operates based on a discretionary model wherein each user is considered as the ultimate owner of her data.[2] As such, users in LAMP express their privacy preferences by assigning *sensitivity labels* to their owned objects, and *security labels* to their friends.

Labels in LAMP are expressed in terms of security or sensitivity levels, types of relationships, and types of objects (see Fig. 1b). Access decisions are taken based on well defined axioms that consider the richness of interaction types and access privileges that OSNs allow. These axioms ensure that subjects can only gain specific privileges on objects, based on the relationship existing between the object sensitivity levels and their own security levels.

To the best of our knowledge, except from the work in [12], which has discussed design principles for privacy settings by considering co-owned aggregate objects as collections of related annotations, LAMP is the first proposal that considers the relationships between aggregate data objects to decompose them to atomic unique levels of ownership, and that uses a labeling strategy to provide more control and richer privacy settings to data owners on all types of objects they create.

We formalize and prove the security and complexity properties of LAMP, and we discuss how it allows users to express a richer set of privacy settings, compared to existing proposals. We conduct performance experiments using different access scenarios simulated on a real OSN graph. We also deployed LAMP as a Facebook

---

[2] Using the labeling strategy of MAC under a decentralized approach has been adopted in other systems, such as Oracle Label Security where labels are used in conjunction with DAC functionalities to provide access policy refinement at a table level [13].

test app and performed a preliminary study on LAMP's usability by comparing LAMP to Facebook privacy settings. For space considerations, we report here the performance experiments and refer the reader to a technical report for the preliminary results of the usability experiments [1].

The remainder of this paper is organized as follows. Section 2 introduces a background on the interactions allowed in OSNs nowadays. Section 3 describes the proposed model; whereas Sect. 4 provides its correctness and complexity properties. Section 5 reports the results of the performed experiments. Finally, Sect. 6 concludes the paper.

2   Background

In this paper, we consider the scenario of general-purpose OSNs that allow users to establish friendship links with each other, and share different types of information. There are number of such OSNs in the online market nowadays, but it remains safe to say that the two worldwide biggest ones currently in the box are Facebook and Google+. Generally, OSN users are associated with an information space typically made of two main blocks: a profile and a wall or timeline. The profile contains personal information, like full name, gender, age, education etc.; whereas the wall organizes, in a graphically timelined manner, the data objects the user shared with her friends or those that her friends have shared with her. Users can upload content of different types into their information space, or interact on their friends' shared information (like, comment, tag, etc.), creating by this aggregate co-owned objects. These aggregate objects are typically made of an information that stands as *independent* by itself, and a tree of objects that are *dependent* on it (see Fig. 2 for an example). Table 1 lists the different types of information created in nowadays OSNs, both dependent and independent. The Friend-Post (FP) type on Table 1 denotes an object posted on a user's wall by one of her friends.

Table 1. Types of information shared in OSNs

Type	Dependent
Text (TX) [text posts & profile data]	Independent
Photo (P)	Independent
Video (V)	Independent
Like (L)	Dependent
Comment (C)	Dependent
Tag (TG)	Dependent
Geo-Location (GL)	Dependent
Friend-Post (FP)	Independent

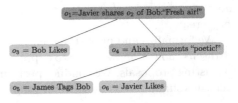

Fig. 2. Typical objects' structure in OSNs

The privacy settings currently available in mainstream OSNs, such as Facebook or Google+, present limitations to the expression of users refined privacy needs, especially w.r.t dependent object types (e.g., no privacy settings for objects of types like (L) and comment (C)). LAMP addresses these limitations and offers a more flexible and a richer privacy setting functionality to OSN users. We define and detail the underlying model in the following section.

3   The LAMP Model

We start by presenting basic definitions, then we define how privacy requirements of users can be expressed using labels. Finally, we introduce the mechanism governing access decisions.

3.1   Basic Definitions

We model an OSN as an undirected graph $FG = (U, FR)$, where U is the set of users, and FR is the set of edges. We say that two users $a, b \in U$ are friends in the OSN if and only if there exists one direct edge connecting them, that is, $\exists e_{a,b} \in FR$.

OSN users create and share different types of information (see Table 1) leveraging on the relationships they establish with others. We define the set of information types in the OSN as $OTS = \{TX, P, V, L, C, TG, GL, FP\}$, and we refer to all pieces of information as an *object*, that we formally define as follows:

Definition 1 (OSN object). *An OSN object o is a tuple (type, owner, parent, children, copyof), where:*[3] *(i)* **type** *$\in OTS$ denotes the type of the object. (ii)* **owner** *$\in U$ denotes the owner of the object. If $o.type \notin \{TG, FP\}$, the owner is the user who generated the object (dependent or independent). Otherwise, it is the user who is tagged or the user on whose wall the friend post is made. (iii)* **parent***: if o is a dependent object, this refers to the object on which it depends. It is set to null, otherwise. (iv)* **children***: is the set of objects that depend on o, as generated by interactions on it, if any. It is set to null, otherwise. (v)* **copyof***: if o is a shared copy of another object $\bar{o}$, this is equal to $\bar{o}$, otherwise it is set to null.*

In addition to the objects that users can create, we consider the existence of another special object type, that we refer to as the *root* object, and that models user walls. We consider that every OSN user owns exactly one *root* object that is created by default upon her subscription to the OSN. Root objects serve for controlling the function of *writing* on users' walls by their friends as we will detail later (see Algorithm 1). A *root* object associated with user a is modelled as $root_a = (root, a, null, null, null)$.

Example 1. Consider the OSN objects in Fig. 2. By Definition 1, object o_1 is modeled as *(TX, Javier, null, $\{o_3, o_4\}$, o_2)*, whereas the tag object o_5 is modeled as *(TG, Bob, o_4, null, null)*.

---

[3] We use the dot notation to refer to the parameters in an object tuple.

Besides creating and sharing objects, there are different types of actions that users can perform on them. We accordingly define the set of controllable privileges in LAMP as $PS = \{read,\ add\text{-}comment,\ add\text{-}like,\ add\text{-}tag,\ share,\ write\}$.[4]

As mentioned earlier, access requirements in LAMP are expressed by means of labels, formally defined in the next section.

3.2 Privacy Requirements Formulation

To express privacy requirements, users assign security labels to each of their owned objects and to each of their friends. By labeling friends, users express the limitations they want to put on them, whereas object labeling serves for expressing the sensitivity of the information and its accessibility criteria. We note that we assume a set of possible groups that users can organize their friends into. These groups are created by users depending on their preferences and can be viewed as similar to users' lists or users' circles as available on Facebook and Google+, respectively. A possible example of a set of user groups might be {friends, colleagues, teammates, schoolmates, family, acquaintances}. This set is created at user's side and is only used for the purpose of creating their friends and objects security labels. In addition, we also assume in the system a totally ordered set of levels $LOS = \{Unclassified\ (UC),\ Very\ Low\ (VL),\ Low\ (L),\ Medium\ (M),\ High\ (H),\ Very\ High\ (VH)\}$, with UC < VL < L < M < H < VH.

We refer to a friend label as *Friend Clearance Label (FCL)* and we formally define it as follows:

Definition 2 (Friend Clearance Label - FCL). *Let $a, b \in U$ be two friends in the OSN (i.e., $\exists e_{a,b} \in FR$). The label $FCL_{a,b}$, assigned by user a to user b, is denoted by the tuple $(CL_{a,b}, TS_{a,b}, GS_{a,b})$, where: (i) $CL_{a,b} \in LOS$ is the clearance level that a grants to b; (ii) $TS_{a,b} \subseteq OTS$ is the set of object types that a wants b to get access to; (iii) $GS_{a,b}$ is the set of groups that a assigns to b.*

We refer to object labels as *Object Sensitivity Labels (OSL)*, and we formally define them as follows:

Definition 3 (Object Sensitivity Label - OSL). *Let $a \in U$ be a user in the OSN and let o be an OSN object such that $o.owner = a$. The label OSL_o of object o is denoted by the tuple (SL_o, TY_o, GS_o), where: (i) $SL_o \in LOS$ is the sensitivity level of o; (ii) $TY_o = o.type$ is the type of o; (iii) GS_o is the set of groups for which object o should be available.*

Example 2. Assume Walt uploads a photo (GP) and assigns to it $OSL_{GP} = (L,\ P,\ \{colleagues,\ family\})$. This means that GP has a low sensitivity and it concerns Walt's colleagues, or family. Assume Walt assigned to his friend Javier an $FCL_{w,j} = (H,\ \{P,\ T,\ V\},\ \{colleagues,\ university\})$. This implies that Walt grants to Javier a high clearance level, allows him to see his photos, texts, and videos, and he considers him a member of the colleagues and university groups.

---

[4] We recall that the *write* privilege refers to posting on friends' walls.

3.3   Access Control Decisions

Access to objects in an OSN can be related to one of the privileges enclosed in the privileges set (PS). To reflect this broader range of privileges, compared to traditional scenarios formalizing only read and write privileges, we refer to access requests as *interaction requests - (IR)*. An IR can be of two types: (1) performed on an object (e.g., read or comment on an object), or (2) made to create an object related to another user (i.e., tag a user or write on her wall). We define an *interaction request* as follows:

Definition 4 (Interaction Request - IR). *Let $a, b \in U$ be two friends in the OSN (i.e., $\exists e_{a,b} \in FR$). An IR by user b on user a is denoted by the tuple $ir_{b,x} = (x, p, b)$, where $p \in PS$ is the requested privilege, and x has one of the following forms: $x = o$, where o is an object s.t. $o.owner = a$; if $p \in \{read, add\text{-}like, add\text{-}comment\}$, or $x = o$, where o is an object s.t. $o.owner = a$ and $o.parent = null$; if $p = share$, or $x = a$, where a is the target user; if $p = write$, or $x = (a, o)$, where a is the target user and o is an object; if $p = add\text{-}tag$.*

Users can explicitly issue a *read* IR on independent objects only. If such a *read* IR is positively evaluated, the system issues, on behalf of the requesting user, *read* IRs on all the children's tree of the granted independent object. This ensures that the children objects are evaluated independently of their parent object and only based on their proper OSLs. We explain this later under Algorithm 1.

Like in standard MAC, the evaluation of an IR is performed based on properties that define orders between subject and object labels. In standard MAC, there are two properties that govern the system, related to the *read* and to the *write* requests, respectively. LAMP requires not only the redefinition of these two properties to account for all the features in the FCLs and the OSLs, but it also requires defining new axioms to take into account the other interactions possible in an OSN.

An order relation among labels must be defined to have the basis on which they can be compared. In LAMP, we refer to this relation as the *dominance relationship*, formally defined as follows:

Definition 5 (Dominance relationship). *Let $a, b \in U$ be two friends in the OSN (i.e., $\exists e_{a,b} \in FR$) and let $FCL_{a,b} = (CL_{a,b}, TS_{a,b}, GS_{a,b})$ be the label a assigned to b. Let o be an object s.t. $o.owner = a$, and let $OSL_o = (SL_o, TY_o, GS_o)$ be its OSL. $FCL_{a,b}$ dominates OSL_o, denoted as $FCL_{a,b} \gg OSL_o$, if an only if,*

$$CL_{a,b} > SL_o \wedge TY_o \in TS_{a,b} \wedge GS_o \cap GS_{a,b} \neq \emptyset$$

Example 3. Consider Example 2. The FCL that Walt assigned to Javier dominates the OSL assigned to GP photo because: (1) the clearance level of Javier (High) is higher than the sensitivity level of the photo (Low); (2) object type photo is in the types set in Javier's label; and (3) the group sets in Javier's and the photo's labels have a group in common (colleague).

The Fundamental Security Property. We are now ready to introduce the first property in LAMP, referred to as the *Fundamental Security Property (FSP)*:

Definition 6 (Fundamental Security Property). *Let $a, b \in U$ be two friends in the OSN (i.e., $\exists e_{a,b} \in FR$) and let $FCL_{a,b}$ be the label a assigned to b. Let o be an object s.t. $o.owner = a$, and let OSL_o be its label. Let $ir_{b,o} = (o, p, b)$ be an IR made by b on o s.t $p \in \{read, share, add\text{-}like, add\text{-}comment\}$. $ir_{b,o}$ satisfies FSP, iff: $FCL_{a,b} \gg OSL_o$.*

Informally, the FSP dictates that to grant a *read, share, add-like,* or *add-comment* IR on an object, the FCL of the requestor must dominate the OSL of the object it targets. A requirement of the FSP is that the requestor and the object owner are friends in the OSN as otherwise the friend label to be compared would not exist. As a consequence, in LAMP, only friends of a user can have access to and interact on her information space. This is not fully aligned with the classical approach of OSNs where there is the possibility of making information available to friends-of-friends or public. Regarding the case of information desired to be made public (i.e., accessible to all users in the OSN), it can be easily enabled by making the object unclassified, and by letting the system assign a default label $FCL_{default} = (UC, GS, OTS)$ to all OSN users who are not direct friends with the object owner, where GS, and OTS are the sets of all groups and of all object types in the OSN, respectively. For other information that is not made publicly available, our approach is to provide users with an environment that facilitates the understanding and control of their objects audiences. This is ensured by the suggested labels assignment, as users can be fully aware of (and track) who might gain access to what, contrary to the approach of allowing the unlimited and uncontrollable friend-of-friend access. However, LAMP can still be extended to cover such a scenario by complementing it with a mechanism for automatic FCLs assignment to friends of friends. This issue is a research subject in itself, that we plan to address as future work.

The FSP is sufficient for all the IRs it targets, except from the *share* one. This is what we address in the following sub-section.

The *Share* Privilege and the Share Up Property. When a *share* IR is granted, it results in the creation of a copy of the original object, that is owned by the sharing user. The problem here is on what should be the label of this shared copy. The simplest design idea is to make the copy inherit the same label as the original object, ensuring by this that only the audience of the original object is allowed to view the shared copy. This will map to what is being the standard in current OSNs, such as Facebook. However, this design choice results in two limitations that could not be desirable: (1) the user who performs the *share* interaction would have no way to influence the privacy settings of the shared copy; and (2) this strategy limits the intended purpose of the *share* functionality, since it does not result in an enlargement of the intended audience. Indeed, when a user allows a friend to share an object, this logically means that the user wants to delegate to her/him the dissemination of that object in order to make it available to a wider audience from the friend's side. Otherwise, if the user wants to limit the visibility of an object strictly to her allowed audience, then what could be the purpose from allowing a *share* interaction on it? Therefore, an alternative design decision, that would offer more flexibility and give meaning to the power of a *share* operation, is to have the shared copy have its distinct object label. However, the copy's label should still respect the privacy of the original object in such a way that the copy might be available to a wider audience without violating the privacy of the original object. Herein, the focus is on two concerns: (1) the shared copy *so* of an object *o* should not be made available to the friends of *o.owner* who are initially not allowed to access *o*; (2) the delegation offered by *o.owner* to the friend who creates the shared copy *so* should respect the sensitivity of *o*, such that *so* is shared only with those friends of *so.owner* who are at least as trusted as the sensitivity of *o*. We present Example 4 for a better illustration of these two concerns.

Example 4. Consider Example 2, and assume that Walt and Javier have Mina as a common friend in the OSN. Let Walt's FCL for Mina be $FCL_{w,m}$ =(VL, {*T*}, {*university*}). Recall that the OSL of Walt's photo is OSL_{GP} =(L, P, {*colleagues, family, university*}). Clearly, Mina does not have access to Walt's photo as $FCL_{w,m}$ does not dominate OSL_{GP}. Assume now that Walt allows Javier to share the photo; hence delegates to him its broader dissemination. This delegation means that Walt entrusts Javier to disseminate the picture to those of his friends that he trusts at least as high as the sensitivity of the photo (i.e., Walt's picture has a Low sensitivity, therefore it should be disseminated to those friends of Javier whom he trusts with at least a Low value). Furthermore, the shared photo by Javier should not be made available to Mina, no matter how Javier trust's in Mina could be different from Walt's.

To address these two concerns, we first introduce an additional axiom, called the *Share Higher Property*. Before formally defining it, we introduce a new required concept that governs the relationship between the label of an object and that of its copies made from a granted *share* IR. We refer to this as the *Not-declassify relationship*:

Definition 7 (Not-declassify relationship). *Let $OSL_o = (SL_o, TY_o, GS_o)$ be the label of an object o. Let $OSL_{\bar{o}} = (SL_{\bar{o}}, TY_{\bar{o}}, GS_{\bar{o}})$ be the label assigned to a copy $\bar{o}$ of o (i.e., $\bar{o}.copyof = o$). Label $OSL_{\bar{o}}$ does not declassify label OSL_o, and we write $OSL_{\bar{o}} \not\preceq OSL_o$, if and only if: $SL_{\bar{o}} \geq SL_o$.*

The Not-declassify relationship requires that the sensitivity level of an object's copy is at least equal to that of the original object. This would ensure that a share action does not declassify the shared information, with the assumption of a delegated trust from the original object's owner to the sharing friend. It is also to be noted that no restriction is made on the groups set parameter of the label. This is because the organization of friends into groups is dependent on each user without necessarily mapping to the groupings adopted by their friends. For example, those who might be family to a user, might be colleagues to another. However, it is worth mentioning that the purpose of the share action is to disseminate objects to wider and different audiences, as long as this does not result in explicitly making the information available to a non-desired friend.

Based on the Not-declassify relationship, the second axiom of LAMP, the *Share Higher Property*, is defined as follows:

Definition 8 (Share Higher Property - SHP). *Let* $a, b \in U$ *be two friends in the OSN (i.e., $\exists e_{a,b} \in FR$), and let o be an object s.t. $o.owner = a$. Let OSL_o be the label a assigned to o. Let $ir_{b,o} = (o, share, b)$ be a share IR made by b on o, and let $OSL_{\bar{\sigma}}$ be the object label that b intends to assign to the copy of o. We say that $ir_{b,o}$ satisfies SHP, if and only if: $OSL_{\bar{\sigma}} \not\preceq OSL_o$.*

Informally, the SHP enforces that users can share their friends' objects only if they assign to the shared copy an OSL that does not declassify the one of the original object. We recall that a *share* IR should first satisfy the FSP. Therefore, only those friends who have a clearance level at least equal to the sensitivity level of the object can perform a *share* IR. This ensures respecting the delegation of objects dissemination to only those friends who are at least as trusted as the sensitivity of the object they are entrusted to share.

The SHP addresses the delegation of dissemination concern, however it does not solve the first concern we discussed earlier related to when an object owner and the sharing friend have a friend in common who is not initially allowed to access the object by the owner (the case of Mina in Example 4). To prevent such *horizontal disclosures*, we enforce the preferences of objects' owners by considering their labels and not the copy's when the requestor, the sharer, and the owner are mutual friends. For the scenario in Example 4, for instance, if Mina issues a *read* IR on the shared copy of Walt's picture from the common friend Javier, the labels assigned by Walt for the original picture and for Mina are used to evaluate the IR, and not the ones assigned by Javier to the shared copy and to Mina. This is enforced by Algorithm 1 as it will be presented later.

The *Add-Tag* and *Write* Privileges and the Write Higher Property.
Both the *add-tag* and the *write* interactions, if granted, result in the creation of new objects, and therefore they bring to the problem of what the labels for these resulting objects should be. For instance, assume Bob has a very high level of trust in Alice and allows her to post on his wall. Alice might hold sensitive information about Bob and, as such, her posts on his wall might reflect some of it. Thus, Bob would want that Alice's posts on his wall be managed with a label that reflects their expected sensitivity; that is, a label that is at least as high as the one he assigned to Alice. On the other hand, if Bob's trust on another user, say Aliah, is low, then he might need to impose more control on her posts on his wall as it could be that she holds some sensitive information about him that she might post to embarrass him, for example. The same applies to the *add-tag* interaction as well. To cope with this, we suggest enforcing two conditions on the labels that requestors of granted *write* or *add-tag* IRs can assign to the resulting objects. The first condition imposes a sensitivity level for the created object that is at least as high as the clearance level that the affected user assigned to the requestor, if this latter is higher than the medium level. For example, if Bob

assigns a high clearance level to Alice, Alice's posts on his wall will have at least a high sensitivity level. However, if the clearance level assigned by the affected user to the requestor is lower than the medium level, its inverse is set as the least requirement for the sensitivity level of the resulting object. For instance, if Bob assigns to Aliah a low clearance level, Aliah's posts on his wall will have a sensitivity level at least equal to the inverse of Aliah's clearance level (i.e., a high sensitivity level).

The second condition imposes that the group set of the resulting object's label is exactly the group set that the affected user specified in her label for the requestor. For example, if Bob assigned the group "colleagues" to Alice, then it is likely that Alice's posts about him will also concern the "colleagues" group. To formalize these conditions, we introduce the third axiom of LAMP, referred to as the *Write Higher Property - (WHT)*:

Definition 9 (Write Higher Property - WHT) *Let $a, b \in U$ be two friends in the OSN (i.e., $\exists e_{a,b} \in FR$) and let $FCL_{a,b}=(CL_{a,b}, TS_{a,b}, GS_{a,b})$ be the label a assigned to b. Let $ir_{b,x} = (x, p, b)$ be an IR such that $p \in \{write, add\text{-}tag\}$ and $x = a$, if $p = write$, $x = (a, ob)$, if $p = add\text{-}tag$, with ob the object to be tagged. Let o be the object resulting from granting $ir_{b,x}$ and OSL_o be its assigned label by b. $ir_{b,x}$ satisfies WHT if and only if: $o.owner = a \wedge OSL_o = (SL_o, TY_o, GS_o)$ s.t., $GS_o = GS_{a,b}$,*

$$TY_o = \begin{cases} TG & \text{if } p=add\text{-}tag. \\ FP & \text{if } p=write. \end{cases}$$

and

$$SL_o \geq \begin{cases} CL_{a,b} & \text{if } CL_{a,b} \geq M. \\ f^{-1}(CL_{a,b}) & \text{otherwise.} \end{cases}$$

With $f^{-1}(y), y \in LOS$ being the inverse function for security levels. For example $f^{-1}(VH) = VL$, $f^{-1}(L) = H$, etc.

Example 5. Consider Example 2, and assume Javier has the right to post on Walt's wall and that he posts on it a video of Walt's graduation ceremony. We recall that Walt assigned to Javier *(H, {P, T, V}, {colleagues, university})*. By the WHT property, the video's owner is Walt, and a possible granted label that Javier can assign to it is: *(H, FP, {colleagues, university})*. This means that the video will be available only to the friends of Walt to whom he assigned a high or a very high clearance level, who belong to the colleagues or to the university groups, and who are allowed to see Walt's friends' posts.

Access Control Enforcement. Putting it up all together, Algorithm 1 defines how access control is enforced in the system based on the privacy preferences of users, as expressed through FCLs and OSLs and on the properties defined above.

Algorithm 1 takes as input an IR and produces as output a *granted* or *denied* message, based on the corresponding properties to the requested privilege. For a *read* IR, the algorithm first checks if the target object is a copy. If it is, the

NoHorDisclosure function is called (lines 3, 4) to rewrite the IR as targeting the original object, as long as the involved parties are mutual friends (lines 34, 39). It is then checked if the retrieved IR satisfies the FSP. If it does, a similar IR is propagated through the children of the target object (i.e., calling the *propagate* procedure in line 6). The procedure traverses the object's tree in a depth first manner, evaluating each child against the FSP. If satisfied, *granted* is returned and the depth traversal continues. Otherwise, *denied* is returned (lines 39–46) and the traversal moves to the next breadth child. In case the input IR does not satisfy the FSP, *denied* is returned (line 8).

For a *write* IR, it is first checked if the requestor has a *write* privilege on the targeted user's wall, by evaluating a *read* IR on the *root* object of the targeted user (lines 10, 11). If this IR satisfies the FSP and the input *write* IR satisfies the WHP, this latter is *granted*, otherwis *denied* is returned (lines 12–15).

In case the input IR is a *share* one (line 16), it is checked if it satisfies both the FSP and the SHP sending *granted* if it does, or *denied* in the failing case.

As for *add-tag* IRs, a *read* IR on the object to be tagged is formulated by the system (line 22). Then it is checked if this system IR satisfies the FSP and if the input *add-tag* IR satisfies the WHP. If the two conditions are satisfied, the input IR is *granted*, otherwise it is *denied*.

Finally, for *add-like* and *add-comment* IRs, they are granted only if they satisfy the FSP and if a system issued *read* IR on the object they target (line 29) is granted (i.e., it satisfies the FSP too) (lines 30–33).

4   Correctness Property

To formalize the correctness property of the system, we define the concept of its *state* as the set, $SIR = \{ir_1, ir_2, ..ir_n\}$, of interaction requests currently granted in the system. We say that the state of the system is correct, and we refer to it as the *correct state*, if and only if $\forall ir_i \in SIR, ir_i$ satisfies all the model's properties. The system changes its state only when a new IR processed by Algorithm 1 returns a granted message. Given a *correct state*, the following holds:[5]

Theorem 1. *Let SIR be the current state of the system. Let ir_{new} be a new interaction request issued to the system. Algorithm 1 issues a granted message if and only if $SIR_{new} = SIR \cup \{ir_{new}\}$ is a correct state.*

We note that changes to labels, either FCLs or OSLs, by a user does not affect the stability of the system, as they concern how the user's data flows to her friends only. That is, if Alice changes the OSL of her photo, this will only result in making it available to a larger audience from her friends, as will be imposed by Algorithm 1. Likewise, changing the FCL of her friend Bob, will result in changing the set of her available objects to Bob, for which the access will always be controlled by Algorithm 1.

---

[5] Related proofs are reported in [1].

Algorithm 1 Access control enforcement

Input: An IR, $ir = (x, p, b)$
Output: *granted* or *denied*
1: **Switch** p **do**
2:     **Case** *read*   ▷ x is an object
3:         **if** $x.copyof \neq null$ **then**
4:             $ir \leftarrow$ **NoHorDisclosure**(ir);
5:         **if** **SatisfyFSP**(ir) **then**
6:             **propagate**(ir);
7:         **else**
8:             **send** *denied*;
9:     **Case** *write*   ▷ x is a target user
10:         $root_x \leftarrow$ **GetRootOf**(x);
11:         $ir_{allowed} \leftarrow (root_x, read, b)$;
12:         **if** **SatisfyFSP**$(ir_{allowed}) \wedge$ **SatisfyWHP**(ir) **then**
13:             **send** *granted*;
14:         **else**
15:             **send** *denied*;
16:     **Case** *share*   ▷ x is an object
17:         **if** **SatisfyFSP**$(ir) \wedge$ **SatisfySHP**(ir) **then**
18:             **send** *granted*;
19:         **else**
20:             **send** *denied*;
21:     **Case** *add-tag*   ▷ x is a pair (usr, obj)
22:         $ir_{allowed} \leftarrow (obj, read, b)$;
23:         $ir \leftarrow (usr, p, b)$;
24:         **if** **SatisfyFSP**$(ir_{allowed}) \wedge$ **SatisfyWHP**(ir) **then**
25:             **send** *granted*;
26:         **else**
27:             **send** *denied*;
28:     **Case** *add-like* $\vee$ *add-comment*   ▷ x is an object
29:         $ir_{read} \leftarrow (x, read, b)$;
30:         **if** **SatisfyFSP**$(ir_{read}) \wedge$ **SatisfyFSP**(ir) **then**
31:             **send** *granted*;
32:         **else**
33:             **send** *denied*;

34: **function NoHorDisclosure**$(ir_{a,o})$
35:     $IR \leftarrow ir_{a,o}$;
36:     **while** $o.copyof \neq null$ **do**
37:         **if** isFriend(a, o.copyof.owner) **then**
38:             $IR \leftarrow ir_{a,o.copyof}$;   ▷ rewrite the IR to target the copied object
39:         $ir_{a,o} \leftarrow ir_{a,o.copyof}$;
        return IR;

40: **procedure PROPAGATE**$(ir_{a,o})$
41:     **send** *granted*;
42:     **while** $ch \leftarrow o.nextChild \neq null$ **do**
43:         $IR \leftarrow (ch, read, a)$;
44:         **if** **SatisfyFSP**(IR) **then**
45:             **propagate**(IR);   ▷ propagate to next in-depth child
46:         **else**
47:             **send** *denied*;   ▷ deny and iterate to next in-breadth child

5   Performance Experiments

In our experiments, we study the performance of LAMP under access scenarios simulated on a real OSN graph. We have implemented a prototype of LAMP as a web application that we interfaced with Facebook graph API. The prototype has been implemented using PHP and the MySQL DBMS. We have been running a usability study, for which preliminary satisfactory results have been obtained. For space limitations, we report these in a technical report [1]. Our experiments have been conducted on a standard PC with a dual core processor of 2.99 GHZ each and 8 GB of RAM.

For performance testing, we exploited the public dataset available for the Slovakian OSN, Pokec.[6] The dataset represents a friendship graph of 1.63 million nodes and 30.6 million edges with a diameter equal to 11; however, it does not contain any data object. As we discuss in [1], the performance is regulated by the number of children in an object dependency tree (i.e., d), and by the number of chained shares an object is subject to (i.e., m). For this, we performed two experiments, by varying both m and d independently. As such, we first simulated share operations along friendship paths of different lengths, and we computed the time required to evaluate an access request on each of the shared copies. Figure 3a reports the achieved results. The x-axis refers to the number of chained shares an object has been subject to, whereas the y-axis refers to the average time in milliseconds required to evaluate an access request on the last shared copy. All the reported numbers are the result of averaging 40 individual instances. As we can see on the figure, the time required to evaluate an access request on a shared copy is directly proportional to the distance between the target shared copy and the original object it refers to (i.e., the number of chained shares). However, the case of a chained share of length 50 requires no more than 80 ms. We can also see that the evaluation time does not follow a perfect linear increase with the number of chained shares. This is because the friendship sub-graph surrounding the sharing path also affects the convergence of the evaluation, as the *NoHorDisclosure* function in Algorithm 1 makes recursive calls as long as a common friendship is found to be between the requestor and the owner of the copied object.

We have also simulated object dependency trees of different sizes (d) varying both their breadth and depth. We considered the worst case scenario whereby the access evaluation on all children of a tree is positive. Figure 3b reports the achieved results by plotting the time in milliseconds (the y-axis) for tree sizes varying from 100 to 10K children.[7] For each reported tree size, the evaluation time has been averaged across 10 different trees by varying their breadth and depth sizes. For all considered trees, the breadth made at least 80 % of the tree's size. This is because on Facebook for instance, and according to the same study mentioned above, most of the interactions are one level likes or one level comments.

As it can be seen on the figure, the amount of time required to evaluate access requests on all the children in an objects dependency tree increases, as expected, almost linearly with the size of the tree. We can see that the evaluation time still remains below 8k ms for trees of 10k children in size.

---

[6] http://snap.stanford.edu/data/soc-pokec.html.

[7] Based on a 2015 study on Facebook, the average likes for personal content is below 100. It is about 100K for business and fans pages: http://www.adweek.com/socialtimes/infographic-quintly-average-like-totals-pages-february-2015/617303.

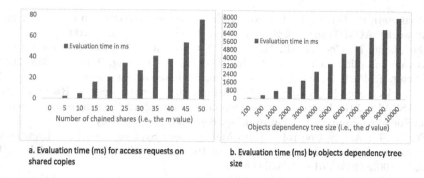

a. Evaluation time (ms) for access requests on shared copies

b. Evaluation time (ms) by objects dependency tree size

Fig. 3. Performance results on LAMP

6   Conclusion and Future Work

In this paper, we presented a label-based access control model for OSNs. The proposed LAMP model considers relationships between objects in an OSN and allows their control at an atomic ownership level, simplifying as such the complexity of addressing data co-ownership of integral elements over which conflictual access policies may be specified. LAMP ensures a flexible and rich set of privacy settings, and empowers data owners to have control over the objects they create at finer granularity levels (e.g., comment, like, etc.). Our method achieves practical performance results and it is also designed to fit within different types of OSNs. Indeed, although we assume an undirected graph model for OSNs, our proposed solution can naturally fit the directed graph model as well, as the FCLs are directional (i.e., $FCL_{A,B}$ and $FCL_{B,A}$ are independently governing the data flow from A to B and from B to A, respectively.)

We are aware of the importance of ensuring usability and friendliness to average OSN users. Our preliminary usability experiments results are satisfactory [1]; however, they remain limited in terms of the number of participants and their representation of average users, but most importantly in terms of the amount of time these participants have been using our app. However, we believe that our model provides a simpler solution compared to other proposals for the management of co-owned data. As such, the first planned extension of this work is on usability experiments that need to be enriched in terms of the representativeness of participants, the statistical relevance of usage time, and the completeness of the interactions available on the app. Moreover, we plan to design accompanying mechanisms for the automatic assignment of friend and object labels based on general policies that the users can set, or based on automated learning strategies.

References

1. Bahri, L., Carminati, B., Ferrari, E., Lucia, W.: Technical report: Lamp - label-based access control for more privacy in online social networks (2016). https://drive.google.com/file/d/0B9hyKuTMyMBzeTUxbGZBWHlQSHc/view

2. Carminati, B., Ferrari, E., Perego, A.: Enforcing access control in web-based social networks. ACM Trans. Inf. System Secur. (TISSEC) **13**(1), 6 (2009)
3. Caviglione, L., Coccoli, M., Merlo, A.: A taxonomy-based model of security and privacy in online social networks. Int. J. Comput. Sci. Eng. **9**(4), 325–338 (2014)
4. Cheng, Y., Park, J., Sandhu, R.: Relationship-based access control for online social networks: beyond user-to-user relationships. In: Privacy, Security, Risk and Trust (PASSAT), 2012 International Conference on and 2012 International Conference on Social Computing (SocialCom), pp. 646–655. IEEE (2012)
5. Ferrari, E.: Access Control in Data Management Systems. Synthesis Lectures on Data Management, Morgan & Claypool Publishers (2010). http://dx.doi.org/10.2200/S00281ED1V01Y201005DTM004
6. Fong, P.W., Siahaan, I.: Relationship-based access control policies and their policy languages. In: Proceedings of the 16th ACM Symposium on Access Control Models and Technologies, pp. 51–60. ACM (2011)
7. Gao, H., Hu, J., Huang, T., Wang, J., Chen, Y.: Security issues in online social networks. IEEE Internet Comput. **15**(4), 56–63 (2011)
8. Hu, H., Ahn, G.J., Jorgensen, J.: Multiparty access control for online social networks: model and mechanisms. IEEE Trans. Knowl. Data Eng. **25**(7), 1614–1627 (2013)
9. Hu, H., Ahn, G.J., Zhao, Z., Yang, D.: Game theoretic analysis of multiparty access control in online social networks. In: Proceedings of the 19th ACM Symposium on Access Control Models and Technologies, pp. 93–102. ACM (2014)
10. Madejski, M., Johnson, M.L., Bellovin, S.M.: The failure of online social network privacy settings. Columbia University Academic Commons (2011)
11. Masoumzadeh, A., Joshi, J.: Osnac: an ontology-based access control model for social networking systems. In: 2010 IEEE Second International Conference on Social Computing (SocialCom), pp. 751–759. IEEE (2010)
12. Mehregan, P., Fong, P.W.L.: Design patterns for multiple stakeholders in social computing. In: Atluri, V., Pernul, G. (eds.) DBSec 2014. LNCS, vol. 8566, pp. 163–178. Springer, Heidelberg (2014)
13. ORACLE: Label security administrator's guide. http://docs.oracle.com/cd/B19306_01/network.102/b14267/intro.htm. Accessed 29 May 2015
14. Pang, J., Zhang, Y.: A new access control scheme for facebook-style social networks. Comput. Secur. **54**, 44–59 (2015)
15. Squicciarini, A.C., Xu, H., Zhang, X.L.: Cope: Enabling collaborative privacy management in online social networks. J. Am. Soc. Inform. Sci. Technol. **62**(3), 521–534 (2011)
16. Such, J.M., Rovatsos, M.: Privacy policy negotiation in social media. arXiv preprint (2014). arXiv:1412.5278

Privacy-Preserving Two-Party Skyline Queries Over Horizontally Partitioned Data

Ling Chen[1][(✉)], Ting Yu[2], and Rada Chirkova[1]

[1] Department of Computer Science, North Carolina State University, Raleigh, USA
{lchen10,rychirko}@ncsu.edu
[2] Qatar Computing Research Institute, Hamad Bin Khalifa University,
Doha, Qatar
tyu@qf.org.qa

Abstract. Skyline queries are an important type of multi-criteria analysis with diverse applications in practice (e.g., personalized services and intelligent transport systems). In this paper, we study how to answer skyline queries efficiently and in a privacy-preserving way when the data are sensitive and distributedly owned by multiple parties. We adopt the classical honest-but-curious attack model, and design a suite of efficient protocols for skyline queries over horizontally partitioned data. We analyze in detail the efficiency of each of the proposed protocols as well as their privacy guarantees.

1 Introduction

Given a set of multi-dimensional vectors, a skyline query [8] is to find all the vectors that are not dominated by any other vector. Skyline queries are widely used in multi-criteria decision making applications, for example, personalized services, intelligent transport systems, location-based services and urban planning.

In this paper, we study how to answer skyline queries over sensitive data distributedly owned by multiple parties who do not fully trust each other. Similar to many past efforts on other data analysis tasks [1,25,28,29], by adopting a secure multi-party computation setting, our goal is to design efficient and privacy-preserving distributed protocols to enable multiple data owners to collaboratively compute skyline queries without revealing their private inputs. Due to space limit, we focus on horizontally partitioned data where similar information about different individuals is collected in different organizations.

Our approach for privacy-preserving skyline queries over horizontally partitioned data utilizes some existing secure protocols for basic operations, such as secure comparison protocols [10,30], secure vector dominance protocols [3,19,20], secure permutation protocols [12], secure equality-testing protocols [13,26], and secure multi-to-sum protocols [26,27]. To securely compute skyline queries, the secure protocol needs to address two problems: (1) how to securely determine

© IFIP International Federation for Information Processing 2016
Published by Springer International Publishing Switzerland 2016. All Rights Reserved
S. Foresti and J. Lopez (Eds.): WISTP 2016, LNCS 9895, pp. 187–203, 2016.
DOI: 10.1007/978-3-319-45931-8_12

whether a vector in one party dominates a vector in the other party? (2) how to securely apply the protocol of (1) to the set of vector pairs formed by pairing a vector V_1 in one party A with each vector in the other party B, with the goal of determining whether V_1 is dominated by any vector in party B or not. To address these two problems, straightforward compositions of such basic building blocks would not offer viable solutions. For example, existing techniques propose secure protocols to perform vector dominance checking, but they cannot be applied directly to address the first problem. The reason is that vector dominance requires each dimensional value in a vector V_1 to be strictly better than the corresponding dimensional value in another vector V_2, while the dominance used in skyline queries (referred to as skyline dominance) allows some dimensional values but not all values in V_1 to be equal to the corresponding dimensional values in V_2. Further, to address the second problem, simply invoking the protocol for the first problem for each pair of vectors when answering skyline queries would unnecessarily reveal sensitive intermediate results, i.e., V_1 is dominated or not dominated by certain vector in the other party.

To address these challenges, we propose three secure protocols. The major novelty of our protocols lies in the following aspects. First, to address the first problem, we propose a novel protocol, enhanced vector dominance protocol (EVDP). Our insight is that for two d-dimensional vectors V_1 and V_2 that are not equal in every dimension, we can obtain the same dominance results for vector dominance and skyline dominance if we improve every value in V_1 by a fixed value. Therefore, EVDP improves every value in V_1 by a fixed value to obtain V_1', and applies a vector dominance protocol over V_1' and V_2 to securely obtain the skyline dominance results of V_1 and V_2. Second, built upon EVDP, we propose three *1-to-N skyline dominance* protocols (HP.1, HP.2, and HP.3) to address the second problem. These protocols determine whether a vector in one party is dominated by any of the N vectors in the other party. By applying these protocols on every vector in each party, we can securely compute the final skyline results without disclosing non-skyline results.

These three proposed protocols provide different levels of protection of the intermediate computation results with different communication and computation costs. HP.1 applies EVDP to determine whether a vector V_a in party A is dominated by any of the n vectors $V_{b_1}, \ldots, V_{b_n}$ in party B, and terminates whenever a dominance is found or when all vectors in party B are compared with. To prevent the disclosure of which vector in party B dominates V_a, HP.1 also employs the secure permutation protocol to permute the order of the vectors in party B. However, such protocol still discloses the intermediate results about at least how many vectors in B do not dominate V_a. To prevent such disclosure, HP.2 and HP.3 improve over HP.1 with different additional costs. HP.2 requires $O(d \cdot 2^n)$ invocations of the multi-to-sum protocol, while HP.3 requires $O(d \cdot n)$ invocations of the multi-to-sum protocol for d-dimensional vectors and $O(n)$ invocations of the secure comparison protocol. When n is relatively small, HP.2 and HP.3 have comparable costs, and HP.3 is preferred when n becomes larger.

2   Skyline Queries

Skyline queries are an important class of preference queries supporting multi-criteria decision making. A skyline query over a d-dimensional data set S returns a subset of S containing d-dimensional vectors that are not dominated by any other vector in S. We assume the existence of a total order relationship on each dimension, and refer to the dominance relationship in skyline queries as skyline dominance:

Definition 1 (Skyline Dominance). *Given two vectors* $V_1 = (a_1, \ldots, a_d)$ *and* $V_2 = (b_1, \ldots, b_d)$, *if for* $i = 1, \ldots, d$, $a_i \succeq b_i$ *and* $\exists j$, $a_j \succ b_j$, *we say that* $V_1 \succ^s V_2$, *where* $\succ^s$ *denotes skyline dominance,* $\succeq$ *denotes better than or equal to, and* $\succ$ *denotes better than.*

Consider the following example of skyline queries. Assume that a user wants to book a hotel for a conference with the goals of *inexpensive* price and *short* distance to the conference venue. Consider four hotels A ($200, 5 miles), B ($150, 2 miles), C ($120, 3 miles), and D ($150, 1 mile). Hotel C is clearly a better candidate than A because C is cheaper and closer to the venue. Therefore, we say that C dominates A. Also, D dominates B since D is as expensive as B but is closer to the venue. However, C does not dominate B since B is closer than C to the venue. Therefore, the skyline results are $\{C, D\}$.

In a straightforward approach for skyline queries, such as Block-Nested-Loops [8], a skyline vector needs to be compared against all other vectors to ensure that no other vectors dominate it. Without loss of generality, we assume that the domain of each dimension is I (the integer domain) and the larger the better, i.e., a bigger value dominates a smaller value. Each dimension can be encoded with l bits, and its value ranges from 0 to $2^l - 1$.

2.1   Horizontally Partitioned Data

We formally define skyline queries over the vectors distributed in two parties, i.e., horizontally partitioned data (HPD):

Definition 2 (Skyline Queries over HPD). *Party A has* m *vectors* $\mathbb{V}_a = (V_{a,1}, \ldots, V_{a,m})$ *and party B has* n *vectors* $\mathbb{V}_b = (V_{b,1}, \ldots, V_{b,n})$. *Vectors in both parties have the same* d *skyline attributes. A skyline query over HPD returns a set of vectors* $\{V_i | V_i \in \mathbb{V}_a \cup \mathbb{V}_b, \nexists V_j \in \mathbb{V}_a \cup \mathbb{V}_b, s.t. V_j \succ^s V_i\}$.

To compute skyline queries over HPD, a straightforward approach is to create a list of all the vectors from two parties and compute skyline vectors over the list of the vectors. A more efficient approach is to compute skyline vectors first in each party (referred to as local skyline vectors) and then compute global skyline vectors from the local skyline vectors, since local non-skyline vectors are guaranteed not to be global skyline vectors.

Application Scenario. A state fellowship is looking for high school student candidates that have high GPA, high SAT score and high ACT score.

Since the candidates are distributed over different high schools within a state, secure skyline queries over the data across different schools are required. The scores of those students that are not selected for the fellowship should not be revealed. To securely select the candidates, high schools can perform privacy-preserving skyline queries with GPA, SAT and ACT scores as the skyline attributes.

2.2 Threat Model

We consider the semi-honest adversarial model, where both parties are honest but curious. Each party knows only its own vectors. The final skyline results are known to both parties. Given a secure protocol that computes the final skyline results, both parties strictly follow the protocol specifications but are willing to learn any information leaked during execution in order to compromise privacy.

3 Secure Multi-party Computation Building Blocks

Secure multi-party computation (SMC) [14,30] is a framework that allows multiple parties to perform rich data analytics over their private data without revealing any information other than the output [2,3,20,21]. We next present some basic SMC protocols that we use in our proposed protocols.

Secure Comparison Protocol. Secure comparison is an important problem in cryptography and its solution serves as a primitive operation in many SMC problems. The goal of this problem is to solve the inequality between two numbers a and b, i.e., whether $a \geq b$, without revealing the actual values of a and b. Cachin [10] proposed a scheme where a semi-trusted third party provides a means for two bidders to determine whose bid is higher in zero knowledge. This scheme assumes that two bidders do not collude with each other. The communication complexity of Cachin's scheme is linear.

Secure Permutation Protocol. A secure permutation protocol is to permute the values in a vector without revealing the values of the vector and the permutation. A typical scenario is that party A has a vector $V_A = (a_1, \ldots, a_d)$ and party B has a private permutation π and a random vector $R = (r_1, \ldots, r_d)$. A secure two-party permutation protocol enables party A to obtain $\pi(V_A + R)$ without party A learning π or R; Party B also should not learn about V_A. Existing research [12] introduces a representative secure protocol based on a homomorphic public key system. The working mechanism is as follows: firstly, party A generates a key pair for a homomorphic public key system and sends the public key to party B. Using the public key, party A then encrypts V_A and sends the result $E(V_A)$ to party B. Party B computes $E(V_A) \cdot E(R) = E(V_A + R)$, permutes $E(V_A + R)$ using π, and then sends the result $\pi(E(V_A + R))$ to party A. Party A decrypts $\pi(E(V_A + R))$ by the private key and gets $D(\pi(E(V_A + R))) = \pi(D(E(V_A + R))) = \pi(V_A + R)$.

Secure Equality-Testing Protocol. An equality-testing protocol is to determine the equality between two numbers without revealing the values of two numbers. A typical solution is to apply a commutative encryption scheme to achieve secure equality testing [13,26].

Secure Vector Dominance Protocol. Suppose party A has a vector $V_A = (a_1, \ldots, a_d)$ and party B has a vector $V_B = (b_1, \ldots, b_d)$. One existing protocol [3, 19,20] is as follows: first, party A and party B use an input disguise method to get a randomized input: $V'_A = (a'_1, \ldots, a'_{4d})$ and $V'_B = (b'_1, \ldots, b'_{4d})$. Such a disguise makes sure that for values in V'_A and V'_B, there will be the same number of $a'_i > b'_i$ situations as that of $a'_i < b'_i$ situations. Let $Z = (1, \ldots, 1, 0, \ldots, 0)$, where the first $2d$ values are all 1 (indicating $a'_i > b'_i$) and the remaining $2d$ values are all 0. Second, party B generates a random permutation π and a random vector R. Party A computes $V''_A = \pi(V'_A + R)$ using the secure permutation protocol while party B computes $V''_B = \pi(V'_B + R)$ and $Z' = \pi(Z)$. Third, party A and party B use a secure comparison protocol, such as Yao's Millionaire protocol, to compare V''_{A_i} and V''_{B_i} where $i = 1, \ldots, 4d$. Party A holds all the comparison results, $U = (u_1, \ldots, u_{4d})$. If $V''_{A_i} > V''_{B_i}$, where $i = 1, \ldots, 4d$, $u_i = 1$, otherwise, $u_i = 0$. Fourth, party A and party B use a secure equality-testing protocol to compare U with Z'. If $U = Z'$, indicating $a'_i > b'_i$ for $i = 1, \ldots, 2d$, then V_A dominates V_B. Otherwise, V_A does not dominate V_B.

Secure Multi-to-Sum Protocol. The multi-to-sum protocol [26,27] is to convert the multiplicative sharing of a secret s to the additive sharing of s. Assume there is a secret s over a ring R and $s = a \cdot b = x + y$. $Pair(a, b)$ is called the multiplicative sharing of s. $Pair(x, y)$ is called the additive sharing of s. Initially, party A holds a while party B holds b such that $a \cdot b = s$. After executing the multi-to-sum protocol, party A holds x and party B holds y such that $x + y = s$, with no information leaked to any of them about s or the multiplicative sharing a and b.

4   Privacy-Preserving Skyline Queries

4.1   Enhanced Vector Dominance Protocol (EVDP)

Existing work proposes a secure vector dominance protocol (VDP) that securely computes the vector dominance of two d-dimensional vectors, but the definition of vector dominance is more strict than skyline dominance.

Definition 3 (Vector Dominance). *Given two vectors $V_1 = (a_1, \ldots, a_d)$ and $V_2 = (b_1, \ldots, b_d)$, if for all $i = 1, \ldots, d$, $a_i \succ b_i$, then we say that $V_1 \succ^v V_2$, where $\succ^v$ denotes vector dominance and $\succ$ denotes better than.*

Table 1 illustrates the differences between vector dominance and skyline dominance using 2-dimensional vectors. As we can see from the second column $((2, 1) \succ (1, 1))$, vector dominance and skyline dominance return different values when (1) every value in V_a is not worse than the corresponding value in V_b and at least one value in V_a is better than the corresponding value in V_b and (2) at least one and at most $d - 1$ values in V_a are the same as the corresponding values

Table 1. Differences between Vector Dominance and Skyline Dominance

Input: V_a, V_b	$(1,1) \succ (1,1)$	$(2,1) \succ (1,1)$	$(2,2) \succ (1,1)$	$(2,0) \succ (1,1)$
Vector dominance	F	F	T	F
Skyline dominance	F	T	T	F
Enhanced vector dominance	T	T	T	F

in V_b. Due to such differences, we cannot directly apply secure vector dominance protocols to answer skyline queries.

To address this problem, we propose an enhanced vector dominance protocol (EVDP), which adapts VDP to support skyline dominance. EVDP accepts as input two vectors $V_a = (a_1, \ldots, a_d)$ and $V_{b_i} = (b_{i,1}, \ldots, b_{i,d})$, and improves V_{b_i} in every dimension to obtain V'_{b_i}: $V'_{b_i} = V_{b_i} + (1, \ldots, 1) = (b_{i,1} + 1, \ldots, b_{i,d} + 1)$. By performing VDP on V'_{b_i} instead of V_{b_i}, EVDP obtains the same dominance results as skyline dominance except when V_{a_i} and V_{b_i} are exactly the same, as shown in the first column in Table 1. In other words, if we assume that V_{b_i} and V_a are not the same in every attribute (referred to as the *inequality assumption*), then the results of EVDP is the same as skyline dominance's.

Checking the inequality assumption allows both parties to know that they have a set of common vectors. We next analyze how such disclosure can be used to infer side information about the other party. First, if a vector V_1 in party A and a vector V_2 in party B are equal, there exists no vector in either party dominating V_1 or V_2, and V_1 and V_2 must belong to the final skyline results, which are known to both parties. Such disclosure cannot help a party infer the values of the remaining vectors in another party. Second, ideally, even if party A sees a vector of its local skyline results V_1 is in the final results, it should not know whether party B has the same vector. Thus, knowing the existence of V_2 can be used by A to infer that the local skyline results of party B do not contain the vectors that can be dominated by V_2. However, such disclosure cannot be directly used by A to infer the complete data distribution of B's vectors.

To securely test the inequality assumption, we adopt equality-testing protocol, which leverages homomorphic encryption to securely identify from two parities all the vectors that have the same attribute values. For these identified vectors, we can safely output them as the final skyline results. Also, since these vectors do not dominate any other vector V' in the local skyline results (otherwise V' would not appear in the local skyline results), we can safely exclude them from the skyline dominance testing against the remaining vectors.

For computing the final skyline results from the remaining vectors, we propose three secure protocols based on EVDP.

4.2 1-to-N Skyline Dominance

As discussed earlier, a straightforward protocol that applies EVDP on each pair of vectors in both parties discloses significant intermediate results. To prevent such disclosure, we define *1-to-N skyline dominance* as the primitive operation in privacy-preserving skyline queries over HPD.

Definition 4 (1-to-N Skyline Dominance). *Party A has one vector $V_a = (a_1, \ldots, a_d)$ and party B has n vectors $V_{b_1} = (b_{1,1}, \ldots, b_{1,d}), \ldots, V_{b_n} = (b_{n,1}, \ldots, b_{n,d})$. 1-to-N skyline dominance returns false if $\nexists V_{b_i}$ s.t. $V_{b_i} \succ^s V_a$; otherwise, returns true.*

Based on this definition, we propose three secure horizontal 1-to-N skyline dominance protocols, referred to as HP.1, HP.2, and HP.3, which securely compute skyline dominance between a vector V_a in Party A and n vectors in party B. To obtain the final skyline results, these protocols are applied $m + n$ times on each vector in parties A and B. One party can easily learn the number of vectors in the local skyline results in the other party (i.e., m or n) during the computation. To prevent the disclosure of m and n, both parties can generate random number of dummy vectors that are guaranteed to be pruned in the computation of final skyline results. The dummy vectors can be generated by randomly selecting out-of-domain values. For example, when each element in a vector is in the range $[0, 1000)$, the dummy vectors can be generated within the range $(-\infty, 0)$. We next present the details of the three protocols.

4.3 Secure Horizontal 1-to-N Skyline Dominance Protocol (HP.1)

To determine whether V_a is dominated by any of the n vectors from party B (1-to-N Skyline Dominance), HP.1 first pairs V_a with each of the vectors in party B and gets pairs of vectors $(V_a, V_{b_1}), \ldots, (V_a, V_{b_n})$. The steps of HP.1 are shown in Algorithm 1. To securely compute skyline queries over HPD, HP.1 prevents two types of disclosure: (1) for each pair (V_a, V_{b_i}), which values and how many values in V_{b_i} dominate the corresponding values in V_a (Steps 1–4); (2) which vector in $\{V_{b_1}, \ldots, V_{b_n}\}$ dominates V_a (Steps 5–6).

In Step 1, party B prepares each of its vectors for EVDP by increasing the values in the vectors.

Steps 2–4 include input disguise, secure permutation and secure comparison, which are adapted from VDP. In Step 2, both parties A and B disguise their vectors to prevent the disclosure of how many values in V_a are better than the values in V_{b_i}. We adopt the disguise algorithm based on [3]: given party A's vector $V_a = (a_1, \ldots, a_d)$, it generates a $4d$-dimension vector $V_a' = (a_1', \ldots, a_{4d}')$, such that

$$a_1' = 2a_1, \qquad \ldots, \qquad a_d' = 2a_d, \qquad (1)$$
$$a_{d+1}' = 2a_1 + 1, \qquad \ldots, \qquad a_{2d}' = 2a_d + 1, \qquad (2)$$
$$a_{2d+1}' = -2a_1, \qquad \ldots, \qquad a_{3d}' = -2a_d, \qquad (3)$$
$$a_{3d+1}' = -(2a_1 + 1), \qquad \ldots, \qquad a_{4d}' = -(2a_d + 1). \qquad (4)$$

Given party B's vector $V_{b_i} = (b_{i,1}, \ldots, b_{i,d})$, it generates a $4d$-dimension vector $V'_{b_i} = (b'_{i,1}, b'_{i,2}, \ldots, b'_{i,4d})$, such that

$$b'_{i,1} = 2b_{i,1} + 1, \qquad \ldots, \qquad b'_{i,d} = 2b_{i,d} + 1, \qquad (5)$$

$$b'_{i,d+1} = 2b_{i,1}, \qquad \ldots, \qquad b'_{i,2d} = 2b_{i,d}, \qquad (6)$$

$$b'_{i,2d+1} = -(2b_{i,1} + 1), \qquad \ldots, \qquad b'_{i,3d} = -(2b_{i,d} + 1), \qquad (7)$$

$$b'_{i,3d+1} = -2b_{i,1}, \qquad \ldots, \qquad b'_{i,4d} = -2b_{i,d}. \qquad (8)$$

This disguise scheme has the following interesting property: for a pair (V'_a, V'_{b_i}), there will be the same number of $a'_j > b'_{i,j}$ situations as that of $a'_j < b'_{i,j}$ situations when $a_j = b_{i,j}$ or $a_j > b_{i,j}$ or $a_j < b_{i,j}$. Thus, we cannot infer how many values in V_1 are greater than the values in V_2 by simply counting the number of "1"s in the comparison vector [3]. Also, we can see that when the d-dimensional vector V'_a dominates V'_{b_i}, the comparison vector must be a $4d$-dimensional vector where the first $2d$ attribute values are all "1" and the remaining $2d$ attribute values are all "0". Thus, we construct $Z = (\underbrace{1, \ldots, 1}_{2d}, \underbrace{0, \ldots, 0}_{2d})$ in Step 2, which is used to determine whether V_a is dominated by V_{b_i} by comparing the permuted Z with the comparison vector noted as $\mathbb{U}$ in HP.1 (Step 6).

In Step 3, HP.1 uses the secure permutation protocol to prevent B from learning the order of the vectors used to perform skyline dominance checking with V_a. Party A generates n random permutations and n random vectors. These permutations and random vectors are used to permute the disguised vectors V'_a, V'_{b_i} and Z. We use n random permutations instead of one to prevent adversaries from guessing the data distribution of the skyline attribute values.

In Step 4, for the ith pair $(V''_{a,i}, V''_{b_i})$, party B applies a secure comparison protocol to obtain comparison results U_i, where $U_i = (u_{i,1}, \ldots, u_{i,4d})$, $u_{i,j} = 1$ if $b''_{i,j} > a''_{i,j}$, and $u_{i,j} = 0$ if $b''_{i,j} \leq a''_{i,j}$ for $j = 1, \ldots, 4d$. If we simply run a secure equality testing protocol for each pair of Z'_i in Z and U_i in $\mathbb{U}$, we will disclose the intermediate results about whether V_a is dominated by V_{b_i} or not.

To prevent disclosure of the intermediate results, HP.1 applies a secure permutation protocol on Z and $\mathbb{U}$ (Step 5). Party A generates a new random permutation π_{n+1} to obtains Z', and party B obtains $\mathbb{U}'$ by using π_{n+1}. Then Z' is compared with $\mathbb{U}'$ by using a secure equality testing protocol: the testing terminates if there is any $U'_i = Z''_i$ or none can be found.

Example. Assume that Party A has $V_a = (1,1)$, and Party B has three vectors: $V_{b_1} = (3,1)$, $V_{b_2} = (2,2)$, and $V_{b_3} = (4,0)$. After Step 1, we have $V_{b_1} = (4,2)$, $V_{b_2} = (3,3)$, and $V_{b_3} = (5,1)$. We then perform input disguise (Step 2): Party A has $V'_a = (2,2,3,3,-2,-2,-3,-3)$ and Z, and Party B has $V'_{b_2} = (7,7,6,6,-7,-7,-6,-6)$. We omit the detailed transformations of V'_{b_1} and V'_{b_3} due to space limitations. In Step 3, assume that $R_2 = (1,1,1,1,1,1,1,1)$ and π_2 simply switches the first $4d$ values with the last $4d$ values: Party A has $V''_{a,2} = (-1,-1,-2,-2,3,3,4,4)$ and $Z'_2 = (0,0,0,0,1,1,1,1)$, and Party B has $V''_{b_2} = (-6,-6,-5,-5,8,8,7,7)$. In Step 4, by applying secure comparison on $V'''_{a,2}$ and V'''_{b_2}, Party B obtains $U_2 = (0,0,0,0,1,1,1,1)$. In Step 5, assume that $R_2' = (2, 2, 2, 2, 2, 2, 2, 2)$ and π_4 permutes $(1, 2, 3)$ to $(2, 1, 3)$: Party A obtains $Z_2'' = (2, 2, 2, 2, 3, 3, 3, 3)$ and $\mathbb{Z}' = (Z_2'', Z_1'', Z_3'')$, and Party B has $U_2' = (2, 2, 2, 2, 3, 3, 3, 3)$ and $\mathbb{U}' = (U_2', U_1', U_3')$ (note that Party B does not know the order of items in $\mathbb{U}'$). In Step 6, Z_2'' and U_2' are first compared and since they are equal, we know that V_a is at least dominated by V_{b_2}.

Communication and Computation Cost. HP.1's communication cost includes the costs for applying the secure permutation protocol, the secure comparison protocol, and the secure equality testing protocol.

For a vector in party $A(B)$, HP.1 needs to apply $n + 1$ $(m + 1)$ times of the secure permutation protocol. We assume each dimension in a vector is an integer that can be encoded with l bits, and its value ranges from 0 to $2^l - 1$. The communication cost of applying one secure permutation protocol is $O(d \cdot l)$ as it uses the homomorphic public key system. As HP.1 is applied m times for vectors in party A and n times for vectors in party B, the cost of the secure permutation protocol is $O(n \cdot m \cdot d \cdot l)$. The computation cost of secure permutation depends on the adopted protocol. A representative protocol (see Sect. 3) requires $O(1)$ encryption/decryption, $O(1)$ modular multiplication to obtain $E(V_A) \cdot E(R)$, and $O(1)$ application of the permutation π, whose cost is $O(d)$ for permuting values in a vector.

The secure comparison protocol is applied to compare corresponding attribute values in two vectors, and thus we need to apply at most $n \cdot 4d$ times of the secure comparison protocol. According to Cachin [10], the communication cost of Cachin's protocol to compare input numbers is $O(l)$. By applying $n + m$ times of HP.1, the communication cost of the secure comparisons is $O((n + m) \cdot d \cdot l)$. The computation cost of one secure comparison includes the costs of one generation of the garbled circuits and one evaluation of the garbled circuits, which also includes the adopted oblivious transfer protocols and encryption/decryption of the values for the gates in the circuits [10, 18, 30]. Latest works on garbled circuits show that 16K-bit integer comparison can be computed within 0.5s [17, 22].

The secure equality testing protocol uses the homomorphic public key system. Thus, the communication cost of the adapted equality testing protocol for evaluating the inequality assumption and the equality testing for determining the skyline dominance are both $O((n + m) \cdot d \cdot l)$. The computation cost is $O(n + m)$ invocations of encryption and $O(n \cdot m \cdot d)$ of comparisons to identify the equal encrypted vectors.

Security Analysis. In HP.1, Steps 1–4 protect the comparison results of a pair (V_a, V_{b_i}). In Step 1, the result is computed locally in party B and no information is disclosed. The input disguise in Step 2 makes sure that if $a_j > b_{i,j}$, we will have $a_j' > b_{i,j}'$, $a_{d+j}' > b_{i,d+j}'$, $a_{2d+j}' < b_{i,2d+j}'$, and $a_{3d+j}' < b_{i,3d+j}'$, preventing the disclosure of the comparison results in Step 4. In Step 3, party A generates the permutations and the random vectors, and thus after permutation party B loses track of the order of the values in the vectors. Party A does not know the values of U_i and is not aware of the comparison results.

Algorithm 1. Secure 1-to-N Skyline Dominance Protocol (HP.1)

Input: Party A has one vector $V_a = (a_1, \ldots, a_d)$ and party B has n vectors $V_{b_1} = (b_{1,1}, \ldots, b_{1,d}), \ldots, V_{b_n} = (b_{n,1}, \ldots, b_{n,d})$.

Output: Whether V_a is dominated by any of the n vectors in party B or not.

1: EVDP preparation:
   Party B : **for** $i = 1$ **to** n **do**
$$V_{b_i} = \text{IMPROVE}(V_{b_i})$$
2: Input disguise:
   Party A : $V_a' = \text{DISGUISE}(V_a)$, $Z = (\underbrace{1, \ldots, 1}_{2d}, \underbrace{0, \ldots, 0}_{2d})$

   Party B : **for** $i = 1$ **to** n **do**
$$V_{b_i}' = \text{DISGUISE}(V_{b_i})$$
3: Secure permutation:
   Party A : **for** $i = 1$ **to** n **do**
           Generate π_i and R_i, $V_{a,i}'' = \pi_i(V_a' + R_i)$, $Z_i' = \pi_i(Z)$
       $\mathbb{Z} = (Z_1', \ldots, Z_n')$
   Party B : **for** $i = 1$ **to** n **do**
$$V_{b_i}'' = \text{SECUREPERMUTATION}(\pi_i, V_{b_i}', R_i)^*$$
4: Secure comparison:
   Party B : **for** $i = 1$ **to** n **do**
$$U_i = \text{SECURECOMPARISON}(V_{a,i}'', V_{b_i}'')$$
       $\mathbb{U} = (U_1, \ldots, U_n)$
5: Secure permutation:
   Party A : Generate π_{n+1}
       for $i = 1$ **to** n **do**
           Generate R_i', $Z_i'' = Z_i' + R_i'$
       $\mathbb{Z}' = \pi_{n+1}(Z_1'', \ldots, Z_n'')$, $\mathbb{R} = (R_1', \ldots, R_n')$
   Party B : $\mathbb{U}' = \text{SECUREPERMUTATION}(\pi_{n+1}, \mathbb{U}, \mathbb{R})$
6: Secure equality testing:
   for $i = 1$ **to** n **do**
       if $\text{SECUREEQUALITYTEST}(U_i', Z_i'')$ **then return true**
   return false

---

* Using the secure permutation protocol, party B gets $V_{b_i}'' = \pi_i(V_{b_i}' + R_i)$.

Steps 5–6 protect the comparison results of the pairs $(V_a, V_{b_i}), \ldots, (V_a, V_{b_n})$. In Step 5, party A generates the permutation π_{n+1} and the random vector $\mathbb{R}$, and thus after permutation party B loses track of the order of the vectors in $\mathbb{U}$. On the other hand, party A knows the order of the vectors $V_{a,i}'', (i = 1, \ldots, n)$ after the permutation. However, since all the $V_{a,i}''$ come from V_a, party A cannot infer more information from the order other than what party A originally knows.

However, step 6 could disclose the intermediate results of at least how many vectors in party B do *not* dominate V_a. In Step 6, parties A and B runs secure equality testing until a pair (V_a, V_{b_i}) is found to be equal. If such a pair is not found, then V_a is not dominated by any vector in party B and no intermediate information is disclosed. But if such a pair is found in the ith secure equality testing, then both parties know that at least i-1 vectors in party B do not dominate V_a in party A.

4.4   Enhanced Secure Horizontal 1-to-N Skyline Dominance Protocol (HP.2)

To prevent the disclosure in HP.1, i.e., V_a in party A is not dominated by at least $i - 1$ vectors in party B, we propose an enhanced secure horizontal 1-to-N skyline dominance protocol (referred to as HP.2), which replaces the secure equality testing (Step 6 in Algorithm 1) with a secure protocol to compute a product of the polynomials: $\prod_{i=1}^{n}(Z_i'' - U_i')$. If there exists i such that $Z_i'' = U_i'$, the product is 0, i.e., V_a in party A is dominated by at least one vector in party B and V_a is not a vector in the final skyline results.

Secure evaluation of the product of polynomials can be achieved by leveraging the existing secure multi-to-sum protocol. The steps of the algorithm is shown in Algorithm 2. We first perform the polynomial expansion and obtain a sum of 2^n products. Each product can be converted from the multiplicative sharing to the additive sharing by the secure multi-to-sum protocol. Each party sums all the additive sharing together. Then each party shares the sum and securely computes the final product value of $\prod_{i=1}^{n}(Z_i'' - U_i')$. If it is equal to 0, there must

---

Algorithm 2. Enhanced Secure 1-to-N Skyline Dominance Protocol (HP.2)

Input: Party A has one vector $V_a = (a_{1,1}, \ldots, a_{1,d})$ and party B has n vectors $V_{b_1} = (b_{1,1}, \ldots, b_{1,d}), \ldots, V_{b_n} = (b_{n,1}, \ldots, b_{n,d})$.

Output: Whether V_a is dominated by any of the n vectors in party B or not.

1: Steps 1 - 5 from HP.1.

2: Secure compute $\prod_{i=1}^{n}(Z_i'' - U_i')$:

$$\prod_{i=1}^{n}(Z_i'' - U_i') = \underbrace{\prod_{i=1}^{n}(Z_i'') + \prod_{i=1}^{n-1}(Z_i'') \cdot (-U_n') + \ldots + Z_1'' \cdot \prod_{i=2}^{n}(-U_i')}_{2^n - 2 \text{ multiplicative sharings:} MS_1, \ldots, MS_{2^n - 2}} + \prod_{i=1}^{n}(-U_i')$$

Party A : **for** $i = 1$ to $2^n - 2$ **do**
$$X_{a_i} = \text{MultiToSum}(MS_i)$$
$$\mathbb{A}_z = \prod_{i=1}^{n}(Z_i'') + \sum_{i=1}^{2^n - 2} X_{a_i}$$

Party B : **for** $i = 1$ to $2^n - 2$ **do**
$$X_{b_i} = \text{MultiToSum}(MS_i)$$
$$\mathbb{B}_z = \prod_{i=1}^{n}(-U_i') + \sum_{i=1}^{2^n - 2} X_{b_i}$$

3: Equality testing:
   if $\mathbb{A}_z + \mathbb{B}_z = 0$ **then return true**
   else return false

---

be at least one factor, i.e., $(Z_i'' - U_i')$, being 0, indicating that V_a in party A is dominated.

Let us walk through the process of polynomial expansion by an example where $n = 2$. Party A holds $\mathbb{Z}' = (Z_1'', Z_2'')$ while party B holds $\mathbb{U}' = (U_1', U_2')$. By polynomial expansion, $\prod_{i=1}^{2}(Z_i'' - U_i') = Z_1'' \cdot Z_2'' - Z_1'' \cdot U_2' - U_1' \cdot Z_2'' + U_1' \cdot U_2'$. Party A holds the multiplicative value of $Z_1'' \cdot Z_2''$ while party B holds the value of $U_1' \cdot U_2'$. We use the secure multi-to-sum protocol to obtain the additive sharing X_a and X_b such that $X_a + X_b = Z_1'' \cdot U_2'$, where X_a is held by party A and X_b is held by party B. We do the same for $U_1' \cdot Z_2''$ with Y_a is held by party A and Y_b is held by party B. Therefore, party A holds the sum $\sum_A = Z_1'' \cdot Z_2'' + X_a + Y_a$ and party B holds the sum $\sum_B = U_1' \cdot U_2' + X_b + Y_b$. Then we adopt the secure sum protocol to obtain $\sum = \sum_A + \sum_B$. If $\sum = 0$, V_a is dominated.

Communication and Computation Cost. HP.2 includes the private permutation protocol, the secure comparison protocol, and the secure equality testing protocol. The analyses of these three protocols are the same as those in HP.1 except that HP.2 replaces Step 6 of HP.1 with the secure evaluation of the product $\prod_{i=1}^{n}(Z_i'' - U_i')$. After the polynomial expansion, this product of polynomials is expanded into 2^n items. Among them, there are $d \cdot (2^n - 2)$ items requiring the multi-to-sum protocol to securely convert the multiplicative sharing to the additive sharing.

To compute the final skyline results, HP.2 is applied $m + n$ times. For party A, it requires $m \cdot d \cdot (2^n - 2)$ invocations of the multi-to-sum protocol. For party B, it requires $n \cdot d \cdot (2^m - 2)$ invocations of the multi-to-sum protocol. In total, the complexity is $O(m \cdot d \cdot (2^n - 2) + n \cdot d \cdot (2^m - 2))$ invocations of the multi-to-sum protocol. Even though the cost of the multi-to-sum protocol is $O(l)$ invocations of OT_2^1 oblivious transfer of strings whose cost is $O(l)$ [26,27], the exponential invocations of the multi-to-sum protocol are expensive.

Security Analysis. HP.2 provides strong security guarantee. Compared with HP.1, in Step 6 of HP.2, the evaluation of $\sum = \prod_{i=1}^{n}(Z_i'' - U_i')$ is protected by the secure multi-to-sum protocol. If $\sum$ is 0, both parties know that V_a is dominated by at least one vector of B. But they cannot infer which vectors in B dominate V_a. If $\sum$ is not 0, both parties know that V_a is not dominated by any vector of B, and thus V_a becomes a vector in the final skyline results.

4.5 Alternative Enhanced Secure Horizontal 1-to-N Skyline Dominance Protocol (HP.3)

As discussed above, the use of polynomial expansion in HP.2 incurs exponential communication and computation costs. To reduce the cost, we further propose a more efficient protocol HP.3. The insight of HP.3 is to replace the secure evaluation of the product $\prod_{i=1}^{n}(Z_i'' - U_i')$ in HP.2 with the secure computation of $(Z_i'' - U_i')^2$. Since $(Z_i'' - U_i')^2$ are all greater than or equal to 0, if the min value of $(Z_i'' - U_i')^2$ is 0, V_a in party A is dominated; otherwise, V_a is not dominated. We next discuss the three new steps of HP.3 in Algorithm 3.

In Step 2, each of $(Z_i'' - U_i')^2$ is expanded into a polynomial, i.e., $(Z_i'' - U_i')^2 = (Z_i'')^2 - 2 \cdot Z_i'' \cdot U_i' + (U_i')^2$, where $2 \cdot Z_i'' \cdot U_i'$ can be converted to the additive sharing using the multi-to-sum protocol and then party A holds X_{a_i} and party B holds X_{b_i}. Then each of $(Z_i'' - U_i')^2$ can be transformed into the additive sharing where party A holds $\mathbb{A}_i = (Z_i'')^2 + X_{a_i}$ and party B holds $\mathbb{B}_i = (U_i')^2 + X_{b_i}$. Therefore, party A holds $\mathbb{A} = (\mathbb{A}_1, \ldots, \mathbb{A}_n)$ and party B holds $\mathbb{B} = (\mathbb{B}_1, \ldots, \mathbb{B}_n)$.

In Step 3, we securely find the min value of $\mathbb{A}_i + \mathbb{B}_i$ using $n - 1$ times of secure comparisons. For example, we test whether $\mathbb{A}_1 + \mathbb{B}_1 < \mathbb{A}_2 + \mathbb{B}_2$, i.e., $\mathbb{A}_1 - \mathbb{A}_2 < \mathbb{B}_2 - \mathbb{B}_1$. If $\mathbb{A}_1 + \mathbb{B}_1 < \mathbb{A}_2 + \mathbb{B}_2$, we keep the pair $(\mathbb{A}_1, \mathbb{B}_1)$ to compare with the next pair $(\mathbb{A}_3, \mathbb{B}_3)$. It requires $n - 1$ times of secure comparisons to find the min value $\mathbb{A}_z + \mathbb{B}_z$.

In Step 4, both parties reveal the values of $\mathbb{A}_z$ and $\mathbb{B}_z$, whose sum is minimum among all, and compute $\mathbb{A}_z + \mathbb{B}_z$, and then test whether the min sum value is equal to 0 or not. If it is 0, V_a in party A is dominated. Otherwise, V_a is a global skyline vector.

Algorithm 3. Alternative Enhanced Secure 1-to-N Skyline Dominance Protocol (HP.3)

Input: Party A has one vector $V_a = (a_{1,1}, \ldots, a_{1,d})$ and party B has n vectors $V_{b_1} = (b_{1,1}, \ldots, b_{1,d}), \ldots, V_{b_n} = (b_{n,1}, \ldots, b_{n,d})$.
Output: Whether V_a is dominated by any of the n vectors in party B or not.

1: Steps 1 - 5 from HP.1.
2: $(Z_i'' - U_i')^2$ computation:
      Party A : **for** $i = 1$ **to** n **do**
   $$X_{a_i} = \text{MULTITOSUM}(Z_i'', U_i')$$
   $$\mathbb{A}_i = (Z_i'')^2 + X_{a_i}$$
      Party B : **for** $i = 1$ **to** n **do**
   $$X_{b_i} = \text{MULTITOSUM}(Z_i'', U_i')$$
   $$\mathbb{B}_i = (U_i')^2 + X_{b_i}$$
3: Min value identification:
      Party A : $\mathbb{A}_z = \mathbb{A}_1$
      Party B : $\mathbb{B}_z = \mathbb{B}_1$
      for $i = 2$ **to** n **do**
        if $\text{SECUREGREATERTHAN}(\mathbb{A}_z - \mathbb{A}_i, \mathbb{B}_i - \mathbb{B}_z)$ **then**
          Party A : $\mathbb{A}_z = \mathbb{A}_i$
          Party B : $\mathbb{B}_z = \mathbb{B}_i$
4: Equality testing:
      if $\mathbb{A}_z + \mathbb{B}_z = 0$ **then return true**
      else return false

Communication and Computation Cost. The analysis of Step 1 in Algorithm 3 is the same as HP.1. For Step 2, it requires $O(d \cdot n)$ invocations of the multi-to-sum protocol to securely convert the multiplicative sharing $Z_i'' \cdot U_i'$ into the additive sharing. For Step 3, it requires $O(n)$ invocations of the secure comparisons to securely identify the pair of $(\mathbb{A}_z, \mathbb{B}_z)$. For Step 4, there is no secure protocol applied and the cost can be ignored. Thus, HP.3 reduces the cost of HP.2 from the exponential invocations of the multi-to-sum protocol to the linear invocations of the multi-to-sum protocol plus the linear invocations of the secure comparison protocol.

Security Analysis. Step 1 of HP.3 is the same as Steps 1–5 of HP.1, and thus protects the comparison results of the pairs (V_a, V_{b_i}). Steps 2–3 protect the information of how many vectors in party B may dominate V_a. The multi-to-sum protocol in Step 2 makes sure that both parties cannot know the sum values of each pair $(\mathbb{A}_i, \mathbb{B}_i)$ while searching for the min sum $\mathbb{A}_z + \mathbb{B}_z$. Assume that after Step 3, both parties know that the ith pair produces the min sum $(\mathbb{A}_z, \mathbb{B}_z)$. Party B does not know the order of vectors as Step 5 in HP.1 (Algorithm 1) permutes the order. Hence, party B cannot infer which vector produces the value $\mathbb{B}_z$. For party A, all vectors are derived from V_a and thus no more information can be inferred by party A regarding which vector in party B contributes to the value $\mathbb{B}_z$.

In Step 4, both parties reveal the values of $(\mathbb{A}_z, \mathbb{B}_z)$ to compute the minimum sum. If $\mathbb{A}_z + \mathbb{B}_z = 0$, both parties learn that V_a is dominated. Party A can learn such result from the output as well. Party B can learn what vectors in A are global skyline vectors from the output and V_a is not among the global skyline vectors. But B does not know the values of V_a, and thus cannot know which vector in A is pruned. In addition, with dummy vectors included in the local skyline results of both parties, knowing that V_a is pruned cannot be used by each party to learn the exact number of the pruned vectors. If $\mathbb{A}_z + \mathbb{B}_z \neq 0$, both parties can learn V_a is not dominated and is a vector in the final skyline results, which can be learned from the output anyway. Since A generates the permutations, A knows the order of vectors in B and the ith vector of B is selected for $(\mathbb{A}_z, \mathbb{B}_z)$. However, A does not know the values of any vector from B and such information cannot be combined with $\mathbb{B}_z$ to infer the value of V_{b_z}. For B, since the permutation π_{n+1} is generated by A, B does not know which vector of B is selected for $(\mathbb{A}_z, \mathbb{B}_z)$, and $\mathbb{A}_z$ cannot be used by B to infer the value of V_a.

4.6   Extension to N-Parties

All the proposed protocols (HP.1, HP.2, and HP.3) can be extended to support the secure communication and computation of N parties ($N > 2$): (1) for party P_1 from N parties, apply the protocols on P_1 and every other $N - 1$ parties, and only output the results of P_1 if the results are not dominated by any vector in the other $N - 1$ parties; (2) P_2 first selects only the vectors that are not dominated by the results output by P_1, then runs the protocols with every other $N - 2$ parties, and outputs the results of P_2; (3) repeat (2) for the remaining parties.

5 Related Work

Yao [30] first proposed the two-party comparison problem (Yao's millionaire protocol) and developed a provably secure solution. Ben-Or et al. [5] and Chaum [11] then proposed secure protocols for computing addition and multiplication (XOR and AND). More recently, the advances in the theory of secure multi-party computations [10,15,16] proved that any multi-party function can be computed securely with certain amount of computation cost.

With these primitives, finding an efficient and practical solution for a specific problem is still not trivial. A line of research has focused on developing efficient secure multi-party communication protocols for specific functions. There exists research work on more generic primitives such as set operations [6,23], top-k queries [28]. More recent work also focuses on secure protocols for vector dominance [19,20]. These focus on finding more efficient solutions to specific problems, which can provide building blocks for more complex applications, such as the problem of skyline queries that our work focuses on.

Another important line of research focuses on creating frameworks and specialized programming languages to implement and run secure multi-party computation protocols. The early approaches include FairplayMP [4], Sharemind [7], and SEPIA [9], which implement generic MPC frameworks that support a similar set of primitives, such as addition, multiplication, comparisons and equality testing. These frameworks either provide specialized programming languages to facilitate the security programming, or allow users to program using standard programming languages and library calls. With the advances of research on garbled circuits [18,24], more efficient framework, ObliVM [22], has been built to make secure computations easier and faster. This framework provides a domain-specific language designed for compiling programs into efficient oblivious representations suitable for secure computations. It also provides MapReduce abstractions that facilitate the parallelization of the compiled program.

Unlike this line of research work that focuses on building efficient generic secure computation frameworks, our work focuses on designing efficient secure protocols that minimize the costs of communication and computation while preserve the privacy of the data in multiple participating parties.

6 Conclusion

Skyline queries are an important type of multi-criteria analysis with diverse applications in practice. In this paper, we adopt the classical honest-but-curious attack model and present a suite of efficient protocols for skyline queries to answer skyline queries in a privacy-preserving way when the data is sensitive and distributedly owned by multiple parties. The secure protocols for horizontally partitioned data take 1-to-N skyline dominance as the primitive secure operation to prevent the revelation of intermediate results. We analyze in detail the efficiency of each protocol and its privacy guarantee.

References

1. Abdel Wahab, O., Hachami, M.O., Zaffari, A., Vivas, M., Dagher, G.G.: Darm: a privacy-preserving approach for distributed association rules mining on horizontally-partitioned data. In: IDEAS (2014)
2. Amirbekyan, A., Estivill-Castro, V.: A new efficient privacy-preserving scalar product protocol. In: AusDM (2007)
3. Atallah, M.J., Du, W.: Secure multi-party computational geometry. In: Dehne, F., Sack, J.-R., Tamassia, R. (eds.) WADS 2001. LNCS, vol. 2125, pp. 165–179. Springer, Heidelberg (2001)
4. Ben-David, A., Nisan, N., Pinkas, B.: Fairplaymp: a system for secure multi-party computation. In: CCS (2008)
5. Ben-Or, M., Goldwasser, S., Wigderson, A.: Completeness theorems for non-cryptographic fault-tolerant distributed computation. In: STOC (1988)
6. Blanton, M., Aguiar, E.: Private and oblivious set and multiset operations. In: ASIACCS (2012)
7. Bogdanov, D., Laur, S., Willemson, J.: Sharemind: a framework for fast privacy-preserving computations. In: Jajodia, S., Lopez, J. (eds.) ESORICS 2008. LNCS, vol. 5283, pp. 192–206. Springer, Heidelberg (2008)
8. Borzsony, S., Kossmann, D., Stocker, K.: The skyline operator. In: ICDE (2001)
9. Burkhart, M., Strasser, M., Many, D., Dimitropoulos, X.: Sepia: privacy-preserving aggregation of multi-domain network events and statistics. In: USENIX Security (2010)
10. Cachin, C.: Efficient private bidding and auctions with an oblivious third party. In: CCS (1999)
11. Chaum, D., Crépeau, C., Damgard, I.: Multiparty unconditionally secure protocols. In: STOC (1988)
12. Du, W., Atallah, M.J.: Protocols for secure remote database access with approximate matching. In: Ghosh, A.K. (ed.) E-Commerce Security and Privacy. Advances in Information Security, vol. 2, pp. 87–111. Springer, New York (2001)
13. Fagin, R., Naor, M., Winkler, P.: Comparing information without leaking it. Commun. ACM **39**(5), 77–85 (1996)
14. Goldreich, O., Micali, S., Wigderson, A.: How to play any mental game. In: STOC (1987)
15. Gordon, D.S., Carmit, H., Katz, J., Lindell, Y.: Complete fairness in secure two-party computation. In: STOC (2008)
16. Harnik, D., Naor, M., Reingold, O., Rosen, A.: Completeness in two-party secure computation: a computational view. In: STOC (2004)
17. Holzer, A., Franz, M., Katzenbeisser, S., Veith, H.: Secure two-party computations in ANSI C. In: CCS (2012)
18. Huang, Y., Evans, D., Katz, J., Malka, L.: Faster secure two-party computation using garbled circuits. In: USENIX Security Symposium (2011)
19. Ibrahim, M.H.: Two-party private vector dominance: the all-or-nothing deal. In: ITNG, pp. 166–171 (2006)
20. Yuan, J., Ye, Q., Wang, H., Pieprzyk, J.: Secure computation of the vector dominance problem. In: Chen, L., Mu, Y., Susilo, W. (eds.) ISPEC 2008. LNCS, vol. 4991, pp. 319–333. Springer, Heidelberg (2008)
21. Laur, S., Talviste, R., Willemson, J.: From oblivious AES to efficient and secure database join in the multiparty setting. In: Jacobson, M., Locasto, M., Mohassel, P., Safavi-Naini, R. (eds.) ACNS 2013. LNCS, vol. 7954, pp. 84–101. Springer, Heidelberg (2013)

22. Liu, C., Wang, X.S., Nayak, K., Huang, Y., Shi, E.: Oblivm: a programming framework for secure computation. In: IEEE Symposium on Security and Privacy (2015)
23. Freedman, M.J., Nissim, K., Pinkas, B.: Efficient private matching and set intersection. In: Cachin, C., Camenisch, J.L. (eds.) EUROCRYPT 2004. LNCS, vol. 3027, pp. 1–19. Springer, Heidelberg (2004)
24. Bellare, M., Hoang, V.T., Keelveedhi, S., Rogaway, P.: Efficient garbling from a fixed-key blockcipher. In: IEEE Symposium on Security and Privacy (2013)
25. Miyaji, A., Rahman, M.S.: Privacy-preserving data mining: a game-theoretic approach. In: Li, Y. (ed.) DBSec. LNCS, vol. 6818, pp. 186–200. Springer, Heidelberg (2011)
26. Naor, M., Pinkas, B.: Oblivious transfer and polynomial evaluation. In: STOC (1999)
27. Naor, M., Pinkas, B.: Efficient oblivious transfer protocols. In: SODA (2001)
28. Vaidya, J., Clifton, C.: Privacy-preserving top-k queries. In: ICDE (2005)
29. Vaidya, J., Kantarcioglu, M., Clifton, C.: Privacy-preserving naive bayes classification. VLDB J. **17**(4), 879–898 (2008)
30. Yao, A.C.: Protocols for secure computations (extended abstract). In: FOCS (1982)

Fault-Channel Watermarks

Peter Samarin[1,2]([✉]), Alexander Skripnik[1], and Kerstin Lemke-Rust[1]

[1] Bonn-Rhein-Sieg University of Applied Sciences, Sankt Augustin, Germany
{peter.samarin,kerstin.lemke-rust}@h-brs.de,
alexander.skripnik@smail.inf.h-brs.de
[2] Ruhr-Universität Bochum, Bochum, Germany

Abstract. We introduce a new approach for securing intellectual property in embedded software implementations by using the response of an implementation to fault injections. In our approach, the implementation serves as its own watermark that is recorded through its fault effects. There is no additional code for the watermark. A simulator that maps the fault injections to the executed instructions aids an automated characterization of program code. We provide a proof-of-concept implementation of our watermarking approach using an 8-bit ATMega163 microcontroller and several assembly implementations of AES encryption. The results show that our method is well-suited for detection of identical software copies. In addition, our method shows robust performance in detection of software copies with a large number of added dummy instructions.

Keywords: Fault-channel watermarks · Watermarking · IP protection · Fault analysis · Embedded software

1 Introduction

A watermark is an identifying information that is embedded in media. Watermarking is of dual use: first, it discourages intellectual property (IP) theft; and second, when such theft has occurred, it allows to prove ownership [13]. The attacker aims to garble the watermark by applying simple transformations of the watermarked media such as additions, distortions, and deletions. The verifier performs a specific test to prove the existence of the watermark, even if it is degraded due to simple transformations.

This paper addresses IP protection of embedded software for which a simple read-out of a suspected program code from the memory of a microcontroller is prevented. The main focus is on authorship watermarks that embed information identifying the author of the software. We act on the software watermark model that has been introduced by Becker et al. [10]. In this model, the verifier needs to have physical access to the device that runs the suspected software. The verifier does not have direct access to the program code of the suspected software. In contrast to previous work, we use the fault-channel of a device to construct a new watermarking scheme. To our best knowledge, this work is the first to implement fault-channels watermarks.

© IFIP International Federation for Information Processing 2016
Published by Springer International Publishing Switzerland 2016. All Rights Reserved
S. Foresti and J. Lopez (Eds.): WISTP 2016, LNCS 9895, pp. 204–219, 2016.
DOI: 10.1007/978-3-319-45931-8_13

2   Related Work

2.1   Fault Analysis

Accidental computation errors in chips caused by high-energetic particles are well known since the 1970s [6]. Since the pioneering work of Boneh et al. [12] a new area of research dedicated to fault attacks on cryptographic implementations has emerged. These kind of attacks aim at determining secret or private cryptographic keys based on erroneous outputs of the implementations. Originally, these attacks were theoretical. Anderson and Kuhn [1,2] reported that fault injections using voltage drops and glitch attacks are indeed practical and already in use in pay-TV hacks to manipulate the program counter of a CPU. A new breakthrough in fault injection was demonstrated by Skorobogatov who uses the impact of light on a de-packaged chip [21]. Until now, the use of laser based fault injection is state-of-the-art. A valuable survey of fault injection techniques and countermeasures is provided in [6].

Microcontrollers that were investigated on non-invasive fault injections have turned out to be vulnerable. Closely related to our work is [5], in which the fault effects of clock glitches of the ATMega163 microcontroller were tested in depth. Similarly, specific instructions of the microcontroller platforms Atmel ATxmega256 and ARM Cortex-M0 were investigated in [17]. Other works characterize the effects of low voltage attacks on the ARM9 microprocessor [8,9].

Secure smartcard chips are usually equipped with effective countermeasures on non-invasive fault attacks such as voltage and clock sensors and usage of an internal clock. Defenses against fault injection using laser light, however, are much more difficult. Because of this we act on the assumption that there are some vulnerabilities left even on a security chip that can be used for semi-invasive fault injection. Our approach on watermarking requires that faults can be introduced, no matter how they are introduced. Even if cryptographic implementations include fault detection mechanisms in software, the execution of such routines can be of use for our watermarking scheme.

2.2   Side-Channel Watermarks

Becker et al. [10,11] propose to use side-channel leakage for watermark detection. It is built upon Differential Power Analysis (DPA) [16]. The watermark is realized by adding extra code for a watermark key, a combination function, and a leakage generator. The leakage generator transmits the result of the combination function through a side channel leakage and it is detected in the same way as with DPA. A main drawback of these schemes is the need for additional code or hardware which is at risk to be localized by reverse engineering of the adversary. Obfuscation can help increasing the efforts for reverse engineering but perfect obfuscation is impossible [7]. A further drawback is that these side-channel watermarks need to be always-on, thereby consuming additional power.

Another side channel approach to watermarking by Durvaux et al. [14] uses soft physical hash functions. This approach is quite similar to ours, as it uses the software implementations as they are, without additional code due to watermarks. The authors use the correlation coefficient as similarity score. For this, they need to transform the side channel traces of the two implementations under test to a fixed length vector. For compression, removal of noisy parts and subsequent fast Fourier transform (FFT) of the data is proposed. From the frequency domain data, the authors extract the values corresponding to frequencies below the clock frequency from both vectors and use them for the similarity score. Experimental results in [14] show that the robustness of this approach is rather low as it is susceptible to the addition of dummy instructions.

Research in building a side-channel based disassembler goes back to the initiating work of Quisquater and Samyde [20]. It aims at extracting executed instructions from the side-channel leakage. Recent work by Strobel et al. [23] reported a 87.69 % success rate on a real application on a PIC16F687 microcontroller by training a classifier with electromagnetic traces obtained by applying multiple EM-probes at different positions of the chip simultaneously.

3   Fault-Channel Watermarks

A fault-channel watermark consists of a well-characterized sequence of fault-sensitive instructions that are embedded in the functional code. It is an important difference to previous work that such a watermark design is part of the functional code, i.e. additional code for the watermark is not needed anymore.

Security Objective. Robustness is the main security objective for authorship watermarks. A watermarking algorithm is robust if it is legible after all possible transformations [18].

Adversary Model. We assume that the adversary obtains the program code of the original embedded software under IP protection. The adversary can insert, delete, and substitute assembly instructions. The adversary may embed the original program code inside a software wrapper, thereby hiding the external interfaces of the original program.

Same as in other state of the art approaches, e.g., [10], our adversary model does not include compiler-based code transformations that require a decompiler for transforming the program code to a high-level programming language.

Verifier Model. We assume that a read-out prevention makes it impossible to directly extract the binary of the code from the memory of the microcontroller. The verifier is assumed to have physical access to the microcontroller and is assumed to be able to repeatedly trigger execution of the suspected code. IP protection and verification is done in three steps: preparation, embedding, and verification.

3.1   Preparation: Characterization of Fault Sensitivity

During the preparation step, a microcontroller architecture is analyzed for its susceptibility to fault attacks. Such an analysis requires equipment for fault injection. As we aim at a cheap and easy-to-setup non-invasive fault injection, methods such as voltage dropping and glitching are preferred. However, this does not exclude more advanced characterization, e.g., using laser light. The aim is to detect and parameterize easily reproducible faults of the microcontroller. The preparation step may include a profiling of specific assembly instructions. Alternatively, existing program code can be scanned with different fault injection parameters at execution time. Using a simulator that maps the fault injection time to the executed instruction, the fault sensitive instruction in the code can be identified.

As result of the preparation step, the designer knows about appropriate fault parameterizations and some fault sensitive assembly instructions, which are a subset of the microcontroller instruction set. For each instruction, an appropriate parameter set for fault induction may be stored.

Example 1. In case of voltage-controllable faults, the parameter set includes fault probability, fault voltage, timing offset within an instruction cycle and timing pulse width.

Example 2. In case of clock-controllable faults, the parameter set includes fault probability and glitch period.

Example 3. In case of laser-controllable faults, the parameter set includes fault probability, XY-coordinates of the chip, timing offset within an instruction cycle, laser wavelength, laser pulse width, and laser energy.

3.2   Embedding

Embedding of the fault sensitive instructions and thereby the watermark occurs during software development. A reference watermark of the finalized implementation is based on a chosen fault injection parameter set of the preparation phase. The implementation is entirely scanned as a function of the timing offset where the fault injection applies. More precisely, the implementation is invoked for each fault injection, and the output of the implementation is recorded. For the next fault injection, the timing offset is increased by a fixed amount that is at maximum one clock period, so that each instruction is tested with at least one fault injection.

As result of each scan, a string is output that denotes the watermark. Each string consists of characters from the same alphabet. For simplicity, we assume the set of $\{0,1,2\}$, where '0' indicates no error, '1' indicates a data output error and '2' indicates an unexpected end of computation (program crash). Table 1 shows an example of a fault injection scan and the resulting string.

Multiple scans of the implementation can be used to build a fault-channel profile of the implementation. For each time offset, the profile specifies the frequency that each character appears [15], i.e., the profile is a two dimensional matrix $P_{y,j}$ for each character y of the alphabet and each timing offset j.

Table 1. An excerpt from a fault injection scan. Fault injection is applied once every clock cycle. An `LDI` instruction takes 1 clock cycle to execute, a `CALL` instruction needs 4 clock cycles, and a `PUSH` needs 2 clock cycles. The scan produces the string '112000002'

Offset (ns)	Instruction	Response to fault injection	Resulting string
400	LDI	data output error	1
900	LDI	data output error	1
1400	LDI	program crash	2
1900	CALL	no error	0
2400		no error	0
2900		no error	0
3400		no error	0
3900	PUSH	no error	0
4400		program crash	2

3.3 Verification

The objective of the verifier is to decide whether a microcontroller under test contains relevant parts of the reference watermark from the embedding phase.

The verifier entirely scans the executable parts of the suspected code with the fault injection parameter set of the embedding phase. For each entire scan, the verifier outputs a string that is built in the same way as in the embedding phase.

Finally, the verifier compares the similarity between the obtained string and the original watermark profile, cf. Sect. 3.3. The existence of the original watermark is successfully proven, if the similarity of the watermark is sufficiently high.

Edit Distance. In order to assess the reproducibility of our results using the same implementation as well as to assess the success of watermark detection when comparing the results with possibly different implementations obtained in the embedding and verification phase, we need to define how we quantitatively compare strings. During the preparation tests, the strings are generally of the same length, however, this does not always hold. In the more general case, we want to compare the string S_1 with length m to the string S_2 with length n. For convenience, we assume that a string starts with the index 1 (as opposed to 0).

The edit distance d_e between two strings is defined as the minimum number of edit operations—insertions, deletions, and substitutions—needed to transform the first string into the second [15] or vice versa. Two strings are said to be similar if their edit distance is significantly small. This concept goes back to Levenshtein and the Levenshtein distance is generally recognized as a famous representative of edit functions, though it is not consistently used in the literature [22].

Algorithm 1 shows how to compute normalized edit distance. The function $t(i, j)$ computes whether the characters $S_1(i)$ and $S_2(j)$ match and assigns the

---

Algorithm 1. Computation of edit distance of transforming S_1 into S_2

Input: Strings S_1 and S_2 with lengths m and n, respectively
Output: d_e - normalized edit distance between S_1 and S_2

1 $D = \text{zeros}(m+1, n+1)$
2 **for** $i = 1 : m$ **do**
3      $D[i, 0] = i$
4 **for** $j = 1 : n$ **do**
5      $D[0, j] = j$
6 **for** $i = 1 : m$ **do**
7   **for** $j = 1 : n$ **do**
8          $D[i, j] = \min(D[i-1, j-1] + t(i, j),$ // match or substitute $S_1(i)$ and $S_2(j)$
9                          $D[i-1, j\ \ \ ] + 1,$ // delete $S_1(i)$ with the cost of 1
10                         $D[i\ \ .\ \ , j-1] + 1)$ // insert $S_2(i)$ with the cost of 1

11 **return** $d_e = \frac{D[m,n]}{max(m,n)}$

---

cost 0 when they do, otherwise the character $S_1(i)$ should be substituted by character $S_2(j)$, in which case the cost is 1. Matrix D saves the traceback that can be used to recover the sequence of steps for optimally transforming S_1 into S_2. The computed edit distance is normalized by the maximum length of both strings, so that the resulting numbers are in range between 0 and 1 and can be compared to each other.

The time and space complexities of Algorithm 1 are in $O(mn)$. However, in our case, it is not necessary to know *how* to transform one string into another, but only how much it costs. Thus, the space requirement can be reduced to $O(m)$, as two rows of matrix D are sufficient to compute the edit distance.

4 Experimental Setup

Figure 1 shows the high-level view of our setup.

ATMega163 Smartcard. In this work we use a smartcard with an ATMega163 microcontroller [3]. It is an 8-bit RISC microcontroller that has 32 general-purpose registers, 16 K bytes flash, and 1024 bytes internal SRAM. It can be driven by a clock with frequencies between 0 and 8 MHz. It features 130 instructions, most of which run in 1 clock cycle [4]. The processor uses two-stage pipelining, so that during execution of one instruction, the next instruction is fetched and decoded.

Before an application can be run on the smartcard, it has to be compiled. This is accomplished using avr-gcc, which produces a hex-file that can be loaded into the flash of the smartcard using a smartcard programmer. Our applications for the smartcard are written in combination of C and assembly language.

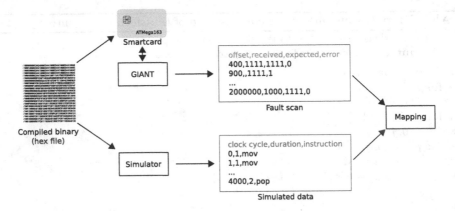

Fig. 1. Data flow of a fault injection scan.

GIAnT. The generic implementation analysis toolkit (GIAnT) is an FPGA-based board for fault injection and side channel analysis [19]. Figure 2 shows the board. The GIAnT board was built using a modular approach, so that each component can be bought separately. The core of the board is a Spartan 6 FPGA that is responsible for communication with the device under test, and performing the fault injections. The board has a slot for inserting a smartcard and can communicate with it using $T = 0$ and $T = 1$ protocols. The board can control the power supply of the smartcard and induce a voltage drop upon request. The GIAnT board was configured to run the smartcards at 2 MHz.

The user can set several parameters, such as the *trigger* type, time *offset* from the trigger after which the fault injection should occur, the *pulse width* of the injection, the *voltage level* during the fault injection, and even a complex voltage pattern with different voltage levels. There are several trigger types: a trigger upon the first input to the smartcard, a trigger upon the first output from the smartcard, and a trigger upon a "HIGH" voltage applied to the programming pin of the smartcard.

To perform a fault injection, the user has to program the GIAnT board, reset the smartcard, feed it with all necessary data to initialize the start up sequence, as the smartcard is reset before doing a fault injection. When the board is ready, the trigger needs to be set, after which the application under test can be executed. The GIAnT board reacts to the trigger and makes the voltage of the smartcard drop at the specified time offset after the trigger for the specified pulse width.

Fault Injection Scan. In this work, we want to perform fault injection scans of suspicious applications. During one such scan, each instruction is disturbed at least once, and the offset is increased by a fixed step size. The result of a fault scan is a dataset that contains the offset of each fault injection performed,

Fig. 2. The GIAnT board.

the received output, the expected output, and whether or not the fault injection cause an error such that the smartcard failed to respond.

ATMega163 Simulator. To understand the impact of a fault injection on any arbitrary instruction, we need to know at what time each instruction is executed. We achieved this by writing an ATMega163 simulator that can load and run an arbitrary hex file compiled for an ATMega163 microcontroller. Our simulator logs executed instructions, the internal state of the CPU, the current number of clock cycles, and the number of clock cycles that an instruction requires to execute.

Mapping Injections to Instructions. The final step is to combine the data obtained from running the fault injection scan with the data from the simulator. The mapping gives us the insight of which instructions are vulnerable to fault injection and at what offset. Further, it allows us to see the dependencies between the opcode, the internal state of the processor, and the applied fault injection.

5 Experimental Results

For our experimental analysis we used several different AES-128 program codes on the ATMega163. Two AES program codes (AES0 and AES1 versions) stem from source codes written in assembly and three program codes (AES2 versions) were generated from one AES source code in C using different compiler versions and options. All AES implementations are embedded into a minimized smartcard operating system that allows to set the AES key and AES plaintext. The AES key and plaintext are fixed for the duration of whole fault scan. One fault injection

Table 2. Scanned AES implementations, their versions, and measurement details

Name	AES0	AES1-v-0	AES1-v-1	AES1-v-2	AES2-v-0	AES2-v-1	AES2-v-2
Language	assembly	assembly	assembly	assembly	C	C	C
Optimization	-	-	-	-	-O3	-O3	-O2
Compiler version	-	-	-	-	4.8.4	4.3.3	4.3.3
N. of clock cycles	5705	4480	4480	5569	12010	12006	21980
N. of instructions	15	28	28	32	38	32	38
Inj. step size	100 ns	100 ns	500 ns	500 ns	500 ns	500 ns	500 ns
Inj. pulse width	500 ns	500 ns	500 ns	500 ns	500 ns	500 ns	500 ns
N. of scans	10	10	5	5	10	10	10
All key bytes	0x0a	0x0a	random	0x0a	0x0a	0x0a	0x0a
All plaintext bytes	0x09	0x09	random	0x09	0x09	0x09	0x09

scan over all 12010 clock cycles of AES2-v-0 implementation requires around 3.3 h, and to scan all 4480 clock cycles of AES1-v-0 requires around 1 h.

Table 2 shows an overview of all implementations and the parameters used to perform fault injection scans. There are three versions of the AES1 implementation: AES1-v-0 and AES1-v-1 use the same program code but different key and plaintext and AES1-v-2 is a modified program code version of AES1 that is generated by adding dummy assembly instructions throughout the whole code.

5.1   Success Probability of Fault Injection

Figure 3 illustrates average success probabilities obtained by applying a fault injection scan of AES0 implementation for each individual assembly instruction at different offsets. The step size of the fault injection offset is 100 ns, which means that there are 5 fault injections per clock cycle. Note that the CPSE instruction needs one clock cycle if the two compared registers are not equal, and two clock cycles if they are equal, in which case the next instruction will be skipped. It was used to check whether the final AES round was reached, so that its two-clock-cycles version is seen only once.

The statistics were computed by aligning all executed instructions and computing the average success at each injection offset. We assume that if an injection occurs during the last 200 ns of an instruction, it contributes to the injection statistics of the next instruction. This is because the pulse width of the injection is 500 ns, which is the same as the clock period the ATMega163. It means that if the injection starts 200 ns before an instruction, it disturbs the previous instruction for 200 ns, and the current one for 300 ns.

From Fig. 3, we learn that a fault injection is most successful when applied 100 ns before each clock cycle. We used this insight to reduce the duration of fault injection scans by setting the offset step size to 500 ns and starting the scan at 400 ns.

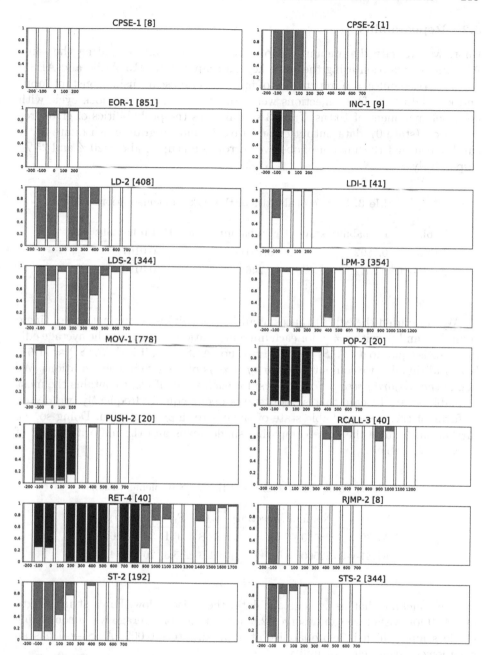

Fig. 3. Probability of fault injection success for all 15 instructions of the AES0 implementation at different offsets. The name of each instruction is followed by the number of clock cycles it takes to execute it. The number of times the instruction is executed during one AES encryption is shown in square brackets. Horizontal axis denotes the offset in nanoseconds, and vertical axis the probability. Fault injections that were not successful are shown in white, fault injections that caused data output errors are shown in gray, and fault injections that resulted in program crash are shown in black.

5.2   Repeatability

First, we evaluate the amount of noise that occurs while repeating the same AES implementation using the same key and input data. For AES0 and AES1-v-0 we carried out $r = 10$ repetitions of fault injection scans using constant input and key data. The fault injections were applied five times per clock cycle with an offset increment of 100 ns. Table 3 summarizes the probabilities of error-free execution (state 0), data output error (state 1) and program crash (state 2). It can be seen that the amount of observed errors sums up to about 20 % and 25 %, respectively.

Table 3. Fault probabilities of the AES implementations

Impl.	Probability state '0'	Probability state '1'	Probability state '2'
AES0	0.7892	0.1941	0.0167
AES1-v-0	0.7342	0.2464	0.0194

We computed the edit distances of all $\frac{r(r-1)}{2}$ pairwise combinations of single strings S_i and S_j with $i \neq j$, for each implementation. For AES0, the average edit distance is equal to $\overline{d_e}(S_i, S_j) \approx 62.8 \pm 6.1$. For AES1-v-0, it is $\overline{d_e}(S_i, S_j) \approx 41.6 \pm 5.3$. Additionally, we computed *majority strings* of the two implementations. We define the *majority string* $\overline{S}$ as follows: for each time offset, it contains the most probable state. In case that several states occur equally frequently, we decide in favor of the more probable state of the entire implementation. Doing so, we further can reduce the noise comparing single scans and the majority string of 9 scans, cf. Table 4.

Table 4. Fault characteristics of the AES implementations

Impl.	No. fault injections	$\overline{d_e}(S_i, S_j)$	$\overline{d_e}(S_i, \overline{S})$
AES0	28550	62.8 ± 6.1	38.0 ± 6.4
AES1-v-0	22500	41.6 ± 5.3	26.7 ± 4.5

We conclude that using constant data, the noise is low. For a string length of 28550 for AES0, we can observe 62.8 mismatches on average when comparing single scans, which is a probability of approximately 0.002. AES1-v-0 has an even lower mismatch probability.

5.3   Comparing Different AES Implementations

Table 5 shows a comparison of all AES implementations. Originally, AES0 and AES1-v-0 were scanned with offset step size of 100 ns, while the other implementations with 500 ns. To compare them to each other, the number of data points of AES0 and AES1-v-0 was reduced to only include injection offsets starting from 400 ns with injection step size of 500 ns.

Table 5. Mean normalized edit distances computed pairwise for all measurements

	AES0	AES1-v-0	AES1-v-1	AES1-v-2	AES2-v-0	AES2-v-1	AES2-v-2
AES0	**0.0032**	0.3537	0.3502	0.3506	0.5281	0.5342	0.7404
AES1-v-0	0.3537	**0.0015**	0.1116	0.2623	0.6272	0.6307	0.7954
AES1-v-1	0.3502	0.1116	**0.0441**	0.2972	0.6269	0.6309	0.7954
AES1-v-2	0.3506	0.2623	0.2972	**0.0288**	0.5529	0.5617	0.7454
AES2-v-0	0.5281	0.6272	0.6269	0.5529	**0.0131**	0.3389	0.4815
AES2-v-1	0.5342	0.6307	0.6309	0.5617	0.3389	**0.0462**	0.4738
AES2-v-2	0.7404	0.7954	0.7954	0.7454	0.4815	0.4738	**0.0169**

Self-distance. Normalized edit distance of each fault injection scan of an implementation to all other scans of the same implementation is small, and significantly smaller than to the scans of all the other implementations. This means that the edit distance is especially well-suited for revealing binaries that were used without modification.

Different Input Data. Implementations AES1-v-0 and AES1-v-1 are identical, however, they are invoked with different key and plaintext. While AES1-v-0 has all key bytes set to 0x0a, and plaintext bytes to 0x09, the AES1-v-1 implementation has the key equal to 0x0b56e9b99f17ee9bc7cacbfbc6e7b1f2, and plaintext set to 0x1d4c2c6300b72ee1b094717c29f46c7d. The normalized edit distance between these two implementations is higher than their respective self-distances, but closer each other than to all other implementations. To minimize the impact of processed data, the IP verifier should use the same data during verification. In situations where it is not possible (for example, the secret key can be set to a fixed value by the attacker), the verifier can precompute a majority string of the original implementation by feeding the algorithm with random data at each fault injection.

Robustness to Dummy Instructions. The AES1-v-2 implementation was designed to simulate an attacker that has taken the original AES1-v-0 implementation and added a significant number of dummy instructions. These instructions are combined in a way that they have no impact on the state, unless the application is scanned by fault injections. For example, it is possible to push an important register onto the stack, modify it, and pop it back, as shown in Listing 1.1. Under normal circumstances, these operations will not have any impact on subsequent computations. However, a successful fault injection on PUSH or POP instructions will change the data in some registers. Since there is always only one injection per program execution, a fault can cause either PUSH or POP to malfunction, so that data used in subsequent computations will be different from the data of the original implementation. Thus, dummy instructions will only add extra characters to the fault injection string at their respective offsets, but will not cause changes in the original fault injection string at other offsets.

```
NOP
PUSH  r0
PUSH  r18
PUSH  r19
PUSH  r30
LDI   r18, 0xff  ;; r18 := 0xff
MOV   r0,  r18   ;; r0  := r18
LDI   r19, 0x7c  ;; r19 := 0x7c
EOR   r30, r0    ;; r30 := r30 xor r0
EOR   r19, r18   ;; r19 := r19 xor r18
MOV   30,  r19   ;; r0  := r18
POP   r30
POP   r19
POP   r18
POP   r0
```

Listing 1.1. Dummy instructions in the key scheduler.

In addition to PUSH and POP instructions, several other *inverse-instructions-pairs* have been used, such as, e.g., NEG-NEG, EOR-EOR, INC-DEC. These instructions, when applied to one and the same register in succession, cause no changes under normal circumstances. However, a successful fault injection will change the content of the register, and influence the remaining computations.

In total, 1029 extra clock cycles have been added in various places throughout the code: in the key scheduler, in MixColumns, in SubBytes, in and outside of the AES rounds. This makes 22.97 % of added dummy clock cycles over the 4480 clock cycles of the initial implementation.

We observed the average normalized edit distance of 0.26 between the original and the modified implementation. Despite all additional instructions, the normalized edit distance between the two implementations is smaller than their normalized edit distances to all other implementations. These results show that our approach is still robust given an amount of 22.97 % added dummy clock cycles.

Durvaux et al. [14] added 52 dummy clock cycles to the total of 2739 clock cycles of the *Furious* implementation of AES, which makes 1.9 % of extra clock cycles. In response, the similarity score changed from 0.9 to 0.55. This might be caused by the use of Pearson's correlation to compute the similarity score between power traces—the correlation is not robust when additional instructions are inserted at several different positions in the code. Furthermore, correlation compares two vectors that must have the same size. Our approach, however, uses edit distance that allows comparison of arbitrary-sized strings. In addition, it is possible to extract matching substrings and see which parts of the original code have been used in the modified implementation.

Compiler Options and Versions. AES2-v-0 and AES2-v-1 stem from one and the same implementation written in C that was compiled using different versions of the avr-gcc compiler. Their duration deviates by only 4 clock cycles, but the generated assembly code is significantly different. This is also reflected in their normalized edit distance—it is much larger then their respective self-distances. However, their mutual normalized edit distance is smaller than their normalized distance to all the other implementations.

The AES2-v-2 implementation was compiled using a different optimization option: -O2, as opposed to -O3. This resulted in larger run time of the AES encryption. This implementation has a low self-distance and a high distance to all other implementations.

6   Conclusion and Future Work

In this work we have presented a new method for software IP protection based on fault analysis that does not require software developers to change or modify their implementations. This method was designed to enable analysis of IP that resides in read-protected memory. To verify whether a suspicious system uses software legitimately, we perform a fault injection scan of the entire implementation, convert the results of the scan into a string, and compare the resulting string to a string obtained from scanning our own implementation. The two strings are compared using normalized edit distance, which tells us how many changes we must apply to one string to transform it into the other.

The method was evaluated by comparing several AES implementations written for an ATMega163 microcontroller. Experimental results show that the method is especially well-suited for comparing compiled binaries and implementations in assembly code that were taken without modifications. There is little variation between the fault injection scans of the same implementation. Different implementations have a high normalized edit distance from each other, such that it is very unlikely that one implementation gets mistaken for another.

The strength of using normalized edit distance becomes apparent when we randomly add dummy instructions to the original code that do not have impact on the state unless a fault injection disturbs their operation. Adding dummy instructions results in an increase of normalized edit distance that is proportional to the number of instructions added normalized by the overall size of the original code. Thus, for 22.97 % additional clock cycles, the normalized edit distance increased of the original and modified AES implementation was equal to 0.26, which means that 26 % of one implementation have to be changed in order to transform it into the other. The robustness of our method is significantly better than the method of [14] that is based on Pearson's correlation, whose performance decreases substantially after adding a very small number of dummy clock cycles.

Edit distance is a global alignment method that compares two strings as a whole and might ignore high local similarity in favor of a better global alignment [15]. A promising direction for future work is the evaluation of local alignment methods that can find substrings of high similarity, which would allow us to identify sub-parts copied from the original code.

Acknowledgements. This work has been supported in parts by the German Federal Ministry of Education and Research (BMBF) through the project DePlagEmSoft, FKZ 03FH015I3.

References

1. Anderson, R.J., Kuhn, M.G.: Tamper resistance - a cautionary note. In: The Second USENIX Workshop on Electronic Commerce Proceedings, pp. 1–11 (1996)
2. Anderson, R., Kuhn, M.: Low cost attacks on tamper resistant devices. In: Christianson, B., Crispo, B., Lomas, M., Roe, M. (eds.) Security Protocols 1997. LNCS, vol. 1361, pp. 125–136. Springer, Heidelberg (1998)
3. Atmel: ATmega163(L) Datasheet (revision E), February 2003
4. Atmel: Atmel AVR 8-bit Instruction Set Manual (revision 0856J), July 2014
5. Balasch, J., Gierlichs, B., Verbauwhede, I.: An in-depth and black-box characterization of the effects of clock glitches on 8-bit MCUs. In: FDTC 2011, pp. 105–114 (2011)
6. Bar-El, H., Choukri, H., Naccache, D., Tunstall, M., Whelan, C.: The sorcerer's apprentice guide to fault attacks. Proc. IEEE **94**(2), 370–382 (2006)
7. Barak, B., Goldreich, O., Impagliazzo, R., Rudich, S., Sahai, A., Vadhan, S.P., Yang, K.: On the (im)possibility of obfuscating programs. In: Kilian, J. (ed.) CRYPTO 2001. LNCS, vol. 2139, pp. 1–18. Springer, Heidelberg (2001)
8. Barenghi, A., Bertoni, G., Parrinello, E., Pelosi, G.: Low voltage fault attacks on the RSA cryptosystem. In: 2009 Workshop on Fault Diagnosis and Tolerance in Cryptography (FDTC), pp. 23–31, September 2009
9. Barenghi, A., Bertoni, G.M., Breveglieri, L., Pellicioli, M., Pelosi, G.: Low voltage fault attacks to AES. In: 2010 IEEE International Symposium on Hardware-Oriented Security and Trust (HOST), pp. 7–12, June 2010
10. Becker, G.T., Burleson, W., Paar, C.: Side-channel watermarks for embedded software. In: 9th IEEE NEWCAS Conference (2011)
11. Becker, G.T., Strobel, D., Paar, C., Burleson, W.: Detecting software theft in embedded systems: a side-channel approach. IEEE Trans. Inf. Forensics Secur. **7**(4), 1144–1154 (2012)
12. Boneh, D., DeMillo, R.A., Lipton, R.J.: On the importance of checking cryptographic protocols for faults. In: Fumy, W. (ed.) EUROCRYPT 1997. LNCS, vol. 1233, pp. 37–51. Springer, Heidelberg (1997)
13. Collberg, C.S., Thomborson, C.D.: Software watermarking: models and dynamic embeddings. In: POPL, pp. 311–324 (1999)
14. Durvaux, F., Gérard, B., Kerckhof, S., Koeune, F., Standaert, F.-X.: Intellectual property protection for integrated systems using soft physical hash functions. In: Lee, D.H., Yung, M. (eds.) WISA 2012. LNCS, vol. 7690, pp. 208–225. Springer, Heidelberg (2012)
15. Gusfield, D.: Algorithms on Strings, Trees, and Sequences. Cambridge University Press, Cambridge (1997)

16. Kocher, P.C., Jaffe, J., Jun, B.: Differential power analysis. In: CRYPTO, pp. 388–397 (1999)
17. Korak, T., Hoefler, M.: On the effects of clock and power supply tampering on two microcontroller platforms. In: 2014 Workshop on Fault Diagnosis and Tolerance in Cryptography, FDTC 2014, pp. 8–17 (2014)
18. Nagra, J., Thomborson, C.D., Collberg, C.S.: A functional taxonomy for software watermarking. In: ACSC, pp. 177–186 (2002)
19. Oswald, D.: GIAnT: Generic Implementation ANalysis Toolkit. SourceForge (2014)
20. Quisquater, J., Samyde, D.: Automatic code recognition for smartcards using a Kohonen neural network. In: Proceedings of the Fifth Smart Card Research and Advanced Application Conference, CARDIS 2002 (2002)
21. Skorobogatov, S.P., Anderson, R.J.: Optical fault induction attacks. In: Kaliski Jr., B.S., Koç, Ç.K., Paar, C. (eds.) CHES 2002. LNCS, vol. 2523, pp. 2–12. Springer, Heidelberg (2003)
22. Smyth, B.: Computing Patterns in Strings. Pearson Education Limited, Essex (2003)
23. Strobel, D., Bache, F., Oswald, D., Schellenberg, F., Paar, C.: SCANDALee: A Side-ChANnel-based DisAssembLer using local electromagnetic emanations. In: Design, Automation, and Test in Europe (DATE), 9–13 March 2015

Short Papers

The Effect of Semantic Elaboration on the Perceived Security and Privacy Risk of Privacy-ABCs — An Empirical Experiment

Ahmad Sabouri[✉]

Deutsche Telekom Chair of Mobile Business & Multilateral Security,
Goethe University Frankfurt, Theodor-W.-Adorno-Platz 4,
60323 Frankfurt, Germany
ahmad.sabouri@m-chair.de

Abstract. Privacy-ABCs are elegant techniques to deliver secure yet privacy-enhanced authentication solutions. The cryptography behind them enables new capabilities, such as selective disclosure of attributes, set membership, and predicates over attributes, which many of them were never experienced by typical users before. Even if the users intuitively accept the existence of such features, they may not be still ready to perceive the semantic of such a proof within the context of authentication. In this work, we argue that additional information is necessary to support the user understand the semantic of their operations. We present the results of our empirical experiment on investigating the effect of providing such a support during authentication with Privacy-ABCs on the perceived security and privacy risk of the users.

1 Introduction

The research community has been trying to enhance the strong authentication techniques to respect the privacy of the users. More specifically, efforts have been dedicated to design schemes for providing data minimization, unlinkability and untraceability during an authentication session. In this regard, *Privacy-preserving Attribute-based Credentials (Privacy-ABCs)*, also known as anonymous credentials, have been in the focus of various recent research projects such as Prime, PrimeLife, FutureID, and ABC4Trust. From the different flavours of Privacy-ABCs, the IBM Idemix and Microsoft U-Prove are among the most prominent ones. Privacy-ABCs are cryptographically proven to be unlinkable and untraceable. Thus, the service providers cannot tell whether two tokens were generated by the same user or not. Also the issuers cannot trace tokens back to the issuance phase and the person behind them, unless the disclosed attributes contains some identifying information.

Privacy-ABCs come with new capabilities such as *selective disclosure of attributes*, *predicate over attributes*, and *proof of set membership*, which mainly

Published by Springer International Publishing Switzerland 2016. All Rights Reserved
S. Foresti and J. Lopez (Eds.): WISTP 2016, LNCS 9895, pp. 223–235, 2016.
DOI: 10.1007/978-3-319-45931-8_14

were never experienced by the users in any of the previous authentication schemes. For instance, using *predicates over attributes*, a user is able to prove facts such as *less than* or *greater than* about their attributes without actually disclosing the attribute value itself. Taking the example of our experiment, a service provider can request a "German" user to prove if her postal code is in the range of 59999 to 61000. In this way, the service provider learns that the user is living in the city of Frankfurt am Main but it does not learn in which district of the city, which could possibly cause leak of information about the financial status. Some scholars [8] reported that users lack an appropriate mental model for such technologies regarding even simpler features, such as combining individual attributes from different credentials in a single authentication. Consequently, we argue in this paper that without additional support regarding the semantic of their actions, the users may not be appropriately influenced by such privacy-enhancing technology regarding their security and privacy risk perception.

In this paper, we demonstrate that the users' perception of security and privacy risks changes, when they are supported with additional information regarding the semantic of their proofs during authentication with Privacy-ABCs. Our findings are based on the results of an empirical experiment with 80 users. We compared the perceived security and privacy risk of two groups of participants who received different treatments during their practice of authentication with Privacy-ABCs. For this experiment, we first implemented an experiment platform where the user could practice authentication with Privacy-ABCs. In the next step, we used the platform to conduct the experiment with the users and afterwards measured their perceived security and privacy risk using part of a systematically developed measurement instrument (cf. Appendix A).

In the rest of this paper, we review the previously conducted related research in Sect. 2. Later on, we explain the details of our experiment in Sect. 3. The results and implications of our experiment are provided in Sect. 4. In the end, we conclude the paper in Sect. 5.

2   Related Works

To the best of our knowledge, there have not been many studies in the literature concerning the human aspects of Privacy-ABCs. Wästlund et al. [8] were the first ones who reported about the challenges to design user-friendly interfaces that convey the privacy benefits of Privacy-ABCs to users. They observed that users were still unfamiliar with the new and rather complex concept of Privacy-ABCs, since no obvious real-world analogies existed that could help them create the correct mental models. Benenson et al. [2,3] investigated one of the ABC4Trust trials using the Technology Acceptance Model (TAM) [4]. Benenson et al. discovered significant negative correlation of Perceived Risk with the Intention to Use, the Perceived Usefulness for the first and secondary goals, the Perceived Ease of Use and the Trust. In the same study, they found the Perceived Risk to be dependent to Perceived Anonymity.

An experts survey was conducted in [7] to predict the factors influencing adoption of Privacy-ABCs. The results indicate that the complexity for the user

Table 1. Measurement instrument for security and privacy risk of using ID+ to authenticate towards Politiks.eu

Items	Concept behind
I think by using ID+ to login to Politiks.eu, my various posts at Politiks.eu become linkable together	Linkability
I believe by using ID+ to login to Politis.eu, I will be able to use the Politiks.eu anonymously/pseudonymously	Anonymity
I think Politiks.eu is not secure enough to be used with ID+	Security
I believe using ID+ to login to Politiks.eu puts other services, which are used with ID+, at risk and enables unauthorised/unwanted actions at those other services	Unwanted Authorization
I believe using ID+ to login to Politiks.eu leads to identity theft or impersonation	Impersonation
I believe that my usage of ID+ to login to Politiks.eu leads to loss of privacy for me because my personal data are collected without my knowledge and consent	Collection
I believe by using ID+ to login to Politiks.eu, I lose control over my personal data	Control
I believe by using ID+ to login to Politiks.eu, my posts at Politiks.eu become known to the ID+ operator.	Traccability

is among the most important factors. In our study, we try to reduce the complexity by providing additional support for the semantic analysis of the *presentation policies* (which are the artefact describing the requested attributes and proofs by service providers) and observe the effect on the perceived security and privacy risks, because perceived risk is reported to be particularly important for the adoption of e-services [6]. The method to influence the perceived risk was chosen based on the recommendations of the warning theory. The warning theory suggests that more specific information about hazards and consequences can reduce uncertainty and enable people to make better-informed cost-benefit trade-off decisions regarding the need to comply [5]. Bal [1] extended this design theory to the field of information privacy warning design by experimentally investigating the effects of explicitness in privacy warnings on individuals' perceived risk and trustworthiness of smartphone apps and observed significant effects.

3   Experiment Design

The experiment was designed to evaluate the effect of additional semantic analysis of the *presentation policy* on the perceived privacy risk by end users. We first implemented the necessary software components to enable authentication with Privacy-ABCs. We called our mock-up Privacy-ABC identity card as "ID+" and let the users try it in our experiment portal, "Politiks.eu". We also adjusted our developed questionnaire for the perceived security and privacy risk to reflect our experiment environment (the details of developing the questionnaire are presented in Appendix A). We used a 7-points Likert scale in the questionnaire ranging from *Strongly disagree* to *Strongly agree*. Table 1 demonstrates the final questionnaire for our experiment. Then, we conducted the experiment through the network of the students at the Goethe University Frankfurt in October and November 2015. In the following sections, we explain the details of our process.

3.1   Experiment Platform Setup

A precondition for our experiment was to set up a platform where scenarios for authenticating with Privacy-ABCs could be tried out. We decided to develop a mock-up prototype which presents the workflow of authenticating with Privacy-ABCs with a more friendly interface than the ABC4Trust reference implementation and better integration into the web browser. We designed the User Agent as a Firefox plugin and integrate it into the browser. We added a button, called "ID" into the toolbar of the Firefox browser, which upon clicking, it would show the users' identity credential in case the smartcard was connected to the computer. In the experiment, the authentication was emulated, therefore, the smart card was employed to provide the feeling of a real process but the users' attributes were actually stored in the browser configurations. A small Java application was developed to run in the background in order to check the status of the smartcard, which allowed the browser plugin to query the status via a Restful web-service call. The plugin was designed to attach specific Javascript codes to the html content of the web-page when opening the experiment portal URL. The Javascript codes would provide the possibility of communicating with the plugin in order to invoke the GUI for authentication with Privacy-ABCs. When a button on the web-page triggers login with Privacy-ABCs, the message is communicated to the plugin. The GUI would pop up as small window next to the "ID" button

1. Open Firefox
2. Plug your smart card into the reader
3. Check your data on the card
4. What information about your is stored on the ID+ smart card?
5. Close the ID+ window
6. Question: *How can you check your data again if you want?*
7. Open "http://politiks.eu"
8. *The portal is introduced!*
9. Login to the "Frankfurt Mayor" discussion
10. Follow the authentication steps
11. What is happening now?
12. Question: *What is the website going to learn about you?*
13. Have a look at the posts
14. Write a post and send it
15. Check your post
16. Log out
17. Login to the "Drug" discussion
18. Follow the authentication steps
19. Question: *What is the website going to learn about you?*
20. Have a look at the posts
21. Write a post and send it.
22. Check your post
23. Log out
24. Login to the "Mayor" discussion again
25. Follow the authentication steps
26. Have a look at your previous posts
27. Write a new post and send it
28. Check your post
29. Log out.

Fig. 1. User tasks list

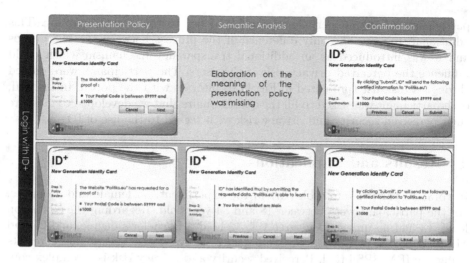

Fig. 2. Experiment process

if the smart card is present. The window guides the user through the steps of authentication and upon completion the user is redirected to the requested page.

3.2   Conducting the Experiment

The experiment was conducted within the student community of the Goethe university Frankfurt. The only limitation was to limit the age to be between 18 and 34. The participants were randomly assigned to one of the two envisioned groups, the "control group" and the the "experiment group". All participants received a brief introduction of ID+ and its privacy-enhancing features. Afterwards, the participants were given a smartcard and were asked to open Firefox and browse to the experiment portal, "http://politiks.eu". In order to urge the need for privacy, we decided the deliver political discussion as the main content of the portal. Two forums were initiated in the portal; one about mayoral election in the city of Frankfurt and one about legalizing drugs. Each forum required the user to authenticate with her ID+ in order to get access to the discussion. The process of authenticating with ID+ for the two groups are shown in Fig. 2. Upon clicking on "Login with ID+" the respective GUI would pop up to guide the participant through the authentication process. The Frankfurt mayoral election forum asked the users to deliver a proof for "Your Postal code is between 59999 and 61000" and the forum on legalizing drugs, would request the users a proof of "Your birth date is before the 01.01.1997". The former policy semantically means that the participant is living in the Frankfurt am Main area as the postal code is following 60xxx format, and therefore the forum ensures that she is a stakeholder. The latter also proves that the participant is older than 18 (by the time of the experiment) and consequently allowed to discuss about drugs. A semantic analysis of the given access policy was presented to the participants of the "experiment group" and not to the "control group". This additional step was the only difference of the process between the two groups and it was introduced as an additional transparency mechanism which could influence the perceived privacy risk of the users. The participants were guided through a task list (presented in Fig. 1) to interact with the portal. In the end, each participant was asked to fill the questionnaire that we developed to measure their perceived security and privacy risk with regard to the use of ID+.

4   Results and Implications

In total 80 participants took part in the experiment, 35 female and 45 males. All the participant were between 18 and 34 years old. Regarding the education level, 13 had no university degree yet, 42 hold a Bachelor's degree, and 25 had Master's degree or above. We statistically analysed the questionnaire results using the IBM SPSS tool. Perceived security and privacy risk is a complex construct and can have various factors. Within the items measuring the perceived security and privacy risk, we covered various aspects namely, Linkability, Traceability, Anonymity, Security, Control, Collection, Impersonation and Unwanted Authorization.

The responses to each of the questions are demonstrated in Fig. 3. The x-axis represents the answers (1 = Strongly Disagree, 2 = Disagree, 3 = Somewhat Disagree, 4 = Neither Agree nor Disagree, 5 = Somewhat Agree, 6 = Agree, 7 = Strongly Agree).

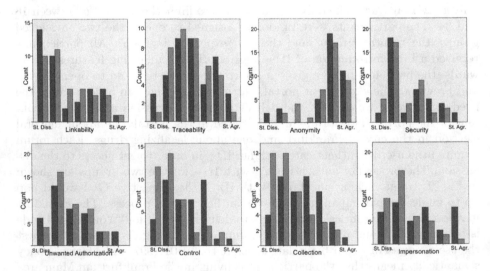

Fig. 3. Participants' answers to the security and privacy risk questions. First column = control group, second column = experiment group

Table 2. Rotated component matrix. Rotation method Varimax with Kaiser normalization

	Component	
	C1	C2
Unlinkability	.150	.736
Anonymity (rev)	.101	.830
Impersonation	.701	.208
Collection	.894	.052
Control	.887	.177
Untraceability	.464	.470
Unwanted Authorization	.467	.448
Security	.603	.358

Comparing the descriptive statistical values for the answers of the control group and the experiment group, we can say both groups *Somewhat Disagreed* to the risk of Linkability ($m_c = 2.85, \sigma_c = 1.96, m_e = 2.95, \sigma_e = 1.78$). With regard to Traceability, both groups had on average a neutral perception ($m_c = 3.98, \sigma_c = 1.72, m_e = 3.75, \sigma_e = 1.46$. The results concerning Anonymity were almost the same for both groups and laid between *Somewhat Agree* and *Agree* ($m_c = 5.60, \sigma_c = 1.67, m_e = 5.50, \sigma_e = 1.41$). For Security, the experiment group demonstrated a slightly stronger disagreement compared to the control group but in general they were both around *Somewhat Disagree* ($m_c = 3.38, \sigma_c = 1.72, m_e = 2.88, \sigma_e = 1.44$). The results also indicate a slight difference concerning perception of Unwanted Authorization but the average on both groups was close to *Somewhat Disagree* ($m_c = 2.93, \sigma_c = 1.46, m_e = 2.75, \sigma_e = 1.13$). The perception of the control group was on average between *Somewhat Disagree* and *Neutral* towards Impersonation while the experiment group's perception was between *Disagree* and *Somewhat Disagree* ($m_c = 3.38, \sigma_c = 1.78, m_e = 2.40, \sigma_e = 1.28$). A similar result was observed for Collection ($m_c = 3.48, \sigma_c = 1.57, m_e = 2.50, \sigma_e = 1.47$), and Control ($m_c = 3.40, \sigma_c = 1.53, m_e = 2.40, \sigma_e = 1.43$).

We performed a *Principal Component Analysis (PCA)* using Varimax rotation with Kaiser Normalization on the security and privacy risk items to investigate whether all the items were loading one "total security and privacy risk" or not. To perform a PCA, the rule of thumb is to have at least 10 participants per variable, which our total number of participants met this requirements for our eight variables. As shown in Table 2, the results indicate that our eight items were loading two components (which we named C1 and C2). Consequently, we calculated component C1 as an un-weighted average of Security, Unwanted Authorization, Impersonation, Collection and Control, and also C2 as the un-weighted average of Unlinkability, Untraceability and Anonymity. Regarding the reliability test, the Bartlett test indicated significant correlation and the Kaiser-Meyer-Olkin (KMO) measure verified the sampling adequacy for the analysis with KMO = .789. Moreover the Cronbach's α was calculated as 0.82 and 0.6 for C1 and C2 respectively.

After identifying the components, we compared the mean value of C1 and C2 between the control group and the experiment group using a *Independent Samples T-test*. As reported in Table 3, the results demonstrate statistically

Table 3. Independent samples T-test

	Leven's Test for Equality of Variance		t-test for Equality of Means							
	F	Sig.	t	df	Sig. (2-tailed)	Mean Diff.	Std. Error Diff.	95% Confidence Interval of the Diff	
								Lower	Upper
C1 Equal variances assumed	3.809	.055	2.887	78	.005	.72500	.25108	.22513	1.22487
Equal variances not assumed			2.887	73.092	.005	.72500	.25108	.22460	1.22540
C2 Equal variances assumed	3.396	.069	.030	78	.976	.00833	.27932	-.54774	.56441
Equal variances not assumed			.030	71.051	.976	.00833	.27932	-.54860	.56527

significant difference of C1 between the two groups, p-value ≤ 0.005, which means that the probability of the corresponding difference in the means to occur by chance is less than or equal to 0.5 %. This shows that the participants of the experiment group perceived less risk (mean diff. = .725) concerning the dimensions of security and privacy covered by C1. Intuitively, the experiment group received additional explicit information with regard to the consequences of delivering the proofs requested by the portal, which made them specially perceive better control over their attributes and their collections.

5   Conclusion

In this work, we designed and conducted an empirical experiment with Privacy-ABCs in order to demonstrate the effect of additional supports to the users with regard to the semantic of the Privacy-ABC proofs. Privacy-ABCs enable new privacy features such as minimal disclosure, predicate over attributes, and set membership. However, users are not very familiar with those concepts and have difficulties to build a mental model of such advanced operations. We argued that additional information explaining the facts and semantics of required Privacy-ABC proofs during an authentication process has an influence on the perceived security and privacy risk of the users. We verified our hypothesis through our experiment, where we examined 80 participants in two groups and measured their perceived security and privacy risk using our systematically developed measurement instrument. Our results demonstrated that the group who received additional information about the semantic of the proofs had a statistically significant difference in some aspects of their perceived security and privacy risk. Despite following methodological approaches, the experiment was conducted through the student network of the Goethe University Frankfurt and the age of the participants were limited to 18–34 years old. Consequently, the results may not be generalizable to users who are significantly different from our sample group.

A   Appendix: Developing a Measurement Instrument

Designing an appropriate and robust measurement instrument is an essential part of any experiment. One of the contributions of this paper is the systematic

Table 4. Facets of risk for the use of identity management systems

Dimension	Definition
Performance Risk	User assessment of potential performance problems and malfunctioning, transaction processing errors, etc., and therefore not delivering the service as promised.
Financial Risk	User assessment of potential financial losses due to the employment of an Identity Service Provider XXX and its login mechanism for accessing Service Provider YYY.
Security & Privacy Risk	User assessment of potential security violation or losses to the privacy and confidentiality of their online/offline identity, personal data, or activities
Time Risk	User assessment of potential losses to convenience, time and effort caused by wasting time researching, setting up, switching and learning how to use the Identity Service Provider XXX login process.
Psychological Risk	User assessment of potential losses to their self-esteem, peace of mind or self-perception (ego) due to worrying, feeling frustrated, foolish, or stressful as a result of employing an Identity Service Provider XXX to login to the Service Provider YYY
Social Risk	User assessment of potential losses to their perceived status in their social group as a result of using and Identity Service Provider XXX to access the Service Provider YYY. The assessment of the probability that consumers believe that they will look foolish to important others
Physical Risk	User assessment of potential losses to their health and their physical status

development of an instrument which measures *multi-faceted risk* of using an identity management solution to access a service. Perceived risk is theorized as being multi-dimensional [11]. Jacoby and Kaplan [13] defined the following five components of risk: financial, performance, physical, psychological, social, and the overall risk. Roselius [18] also identified a sixth dimension called Time loss. Featherman and Pavlou [12] proposed to consider privacy risk in the context of e-commerce instead of the physical risk which seems to be very unlikely. Since then multi-faceted risk has been considered in various studies such as adoption of Internet Banking [14], initial acceptance of emerging technologies [15], and self-service technologies and e-services [11]. Table 4 introduces the dimensions we considered in our instrument.

In this work, we followed the three stages proposed by Moore and Benbasat [16] in order to develop an instrument to measure the multi-faceted risk of using an identity management solution to authenticate towards a service. The first

Table 5. The results of the constructs validity test rounds

Construct	Round 1			Round 2		
	Items	P_{sa}	C_{sv}	Items	P_{sa}	C_{sv}
Performance Risk	3	0.84	0.78	3	0.90	0.86
Financial Risk	3	0.90	0.80	3	1.00	1.00
Security & Privacy Risk	8	0.83	0.77	8	1.00	1.00
Time Risk	2	0.92	0.85	2	0.86	0.71
Psychological Risk	2	0.55	0.28	2	1.00	1.00
Social Risk	2	0.93	0.88	2	0.93	0.86
Physical Risk	3	0.96	0.93	3	1.00	1.00

stage aims at the identification of existing items and the creation of new ones which fit to the definition of the respective constructs.

The second stage focuses on assessing the construct validity and refining ambiguous items. This stage was done following the approach by Anderson and Gerbing [10] by a pretest assessment of the substantive validities of the measures, which is achieved by an *item-sorting task*. In this iterative exercise, some representatives of the population were asked to judge each item and assign it to the construct to which they think the item belongs. After carrying out each round, two indices were calculated: *proportion of substantive agreement*, P_{sa}, and *substantive validity coefficient*, Csv. The indices range from 0.0 to 1.0 and from -1.0 to 1.0 respectively.

P_{sa} is defined as the proportion of respondents who assign an item to its intended construct. The equation for this calculation is: $P_{sa} = nc/N$ where nc represents the number of people assigning an item to its posited construct and N represents the total number of respondents. Csv represents the extent to which respondents assign an item to its posited construct more than to any other construct. The formula for this index is: $C_{sv} = (nc - no)/N$, where nc and N are defined as before and no indicates the highest number of assignments of the item to any other construct.

Larger values for both indices show greater substantive validity and the recommended threshold is 0.5. We conducted the pretest with the help of 20 participants. Even though the majority of the constructs met the threshold, we had to do some refinements in order to improve the items and remove ambiguity. The second round was performed by involving 7 participants, which verified the validity of all the constructs. Table 5 represents the results of the tests.

The final version of the multi-faceted risk measurement instrument is as follows:

Performance:

- Identity Service Provider XXX does not perform reliable enough to guarantee access to Service Provider YYY at anytime. (adapted from [11])
- Identity Service Provider XXX goes down (unreachable) and therefore creates problem with my access to Service Provider YYY. (adapted from [11])

- In future Identity Service Provider XXX discontinues its service and incurs trouble for me to access Service Provider. (new based on the identified risks by [9])

Financial:

- Using Identity Service Provider XXX to login to Service Provider YYY leads to financial loss for me. (adapted from [11])
- Using Identity Service Provider XXX to login to Service Provider YYY stands me to lose money. (adapted from [12])
- Using Identity Service Provider XXX to login to Service Provider YYY causes undesired/unintended withdrawal from my financial (e.g. bank) accounts. (adapted from [12])

Security and Privacy:

- If I use Identity Service Provider XXX to login to Service Provider YYY, my various transactions/service usages at Service Provider YYY become linkable together. (new based on terminology by [17])
- Using Identity Service Provider XXX to login to Service Provider YYY, I will be able to use the service anonymously/pseudonymously. (new based on terminology by [17])
- Service Provider YYY is not secure enough to be linked to Identity Service Provider XXX. (new)
- Using Identity Service Provider XXX to login to Service Provider YYY puts other service providers, which are linked to Identity Service Provider XXX, at risk and enables unauthorized/unwanted actions at those other services. (new due to widespread use of OAuth)
- Using Identity Service Provider XXX to login to Service Provider YYY leads to identity theft or impersonation. (new based on the identified risks by [9])
- My usage of Identity Service Provider XXX to login to Service Provider YYY leads to loss of privacy for me because my personal data are collected without my knowledge and consent. (adapted from [12])
- Using Identity Service Provider XXX to login to Service Provider YYY, I lose control over my personal data. (adapted from [11])
- Using Identity Service Provider XXX to login to Service Provider YYY, my usage of Service Provider YYY becomes known to Identity Service Provider XXX. (new based on terminology by [17])

Time:

- I have to waste a lot of time if I need to switch from Identity Service Provider XXX to another one in the future for accessing Service Provider YYY. (adapted from [11])
- I have to spend lots of time on setting up and learning how to use Identity Service Provider XXX to login to Service Provider YYY. (new)

Psychological:

- Using Identity Service Provider XXX to login to Service Provider YYY makes me nervous or anxious. (new)
- Using Identity Service Provider XXX to login to Service Provider YYY makes me feel worried. (adapted from [11])

Social:

- Using Identity Service Provider XXX to login to Service Provider YYY harms the way others think of me. (adapted from [11])
- Using Identity Service Provider XXX to login to Service Provider YYY leads to a loss of status and reputation for me because my friends and relatives will think less highly of me. (adapted from [11])

Physical:

- Logging into Service Provider YYY using Identity Service Provider XXX is not safe; i. e. may be (or become) harmful or injurious to my health. (adapted from [13])
- Using Identity Service Provider XXX to login to Service Provider YYY leads to physical harm by governmental organizations. (new)
- I will get physically hurt by others if I login to Service Provider YYY using Identity Service Provider XXX. (new)

References

1. Bal, G.: Explicitness of consequence information in privacy warnings: experimentally investigating the effects on perceived risk, trust, and privacy information quality. In: Proceedings of ICIS 2014, Auckland, New Zealand, 14–17 December 2014
2. Benenson, Z., Girard, A., Krontiris, I., Liagkou, V., Rannenberg, K., Stamatiou, Y.: User acceptance of privacy-ABCs: an exploratory study. In: Tryfonas, T., Askoxylakis, I. (eds.) HAS 2014. LNCS, vol. 8533, pp. 375–386. Springer, Heidelberg (2014)
3. Benenson, Z., et al.: User acceptance factors for anonymous credentials: an empirical investigation. In: Proceedings of WEIS (2015)
4. Davis, F.D.: Perceived usefulness, perceived ease of use, and user acceptance of information technology. MIS Q. **13**, 319–340 (1989)
5. Laughery, K.R., Wogalter, M.S.: Designing effective warnings. Rev. Hum. Factors Ergon. **2**(1), 241–271 (2006)
6. Pavlou, P.A.: Consumer acceptance of electronic commerce: integrating trust and risk with the technology acceptance model. Int. J. Electron. Commer. **7**(3), 101–134 (2003)
7. Sabouri, A.: Understanding the determinants of privacy-ABC technologies adoption by service providers. In: Proceedings of I3E 2015, Delft, The Netherlands, 13–15 October 2015, pp. 119–132 (2015)

8. Wästlund, E., Angulo, J., Fischer-Hübner, S.: Evoking comprehensive mental models of anonymous credentials. In: Camenisch, J., Kesdogan, D. (eds.) iNetSec 2011. LNCS, vol. 7039, pp. 1–14. Springer, Heidelberg (2012)
9. Ackermann, T., Widjaja, T., Benlian, A., Buxmann, P.: Perceived it security risks of cloud computing: conceptualization and scale development (2012)
10. Anderson, J.C., Gerbing, D.W., Hunter, J.E.: On the assessment of unidimensional measurement: internal and external consistency, and overall consistency criteria. J. Mark. Res. **24**, 432–437 (1987)
11. Featherman, M.S., Hajli, N.: Self-service technologies and e-services risks in social commerce era. J. Bus. Ethics, 1–19 (2015)
12. Featherman, M.S., Pavlou, P.A.: Predicting e-services adoption: a perceived risk facets perspective. Int. J. Hum. Comput. Stud. **59**(4), 451–474 (2003)
13. Jacoby, J., Kaplan, L.B.: The components of perceived risk. Adv. Consum. Res. **3**(3), 382–383 (1972)
14. Lee, M.C.: Factors influencing the adoption of internet banking: an integration of tam and tpb with perceived risk and perceived benefit. Electron. Commer. Res. Appl. **8**(3), 130–141 (2009)
15. Luo, X., Li, H., Zhang, J., Shim, J.: Examining multi-dimensional trust and multi-faceted risk in initial acceptance of emerging technologies: an empirical study of mobile banking services. Decis. Support Syst. **49**(2), 222–234 (2010)
16. Moore, G.C., Benbasat, I.: Development of an instrument to measure the perceptions of adopting an information technology innovation. Inf. Syst. Res. **2**(3), 192–222 (1991)
17. Pfitzmann, A., Hansen, M.: A terminology for talking about privacy by data minimization: anonymity, unlinkability, undetectability, unobservability, pseudonymity, and identity management (2010)
18. Roselius, T.: Consumer rankings of risk reduction methods. J. Mark., 56–61 (1971)

Delegating Biometric Authentication with the Sumcheck Protocol

Hervé Chabanne[1], Julien Keuffer[2(✉)], and Roch Lescuyer[3]

[1] Safran Identity & Security, Télécom ParisTech, Issy-Les-Moulineaux, France
herve.chabanne@morpho.com
[2] Safran Identity & Security, Eurecom, Issy-Les-Moulineaux, France
julien.keuffer@morpho.com
[3] Safran Identity & Security, Issy-Les-Moulineaux, France
roch.lescuyer@morpho.com

Abstract. In this paper, we apply the Sumcheck protocol to verify the Euclidean (resp. Hamming) distance computation in the case of facial (resp. iris) recognition. In particular, we consider a border crossing use case where, thanks to an interactive protocol, we delegate the authentication to the traveller. Verifiable computation aims to give the result of a computation and a proof of its correctness. In our case, the traveller takes over the authentication process and makes a proof that he did it correctly leaving to the authorities to check its validity. We integrate privacy preserving techniques to avoid that an eavesdropper gets information about the biometric data of the traveller during his interactions with the authorities. We provide implementation figures for our proposal showing that it is practical.

Keywords: Biometrics · Verifiable computing · Authentication

1 Introduction

1.1 Motivation

In order to increase the throughput in border crossing, controls operated by officers could be replaced with automated systems. Such systems often use biometrics to authenticate the travellers: a comparison is made between an official document such as a biometric passport and the traveller who needs to prove his identity. However biometric data need to be collected from the traveller to be compared with data stored on the official document and this step of the process can be time consuming. Delegating a part of the process to the traveller can save time but raises a confidence problem: how can the authority be sure that the traveller really ran the computation?

We use verifiable computing as a tool to address this problem. A verifiable computation system allows a *verifier* to delegate the computation of a function

© IFIP International Federation for Information Processing 2016
Published by Springer International Publishing Switzerland 2016. All Rights Reserved
S. Foresti and J. Lopez (Eds.): WISTP 2016, LNCS 9895, pp. 236–244, 2016.
DOI: 10.1007/978-3-319-45931-8_15

to a *prover*. Upon completion of the computation, the prover returns the result and a proof of the computation. In our use case, the traveller's smart device has the role of the prover and has thus restricted computational power and storage capacity. We stress that this reverses the classical roles played by the verifier and the prover in most of verifiable computing scenarios, where a weak verifier usually delegates computations to a powerful but untrusted prover. The choice of the underlying verifying system has thus been driven according to this configuration. In particular, the requirements for the prover and the targeted computation led us to choose an interactive proof protocol, namely the SUMCHECK protocol [15].

1.2 Background on Biometrics

A biometric system is a pattern recognition system, which makes biometric data acquisition from an individual, then extracts a feature set from the acquired data which gives a *biometric template*. In an *authentication* scheme, the template is then compared against a referenced template and in an *identification* scheme it is compared against a database of templates. Due to external conditions such as light, moisture or the sensor used for the capture, two templates computed from the same individual can vary. However, the variation is expected to be small enough to be able to discriminate two templates coming from the same person from two templates coming from different individuals. This is why the comparison of two templates is usually a matching score, reflecting a similarity rate between the two data. A matching threshold has to be defined to discriminate the templates belonging to the same individual or not. Ideally, if the score of two templates is lower than the threshold, they belong to the same individual. However, in biometric systems, two different individuals can have a matching score lower than the threshold, which leads to the definition of the *false acceptance rate* (FAR) and the *false rejection rate* (FRR), see [13] for details.

In our scenario, we need an automated face recognition system. Today, many systems performing face recognition use machine learning techniques to transform a face picture into a biometric template. The model called convolution neural network (CNN) [14] has shown excellent results [18,22]. CNNs have millions of parameters that are tuned in a learning phase, using a face database for the training. Once the training phase is over, the CNN can embed a picture in a Euclidean space where two vectors representing the same face are closer than two vectors that come from different faces, enabling face recognition.

1.3 Background on Verifiable Computation

Although the problem of verifying computations has been theoretically solved with tools from complexity theory and cryptography [1,16], new challenges raised by verifiability in the setting of cloud computing recently attracted the interest of researchers. Huge progresses have been made and several research teams succeeded in implementing verifiable computing systems. All these systems start by turning the function to verify into a circuit composed of multiplication and addition gates and then perform verification on the circuit.

A first line of work has built on a refined version of probabilistically checkable proofs (PCP) [12] and resulted in a verifiable system called Pepper [20], which has been refined since [19,24]. The second line was opened by Gennaro *et al.* [9], who achieved a breakthrough by building efficient objects to verify computations called quadratic arithmetic programs (QAPs), resulting in an efficient system called Pinocchio [17]. Pinocchio and its refined version [7] allow public verifiability: anyone who has access to the public verification key can verify proofs. Moreover, the prover can make his proof zero-knowledge: he supplies a private input to the computation and builds a proof of the correctness of the result without revealing his input to the verifier. Finally, a system called TinyRAM and designed by Ben-Sasson *et al.* [3] uses QAPs and has the ability to verify a larger class of computations by modelling programs using RAM. The third line of work relied on the notion of interactive proofs, which was introduced by Goldwasser *et al.* [11]. In the verifiable computing setting, the verifier checks that the result of the computation is correct during a sequence of interactions with the prover. The more the verifier asks queries, the less the prover has chance to cheat. Goldwasser *et al.* [10] introduced an efficient protocol, later optimized and implemented by Cormode *et al.* [5]. The last version of this protocol, due to Thaler [23], is currently one of the fastest scheme for verifiable computing. Furthermore, Thaler proposed an implementation of matrix multiplication and also showed that the the main tool of interactive proofs protocols, namely the SUMCHECK protocol [15], can be used to design an efficient protocol for matrix multiplication verification.

However all the systems described above are only *nearly practical* for generic computations. The different systems all have advantages and drawbacks, depending on the type of computations to be verified. One important thing is that all systems building upon PCPs and QAPs need precomputations and amortize their costs by using the verified function several times. The fastest system needs no precomputation and uses the CMT protocol but it cannot handle general computations. Systems based on QAPs and on PCPs have better expressiveness and allow fast verification but the prover's overhead costs compared to native execution of the same computation is consequent. See [25] for comparisons between the different existing systems.

Cormode *et al.* [6] suggested that the SUMCHECK protocol could be used to verify an inner product in the setting of data streaming, where the verifier cannot store the inputs and has to update his computations while he is parsing the data. The recent work of [4] studies the use of verifiable computing for biometric verification in a non-interactive setting *i.e.* where the prover computes a proof without interacting with the verifier. In contrast, we focus on interactive proofs to design and implement a protocol which aims at verifying several distances used in biometric matchings and adapt the SUMCHECK protocol [15].

2   Use-Case: Fast Border Control

In many places, people living next to another country frequently cross the border with their cars to go to work. We want here to design an automated system to

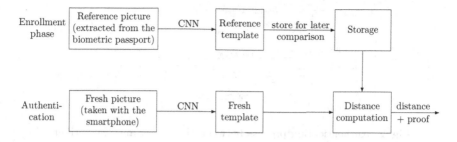

Fig. 1. The biometric matching process

reduce the waiting time, taking profit of the waiting time in the cars queuing line. Our idea is to let the driver perform himself his face verification against his passport photo while crossing the border. Such operations could be performed by a dedicated application installed on his smartphone. At the end, the customs authority will get from this application: a fresh photograph, the official one and a proof that both belong to the same person (Fig. 2). A high-level description of our solution (see also Fig. 1):

- The traveller (who plays the role of the prover) uses a wireless communication device of the mobile to get the picture stored in his biometric passport.
- The picture is turned into a reference template using a CNN.
- The traveller takes a fresh picture of his face and uses the same CNN to create a biometric template.
- A biometric matching is performed on the traveller's mobile and interactions between the traveller and the automated border control device lead to a proof that the matching was correctly computed. The interaction begins with the prover sending two templates and the result of the distance computation to the verifier. The proof is stored on the mobile for a later examination.

We emphasize that our contribution is limited to the application of verifiable computation on distance computations involved in biometric matchings. This is only a part of what is needed to address the whole problem. For instance, liveness detection or verifying the CNN output seem necessary but those topics are outside the scope of this paper. Our purpose here is to deal with a realistic use case for a delegation of a verifiable face matching algorithm. Since a CNN embeds a pictures in a Euclidean space, the verifiable biometric matching involves a distance computation which is compared to a threshold. We first show how to verify an inner product and then extend the verification to euclidean distance computing.

3   The Sumcheck Protocol and Verifiable Distances

In the SUMCHECK protocol [15], a prover $\mathcal{P}$ wants to convince a verifier $\mathcal{V}$ that he knows the value of the expression: $H = \sum\limits_{x_1 \in \{0,1\}} \sum\limits_{x_2 \in \{0,1\}} \dots \sum\limits_{x_n \in \{0,1\}} g(x_1, \dots, x_n),$

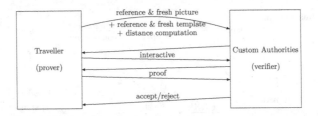

Fig. 2. Authentication process between the prover and the verifier

where g is a multivariate polynomial defined over a finite field. If g has n variables, the protocol has n rounds. In each round, the verifier picks a random value from a finite field and challenges the prover to compute a polynomial derived from the initial polynomial to verify. This polynomial is sent by the prover to the verifier and few computations are needed to check that it is linked to the previous one. If the check succeeds, the verifier can accept the new polynomial as a claim for the initial value. At the end, the verifier has to evaluate the original polynomial in a single value to decide if he accepts the initial claim with high probability. This is the only step where the verifier has a computing challenge.

Verifiable Inner Product. We now give details on how we adapt the SUM-CHECK protocol to obtain a verifiable inner product and verifiable distance computations. Consider two vectors $a, b \in \mathbb{Z}^n$. The inner product of a and b is defined by: $H = \sum_{i=0}^{n-1} a_i \cdot b_i$. Denoting $d = \log n$, the expression giving H can be rewritten, considering a and b as functions defined over $\{1, \ldots, n\}$ such that: $a : i \mapsto a_i$ and $b : i \mapsto b_i$. If the index i is written as a binary vector, $i = \sum_{k=1}^{d} i_k 2^{k-1} = (i_1, \ldots, i_d)$ then a and b define multivariate polynomials:

$$a : (i_1, \ldots, i_d) \mapsto a_i \text{ and } H = \sum_{i_1 \in \{0,1\}} \cdots \sum_{i_d \in \{0,1\}} a(i_1, \ldots, i_d) \cdot b(i_1, \ldots, i_d)$$

To increase the possibility of catching a lie from a cheating prover, the SUMCHECK protocol uses polynomials defined over a large finite field, which agree with a and b over $\{0,1\}^d$ and called low-degree extensions and denoted $\tilde{a}$ and $\tilde{b}$. The above relation still holds with low-degree extensions of a and b.

Squared Euclidean Distance. The protocol described in Sect. 3 can be adapted straightforwardly to verify Euclidean distance. Indeed, given two n-components biometric templates a and b, their squared Euclidean distance is:

$$d_E(a,b) = \sum_{i=1}^{n} (a_i - b_i)^2 = \sum_{i=1}^{n} a_i^2 + b_i^2 - 2a_i \cdot b_i \tag{1}$$

Denoting $d = \log_2 n$, we have to verify with the SUMCHECK protocol the evaluation of the polynomial g over $\{0,1\}^d$:

$$g(x_1, \ldots, x_d) = \tilde{a}(x_1, \ldots, x_d)^2 + \tilde{b}(x_1, \ldots, x_d)^2 - 2\tilde{a}(x_1, \ldots, x_d) \cdot \tilde{b}(x_1, \ldots, x_d) \quad (2)$$

The same ideas can be adapted to verify the distance involved in iris recognition, which is a weighted Hamming distance [8].

4   Adding Data Privacy to the Protocol

At the beginning of the protocol described in Sect. 2, the driver has to send his reference and his fresh templates to the authorities for the verification process. Since biometric template cannot be revoked, we propose to add masking techniques for the templates [2]. In our context, this means that the driver has to pick a random permutation of the template coordinates and a random vector of the same size than the template. More precisely, a template $t = (t_1, \ldots, t_n)$ masked becomes $t_{masked} = \pi(t) + (r_1, \ldots, r_n)$ where π is a random permutation of the n coordinates and $(r_1, \ldots, r_n)$ is a n components vector of $\mathbb{F}_p^n$.

So if t_{ref} and t are masked with the *same* permutation and random vector, computing their distance involves computing their difference:

$$\pi(t_{ref}) + (r_1, \ldots, r_n) - (\pi(t) + (r_1, \ldots, r_n)) = \pi(t_{ref}) - \pi(t) = \pi(t_{ref} - t)$$

And the scalar product of this difference has the same value than the scalar product computed on the vectors without masks: since π permutes the same coordinates on t and t_{ref}, the difference vector masked is the permutation of the original difference vector and computing the scalar product on this masked vector will give the same result.

The distance computation with masked templates gives information about the distance between the templates and the differences between the coordinates of the templates. But linking these differences coordinates to the unmasked template coordinates is hard because of the number of possible permutations and vectors.

We also stress that the driver has to store the permutation and the random vector. Therefore if the authorities have a doubt about the identity of the driver, the driver has everything on his phone to unmask the templates and compute the distance between them. Similar techniques can be used for iris recognition.

5   Experimental Results

We implement a verified inner product using the SUMCHECK protocol, the computations being over the prime finite field $\mathbb{F}_p$ where $p = 2^{61} - 1$. The size of a field element is thus inferior to the machine word size and the probability of being fooled by a dishonest prover is small, see Table 1. Note that optimizations are possible for the verifier but since in our use case the verifier has computational power, we did not implement them.

We run our benchmarks on random vectors of different sizes composed of natural numbers. Dealing with negative numbers or with floating-point rationals is possible with an additional step, *e.g.* the computations over negative numbers are mapped to computations over a finite field large enough so that the mapping is a one-to-one function [21]. This step is done before the prove and verify steps. The protocol has therefore to be implemented in a larger field at the cost of a decrease of performances.

Communication Costs and Security. For input vectors of size n, the SUM-CHECK protocol has $\log_2 n$ rounds, the verifier sends one field element per round (the random challenge, see Sect. 3) and the prover three (the three values needed to interpolate round k polynomial). Not taking into account the sending of the input values, we obtain that the total communication during the protocol is $4\log_2(n) + 1$ field elements.

The security of the SUMCHECK protocol is the probability that a cheating prover builds a proof of a false result that will be accepted by the verifier, this value is given in Table 1 for different input sizes.

Benchmarks. We run experiments on a laptop with a 2 GHz Intel Core i5 processor with 8 GB of RAM. The implementation is written in C++. Table 1 gives the average times of 1000 computations for each vector size. We note that this technique does not need the notion of arithmetic circuits. Using the optimized version of the CMT protocol (see Sect. 1) would lead to a slower protocol with two times more communication costs.

Table 1. Benchmark of the verified inner product of two n-components vectors

n	Inner prod. (ms)	Prover time (ms)	Verifier time (ms)	Security	Communication
128	$< 10^{-4}$	0.01	0.032	2^{-54}	232 B
256	0.0031	0.017	0.053	2^{-54}	264 B
512	0.0032	0.042	0.098	2^{-53}	296 B
1024	0.0032	0.065	0.25	2^{-53}	328 B
4096	0.0077	0.31	1.13	2^{-52}	392 B
2^{20}	3	122	600	2^{-51}	648 B

Acknowledgements. This work has been partially funded by the European H2020 TREDISEC (ICT-2014-644412) and the French ANR BIOPRIV (ANR-12-INSE-0013) projects.

References

1. Arora, S., Safra, S.: Probabilistic checking of proofs: a new characterization of NP. J. ACM **45**, 70–122 (1998)

2. Atallah, M.J., Frikken, K.B., Goodrich, M.T., Tamassia, R.: Secure biometric authentication for weak computational devices. In: Patrick, A., Yung, M. (eds.) FC 2005. LNCS, vol. 3570, pp. 357–371. Springer, Heidelberg (2005)
3. Ben-Sasson, E., Chiesa, A., Genkin, D., Tromer, E., Virza, M.: SNARKs for C: verifying program executions succinctly and in zero knowledge. In: Canetti, R., Garay, J.A. (eds.) CRYPTO 2013, Part II. LNCS, vol. 8043, pp. 90–108. Springer, Heidelberg (2013)
4. Bringer, J., Chabanne, H., Kraiem, F., Lescuyer, R., Soria-Vazquez, E.: Some applications of verifiable computation to biometric verification. In: 2015 IEEE International Workshop on Information Forensics and Security, WIFS (2015)
5. Cormode, G., Mitzenmacher, M., Thaler, J.: Practical verified computation with streaming interactive proofs. In: ITCS 2012, pp. 90–112 (2012)
6. Cormode, G., Thaler, J., Yi, K.: Verifying computations with streaming interactive proofs. In: Conference on Very Large Data Bases - VLDB 2012 (2012)
7. Costello, C., Fournet, C., Howell, J., Kohlweiss, M., Kreuter, B., Naehrig, M., Parno, B., Zahur, S.: Geppetto: versatile verifiable computation. In: Proceedings of the IEEE Symposium on Security and Privacy (2015)
8. Daugman, J.: How iris recognition works. IEEE Trans. Circuits Syst. Video Technol. **14**(1), 21–30 (2004)
9. Gennaro, R., Gentry, C., Parno, B., Raykova, M.: Quadratic span programs and succinct NIZKs without PCPs. In: Johansson, T., Nguyen, P.Q. (eds.) EUROCRYPT 2013. LNCS, vol. 7881, pp. 626–645. Springer, Heidelberg (2013)
10. Goldwasser, S., Kalai, Y.T., Rothblum, G.N.: Delegating computation: interactive proofs for muggles. In: STOC 2008, pp. 113–122 (2008)
11. Goldwasser, S., Micali, S., Rackoff, C.: The knowledge complexity of interactive proof-systems. In: Proceedings of the Seventeenth Annual ACM Symposium on Theory of Computing, STOC 1985 (1985)
12. Ishai, Y., Kushilevitz, E., Ostrovsky, R.: Efficient arguments without short PCPS. In: IEEE Conference on Computational Complexity (CCC 2007) (2007)
13. Jain, A.K., Ross, A., Prabhakar, S.: An introduction to biometric recognition. IEEE Trans. Circuits Syst. Video Technol. **14**(1), 4–20 (2004)
14. LeCun, Y., Bottou, L., Bengio, Y., Haffner, P.: Gradient-based learning applied to document recognition. Proc. IEEE **86**(11), 2278–2324 (1998)
15. Lund, C., Fortnow, L., Karloff, H., Nisan, N.: Algebraic methods for interactive proof systems. J. ACM **39**, 859–868 (1992)
16. Micali, S.: Computationally sound proofs. SIAM J. Comput. **30**, 1253–1298 (2000)
17. Parno, B., Howell, J., Gentry, C., Raykova, M.: Pinocchio: nearly practical verifiable computation. In: IEEE Symposium on Security and Privacy, SP 2013 (2013)
18. Schroff, F., Kalenichenko, D., Philbin, J.: Facenet: A unified embedding for face recognition and clustering. In: The IEEE Conference on Computer Vision and Pattern Recognition (CVPR), June 2015
19. Setty, S., Braun, B., Vu, V., Blumberg, A., Parno, B., Walfish, M.: Resolving the conflict between generality and plausibility in verified computation. In: EuroSys (2013)
20. Setty, S., McPherson, R., Blumberg, A.J., Walfish, M.: Making argument systems for outsourced computation practical (sometimes). In: NDSS (2012)
21. Setty, S.T.V., Vu, V., Panpalia, N., Braun, B., Blumberg, A.J., Walfish, M.: Taking proof-based verified computation a few steps closer to practicality. In: USENIX Security Symposium, pp. 253–268. USENIX Association (2012)

22. Taigman, Y., Yang, M., Ranzato, M.A., Wolf, L.: Deepface: closing the gap to human-level performance in face verification. In: The IEEE Conference on Computer Vision and Pattern Recognition (CVPR), June 2014
23. Thaler, J.: Time-optimal interactive proofs for circuit evaluation. In: Canetti, R., Garay, J.A. (eds.) CRYPTO 2013, Part II. LNCS, vol. 8043, pp. 71–89. Springer, Heidelberg (2013)
24. Wahby, R.S., Setty, S., Ren, Z., Blumberg, A.J., Walfish, M.: Efficient RAM and control flow in verifiable outsourced computation. In: NDSS (2015)
25. Walfish, M., Blumberg, A.J.: Verifying computations without reexecuting them: from theoretical possibility to near-practicality. Commun. ACM (2015)

Password Generators: Old Ideas and New

Fatma Al Maqbali and Chris J. Mitchell[✉]

Information Security Group, Royal Holloway, University of London, Egham, UK
fatmaa.soh@cas.edu.om, me@chrismitchell.net

Abstract. *Password generators* that generate site-specific passwords on demand are an alternative to password managers. Over the last 15 years a range of such systems have been described. We propose the first general model for such systems, and critically examine options for instantiating it. The model enables an objective assessment of the design of such systems; it has also been used to sketch a possible new scheme, AutoPass, intended to incorporate the best features of the prior art while addressing many of the shortcomings of existing systems.

1 Introduction

Passwords remain a very widely used method for user authentication, despite widely shared concerns about the level of security they provide. There are many potential replacement technologies, including combinations of biometrics and trusted personal devices (e.g. as supported by protocols such as FIDO UAF [3]), but it seems likely that it will be some time before passwords are relegated to history. Given their current and likely future wide use, finding ways of improving the use and management of passwords remains a vitally important issue. We focus here on an important practical matter, namely how to make password-based user authentication to a website both more secure and more convenient.

An important class of schemes designed to ease password use are *password managers* (what McCarney [12] calls *retrieval password managers*). A password manager stores user passwords and produces them when required (e.g. by auto-filling-in login pages). Passwords can be stored either locally or on a trusted server; most browsers provide a local-storage password manager. However, the shortcomings of password managers have also been widely documented (see, e.g., McCarney [12]). Passwords stored on a user platform restrict user mobility, since they are not available when a user switches platform, e.g. from a laptop to a tablet or phone. However, if passwords are stored 'in the cloud', then there is a danger of compromise through poorly configured and managed servers, [2,8,13].

An alternative approach, which we consider here, involves generating site-specific passwords on demand from a combination of inputs, including those supplied by the user and those based on the site itself. A number of schemes have been proposed but, apart from a brief summary by McCarney [12], they have

© IFIP International Federation for Information Processing 2016
Published by Springer International Publishing Switzerland 2016. All Rights Reserved
S. Foresti and J. Lopez (Eds.): WISTP 2016, LNCS 9895, pp. 245–253, 2016.
DOI: 10.1007/978-3-319-45931-8_16

not been studied in a more general setting. The main purposes of this paper are to (a) provide a general model for password generation schemes, and (b) use the model to propose a new system combining the best features of existing schemes. This is the first time these schemes have been considered in a unified way.

2   Password Generators — A General Model

Password generators simplify user password management by generating site-specific passwords on demand from a small set of inputs. The term has also been used to describe the generation random or pseudorandom passwords which a user must remember; however, we use the term for schemes that generate a password in a repeatable way. We focus on the general properties of such schemes and options for operation. The schemes have been briefly considered previously by McCarney [12] under the name *generative password managers*.

2.1   A Model

A password generator is functionality on an end-user platform to support password-based user authentication to a remote server (assumed to be a web site). It generates, on demand, a site-unique password for use in authentication. Clearly this password also needs to be available to the web site authenticating the user; the *registration* step, in which the password is set up, is discussed further in Sect. 2.3 below. A password generator has the following components.

– A set of *input values* is used to determine the password for a site; some must be site-specific so the generated password is site-specific. The values could be: stored (locally or online), based on characteristics of the authenticating site, user-entered, or some combination of types.
– A *password generation function* combines the input values to generate an appropriate password. This function must meet the requirements of the authenticating web site; e.g. one web site might forbid non-alphanumeric characters in a password, whereas another might insist that a password contains at least one such character. A password generation function must therefore be customisable.
– A *password output method* transfers the password to the authenticating site, e.g. by displaying the generated password to the user.

All this functionality needs to be implemented on the user platform. There are various possibilities for implementation, e.g. as a stand-alone application or a browser plug-in; these issues are discussed further in Sect. 3 below.

2.2   Examples

We next briefly outline some existing proposals for password generation schemes, presented in chronological order of publication. The functional components of the various examples are considered in greater detail in Sect. 3 below.

The *Site-Specific Passwords (SSP)* scheme proposed by Karp [7] in 2002/03 is one of the earliest proposed examples. It generates a site-specific password by combining a long-term (global) user master password and an easy-to-remember name for the web site, as chosen by the user. *PwdHash*, due to Ross et al. [14], generates a site-specific password by combining a long-term master password, data associated with the web site, and (optionally) a second global password stored on the platform. The 2005 *Password Multiplier* scheme of Halderman, Waters and Felten, [4], computes a site-specific password as a function of a long-term master password, the web site name, and the user name for the user at the web site concerned. Wolf and Schneider's 2006 *PasswordSitter* [15] scheme generates a site-specific password as a function of a long-term master password, the user identity, the application/service name, and some configurable parameters. *Passpet*, due to Yee and Sitaker [16] and also published in 2006, takes a very similar approach to SSP, i.e. the site-specific password is a function of a long-term master password and a user-chosen name for the web site known as a *petname*. Each petname has an associated icon, which is automatically displayed to the user and is intended to reduce the risk of phishing attacks. *ObPwd*, due to Mannan et al. [1,9–11], first surfaced in 2008. It takes a somewhat different approach by generating a site-specific password as a function of a user-selected (site-specific) object (e.g. a file), together with a number of optional parameters, including a long-term master password (referred to as a *salt*), and the web site URL. Finally, *PALPAS* was published in 2015 [5]. PALPAS generates passwords complying with site-specific requirements using server-provided password policy data, a stored secret value (the *seed*), and a site- and user-specific secret value (the *salt*) that is synchronised across all the user devices using the server.

2.3   Registration and Configuration

We only consider schemes whose operation is completely transparent to the authenticating website. As a result, the 'normal' website registration procedure, where the user selects a password and sends it to the site, is assumed to be used. This means that the password generation process needs to be in place *before* the registration procedure, or the introduction of a password generator will require the user to modify their password. A possible way of avoiding the need to change passwords is examined in Sect. 4 below.

A password generator may need to store configuration data. Such data can be divided into: *global configuration data*, i.e. values unique to the user, used to help generate all passwords for that user, and *site-specific configuration data*, i.e. values used to help generate a password for a specific site. Not all schemes use configuration data, although building a workable system without at least some global configuration data seems challenging. However, the use of configuration data is clearly a major barrier to portability. That is, for a user with multiple platforms, the configuration data must be kept synchronised across all these platforms, a non-trivial task — exactly the issue addressed in a recent paper by Horsch, Hülsing and Buchmann [5].

3   Components of the Model

Inputs to Password Generation: The following data input types have been employed in existing schemes. A **master password** is a user-specific long-term secret value; this could either be a **user-entered password**, i.e. entered by the user whenever a password is to be generated, or a **stored password**, i.e. a user-specific secret value stored as global configuration data. A **site name** is a name for the authenticating site; this could take a variety of forms, including a **user site name**, i.e., a name for a site chosen by a user, all or part of the site's **URL**, or a **site-specific secret**, e.g. a random value associated with the site URL. A **digital object** is anything available on the user platform which could be used as input to the password generation process, e.g. a file or a selected block of text on the target web site. A **password policy** is information governing the nature of the password generated, e.g. the set of acceptable symbols.

Generating the Password: Combining inputs to generate a password can be done variously. All approaches involve a 2-stage process, i.e. first combining inputs to generate a bit-string, then formatting the bit-string to obtain a password in the desired format. Horsch et al. [6] propose an XML syntax, the *Password Requirements Markup Language (PRML)*, designed specifically to enable requirements on passwords, as needed in the second stage, to be specified.

Password Output and Use: There are many ways in which a generated password could be transferred to the password field of a login page. Simplest is **manual copy and paste**, as used by SSP [7], where the password generator displays the password, and the user copies it to the login page. A slightly more automated approach is **copy to clipboard** in which the generated password is copied to the clipboard; for security reasons the password can be made to only reside in the clipboard for a limited period, e.g. in PasswordSitter the generated password is saved to the clipboard for 60 seconds before being deleted [15]. The simplest approach for the user is probably **automatic copying to the target password field**; this can either be done automatically, as is the case for PwdHash in the web page implementation [14] and the ObPwd Firefox browser extension [9]. Alternatively it can require the user to perform an action, e.g. clicking a specific key combination, before copying; PassPet requires the user to click on a screen button, [16], and Password Multiplier, [4], requires the user to double click the password field or press *ctrl+P* to trigger password copying.

Approaches to Implementation: A password generator can be implemented as a **browser add-on**, e.g. as a **browser plug-in**, **browser extension** or **signed browser applet**. Many existing password generator schemes adopt this approach, at least as one option, including [4,14–16]. An alternative is to implement the scheme as a **stand-alone application**, e.g. to run on a phone, tablet or desktop. Such an approach is adopted by SSP; ObPwd, [9], is also available as both a browser extension and a mobile app. A somewhat different approach is to use a **web-based application**, either running on a remote server or executing on the user platform as a dynamically downloaded JavaScript.

4   Improving System Operation

We next consider ways to improve password generators. In Sect. 5 we consider how these might be integrated into a novel system.

We have mentioned certain types of configuration data, including global data, such as master secrets, and site-specific data, e.g. password policy values, possibly specified in PRML [6]. We now introduce two new configuration data types.

- A *password offset* (site-specific configuration data) allows users to continue using existing passwords after introducing use of a password generator. It also help when specific password values are imposed on users, or when users need to change their passwords. Addressing such requirements previously has been problematic.

    A password offset is as an input to the second stage of password generation. A password offset induces this stage to generate a specific password value. E.g., suppose a password policy dictates that a password must be a string of letters and numerals, where each such character is internally represented as a numeric value in the range 0–61. After converting the bit-string to a string of alphanumeric characters of the desired length, and given a 'desired password' consisting of an alphanumeric string of the same length, the password offset could simply be the character-wise modulo 62 difference between the two strings[1]. Changing a password can be easily implemented by changing the offset, either to a random value (randomising the password choice), or to a chosen value if the new password value is chosen by the user.

    If implemented appropriately, this offset is not hugely confidential, since it need not reveal anything about the actual password value. Of course, if an 'old' password is compromised, and the old and new offsets are also revealed, then this could compromise the new password value.

- A password generator might generate a password for one site using a different set of input types to those used to generate a password for another site. E.g., a password for a mission-critical site (e.g. a bank account) might be generated using a large set of input values, e.g. including a digital object, whereas a password for a less sensitive site could be generated using a master secret and site name only. Such a possibility could be captured using site-specific configuration data, referred to here as *password input parameters*.

- A system might also store *password reminders* as site-specific configuration data. E.g., when using a digital object as input, a user could specify a phrase as a reminder of the chosen value (without specifying it precisely). This could be revealed on demand via the password generator user interface.

Storing configuration data on a user platform creates a major barrier to portability; it also poses a security risk through possible platform compromise, although much of the configuration data we have discussed is not necessarily confidential. The 'obvious' solution is to use a server to store configuration data,

---

[1] Such an idea is widely implemented to enable credit/debit card holders to select their own PIN value.

or at least the less sensitive such data, much as many password managers keep passwords in the cloud. While it would seem prudent to keep a master secret on the user platform, all site-specific configuration data could be held in the cloud. This type of solution is advocated by Horsch et al. [5,6].

If the site-specific configuration data is all non-confidential, then there is no need for a highly trusted server, a great advantage by comparison with some server-based password managers. Server use need not impact password availability, since a password generator could cache a copy of the configuration data downloaded from the server, addressing short-term loss of server availability.

5   AutoPass: A New Proposal

We now outline AutoPass (from 'automatic password generator'), a novel password generation scheme combining the best features of the prior art together with the novel ideas introduced in this paper, particularly those devised to address some of the shortcomings of previously proposed schemes. AutoPass uses all the types of input given in Sect. 3 to generate a password, since they all contribute to security in different ways. Following the approach of PALPAS, [5], we also make use of a server to store non-sensitive configuration data, such as website password policies.

5.1   Operation

Following Sect. 2, to describe AutoPass we must define: (a) the input types, (b) how the password is generated, and (c) how the password is output, together with the implementation strategy. We cover these points in turn. Since we also propose the use of a cloud service to support AutoPass operation, we also briefly sketch its operation.

– For **inputs**, we propose the use of a **master password**, stored by the system (as global configuration data), and a password (or PIN) to be entered by the user. We also propose use of the first part of the **URL** of the site, where, depending on the implementation, this should also be stored as part of the site-specific configuration and used to retrieve the other site-specific data. The master password can be held encrypted by a key derived from the user password. We also propose the optional use of a **digital object**, where use of this option is indicated in the site-specific configuration data.
– The first stage of **password generation** adopts a two-level hash approach, giving some protection against brute force attacks. The second stage, i.e. **encoding**, uses the AutoPass cloud service to retrieve the password policy for the web site being visited (cf. PALPAS [5]); this policy could be encoded using PRML, [6]. It also uses other cloud-stored configuration data, notably the password offset, password input parameters, and password reminders introduced in Sect. 2.3.

- The precise option for **password output and use** depends on the implementation. Where possible, auto-filling the password is desirable; where this is impossible, the copy to clipboard/paste buffer approach is advocated.
- **Implementation** as a browser add-on is probably the best option, not least in giving simple access to the web page of the target site, although a range of options may need to be pursued depending on the platform type.

We next consider the AutoPass Cloud Service, which will be required to store two main types of data. *User-independent data* will be accessed by AutoPass users, and will include non-sensitive site-specific data, e.g. password policies. Even if corrupted by a malicious party, it would at worst cause a denial of service. *User-specific data* will only be accessed by a single user, and includes a range of password configuration data. Although this data is not highly confidential, access to it will need to be restricted to the user to whom it belongs, e.g. via a one-off login process in the local AutoPass application (with access permissions encoded in a cookie stored in the user platform).

Any cloud service has associated risks arising from non-availability; however, this can be addressed through caching. The local AutoPass app should maintain a copy of the data downloaded from the cloud service; since this data is not likely to change very quickly, the cached data should normally be sufficient. To avoid risks arising from fake AutoPass services, e.g. using DNS spoofing, the cloud service could sign all provided data, and the AutoPass app could verify signatures using a built-in copy of the cloud public key.

5.2 Assessment

AutoPass incorporates both the best features of the existing password generation schemes and certain novel features, notably the use of password configuration data (see Sect. 4). A full assessment of AutoPass will require prototyping and user testing. Nonetheless, we can at least consider the known issues in existing systems and see whether AutoPass addresses these concerns.

By using a combination of stored secret and memorised password/PIN as inputs to the generation process, we enable strong passwords to be generated while protecting against compromise through platform loss. Use of the URL enables automatic generation of site-specific passwords, and optional use of digital objects enables passwords of varying strength to be generated without imposing an unnecessarily onerous load on the user for 'everyday' use. URL use has residual problems, notably if a site URL changes, but user site names also have problems. In this connection, an advantage of AutoPass is that password offsets enable a generated password to remain constant even if a URL changes.

Use of cloud-served password policies solves problems relating to site-specific password requirements. Continued use of existing passwords and the need to change passwords are addressed by use of cloud-stored password configuration data. Password generation/synchronisation issues arising from use of multiple platforms can also be addressed through use of a cloud service. Of course, use of a cloud service brings with it certain availability and security risks; however, by only storing non-sensitive data in the cloud and using caching, these problems are largely addressed.

6   Concluding Remarks

We introduced a general model for password generation, and considered existing proposals in the context of this model. The model enables us to propose certain new options to enhance such schemes. The operation of a novel scheme, AutoPass, has been sketched, but has not yet been tested in practice. The next step is to prototype AutoPass, both to verify that the underlying idea works and also as a basis for practical user trials.

References

1. Biddle, R., Mannan, M., van Oorschot, P.C., Whalen, T.: User study, analysis, and usable security of passwords based on digital objects. IEEE Trans. Inf. Foren. Secur. **6**(3–2), 970–979 (2011)
2. Cluley, G.: Lastpass vulnerability potentially exposed passwords for internet explorer users, August 2013. https://www.grahamcluley.com/2013/08/lastpass-vulnerability/
3. FIDO Alliance: FIDO UAF Protocol Specification v1.0: FIDO Alliance Proposed Standard 08, December 2014
4. Halderman, J.A., Waters, B., Felten, E.W.: A convenient method for securely managing passwords. In: Ellis, A., Hagino, T. (eds.) Proceedings of the WWW 2005, pp. 471–479. ACM, May 2005
5. Horsch, M., Hülsing, A., Buchmann, J.A.: PALPAS - passwordless password synchronization (2015). arXiv:1506.04549v1 [cs.CR]. http://arxiv.org/abs/1506.04549
6. Horsch, M., Schlipf, M., Braun, J., Buchmann, J.A.: Password requirements markup language. In: Liu, J.K., Steinfeld, R. (eds.) ACISP 2016, Part I. LNCS, vol. 9722, pp. 426–439. Springer, Switzerland (2016)
7. Karp, A.H.: Site-specific passwords. Technical report HPL-2002-39 (R.1), HP Laboratories, Palo Alto, May 2003
8. Kelly, S.M.: Lastpass passwords exposed for some internet explorer users, mashableUK, August 2013. http://mashable.com/2013/08/19/lastpass-password-bug/
9. Mannan, M., van Oorschot, P.C.: Passwords for both mobile and desktop computers: ObPwd for Firefox and Android. USENIX; login **37**(4), 28–37 (2012)
10. Mannan, M., van Oorschot, P.C.: Digital objects as passwords. In: Provos, N. (ed.) Proceedings of the HotSec 2008. USENIX Association, July 2008
11. Mannan, M., Whalen, T., Biddle, R., van Oorschot, P.C.: The usable security of passwords based on digital objects: from design and analysis to user study. Technical report TR-10-02, School of Computer Sciemce, Carleton University, February 2010. https://www.scs.carleton.ca/sites/default/files/tr/TR-10-02.pdf
12. McCarney, D.: Password managers: comparative evaluation, design, implementation and empirical analysis. Master's thesis, Carleton University, August 2013
13. Pauli, D.: KeePass looter: password plunderer rinses pwned sysadmins. The Register, November 2015. http://www.theregister.co.uk/2015/11/03/keepass_looter_the_password_plunderer_to_hose_pwned_sys_admins/

14. Ross, B., Jackson, C., Miyake, N., Boneh, D., Mitchell, J.C.: Stronger password authentication using browser extensions. In: McDaniel, P. (ed.) Proceedings of the 14th USENIX Security Symposium. USENIX Association, July/August 2005
15. Wolf, R., Schneider, M.: The passwordsitter. Technical report, Fraunhofer Institute for Secure Information Technology (SIT), May 2006
16. Yee, K.P., Sitaker, K.: Passpet: convenient password management and phishing protection. In: Cranor, L.F. (ed.) Proceedings of the SOUPS 2006. ACM International Conference Proceeding Series, vol. 149, pp. 32–43. ACM, July 2006

Provable Network Activity for Protecting Users Against False Accusation

Panagiotis Papadopoulos[1]([⊠]), Elias Athanasopoulos[2], Eleni Kosta[4],
George Siganos[3], Angelos D. Keromytis[5], and Evangelos P. Markatos[1]

[1] FORTH - Institute of Computer Science, Heraklion, Greece
panpap@ics.forth.gr
[2] Vrije Universiteit Amsterdam, Amsterdam, Netherlands
[3] Qatar Computing Research Institute, HBKU, Doha, Qatar
[4] Tilburg Law School, Tilburg University, Tilburg, Netherlands
[5] Columbia University, New York, USA

Abstract. With the proliferation of the World Wide Web, data traces
that correspond to users' network activity can be collected by several
Internet actors, including (i) web sites, (ii) smartphone apps, and even
(iii) Internet Service Providers. Given that the collection and storage of
these data are beyond the control of the end user, these data traces can
be easily manipulated, if not, tampered with. The result of such manipulated digital traces can be severe: Innocent users can be shamed or even
wrongfully accused of carrying out illegal transactions.

To eliminate these potential accusations on innocent users, we introduce *Provable Network Activity (PNA)*: a framework with which the ISPs
can give the end users control of their stored traces. The framework guarantees that the information collected for the end users is accurate and
will remain accurate for as long as it is stored. Our implementation and
preliminary evaluation suggest that PNA is fast, easy to deploy, and
introduces zero network latency to the end clients.

1 Introduction

Over the past few years the degree to which computers are involved in evidence
collection for crime and security investigations has profoundly changed. A couple
of decades ago there were few cases that could be associated with cyber crime.
Nowadays, there is hardly ever a case that does not involve a computer or a
smartphone. Data from such devices are so important that even the FBI [5] or
the government's prosecutors [8] want to get access to them almost at any cost.

Unfortunately, despite their importance, data collected by our digital
infrastructure today are not necessarily trustworthy. Indeed, malicious attackers
or even rogue insiders may tamper with the process of collecting and/or storing
data and may add *fake* data about individual users. Such fake data may later
be used to ridicule and slander users, or worse, accuse them of questionable or

Published by Springer International Publishing Switzerland 2016. All Rights Reserved
S. Foresti and J. Lopez (Eds.): WISTP 2016, LNCS 9895, pp. 254–261, 2016.
DOI: 10.1007/978-3-319-45931-8_17

even illegal activities. Although fake digital evidence usually does not stand in a court of law, it is often enough to send people to jail [7].

In this paper we propose that data collection processes should actively involve the users concerned. We advocate that the users should not only give their consent in all data collections, but should also make sure that *the collected data are accurate* and will always *remain accurate* for as long as they are stored. To do so, we involve the user in every step of the process: (i) users collect, (ii) users double check, (iii) users sign, and finally, (iv) users encrypt the collected data.

Our proposal is Provable Network Activity (PNA): an architecture that enables both clients and ISPs to collaborate in the data collection process and make sure that the collected data are accurate. PNA works as follows:

– A client who wants to gain control of her traffic and data, and ensure their authenticity can simply register to the service by providing her ISP with her public key. Then, she installs a software responsible for signing all outgoing traffic, before it is sent to the ISP, with her private key[1].
– If the ISP receives traffic from the client *without* receiving the corresponding signature, the traffic is blocked[2].
– If the ISP receives a valid signature, it keeps a record of the access in its log.

2   Threat Model

In this paper we focus on protecting innocent users from false accusations based on fake network logs. We assume that the user's access logs have been collected by a local ISP (or similar service). We also assume that, at some point in time (either during the collection process or later), the logs were tampered with, maybe by intruders, or even by insiders.

More precisely, the setup is composed by three different entities: (i) the user U, (ii) the last-mile ISP I, and (iii) an web site s hosting offensive or even illegal content. We make the following assumptions:

– user U never accessed web site s (via ISP I).
– although ISP I is considered generally trusted, its data logs may be tampered with to show that U has accessed s [10].

3   Provable Network Activity

Traditional data collection has been done by the ISPs without consulting the users at all. That is, ISPs collected data about the users *without the users being able to verify that the collected data are correct* and that the data will remain correct for as long as they are stored.

We advocate that this approach should change. Data should not be collected without the user being able to verify that the data are (and will remain) correct.

---

[1] The exact details of the key management process is beyond the scope of this paper.
[2] Note that this service works on an *opt-in* basis.

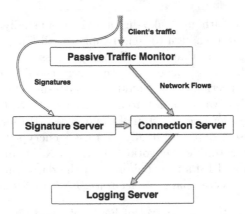

Fig. 1. Overview of the PNA components and their interconnections on the ISP side.

To bring the user back in the game, PNA proposes that the collected data (i) should be reviewed by a user's application (ii) should be signed by the user, and (iii) should be encrypted by the user. Any attempts to tamper with the data will stumble upon the signing and encryption process which becomes impossible (or obviously detectable) without the user's cryptographic keys.

3.1   Client Side

Key Management. The client is responsible for generating a public-private key pair, and is responsible for the security of her private key[3]. The client at any time can replace her public-private key pair, but it is her responsibility to store the old private key and update the public key provided to the provider.

Daemon. A daemon runs in the client's computer and passively monitors all outgoing traffic. For each outgoing flow a signature is computed. The signature is computed on the tuple (destination IP address, port number, protocol, timestamp) by first using SHA and then encrypting with the user's private key. The daemon then sends the tuple plus the signature of the tuple to the ISP's server[4]. This signature is a proof generated by the client that the client *did make* this network connection. If the ISP does not receive such a proof, it will not allow the connection to be established.

3.2   ISP Side

For each client connection (e.g. network flow), the ISP expects to receive a signature from the client. If the signature is received, the connection is allowed

---

[3] For simplicity, we describe our approach as if the user has one device, but it can be easily generalized to include several devices and users, as well.

[4] Note, that we do not use the source IP/port, since usually NAT/Proxies overwrite the source part [4].

to proceed and a log record is generated. If the signature is not received, or is not valid, the connection is not allowed to proceed.

The infrastructure on the ISP side consists of the following entities: (i) a *Passive Traffic Monitor*, (ii) a *Signature Server* that is interacting with the client-side, (iii) a *Connection Server* that maintains the connections and enforces policy, and (iv) a *Logging Server* that provides persistence in a privacy-preserving way.

- **Passive Traffic Monitor.** The ISP passively monitors all traffic to identify new flows. For each new flow identified, the monitor creates a new record to characterize the flow, and sends the record to the Connection Server that handles the policy.
- **Signature Server.** The Signature Server acts as a gateway to the system. It receives signatures from the client side and forwards them to the Connection Server.
- **Connection Server.** The Connection Server collects information (i) from the Passive Traffic Monitor and (ii) from the Signature Server, and makes sure that for each flow received by the Passive Traffic Monitor a corresponding signature is received from the Signature Server. If a signature is not received (or is not valid) for a given flow, the flow is blocked/terminated.
- **Logging Server.** The Logging Server is responsible for storing all signatures for each subscriber.

3.3   Privacy-Preserving Logging

The approach described so far keeps a record only of the IP addresses really accessed by the client:

- If an attacker tries to add a record to the log, this record will just not have the client's signature, and therefore it will be easily singled out as fake.
- If the client tries to access an IP address without providing a signed record for this access, the ISP will clock/reset the access.

Therefore, the log will be an always accurate record of the user's activity. Unfortunately, keeping the log as described so far may seriously violate the user's privacy. Indeed, if the log is leaked, then all the user's accesses will be easily visible. Encrypting the log with an ISP's key does not help either. A malicious attacker may accuse the client of illegal activity just to force the client to reveal the entire log in order to prove that the illegal activity is not there. Such an approach will help the user demonstrate her innocence, at the price of her privacy. It seems therefore that there is a dilemma the user needs to choose from: *either* demonstrate her innocence *or* protect her privacy. In this paper we believe that this is a *false dilemma*. We believe we can do both: i.e. *both* demonstrate the client's innocence *and* protect the client's privacy at the same time. To do so, instead of keeping each signed record, we keep a *hash* of it. We use bcrypt [9] in order to hash all network signatures.

4 Implementation

4.1 PNA Prototype

We implemented PNA in Linux using `libpcap` a building block for capturing network traffic, and OpenSSL a module that provides all cryptographic operations. The implementation was rather straightforward: all software is written in C++ totalling around 2,000 lines of code.

Client-Side Implementation. A Linux-based host runs the code for the client: a DSL subscriber. This host runs the daemon software as we described in Sect. 3.1. The daemon initially connects to a predefined port of a Linux-based server, which is run by the ISP. In parallel, the daemon monitors all TCP/UDP traffic and captures (i) all TCP packets having the `TCP-SYN` flag on and (ii) all UDP packets. For each TCP-SYN packet and for each UDP packet that starts a new flow, the client daemon generates a signature of the packet with the user's private key and sends it to the server using the established connection.

ISP-side Implementation. At ISP side, the server runs the passive traffic monitor, as we described in Sect. 3.2, for capturing all incoming traffic and infer (i) new TCP flows (by inspecting the `TCP-SYN` flag), and (ii) new UDP flows. The monitor uses Redis, an open source in-memory key-value store for maintaining all identified UDP flows. In addition, it also runs the signature module, which listens to a predefined port for incoming signatures by the client. The server verifies each incoming signature, by decrypting it using the user's public key. If the signature is valid, it is forwarded to the logging server and it is stored using bcrypt [9]. Otherwise, (i) if the signature is not valid, or (ii) if the signature is not sent by the client, or (iii) if the signature arrives too late, the connection is terminated. TCP/IP connections area terminated by an explicit `TCP-RST` to the user's host. For UDP connections, the flow is just blocked.

For the asymmetric encryption/decryption, the RSA algorithm is used with `PKCS1` padding as provided by OpenSSL). The length of the keys is 2048 bits. For hashing before encrypting we use `SHA512` as provided by OpenSSL. For bcrypt we use the implementation as provided by the original paper [9].

5 Evaluation

5.1 Client Side

The cryptographic overhead is the only *computational* overhead we impose on the client side. More specifically, the client needs to sign every new flow and send this signature to the ISP in time no more than T. To quantify the latency imposed by this required cryptographic operations, we perform 10,000 private-key encryptions for a testing tuple and we measure the average latency. In this experiment we use OpenSSL's RSA implementation with keys of length of 2048

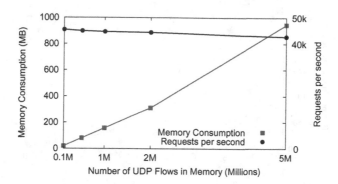

Fig. 2. Passive monitor performance. We see that even for 5 million flows, the server requires less that 1 GB of memory.

bits in two devices: a Linux desktop and a Mac OS laptop. In both cases, the overhead per encryption was less than 10 ms. This means that a typical computer can handle more than a hundred of new flows (i.e. new signatures) per second.

5.2   ISP Side

Passive Traffic Monitor (PTM). As we described in previous section, PTM is responsible for identifying new network flows. While this operation is straightforward when the flows are TCP, in the case of UDP flows it is not that trivial. For each UDP packet, a query needs to be sent to the key-value store to check if this UDP flow has been encountered in the past. Given this complexity, we focus on the UDP flows identification, which evidently is the most expensive part of this component.

To measure the performance of PTM, we simulate traffic sent from client to ISP, containing various number UDP flows (ranging from 100 K to 5 M). The UDP packets of these flows are distributed using a long-tail distribution (80 % of the packets are distributed to 20 % of the flows). In Fig. 2, we can see the results, where it seems that our server is able to process more than 40 K reqs/sec.

In the same experiment, we measure the memory requirements of our system. In Fig. 2, we can see that, as expected, the memory consumption demands grow linearly with the number of UDP flows. Indeed, we see that even if we have as many as 5M UDP flows we probably need less than 1 GB of memory to store all data. Of course, this is a trivial amount of memory for contemporary servers.

Logging Server. This is the component responsible for securely storing the signatures in a privacy-preserving fashion. The main bottleneck in the logging server is the computation of the hash key using bcrypt. To measure this computation overhead we stress a desktop equipped with one Quad-core Intel processor at 2.4G to identify how many bcrypt operations per second can achieve and in Fig. 3 we plot the results. As we see, we can have more than 2000 bcrypt operations per second, and consequently, we can process more than 2000 new flows

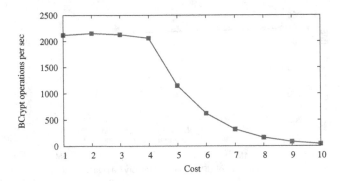

Fig. 3. Bcrypt performance as a function of the value of *cost*. Up to cost = 4, the single CPU can perform more than 2,000 operations per second.

per second. Additionally, recall that it is an off-line operation, and thus does not increase the typical packet routing operation of the ISP.

It is worth mentioning at this point, that bcrypt wastes computational resources on purpose for prohibiting massive in-parallel cracking of the generated hash products and resist dictionary attacks. To achieve that, bcrypt uses *cost* parameter. In our experiment, we explore how this parameter affects the overall calculation performance by testing various values of *cost*. As we can see, up to cost = 4, the single CPU can still perform more than 2,000 operations per second. As a result, even when using a cost value able to sky-rocket the amount of work required by an attacker to reveal the network logs, it is not capable of degrading the system's performance.

6   Related Work

Pretty Good Packet Authentication (PGPA) [6]) is a system that hashes all user's outgoing traffic and stores it to a device. The device must be placed between client and ISP: either towards the user's side, i.e. in her household, or it can be hosted by the ISP. Packet Attestation (PA) [2] suggests installing special monitors, independent of the current Internet's routing infrastructure, in every Autonomous System (AS). These monitors hash and collect all user traffic, and they can attest if the traffic is authentic under a particular case, where a user is accused for receiving offensive traffic. Clue [1] attempts to bring the notion of physical evidence, such as DNA, in the digital world. More precisely, Clue uses Group Signatures [3] for delivering a scheme, where each Internet packet can be attributed to its original source. All these systems propose major reconstruction of fundamental parts of today's Internet. We agree with a large fraction of these proposals and we believe that a clean-slate design will terminate a rich collection of problems that we exhibit today. However, deployment is not always trivial. Changing fundamental Internet-core concepts, such as routing or addressing, is really hard.

7   Conclusion

In this paper we designed, implemented, and evaluated PNA, a framework which gives end users control of their own traces as they recorded by their last-mile ISP. PNA empowers users with the ability to double check the data collected about them and to make sure that these collected data are correct and *will remain correct for as long as they are stored* in the ISP's logs. To do so, users explicitly sign each network flow. The ISP makes sure that each network flow is accompanied by the associated signature. If a signature is not received, the ISP blocks the flow. To ensure the correctness of the log, the ISP stores *both* the network flow records *end* their associated signatures. In this way, tampering with the stored data is extremely difficult: even if attackers manage to add records to the log, they will not be able to add the corresponding signatures. Our preliminary implementation and evaluation shows that our system does not impose any extra latency to the end user and has low computational requirements.

Acknowledgements. This work was supported in part by the project GCC, funded by the Prevention of and Fight against Crime Programme of the European Commission – Directorate-General Home Affairs under Grant Agreement HOME/2011/ISEC/AG/INT/4000002166. This project has received funding from the European Unions Horizon 2020 research and innovation programme under the Marie Skodowska-Curie grant agreement No 316808. This publication reflects the views only of the authors, and the European Commission cannot be held responsible for any use which may be made of the information contained therein.

References

1. Afanasyev, M., Kohno, T., Ma, J., Murphy, N., Savage, S., Snoeren, A.C., Voelker, G.M.: Privacy-preserving network forensics. Commun. ACM **54**, 78–87 (2011)
2. Haeberlen, A., Fonseca, P., Rodrigues, R., Druschel, P.: Fighting cybercrime with packet attestation (2011). http://repository.upenn.edu/cgi/viewcontent.cgi?article=1652&context=cis_papers
3. Chaum, D., van Heyst, E.: Group signatures. In: Davies, D.W. (ed.) EUROCRYPT 1991. LNCS, vol. 547, pp. 257–265. Springer, Heidelberg (1991)
4. Clayton, R.: Mobile internet access data retention (not!) (2012). http://www.lightbluetouchpaper.org/2010/01/14/mobile-internet-access-data-retention-not/
5. Digital trends staff: Apple vs. the FBI: a complete timeline of the war over tech encryption (2016). http://www.digitaltrends.com/mobile/apple-encryption-court-order-news/
6. Haeberlen, A., Rodrigues, R., Gummadi, K., Druschel, P.: Pretty good packet authentication. In: Proceedings of the Fourth Workshop HotDep 2008 (2008)
7. India News: Techie jailed due to Airtel mistake (2012). http://twocircles.net/node/25440
8. Kravets, D.: Twitter reluctantly coughs up occupy protesters data (2012). https://www.wired.com/2012/09/twitter-occupy-data/
9. Provos, N., Mazières, D.: A future-adaptive password scheme. In: ATEC 1999. http://dl.acm.org/citation.cfm?id=1268708.1268740
10. Stolfo, S.J., Bellovin, S.M., Keromytis, A.D., Hershkop, S., Smith, S.W., Sinclair, S. (eds.): Insider Attack and Cyber Security - Beyond the Hacker. Advances in Information Security, vol. 39. Springer, US (2008)

Combining Third Party Components Securely in Automotive Systems

Madeline Cheah(✉), Siraj A. Shaikh, Jeremy Bryans, and Hoang Nga Nguyen

Centre for Mobility and Transport Research, Coventry University, Coventry, UK
cheahh2@uni.coventry.ac.uk,
{siraj.shaikh,jeremy.bryans,hoang.nguyen}@coventry.ac.uk

Abstract. Vehicle manufacturers routinely integrate third-party components and combining them securely into a larger system is a challenge, particularly when accurate specifications are not available. In this paper, we propose a methodology for users to introduce or strengthen security of these composed systems without requiring full knowledge of commercially sensitive sub-components. This methodology is supported by attack trees, which allow for systematic enumeration of black box components, the results of which are then incorporated into further design processes. We apply the methodology to a Bluetooth-enabled automotive infotainment unit, and find a legitimate Bluetooth feature that contributes to the insecurity of a system. Furthermore, we recommend a variety of follow-on processes to further strengthen the security of the system through the next iteration of design.

Keywords: Automotive security · Attack trees · Secure design · Security testing · Bluetooth

1 Introduction

Automotive security has become an issue with the advent of smarter vehicles, which incorporate a large variety of external facing interfaces that could be used to maliciously affect vehicles. The context of our work is the way in which various components are combined to achieve the final vehicle product. Components are often generic with many general purpose features. This promotes their reuse, which drives overall costs within the supply chain down. Larger components are often provided as whole "off-the-shelf" subsystems (for example an infotainment unit), with each component originating with a different manufacturer. Within the automotive supply chain, system integrators often do not have the final detailed designs of the components, especially where these components represent intellectual property such as source code. Components for which no privileged information is available are often referred to as "black boxes" [11], with "white boxes" being those for which all information is available. This distinction becomes important when testing the integrated system [13].

© IFIP International Federation for Information Processing 2016
Published by Springer International Publishing Switzerland 2016. All Rights Reserved
S. Foresti and J. Lopez (Eds.): WISTP 2016, LNCS 9895, pp. 262–269, 2016.
DOI: 10.1007/978-3-319-45931-8_18

The contribution of this paper is a methodology for the secure combination of third party components. The methodology includes a systematic and semi-automated penetration testing process supported by attack trees. This leads to the identification of additional security requirements over and above the functional and integration requirements that already exist for the system, which can then be used to improve the design of the system with respect to security. The motive for beginning the process with testing is to acquire confidence with regard to the overall implementation. The testing process moves knowledge of the component along the black-white spectrum, where we can then extract requirements for secure behaviour in the given context to help mitigate security flaws. This is particularly valuable where a system contains many third party components of which even the original equipment manufacturer (OEM) may not have complete sight because of commercial sensitivities.

The remainder of this paper is structured as follows: we review related work in Sect. 2, followed by an outline of our proposed methodology in Sect. 3. We then apply this methodology to a case study in Sect. 4. We discuss the implications thereof and our conclusions in Sect. 5.

2   Related Work

There are comparative approaches to each of the stages of our methodology, and as such our survey has been divided into categories of gathering security requirements, threat assessment and attack trees, along with a brief discussion on the automotive specific cybersecurity standard J3061.

Security Requirements. Similar methods for gathering security requirements have been proposed by [6], in that security requirements are linked to possible attacks. A key difference to our methodology however is that a functional model of the system is required, which is more information than is usually available in a black box system. Attack trees in a requirements gathering and actioning process are also used in the System Quality Requirements Engineering (SQUARE) methodology [7]. However, use cases in this methodology concentrated on application to a company's procedures rather than embedded systems.

Threat Assessment. This process determines threats (defined as potential negative events that could compromise an asset) to the surface of the target system, typically by looking at the potential malicious actions. In the automotive domain, empirical studies have already shown that attacks on vehicular components are possible [3]. However, despite impressive experimental analyses, actions taken to compromise the vehicle and their results were not systematised. This, in addition to the "grey box" nature of automotive components led us to penetration testing for threat assessment, supported by attack trees, in order to determine the initial security state of the system relative to the target attack goal.

Attack Trees. Attack trees are diagrams modelling the potential actions of an attacker to reach an attack goal [19]. They have been discussed as a possible threat modelling technique in the automotive specific SAE cybersecurity standard J3061 [18], which draws from the "E-safety vehicle intrusion protected applications" (EVITA) project. It is for this reason that we have chosen to use this method. Furthermore, attack trees can help inform threat assessment even in an informal capacity [16]. Formal methods such as attack graphs are not feasible as there is not enough up-front information about the target system.

These trees can be represented diagrammatically or textually. Logic gates (AND and OR) are also commonly used within these trees. Where AND is used, an attack (parent node) is considered complete only if all steps have been completed. Where OR is used, the parent node is complete if at least one of the steps is completed. These gates are also sometimes referred to as conjunctive and disjunctive refinements respectively [12]. For application purposes, where temporal order may be a concern, sequential AND (SAND) could also be used.

A related approach is the formation of "anti-models" [10], depicting how model elements may be threatened (analogous to attack trees). However, these anti-models are derived from the model of the system-to-be (with attendant high informational needs), which makes it less suitable for a black-box system. Even where there are methods that allow for only partial specifications (such as the framework based on Model Driven Engineering) [9], perfectly legitimate behaviour in those specifications could actually be a weakness in terms of the larger system boundary.

EVITA and J3061. EVITA elaborates on some of the possible usages of attack trees. Deliverable 2.3 also includes an outline in which security requirements could be traced back to the attack tree [5]. This is, broadly, along similar lines to our work (although we begin with less knowledge of functionality and other requirements). Additionally, the "dark-side scenario analysis", closest to our security testing process, places particular emphasis on risk assessment, whereas the purposes of our own methodology would be to identify specific insecurities relating to an attack goal without looking at the motivations behind it. J3061 [18] also outlines the use of attack trees (in reference to EVITA). The standard also notes that it may only be possible to consider high-level concepts early in the product development cycle. Security analysts or designers could use our methodology as a way of gathering low level requirements for the next design iteration.

In summary, many of the comparative methodologies reviewed above require in-depth knowledge of the system. Our proposed methodology addresses specifically the problem of a black box with many layers of obscurity, all of which may be individually secure, but may exhibit system-wide insecurities.

3   Proposed Methodology

The methodology adopted in this paper is as follows:

Step 1 - Security testing: Since full specifications are generally unavailable, we begin with security testing (more specifically penetration testing) to probe the black box. This is systematised using attack tree methodology. Initial attack trees are first defined relative to an attack goal. These goals can be as low level (flood an open port with data) or high level (denial of service) as needed and tailored to the target interface.

Step 2 - Inferring requirements: Requirements can be extracted from whichever attack proved successful through a process of inference, and is essentially a negation of observed undesirable behaviours found from testing. The determination of security requirements at this stage can be cross-referenced back to the attack tree. This allows for specific insecurities to be addressed as well as separation of security requirements from other types of requirements (known to be useful for interaction analysis [10]).

Step 3 - Suggesting specifications: Once the requirements gathering phase is considered complete, possible specifications could be suggested using a process such as design space exploration. There may be a number of different design choices (and therefore specifications) that could be made to mitigate the threat. These derived specifications could be cross-referenced with other subsets of specifications (such as safety), and where there are contradictions, could help clarify design choices. Where there are no conflicts, the derived security specifications from our process could be added to the overall set of specifications.

Step 4 - Incorporation of specifications into existing processes: Agreed specifications can be sent down the supply chain. Alternatively, the end user could follow up with in-house model-based design and testing processes. We discuss the latter within the context of our case study (see Sect. 4). The reason for keeping such flexibility is to enable incorporation of this methodology into the wider processes that might be carried out by the end user.

4   Case Study: Automotive Infotainment Unit

For this paper we concentrate on the infotainment unit, where diverse technologies are integrated to deliver functionality such as hands-free communication. We demonstrate the proposed methodology using a case study below. Although this case study came from a single vehicle, it can be reasonably assumed that vehicles of the same make, model and age would share the same weaknesses as production lines are standardised.

Step 1 - security testing: The security testing process was focused on the Bluetooth interface because it is a viable attack vector [15], and because of its ubiquity in cars (an estimated nine million vehicles have implemented this technology [8]). As a vector, it can be used to mount many attacks [4] ranging from denial of service to man-in-the-middle attacks. Implementations can also differ greatly, with various "profiles" available to customise the technology.

The building of the initial attack tree was manually guided, using known vulnerabilities in other Bluetooth applications and surveyed from literature and the National Vulnerability Database [14]. We then evaluated the Bluetooth interface of an automotive infotainment unit using this attack tree (Fig. 1). A number of

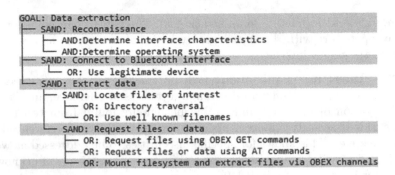

Fig. 1. Attack tree focusing on extracting data via mounting the filesystem

undesirable behaviours were found, including the ability to mount the filesystem of the infotainment unit and read its contents. This was possible because of the presence of the Object Exchange File Transfer Profile (OBEXFTP) service [1]. We highlight this as an example for the remainder of the paper.

Step 2 - inferring requirements: After having connected to the interface using a legitimate pairing and device (the connection, vehicle or device had not been tampered with in any way), we mounted the file system. Being able to mount the filesystem through Bluetooth could lead to injection of malware, directory traversal and data extraction, manipulation or destruction. As such it is undesirable behaviour, so our inferred requirement from this would be "no unauthorised external agency should be able to see or influence the vehicular operating system's filesystem".

Step 3 - suggesting specifications: Based on the case study attack tree, we could fulfil the requirement above by creating specifications that either (a) remove the ability to request files or data (could conflict with functional requirements); (b) remove the ability to mount the filesystem (may have functional or cost implications) or (c) allow the above, but remove support for extracting, deleting or creating (injecting) files (which would conflict with the required functionality of the FTP server role as specified by Bluetooth SIG [1]).

Step 4 - model-based design and formal verification: Formal analyses of the Bluetooth protocol and its authentication and secrecy properties exist [2]. However, we are not attacking the protocol, but rather probing the larger system in which it resides. This is an example of two components in themselves being secure, but exhibiting insecure behaviour when combined into a larger system. Additionally, all users of the Bluetooth system in this test vehicle are able to use all services offered regardless of who they are. Authentication thus becomes irrelevant. Therefore a more appropriate analysis would be reachability, to demonstrate that such an insecure system state could not be reached through the pathways dictated by the attack tree.

We use the process algebra CSP (Communicating Sequential Processes) to describe a specification of the inferred requirements. We choose CSP because it

channel $pair, connect, advertise\_service, service\_discovery$
channel $service1, service2, displayfs$
channel $obexftp : OBEXFTP\_CMD$
datatype $OBEXFTP\_CMD =$
    $Selectserver|NavigateFolder|MountFS|Push|Pull|$
    $CreateFolder|Copy|Move|Rename|Delete|SetPermission$
$BT = pair \rightarrow connect \rightarrow advertise\_service \rightarrow OFFER\_SERVICE$
$OFFER\_SERVICE =$
        $service1 \rightarrow OFFER\_SERVICE$
    $\Box\ service2 \rightarrow OFFER\_SERVICE$
    $\Box\ ..$
    $\Box\ obexftp?cmd$
        if $cmd == MountFS$ then
                $displayfs \rightarrow OFFER\_SERVICE$
            else $OFFER\_SERVICE$
$USER = pair \rightarrow connect \rightarrow service\_discovery \rightarrow USE\_SERVICE$
$USE\_SERVICE =$
        $service1 \rightarrow USE\_SERVICE$
    $\sqcap\ service2 \rightarrow USE\_SERVICE$
    $\sqcap\ ..$
    $\sqcap\ obexftp!MountFS \rightarrow displayfs \rightarrow USE\_SERVICE$
$IMPL = BT\ \underset{\alpha_{BT} \cap \alpha_{USER}}{\parallel}\ USER$

Fig. 2. Small illustrative model of the OBEXFTP service

Suggested (property-oriented) specification:
$SPEC = CHAOS_{\alpha_{IMPL} \setminus \{displayfs\}}$
Refinement assertion:
assert $SPEC \sqsubseteq_{traces} IMPL$
Result: FAIL

Fig. 3. Example specification and verification

is able to represent and combine the message passing choreography expected by individual components. A complete introduction may be found in [17].

The specification for the Bluetooth FTP is available [1] and so we developed a small illustrative CSP model (Fig. 2). We then developed a suggested specification from our inferred requirement, such as never displaying the filesystem (see Fig. 3) which fails during the verification process with trace $\langle pair, connect,$ $service\_discovery, advertise\_service, obexftp.MountFS, displayfs \rangle$. If, however, we removed OBEXFTP, and assuming none of the other services offered the ability to mount a filesystem, it would verify correctly.

We use this exercise to show that the inferred requirement is not met by the standard FTP specification (that a server must respond to a request from a client for "Folder Listing Objects") and is, in fact, contradictory. Thus, any attempt to remove support whilst still maintaining the profile would be breaking Bluetooth's specification.

Here, the model and example specification is simplistic enough to make it self-evident that the removal of OBEXFTP would allow for successful verification. This exercise would add value provided: (a) the systems are sufficiently complex; (b) we can create a more accurate model of the system under investigation, or (c) there is more than one path to mount the filesystem (or, more generally, to achieve any other undesirable behaviour).

5   Discussion and Conclusion

Our methodology is suited for tiered supply chains, as there is no need to have complete specifications of the integrated item for security testing. It also reflects real world security issues that have arisen through the testing process. The attack tree methodology allows for systematisation and traceability, especially where design choices are concerned. These choices could also be cross-referenced against scenarios that were posited in attack trees but were not tested. Any security requirements gathered can be kept separate for interaction analysis and allows for reasoning about alternatives. The formal exercise could allow for clarification of ambiguities, and using a verifier leads to a higher level of confidence in the resulting design (albeit dependent on the model constructed). Limitations include the fact that the initial creation of the attack tree is manually guided although domain expert input in reviewing the tree and repeated testing over more vehicles would mitigate this. There is also a one-off cost of building these trees, although reuse is possible in future testing processes. As testing scope expands, trees could also become crowded, and so tree navigation will be essential. Problems with scalability could also be mitigated using mechanical tools such as design space exploration. Furthermore, the data available to construct the model at the end of the process directly impacts the quality of the model created.

In this paper, we have presented a methodology for securely combining third party components into a wider system and applied it in the context of an automotive head unit using the Bluetooth interface. We have found weaknesses through structured security testing, and using the case study of being able to mount the filesystem through Bluetooth, we demonstrated how to infer security requirements and suggest specifications. We have also recommended follow-on processes that we envisage end users would find constructive in strengthening the security of their systems. Future work would include refining the process by applying the methodology to a more significant case study, with different attack goals. Through both of these, we also aim to acquire enough information as to be more concrete with regards to formal processes. Ultimately, we wish to position this methodology in a larger design process such as that espoused by standards such as J3061.

Acknowledgements. The authors would like to thank Olivier Haas (Coventry University) and Alastair Ruddle (HORIBA MIRA) for valuable comments.

References

1. Bluetooth SIG Inc.: Bluetooth Specification: File Transfer Profile (FTP) (2012)
2. Chang, R., Shmatikov, V.: Formal analysis of authentication in bluetooth device pairing. In: Foundations of Computer Security and Automated Reasoning for Security Protocol Analysis, p. 45. Wroclaw, Poland (2007)
3. Checkoway, S., McCoy, D., Kantor, B., Anderson, D., Shacham, H., Savage, S., Koscher, K., Czeskis, A., Roesner, F., Kohno, T.: Comprehensive experimental analyses of automotive attack surfaces. In: Proceedings of 20th USENIX Security Symp. pp. 77–92. USENIX Assoc., San Francisco, August 2011
4. Dunning, J.P.: Taming the blue beast: a survey of bluetooth based threats. IEEE Secur. Priv. **8**(2), 20–27 (2010)
5. EVITA Project: Deliverable D2.3 - Security requirements for automotive on-board networks based on dark-side scenarios. Technical report (2009)
6. Fuchs, A., Rieke, R.: Identification of security requirements in systems of systems by functional security analysis. In: Lemos, R., Gacek, C., Casimiro, A. (eds.) Architecting Dependable Systems VII. LNCS, vol. 6420, pp. 74–96. Springer, Heidelberg (2010)
7. Gordon, D., Stehney, T., Wattas, N., Yu, E.: System Quality Requirements Engineering (SQUARE) Methodology: Case Study on Asset Management System. Techniacl report Carnegic Mellon University, Pittsburgh, May 2005
8. GSMA: Connected Car Forecast: Global Connected Car Market to Grow Threefold within Five Years. Technical report, GSMA (2013). http://www.gsma.com/connectedliving/wp-content/uploads/2013/06/cl_ma_forecast_06_13.pdf
9. Idrees, M.S., Roudier, Y., Apvrille, L.: A framework towards the efficient identification and modeling of security requirements. In: Proceedings of the 5th Conference on Network Architecture and Information Systems, pp. 1–15. Menton, France, May 2010
10. van Lamsweerde, A.: Elaborating security requirements by construction of intentional anti-models. In: Proceedings of 26th International Conference on Software Engineering, p. 10. IEEE Computer Society, Edinburgh, May 2004
11. Liu, B., Shi, L., Cai, Z., Li, M.: Software vulnerability discovery techniques: a survey. In: Proceedings of the 4th International Conference on Multimedia Information Networking and Security. IEEE, Nanjing, China (2012)
12. Mauw, S., Oostdijk, M.: Foundations of attack trees. In: Won, D.H., Kim, S. (eds.) ICISC 2005. LNCS, vol. 3935, pp. 186–198. Springer, Heidelberg (2006)
13. Midian, P.: Perspectives on penetration testing - Black box vs. white box. Netw. Secur. **2002**(11), 10–12 (2002)
14. National Institute of Standards and Technology: National Vulnerability Database
15. Oka, D.K., Furue, T., Langenhop, L., Nishimura, T.: Survey of vehicle iot bluetooth devices. In: Proceedings of the IEEE 7th International Conference on Service-Oriented Computing and Applications, pp. 260–264. IEEE, Matsue, Japan, November 2014
16. Opdahl, A.L., Sindre, G.: Experimental comparison of attack trees and misuse cases for security threat identification. Inf. Softw. Technol. **51**(5), 916–932 (2009)
17. Roscoe, A.: Understanding Concurrent Systems, 1st edn. Springer, London (2010)
18. SAE International: J3061: Cybersecurity Guidebook for Cyber-Physical Vehicle Systems (2016). http://standards.sae.org/j3061_201601/
19. Schneier, B.: Attack trees: modeling security threats (1999). http://www.schneier.com/paper-attacktrees-ddj-ft.html

Author Index

Printed in the United States
By Bookmasters